# Baby Care

*Dedicated to the memory of my mother,*

*Madge Claxton, 1889–1987.*

*A wise woman, greatly loved.*

# Baby Care

## Nurturing your baby, your way

## Rhodanthe Lipsett

**Edited by Dr Jenny Browne, RM, MEd, PhD**

FINCH PUBLISHING

SYDNEY

**Baby Care: Nurturing your baby, your way**
First published as *No One Right Way* in 2004 and in 2007 by Sea Change Publishing.
This revised and updated edition published in 2012 in Australia and New Zealand by
Finch Publishing Pty Limited, ABN 49 057 285 248, Suite 2207, 4 Daydream Street,
Warriewood, NSW, 2102, Australia.

13 12    8 7 6 5 4 3 2 1

The National Library of Australia Cataloguing-in-Publication entry:

Lipsett, Rhodanthe.
Baby Care : nurturing your baby, your way / Rhodanthe Lipsett.
9781921462306 (pbk.)
Includes index.
Infants--Care--Australia--Handbooks, manuals, etc.
Infants--Health and hygiene--Australia--Handbooks, manuals, etc.
Child care--Australia--Handbooks, manuals etc
Child development--Australia--Handbooks, manuals, etc.
Child psychology--Australia--Handbooks, manuals, etc.
649.1220994

Edited by Jenny Browne and Karen Gee
Editorial assistance by Catherine Page
Text typeset by Jo Hunt
Cover design by Creation Graphics
Cover image courtesy of iStock International
Printed by Griffin Press

We would like to thank the following people for use of their photos in this edition: Katy
Brack, Boyd Attewell and Cathy Spencer.

**Finch titles** can be viewed and purchased at www.finch.com.au

# Praise for the first edition of
# *Baby Care (No One Right Way)*

'The theme for this book is set out in Rhodanthe Lipsett's introduction where she tells of one of the best lessons she learnt early in her professional career: "There is no one right way of doing things. Sometimes rules need to be changed to fit particular circumstances." Here parents will find reassuring, practical advice, which will encourage them, as well as help them. New parents, in particular, will gain from these insights.'

**Professor Kim Oates, MD, MHP, FRACP, Former Chief Executive, The Children's Hospital at Westmead**

'Initially, I thought the book would be a wonderful resource for new parents and their families; as I read I realised the depth of knowledge contained in your ideas, and the simplicity in which you have presented it make it ideal, for not just parents, but for students of midwifery and nursing (and indeed those who have already graduated in their profession) – many of whom are not parents, and yet are called upon for advice. The book is comprehensive and honest giving every side of the die, empowering new parents to watch, and grow with their baby. Your words reinforce their innate skills to parent – to trust their instincts. Your book not only nurtures the new baby, but also swaddles the new parents – congratulations. I will have a copy in my library and recommend it to new mothers and new midwives alike.'

**Shannon Morris, Independent Midwife, Antenatal Education Co-ordinator Birth and Parenting Classes, Queanbeyan District Hospital, NSW**

'This comprehensive resource, based upon years of hands-on experience and current evidence, guides parents in developing critical parenting skills which will serve them and their children for a lifetime. The joy of this book is that it supports parents to find a way of knowing and doing that suits them and their babies best thereby building capacity and promoting resilience. Parents, grandparents, midwives, maternal and child health nurses and other health professionals will all find this book an invaluable resource.'

**Lynne Johnson, President, and Mary Kirk, Director of Nursing/Executive Officer Canberra Mothercraft Society Inc**

'I believe that this book will fill a need for common sense and practicality to prevail in women's lives. When there is so much information around that is based on old wives' tales, culture, evidence and women's stories it is nice to have all this information in one place. As you quite clearly state there is no one right way and women need to be convinced of this. Reading your book will help them.'

**Dr Pauline Glover RM FACM, Course Coordinator: Midwifery Programs School of Nursing & Midwifery, Flinders University, Adelaide**

'I found it enormously comprehensive and thoughtful. I showed it to a friend who said – thank God – everyone tells you about how to get through the birth, but nobody tells you what happens next, and you are left with this tiny baby you need to care for, but don't know where to start. So I can see that it will be of great use to many people. I really liked the practical chapter on first aid, and found the detailed advice in many of the areas very straightforward and easy to understand. So many thanks for sharing it with me.'

**Laurann Yen, General Manager, Community Health ACT**

'I was especially heartened to recognise the value you placed on the intuition of both mothers and midwives as I believe the "art" of midwifery is being lost amid medical procedures and machines that go ping! Sensible reassurance, acknowledgement of difference and real stories from real people, all knitted t ogether with your amazing experience and love of what you did makes your book truly inspirational and precious.'

**Tory Howell, Student Midwife, Bachelor Midwifery, Flinders University SA**

'This is a delightfully practical and supportive book for new parents, new midwives and new doctors – in fact for anyone with an interest in parenting.'

**Karen Guilliland, Reg Midwife, Reg Nurse and Obstetric Nurse, MA: MNZM New Zealand College of Midwives (Inc.)**

'I believe Rhodanthe's manuscript makes an important and comprehensive contribution to newborn care – an area that needs but has not received systemic attention to this date. I think that she brings a fresh perspective to the topic.'

**Danielle Cronin, Health Reporter, *The Canberra Times***

# Contents

# Acknowledgements

This edition has been undertaken in the shared spirit personified by Rhodanthe in everything she does for women, babies and families and midwifery. Rhodanthe asked me to edit this edition, which I have done with the help of many wonderful people who were prepared to read, comment, update, suggest, rewrite, renew and approve of Rhodanthe's wonderful, useful words. Rhodanthe has been diligent too in approving the reviewers' suggestions and making others.

As this has been a quite major revision in some parts, we have chosen to name the people who gave their time freely (and for free!) to review each chapter:

- Roslyn Woolley, RM, Grad Dip Mid – Chapter 1, 'Preparing for parenthood' and Chapter 2, 'Pregnancy'
- Alison Chandra, RM RN, B. App. Sci. – Chapter 3, 'The birth experience'
- Virginia Proust, RN RM, B. App. Sc. Health Ed. – Chapter 4, 'Following birth'
- Emma Baldock, RM, RN, Infant Welfare Cert, B App Sci (Health Ed), M Ed (Counselling Research), Grad Cert Prof Stud (Counselling Supervision) – Chapter 5, 'On being a parent'
- Judy Lamond, RM, RN, BNurs, Grad Dip in Prof Del in Ed, Master Ed Leadership, Grad Cert in Child and Family Health – Chapter 6, 'Communicating', Chapter 7, 'Problems' and Chapter 16, 'Formula (bottle) feeding'
- Michelle McCoombe, RM, Grad Dip Mid – Chapter 8, 'Sex following birth'
- Dr Marian Currie, RN RM Perinatal Cert B.App Sci (Nursing) GDPH PhD – Chapter 9, 'Depression following birth'

- Raelene Garret-Rumba – Chapter 11, 'Breastfeeding', Chapter 12, 'How breastfeeding works', Chapter 13, 'How to breastfeed' and Chapter 18, 'Settling, sleeping and wakefulness'
- Penny Maher – Chapter 15, 'Expressing, using and storing breastmilk' and Chapter 21, 'Feeding problems'
- Raelene Garret-Rumba and Penny Maher – Chapter 10, 'Feeding your baby' and Chapter 16, 'Formula (bottle) feeding'
- Edwina Biro, RN RM BNurs, Grad. Dip Mid, M.Mid Stud – Chapter 14, 'Questions frequently asked by breastfeeding mothers'
- Dr Jan Taylor RM, MN PhD – Chapter 17, 'Daily care'
- Jon Darvill, RN, MN – Chapter 19, 'Growth and development' and Chapter 23, 'Safety and first aid'
- Dr Sue Packer, MBBS, AM, FRACP – Chapter 20, 'Health and illness'
- Rosie Reilly provided excellent advice for the immunisation chapter.

Roslyn Woolley, Edwina Biro and Kate Lipsett assisted in many ways with drafts and sources.

That being said, we have taken liberties with the reviewers' advice and suggestions where it seemed appropriate for the whole of the book, so the final responsibility for content and process is of course Rhodanthe's and mine.

**Dr Jenny Browne**
Associate Professor in Midwifery
University of Canberra, ACT

# Foreword

This book is written to support new parents. I imagine it is first-time mothers and fathers who will rely on it most; women (and men) who because of today's small families and often heavy work and study commitments have little previous experience on which to rely. Families are looking for information and reassurance as they move from often fearful 'coping' to the confidence that only time and experience can build. Rhodanthe Lipsett has accompanied many of us on that often lonely and challenging journey towards the ultimate fulfilment of motherhood and fatherhood and the confidence we eventually develop when we realise that there is no 'one right way'.

Our work and that of colleagues shows many contemporary families, used to ready access to information and often pressed by time, are seeking a resource like this book. The book meets the particular needs of those early weeks and months when motherhood and fatherhood are most difficult because we lack experience in this new role. At the same time we are also getting to know and understand our new and uniquely different babies. This is the time when we are trying so hard to do the best for our babies and at the same time feel most vulnerable.

This book sets out to inform and explain without taking from parents (mostly mothers, given the way most families organise these first few months) their own inherent capacity to know and best manage this experience themselves. Parents, and those planning parenthood, have to sift the useful and correct information from all the advice given. Determining what is best for their baby can only happen after the baby is born. It is then, as we try to respond to cues and build a comfortable and nurturing relationship with this small but definite person, we discover that they themselves influence and shape this relationship astoundingly effectively. This process of negotiation is well described in this book. Rhodanthe allows us to explore, test out and learn about parenting and this baby at the same time. She provides immensely practical information and 'tips' that inspire confidence and that help us become effective, comfortable and to enjoy the role of parent of a small infant as quickly as possible.

I am delighted to commend this book to women and men contemplating or experiencing new parenting and to their mothers and all those 'others' who are trying to help.

**Professor Lesley Barclay, AO, PhD**
Director, University Centre of Rural Health,
North Coast, University of Sydney, Wollongong,
Southern Cross, Western Sydney and North Coast AMS

# Preface

The seeds for this book were planted more than half a century ago when I was a pupil midwife in a large outback Australian hospital.

On one particular morning an Aboriginal grandmother and her 16-year-old granddaughter, Mary, arrived at the hospital. Mary was in advanced labour. The grandmother was taken to the office to provide the admission information and I was left to take care of Mary. I was about to suggest to Mary that she come with me from the foyer of the maternity unit where we were standing to the admitting room. Before we could move, she was gripped by a very strong contraction. Her grandmother had vanished, her pain was severe and the strange environment frightening. She was distressed. Against the wall was a polished timber table complete with a fine maidenhair fern in a large ceramic pot. Mary dived beneath the table. I dropped to all fours and was trying to persuade her to come out, when in through the door swept the delivery suite supervisor – a dignified midwife of ample proportion – who was held in awe by all the pupil midwives. Her standards were exacting and she demanded a high performance from each of her pupils.

'Nurse! What on earth are you doing?' I explained the situation, and the next moment she too was down on the floor. Her stern expression softened and her voice became warm and encouraging. In response to Sister's coaxing Mary timidly crept out, but as she was helped to her feet, she was caught again by another strong contraction. She made no sound but flung her arms round Sister's neck, where she was comfortingly held. Sister's beautifully starched white veil slid down over one ear, but was totally ignored as she continued to reassure Mary.

I gathered my scattered wits. 'Sister, shall I collect the "prep" tray and take it to the anteroom?' Sister looked down at the frightened girl.

'No, nurse. I do not believe that Mary could handle a prep.'

My world rocked. I firmly believed that all mothers should have a perineum-shave and an enema before giving birth. Next I offered to go into the delivery room and put up the stirrups – a routine procedure in preparation for the birth of a baby in those days. Again Sister looked at Mary's frightened face. 'No nurse, I do not think that Mary could handle stirrups. At least we have persuaded her to lie on this trolley.' A further blow to another of my assumptions – that stirrups were to be used for all normal births in the labour ward.

Sister continued, 'In fact I think that I will be delivering this baby on the trolley if I can persuade her to stay on it. However, you had better bring in a mattress and put it on the floor just in case we need it.' Another strong contraction. Mary scrambled off the trolley and went down on hands and knees. 'Baby stuck, baby stuck. Gran says rock.' As Mary rocked back and forth I looked helplessly at Sister. 'Just rub her back firmly while I grab some gloves,' she said. Suddenly Mary climbed back onto the trolley. 'Baby come, baby come,' she panted. Sister was prepared, gloved hands ready. Another push and the baby boy arrived. As the cord was cut I expected Sister to hand the baby to me to take to the nursery to be bathed and weighed.

'No, nurse. Mary will be very upset if you take the baby. Get a bassinet from the nursery and put it beside bed nine.' She gently placed the little blood-covered baby into his mother's arms and told me that we would bath and weigh him beside Mary's bed. 'It is likely that he will not go into the bassinet at all but spend his time in the bed with his mother,' Sister explained. This is just what happened and Mary went home two days later instead of on day seven or eight as was customary then.

This birth occurred in the days when rules were rigid. There were certain ways things were to be done and we were expected to carry out our duties accordingly. The babies were kept in the nursery and could only be viewed through the glass window, even by the fathers. They only left the nursery to be fed, and this with stop-watch precision – ten minutes on each breast and then back to their bassinets.

I was still reeling from the morning's events when Sister appeared at my elbow, stiffly starched and immaculate once more. I was writing my report of the birth of Mary's baby. She fixed me with her firm eye: 'Well nurse, tell me, what did you learn this morning?'

I thought for a minute and then replied, 'I guess Sister, what I really learnt was that there is "no one right way" of doing things. Sometimes rules need to be changed to fit particular circumstances.'

She smiled. 'Quite right, see that you remember that.' And she swept off into her office.

I have never forgotten that lesson.

Babies are babies for such a short time that parents need to be able to delight in them and avoid unnecessary worries. Babies are a wonder and miracle of nature. Sadly, many parents find that the care and responsibility of their new baby is overwhelming; they become anxious and then doubt themselves when they need not do so.

They need to know that there are often many options from which to choose. They need to get sound information, and to feel free to question any advice they do not understand or which causes them anxiety. They need to know that care will vary from day to day and must be suited to each individual baby.

I wrote this book because I felt there was a place for one that addressed *in detail* the difficulties faced by parents in the early days and weeks after the birth of their babies. My aim is to inform, assist, inspire and encourage parents – particularly mothers, who are most often the principal caregivers – so that they can have more 'up times' than 'down times'. If they can experience less anxiety and greater confidence in these early weeks, I believe it can set the pattern for the months and years ahead.

Here I offer much of the knowledge I gained during my career as I shared experiences with colleagues, cared for and worked with mothers, fathers and their babies and reared my own children. I have concentrated on the very young baby, referring to older babies when appropriate. The same basic principles of care apply as a baby grows. I have repeated parts of some sections to explain a particular point being discussed.

Rhodanthe Lipsett

# 1

# Preparing for parenthood

**B**ecause parents' readiness to begin nurturing their newborn baby can be affected by the woman's experiences during pregnancy, labour and birthing, it is important to think about the preparations you wish to make for this special event. As women you will want to consider where, how and with whom you wish to give birth, remembering that information empowers you and yours. Today men are participating more and more in preparing and caring for their babies, so much of the information in this book applies to men as well as to women, who are still usually the primary caregivers in our society.

If you are planning to have a baby or you are already pregnant, it can be helpful to recognise that there will be inevitable changes when you become a parent. You will be thrust into a new and vitally important role which will absorb massive amounts of your time and energy as you provide the nurturing, the loving care and guidance your baby will need. This responsibility will continue for many years and you can expect your emotional ties to bind you permanently. The demands will be great but the rewards can make all the effort worthwhile.

Sometimes a baby is conceived accidentally and parents' feelings can be very mixed. The initial reaction can be delight but it may cause dismay and even panic depending on the circumstances at the time. Following the initial shock it is often possible to accept the fact that a baby is coming and to concentrate on ways to adapt to the reality and move on to accept and, in time, even enjoy the pregnancy.

Before your baby is born you could think of some ways to make life simpler and consider new plans you need to make. For example, think about how you can minimise housework and streamline shopping and cooking, and how you can obtain the rest you need as you manage your baby's frequent feeding and wakeful times. You could investigate

childcare facilities if you plan to return to work outside your home. It can be helpful to attend to some of the paperwork which must be done, e.g. filling out the form for the Family Tax Benefit (and Parenting Allowance if applicable), which can be done up to three months before the birth of your child.

Know that you will be continually learning. It is likely that your daily routine will often be turned upside-down and you may feel that you are no longer in control. If you can accept this, and even find something to laugh about, you can expect life to become easier as time passes. Parents need to talk together, negotiate differences and find ways to have some 'time out' alone and with each other. Lone parents really do need special support. Apart from regaining strength following the birth, lone parents have the sole responsibility for the new baby whom they are learning to know and care for, plus all the normal day-to-day chores. Somehow find a way of taking needed rest whenever possible, particularly during the first six weeks. Enlist friends and family and look for outside help. You can contact Lone Parent Family Support and other such groups.

If you understand, before your baby arrives, that mixed feelings are normal – joy and delight one minute, anxiety and frustration the next – you can be accepting of these feelings. If you are able to make adjustments without feeling guilty, you will be able to plan and make decisions to benefit you all.

**When planning to have a baby you can aim to:**
- have good health before conception and during pregnancy
- produce a healthy baby as easily as possible
- regain strength rapidly following birth
- begin caring effectively for this new individual.

You will do these things best if you plan well and have a relaxed understanding of yourself and your own reactions to new situations. It is important not to have rigid expectations of the experience ahead. Each woman reacts in her own way to conception, pregnancy, labour, birth and the reality of the newly separate but dependent life. Rigid expectations can affect your response to this experience and to your new baby. Mothers are often surprised and disappointed if their experience of birth and/or their new baby differs from their expectations. If you are aware of this possibility you can avoid unrealistic hopes and expectations, which will help you to emerge positively from your experiences – whatever they may be.

Obtaining information is the basis for planning and understanding. You need to feel confident that the information you receive is sound. Identify the types of care available and question anything you feel is unclear or anything you doubt. You will then be in a position to make informed choices.

**It will help to know:**

- how to plan and achieve optimum health before conception and beyond (there are suggestions following)
- what environmental factors, both at home and in the workplace, might affect your developing baby
- the health professionals available to offer any help you need in planning for pregnancy and to provide care during your pregnancy, birth and afterwards
- where you can give birth, the atmosphere, attitudes and policies of each place, booking-in arrangements
- what feelings and physical changes you can expect during pregnancy and beyond
- how to recognise the onset of labour
- what you will need to have ready for the birth and subsequent care of your baby
- how to finance the birth and the raising of your baby within the family budget – what health costs are covered by government (Medicare) or private health insurance and what gap you will have to meet; also, what other benefits from the government you may be eligible for following the birth.

# Preconception care

Parents' own health can affect that of their baby, so aim to be in the best health possible for at least three months before conception. Midwives and doctors – referred to as your health advisers in this book – can advise you on preconception care.

Alcohol drunk by the mother travels through her bloodstream and so to her developing baby. There is then a risk of birth defects and permanent brain damage. Although strictly limited amounts were formerly considered acceptable, it is now widely advised (by the National Health and Medical Research Council, for example) that for women who are pregnant or planning a pregnancy, not drinking at all is the safest option.

**To maximise health during pregnancy you can also follow these guidelines:**

- Choose a wide range of food and limit caffeine intake.
- Take a folic acid supplement as recommended by your health adviser. When taken before conception and in early pregnancy (until twelve weeks) it helps to guard against neural tube defects such as spina bifida.
- Take no illicit drugs.
- If possible avoid any drugs, including over-the-counter medications. If you take routine medication or need prescribed medication for a temporary condition, let your doctor know that you are hoping to become, or may be, pregnant.
- Balance exercise and rest.
- Do not smoke, particularly during pregnancy and your baby's first year.

# Genetic counselling

If you have concerns about your own or your partner's family history, or concerns about your age, it is important to discuss these with your health adviser either before or early in pregnancy. You may be referred to or prefer to seek advice from a genetic counsellor. There are informative pamphlets available too. It is important that you receive correct information early, preferably prior to ten weeks of pregnancy, so that you have time to decide which, if any, tests you will have.

# Equipping the household

There is a wide range of items on offer for the new baby. Babies grow fast and will rapidly outgrow many items of clothing, so it pays to be selective. Remember that you may also receive gifts and/or offers of equipment and clothing from family and friends.

It is important to check that all pieces of baby equipment, both old and new, meet safety standards. Kidsafe, formerly the Child Accident Prevention Foundation of Australia, offers valuable information to help you choose and use wisely. Look for the Australian Standards Mark when shopping: it indicates that the particular item meets minimum safety standards.

You can consider buying pre-owned items, particularly things such as cots (use a new mattress), change tables, prams and baths, to mention a few. If you do get a pre-owned baby capsule for the car it must: be in perfect order; not have been in an accident; and have no mould on the straps. Capsules must be correctly installed and must meet legal requirements.

An advertisement in the local paper may produce some of these in excellent order at a fraction of their new cost. The articles can be scrubbed and aired in the sunshine. (If items are painted, check that the paint is lead free – older babies will often chew on the top of a cot rail.) If you cannot be sure, have it stripped and repainted with varnish or lead-free paint. Do not do the stripping and repainting yourself while pregnant. Lead is toxic. Check that any pre-owned item you acquire meets safety standards.

Hazards which can lead to injury or death are exposed nuts, bolts or any sharp or rough piece. Loose harnesses, straps, strings, ribbons and buttons can cause choking. Be vigilant and make sure there are no loose pieces of cotton or wool which can wrap around fingers or toes, cutting off circulation. Wide gaps between cot and playpen bars can entrap a head, limbs and/or fingers (see below in 'For sleeping'). Check brakes on prams or strollers. Harnesses must be correctly attached; a good harness is made of webbing and has shoulder, lap and crotch straps.

Suffocation can occur where there are pillows, bumpers or unsewn flaps on mattress covers – you can buy safe waterproof covers for the mattress. Never have fine plastic near your baby (sometimes it is left on new mattresses). Fine plastic is dangerous because of the very high risk of suffocation.

## For the laundry

If using cloth nappies, you will need a nappy bucket with a lid. Tap squirters are not necessary but are helpful. One can be used to wash off the poo, after any bulk has been flushed down the toilet, before placing the nappy in the bucket. The Potty Pail nappy sprayer hose is one such device on the market.

## For bathing

Babies are bathed in baby baths, large kitchen sinks and often in laundry tubs. If using the laundry tub or kitchen sink, take care that your baby is not bumped against or burnt on a hot tap – if it is possible, run cold water through the tap prior to bathing to cool the tap down. There will probably be an adjoining bench top, or you

may have a portable change table which you can place close by. You may want a container for soiled clothes. Have two towels – one large body towel and a second, smaller face towel – some cotton wool, and a brush if your baby has hair. You may also choose to use aqueous cream as a soap alternative; it is hypoallergenic and pH balanced, and suitable for all sensitive skin including baby's. Although sprinkling a little talcum powder on baby's bottom used to be in vogue, it is no longer recommended by most professionals, including the American Academy of Pediatrics. Baby powder is unsafe because it contains various combinations of finely ground particles that are easily carried through the air in the same way as dust is. These powders can be easily inhaled and irritate the baby's lungs, possibly resulting in breathing difficulties or worse. Cornstarch has been marketed as an alternative to talcum powder; while cornstarch particles are slightly larger and less airborne than those in talcum powder, they can still pose a risk to your baby.

You can have a small jar containing zinc and castor oil cream which can be used if there is any sign of a nappy rash – it does not need to be used routinely. For cloth nappies use safety pins with snap locks or the plastic nappy fasteners; many cloth nappies today are self-fastening (usually with velcro tabs that can be folded in during washing so they don't catch and pull).

## *For sleeping*

Parents may choose to use a bassinet or cradle for young babies but they usually outgrow them within six months. You might instead use a cot or pram or a combination of these from birth. You will need to check the safety features. In a safe cot the spaces between the slats will be between 5 and 9.5 centimetres. The sides should be at least 60 centimetres above the level of the mattress and there should be no footholds which a toddler can use to climb out. The cot needs rounded corners and safety catches and no projecting pieces that may catch on clothing. Mattresses must fit closely to the sides, head and foot of the cot, pram or cradle so that legs and arms are not at risk of being caught in any gap. Fit a new mattress into a pre-owned bed. Bumpers and pillows are not recommended as there is a risk of suffocation. Don't have anything suspended across the cot in which small fingers can become entangled.

Cradles are popular and often settle a restless baby. It is important that your baby is never left unattended in a freely rocking cradle. They need to have a locking pin bolted into place and the maximum tilt should be no more than 10 degrees. If able to roll forward onto the face, a baby risks suffocation or injury.

Make up the cot or cradle so that your baby's feet are close enough to the bottom end to prevent your baby slipping down beneath the bed clothes – see below.

## Sheets

You can use cotton or flannelette sheets. The latter are warmer in winter. If it is very cold a blanket can be used in place of a bottom sheet. A rectangular piece of cotton sheeting can be placed under your baby's head, to cover the woollen blanket, as some babies are sensitive to wool; this sheeting can also catch any spills. To keep it in place, have it large enough to tuck well under each side of the mattress.

## Blankets

These may be woollen, a wool mix, cotton or acrylic. You can use two cot-size or one single bed blanket. If using a single bed blanket you can make the cot draught-proof by placing the blanket beneath the mattress with its length across the cot at your baby's shoulder height. Place it so that your baby's feet almost reach the bottom of the cot. SIDS and Kids have a detailed description of safe sleeping and helpful photos on their website, <http://www.sidsandkids.org/safe-sleeping>.This will help to prevent an active baby wriggling down under the covers. To cover your baby bring up one side of the blanket across the baby and tuck it under the mattress on the other side. If a second thickness is needed bring the free piece on the other side across and tuck it under the mattress. The surplus at the end can be tucked beneath the foot of the mattress. It is unlikely that you will need any of this spare part of the blanket as cover. If a little more warmth is needed it is better to dress the baby in a woollen cardigan or jumper over the lighter clothing rather than add more bedclothes; this way there is less risk of overheating your baby (see 'Keeping your baby comfortable' in Chapter 17 and 'SIDS' in Chapter 18).

Further suggestions: one or two colourful cot covers; a green mosquito net (green reduces glare) and an elastic band to hold the net in place. Nets can become dusty so they will need regular washing. Be aware of the risk posed by cats, particularly if you have one in the house or if your baby sleeps outside in the pram – they love to snuggle next to *or on top of* a warm baby. You could use a strong cat net. The pram must be deep enough and the net stretched tightly enough to prevent the weight of a cat settling on your baby.

If you use a hot water bottle to warm the cot in cold weather, remove it before you put your baby down. Do not use electric blankets: electricity and wet nappies are dangerous together. Babies can quickly overheat, sweat and become dehydrated. An over-heated baby is at increased risk of SIDS. Take care with heaters: do not have them near the cot. Never leave a bar radiator heater in the baby's room or allow your baby to be placed near one.

## Change tables

These are not essential but can be useful. Check that the height is right for you. They must be stable and have raised mattress edges or rails and a safety strap. Even so, no baby should ever be left unattended on one, as falls causing injury do occur. If you turn away from your baby to reach for something, always keep your hand firmly on your baby's body to prevent a fall.

## Playpens

Check the safety features. Any hinges need to lock firmly so that there is no risk to small fingers. Wooden rods or slats need to be close enough for safety (see the information on cots in 'For sleeping' above). If the playpen has meshed sides, take care that buttons are not caught in the mesh. A playpen has limited use but can be helpful if the phone or doorbell rings.

If the playpen has a base it reduces floor draughts which can be chilling and, when able to stand, your baby will not be able to push it across the floor. Once mobile, babies can become unhappy if kept in the playpen for long periods – it can feel like a prison. If your baby becomes used to it before starting to crawl, it is likely to be accepted happily for short times later. A playpen which can also be used as a portable cot probably provides the best value.

## Clothing for your baby

Have easy-care clothing which is comfortable, safe and practical for laundering, dressing and undressing. Natural fibres such as cotton, bamboo and wool allow ventilation and are cooler and warmer than synthetics. Always look for non-flammable material plus low fire-risk clothes. When buying clothing, remember that babies grow fast. Items you will need following birth will depend on the climate and season – whether it is hot or cold. Home delivery may be arranged through mail order catalogues, the Internet and over the phone. This can save busy mothers trips to department stores.

Many mothers make use of secondhand clothing and obtain it from op shops, garage sales, fetes and friends.

## Singlets

These come in both cotton and wool. It is useful to have some of each and use them according to the temperature around your baby. Usually cotton singlets are enough unless the temperature around your baby is cold. On a cold day you can add warmer outer clothes such as a woollen jumper or cardigan. If you use a woollen singlet, check that your baby does not become too hot (see 'Keeping your baby comfortable' in Chapter 17').

## Nighties and all-in-one cotton suits

In a hot environment, gowns can be more comfortable, particularly if made of very light cotton. Generally, cotton all-in-one grow-suits (sometimes called a 'onesie') are popular but are heavier and enclose the feet which can be a disadvantage in hot weather. It is important that the nappy can be easily changed without completely removing the all-in-one suit. As your baby grows it is important to check that an all-in-one suit still allows ample room for legs, feet and toes. Winter fabrics can be lightweight woollen, woollen mix or bamboo, which are comfortable to wear. Both wool and bamboo are sustainable and naturally thermal regulating, meaning your baby will stay cool in summer and warm in winter. Many synthetic fabrics provide little warmth and don't breathe. Back openings are easy for dressing and undressing, but avoid large raised buttons that would be uncomfortable to lie on. Mothers usually prefer the small snaps for closing. Nighties allow for easier nappy changing in the newborn and at night when you want to disturb your baby as little as possible.

## Bootees and mittens

Bootees must not restrict your baby's feet. Toes and fingers can be caught in open-patterned knitted or crocheted garments. As already mentioned, it is important to check that there are no loose threads to wind around fingers or toes and possibly cut off the circulation. You may prefer socks, which do not fall off as easily.

## *Baby rugs and wraps*

New babies often sleep more comfortably if wrapped. In cooler weather bunny rugs made of brushed cotton or a wool blend will be warmer. Soft, light woollen fabrics can be used. If using a sleeping bag check that your baby does not become over-heated. A well fitting armless sleeping bag is recommended by SIDS and Kids as it keeps baby warm without the risk of loose blankets covering baby's face. If you have a knitted shawl with an open pattern, remember the danger of fingers or toes being caught. If your baby likes to be wrapped in summer you could use muslin or a light cotton wrap.

## *Bibs*

Towelling bibs are absorbent and soft. Bibs which pull over the baby's head are much easier to manage than those with ties. Large bibs protect the clothing better than small ones. Make sure that they are not backed with soft plastic, because of the risk of suffocation, and remove the bib before putting your baby down to sleep.

## *Hats*

If out of doors and in the sun, your baby will need a hat. Similarly, if outside in cold weather your baby will need a warm woolly cap. Babies can rapidly lose heat through the head. However, one of the recommendations of the National SIDS Council of Australia is that babies are not left to sleep alone if wearing a head cover of any sort, as it could slip over the baby's face.

## *Nappies*

There is the choice between cloth and disposable nappies. Cloth nappies are reusable. It is advisable to wash nappies and clothes with pure soap, preferably one containing no phosphates. Gauze nappies are soft, comfortable and cooler in hot weather. (These are not available in all baby departments but you might find them online.) Terry towelling ones are thicker, more absorbent and comfortable to wear. Flannelette are cheaper but less absorbent. Hemp and bamboo nappies are also available; they are generally highly absorbent and come in a wide range of sizes, colours and fastening options – search online to find the style you feel most comfortable with. Later, you can use cloth nappies in other ways, for example, you can cut them to make face washers, bibs and small towels.

Bacteria, which cause illness and/or nappy rash, multiply in the faeces (poo) and urine, and must be killed. Cloth nappies, completely submerged in an anti-bacterial solution for the recommended time – this is usually at least six hours – may be washed in warm water. The chemical solution needs to be changed daily. If not pre-soaked in such a solution use hot water – between 60°C and 80°C – for washing nappies. Use the longest wash cycle. Sun and frost are good bleaching agents and reduce the need to use bleaches which are expensive and environmentally unfriendly.

Most of the so-called 'disposable' nappies are also an environmental problem. Put into the garbage they take up enormous space in landfill. Groundwater may be contaminated by bacteria from these soiled nappies and there are possible health risks from dioxins which may be left in the nappy pulp when chlorine processes are used in manufacture. However, today there are manufacturers who do not use chlorine-based processes so check the packaging. Disposable nappies are expensive and are bulky to carry home with the shopping. You can buy from mail order companies and this can be a cheaper option. However, disposable nappies are most useful in emergencies and when travelling. Sometimes they are used just at night because they are very absorbent. If using disposables, realise that disposable nappies do not feel wet like cloth nappies, so take care that you change your baby often enough to prevent nappy rash.

Now there is a product from Tasmania, Weenees (by Eenee Designs), which you may choose to investigate. These are waterproof baby pants plus inner pads. The pads are changed and can be flushed down the toilet. Weenees have the convenience of standard disposable nappies while being 100 per cent compostable and biodegradable. Normal cloth nappies can be also be used inside the baby pants without the need for pins. The baby pants are machine washable. The soft inner lining is waterproof but lets in air, helping to prevent sweating and rashes.

## Nappy service

This service may be available in your area. Wet and soiled nappies are collected and a fresh supply left once or twice weekly. You may find that the cost of a nappy service is comparable to the cost of disposables. If you use this service, and you have options, try to find a company which avoids using strong detergents. They are not kind to your baby's skin or the environment.

## Nappy liners

Fabric liners are used inside cloth nappies. These can be washed and reused. Because they draw moisture away from your baby's skin they reduce discomfort and lessen the likelihood of nappy rash. There are also disposable nappy liners. If these are only wet you can wash and reuse them two or three times before discarding them. The nappy liners hold much of the bowel motion. Rinse the faeces down the toilet before placing the liner in the nappy bucket or disposing of it. You can also use flushable liners and place both the faeces and liner straight into the toilet.

## Nappy covers

These are available in flannel, woollen knits (these are usually hand-knits), PUL (a breathable, knitted polyester) or cotton, e.g. fluffies. They are sometimes called pilchers or over-pants. They prevent your baby feeling cold in a wet nappy and help to keep clothing and bed dry. You can make your own. Buy a piece of flannel measuring 90 centimetres by 140 centimetres from which you can cut four triangular pieces which can be pinned over the cloth nappy. Plastic nappy pants which fit closely around the thighs and waist do not allow circulation of air and can keep your baby's skin moist, steamy and prone to nappy rash. Except for really short periods they are not advised. If you use them, check that they are not too tight around the waist or thighs.

## *A sample clothing list*

**Nappies:** you will need 24 to 30 cloth nappies or waterproof baby pants with the flushable pads (e.g. Weenees) or at least five or six packets of other disposable nappies.

**Nappy liners:** a box of disposable liners and/or three or four cloth nappy liners – particularly useful at night.

**Nappy pants or fluffies:** six or seven.

**Cotton singlets:** four to six. Remember that your baby will grow rapidly so do not have too many of the same size.

**Woollen cardigans or jumpers:** three or four.

**Long or short gowns or all-in-one stretch suits:** three or four.

**Hats:** sun hat and a warm cap – one of each.

**Bibs:** six or more.

**Wraps:** light wraps – two or three; warm bunny rugs – four or more.

# 2

# Pregnancy

If you are planning to have or are having a baby, you need to find knowledgeable and supportive professional caregivers in whom you feel confident – those who will provide skilled care and the information you need, preferably before conception and then throughout the pregnancy, birth and the postnatal period.

# How some mothers reacted to pregnancy and birth

**Gemma:** *'When we found out I was pregnant David and I were devastated. We weren't sure we wanted a child but we were sure that the timing was a disaster. We'd just bought an old house and we needed both our incomes to meet the repayments and buy the materials for repairs. What to do? We briefly considered an abortion but neither of us could face that. David said that I would have to decide whether to give up work or keep on. Whatever we considered, the problems seemed really grim. Apart from all that I had never even held a baby, knew nothing about them and wasn't sure that I wanted to find out.*

*I did go to the antenatal classes and felt out of it for the first two or three visits. The other mothers or couples seemed so happy and enthusiastic that I felt guilty for being different. Then I met Molly. She was a single girl and things were far worse for her. We supported each other and things improved. It wasn't till I felt Michael moving that I really faced up to the fact that this baby was coming. I had to have a caesarean. I didn't feel a rush of maternal love for Michael but David was wrapped in him at once – this didn't make me feel any better. I breastfed but resented his frequent feeding.*

*The best thing that happened was that Sue, one of the postnatal midwives, saw that I was upset. She just sat with me for a while and then said 'Would you like to tell me?' She accepted the way I was feeling and pointed out that Michael would be likely to sleep much better and that I would be more relaxed if I just fed him when he was hungry. She had a theory that caesarean babies need extra touching and holding because they had missed out on the experience of passing through the birth canal. Michael is now three months old. He is fully breastfed. When he started smiling I began to love and enjoy him but it's still all happening slowly. We've found a nice motherly woman with school age children nearby, who is willing to care for Michael while we are at work. Her own children are bright and happy. We can trust her with Michael. I leave expressed breastmilk for her to give him. Life isn't all easy – I feel trapped at times but it's settling down and now we are really happy that we have him.'*

**Alicia:** *'My main worry is: do I go back to work or do I stay at home? I'm in a no-win situation. I know I will feel guilty whichever decision I make. Henry's no help, he says it is up to me. Whatever we mothers do is wrong. If we go back to work we are selfish and putting our own interests ahead of the baby. If we stay at home we will vegetate and become dull and uninteresting and add a heavy load to our husbands, who have then to be the only income earners. It's all so confusing.'*

**Elke:** *'When we found out that I really was pregnant, Xavier and I were euphoric. We had been trying for the last five years and had more or less given up hope. I could even live with morning sickness and be happy. We haven't much money but we can live without the restaurants and weekends away – I can even pass my favourite dress shop without wanting to buy. Already Xave is stripping and painting an old cot although I am only two months pregnant. I suppose reality will hit us when our baby is born but I can't imagine anything really getting us down. There is nothing worse than desperately wanting a baby and the same old curse keeps turning up.'*

Your initial reaction to your pregnancy will depend on a number of factors, especially on whether it is planned. Very often feelings are mixed and vary from day to day. Happy anticipation can be mixed with worries about health, changing circumstances, the effect on your relationship with your partner and feelings about your ability to care for your new baby. Many people will offer advice and relate stories of their own pregnancies and experiences, which may encourage you or cause you needless anxiety depending on the details. No two pregnancies are the same. Should problems develop during your pregnancy, regular checks can help to detect them early so that their impact may be minimised.

## Antenatal care

Antenatal care is usually provided by a midwife, a family doctor, a specialist obstetrician, or by a combination of healthcare providers. It is designed to monitor your health and that of your developing baby and provide you with opportunities to discuss your pregnancy, birth and postnatal care. It is common to book in for regular antenatal care after twelve to fourteen weeks. However, it is not uncommon for lots of hospitals or services to have long waiting lists, so no harm can be done by making contact much earlier in your pregnancy. You may wish to see your doctor or midwife earlier, particularly if you are considering early pregnancy tests or you are unsure of your due date. It is usual for pregnant women to be checked at regular intervals throughout pregnancy.

At your first visit you will be asked questions about any previous pregnancies, your general health and family history. You can expect a full physical and gynaecological examination. Routine tests will be explained, planned or performed. You will also be able to ask any questions you may have.

Many women find antenatal education (parent preparation classes) very helpful. A support person/s can attend with you. Sharing with other expectant parents can be a benefit and lasting friendships are often made. The classes are usually conducted by the hospital or birth centre where you have planned to have your baby. If you are having a home birth, your midwife will advise you. Your health adviser or local hospital will be able to tell you what classes are available in your area. These classes are usually relaxed and friendly, with ample time to discuss any aspects of pregnancy, labour, birth and the early postnatal period.

Breastfeeding is best for your baby. So early in pregnancy the first step is to think positively and accept that you can and will breastfeed.

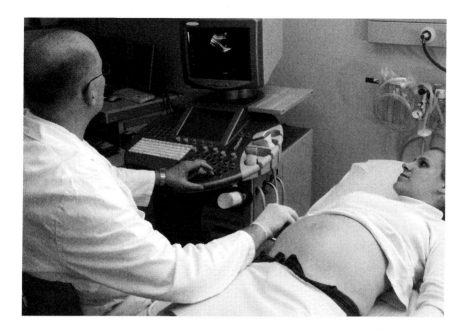

Your body will certainly be getting ready to do so. Look for midwives and/or doctors who truly support breastfeeding. There are maternity units which have been accredited as Baby Friendly (see the 'Hospitals' section in Chapter 3, 'The birth experience'). You can ask when booking in for the birth. You can also contact the Australian Breastfeeding Association (ABA) and Lactation Consultants of Australia and New Zealand (LCANZ), both of which offer help before and after the birth of your baby.

## Pathology tests and investigations

There is a wide range of tests available to you. Your health adviser will provide details of all the recommended tests for you and your baby. Some are recommended at the beginning of pregnancy and others at later stages. You can discuss these so that you can understand their purpose and make an informed choice about those you wish to have done.

# Managing your food

Your health is always affected by what you eat. An ideal time to check your nutrition is when starting a family, the particular motivation being the health and wellbeing of your new baby. Good nutrition does not depend on elaborate and time-consuming cooking. Choose a variety of nutritious, simply prepared food (minimally processed and low in additives). Avoid artificial sweeteners such as saccharin and cyclamates. Perishables need to be eaten when they are as fresh as possible.

If you suffer from food allergies, discuss these with your health adviser. Avoid any foods you develop an aversion to and do not 'binge' – that is, eat any one food in excess. Craving can indicate a sensitivity to a particular food.

The body needs the equivalent of six to eight or more glasses of water daily. It is valuable to drink water itself instead of just having tea or coffee. Unsweetened pure fruit juice is preferable to sweetened drinks, cordials and other soft drinks. Remember to limit your intake of caffeine, which is present in tea, coffee, cocoa (and therefore chocolate) and cola. If you have reason to think that caffeine disagrees with you, avoid it. Two cups of fluid containing caffeine, preferably weak, is considered the daily maximum; less would be preferable, both during pregnancy and while breastfeeding.

Because of the risk of the infection listeriosis, mothers are advised to avoid eating any unpasteurised cheese such as farm cheese, camembert, brie, ricotta, etc. unless they are used in a cooked dish and eaten hot. Other foods that may contain listeria are raw and smoked seafood, takeaway salads, cold meat and pate. The infection typically produces mild flu-like symptoms in the mother but if transmitted to her developing baby she may miscarry, have a premature birth, or have a stillbirth. Her baby may suffer severe illness.

Fish is an excellent source of protein and the valuable omega 3 fatty acids but some of the larger fish higher up the food chain, such as tuna and swordfish, may contain mercury and are better avoided. Soft boiled eggs may contain salmonella but well-cooked scrambled egg is considered safe. You can talk with your health adviser about such foods or discuss them with a dietitian.

## Food and morning sickness

Some mothers experience nausea and/or vomiting, particularly during the first three months. It is often worst first thing in the morning, although vomiting can occur at other times during the day. It is usually due to the production of hormones needed for the early development of the baby.

**You can try:**

- eating a piece of dry toast, a plain biscuit or a piece of fruit before getting up
- drinking very weak black or ginger tea, a small glass of ginger ale, soda water or tomato juice
- having small nutritious meals (four to six per day); they may be better tolerated than large meals and will help to keep the blood sugar levels within normal limits
- having steamed rather than fried food to reduce fat intake; if the vomiting persists, discuss this with your health adviser
- resting as much as possible – this can reduce persistent vomiting.

## Constipation and possibly haemorrhoids

To reduce the risks of these two conditions aim to:

- increase your fluid intake (aim for at least two to three litres a day)
- eat more vegetables and fruit, both fresh and dried – prunes and figs may help
- choose wholegrain breads and cereals, and you could add three or four teaspoons of unprocessed bran
- increase your intake of legumes and nuts
- take moderate exercise such as walking and swimming.

Should nausea, constipation and/or haemorrhoids persist, discuss these with your health adviser. Iron supplements in early pregnancy may increase constipation. Having a daily bowel movement at a regular time may help.

## *Vegetarian mothers*

It is not difficult to have a balance of all the nutrients you need if you plan carefully. Take particular care that you have enough high quality protein and vitamin B12, iron and calcium. There is high quality protein in eggs, dairy and soy products. Dairy products are rich in calcium, and there are soy products which are fortified with calcium. You can obtain vitamin B12 from milk, eggs, mature cheese, brewers' yeast and fortified soy drink. Discuss your need for vitamin B12 with your health adviser – you may need a supplement. Because there is no red meat in the diet an iron supplement may be needed. An excellent book for vegetarian mothers is *Diet For a Small Planet* by Frances Moore Lappé, published by Ballantyne. It provides useful recipes and combinations of foodstuffs, particularly the meatless proteins, to maximise their nutritional value.

Select a variety of foods from the major groups. If you do not eat meat and fish you need to carefully combine foods which complement each other to supply complete protein. This occurs, for example, when

milk or milk products are added to cereals. Cereal foods with legumes and nuts complement one another to provide a meal with high quality protein.

## Vegan mothers

Because a vegan diet contains no animal products at all, if you choose this diet you will need to pay particular attention to obtaining enough iron, vitamin B12 and calcium. Supplements are usually needed. Balance the proteins you eat: see the above information on vegetarian mothers. Discuss your diet with your health adviser.

## Mothers who follow other traditional cultural eating practices

These mothers usually produce healthy babies. The traditional foods in appropriate quantities and balance in their countries of origin provide the necessary nutrients. If this were not so these cultures would not have healthy mothers and babies. If yours is such a diet it is likely that your health adviser will discuss any particular nutritional needs with you.

Sources of information about nutrition and diet are: the healthcare professionals caring for you; a dietitian at a hospital (if you are unable to visit you can obtain telephone advice); books on nutrition obtainable at the library or bookshop.

You need variety to meet your nutritional needs for carbohydrate, fat, protein, minerals, vitamins, water, bulk and fibre. No single food is adequate in all respects.

## Vitamins and minerals

Good quality food – some from each group – should provide the vitamins and minerals needed but, in addition, you are most likely to be advised to take a folic acid supplement for twelve weeks before conception and for twelve weeks in early pregnancy to guard the growing baby against neural tube defects such as spina bifida. An iron supplement may also be useful in the prevention of anaemia. Your health adviser will discuss supplements with you. Black stools (faeces) are a harmless side effect of an iron supplement; constipation can be more troublesome and is usually improved by increasing water and fibre in your diet and by daily exercise.

## Selecting and preparing food

Choose a wide range of foodstuffs, minimise processed food and use the freshest food available. Frozen or tinned fruit and vegetables can be more nutritious than tired, limp produce. Look for those with low or no added salt or sugar. Keep your daily intake of fat, salt and sugar low. Minimise fried, fatty foods: oily chips, sausage rolls, meat pies and spring rolls, etc. Sugary items may include breakfast cereals, biscuits, cakes, chocolates, sweets, soft drinks and so on.

## Eating

Plan regular meals. You can have breakfast, a light meal and a main meal, and a drink whenever you feel thirsty. If hungry between meals have a nutritious snack such as bread or plain biscuits with cheese, a piece of fruit or some yoghurt. A few nuts with some dried sultanas or raisins can also be satisfying. Do not eat 'on the run'. Relax and enjoy your food.

Here is a possible menu for a day:

**Breakfast:** Orange juice (preferably freshly squeezed) and/or one or two pieces of fruit, cereal with milk, toast with butter or table margarine. You could have an egg, cheese or baked beans with bread or toast. You might enjoy a glass of milk or have water, tea or coffee. You might choose decaffeinated tea or coffee.

**Light meal:** A light meal may include fresh salad or some vegetables with eggs, meat, chicken, fish or cheese. Bread with butter or table margarine, a piece of fresh fruit with yoghurt and a drink.

**Main meal:** Meat, fish, poultry, cheese, eggs, legumes; pasta or rice; potato and other vegetables or salad.

**Dessert:** Dessert could be a milk pudding, yoghurt or a glass of milk; fresh fruit and a drink of your choice.

# Preparing for breastfeeding

| You can | Why? |
|---|---|
| Aim to be relaxed and confident in your ability to breastfeed | Milk production is a normal stage of reproduction. After birth your breasts will automatically make enough milk for your baby |
| Take care of your health: eat simple nourishing food and balance your rest and exercise | Good health is a major factor in maintaining your wellbeing and milk supply |
| Involve your partner and/or other supportive people in your preparations. They can share in gathering information about breastfeeding | Mutual support and working together will help you breastfeed successfully. Studies have shown that if others, particulary a partner, are supportive of breastfeeding it is far more likely to be successful |
| Contact local groups of breastfeeding mothers, for example the Australian Breastfeeding Association (ABA), and spend time with such a group where you can watch, learn and socialise. You can talk with members of the Australian Lactation Consultants Association (ALCA) during your pregnancy | Being with and talking to breastfeeding women can give you information and strengthen your confidence in your own ability to breastfeed |
| Get to know your breasts and nipples. Learn to feel comfortable handling them. Understand the changes that occur with pregnancy and lactation (see below) | You will be able to take steps to avoid or minimise any breast and nipple problems |
| If you have questions ask your midwife, doctor or other health adviser experienced in breastfeeding. Do not be distressed if you receive conflicting advice. Find what approach works best for you and rely on your knowledge of your body and your baby | Having knowledge helps to reduce any anxieties you may have |

## Changes to the breasts during pregnancy

Pregnancy is controlled by a number of hormones and these affect the breasts almost immediately. They may feel tender, tingly or full and surface veins may appear. They will increase in size as glandular tissue and milk ducts multiply, and around four to five months into pregnancy you may need a larger bra. Occasionally the capacity in some breasts is a little less than average and when the baby is born it may be necessary to feed a little more frequently. However, this is not related to breast size.

Before the first pregnancy the areola – the area around the nipple – is usually pink. It darkens during pregnancy and then remains dark. Small 'bumps' around the areola, known as Montgomery's tubercles, will enlarge. They produce oily secretions which condition and protect the nipples and areola, and are antibacterial. The nipples change in shape and become protractile – that is, they can readily stretch out. This helps the baby to draw the nipple well back into the mouth along with some or all of the areola and part of the breast when feeding. Around the fifth month of pregnancy the breasts begin to secrete a small amount of sticky, yellowish fluid, known as colostrum. You may not notice this. The colostrum will provide your baby's first feeds for two or three days after birth before the breastmilk 'comes in'.

## Antenatal care of breasts and nipples

Most pregnant women need no special preparation of their breasts and nipples during pregnancy besides their usual personal hygiene. Nipples need no creams.

Avoid soap on nipples and breasts so that the natural oily secretions are not removed; just pat dry after a shower and avoid rough drying which can be damaging.

Some women have flat or inverted nipples which do not become erect when stimulated. If the nipple stands out when the areola is pressed between finger and thumb the baby is likely to attach easily and no nipple treatment is needed. During pregnancy nipples improve naturally. The oestrogens (hormones) in the body affect the breast tissue behind the nipples and make them more protractile. Various treatments for flat/inverted nipples have been tried.

There are mothers who feel that a set of exercises – called Hoffman's exercises – are helpful but at present there is no scientific evidence to support this. If you wish to try them, the following description may help you. To use Hoffman's exercises, imagine a cross on your nipple. Along one line of the cross you place a thumb on each side of your nipple at the very base. Now firmly press in against the breast tissue. As you are doing this, also pull your thumbs away from each other. The idea is to try to loosen the tightness at the base and stretch out the nipple. You will see the nipple move up and outward. It is recommended that you do this first thing in the morning. Repeat the stretch five times, first along one line of the cross and then five times along the other.

There is a device – the Niplette – that some pregnant women use. The Niplette is placed over the nipple and as air is withdrawn using a small syringe the inverted nipple is sucked into it. If you use this device, always control the amount of suction you apply. Do not overdo it. The aim is to gently stretch the nipple as the plunger in the syringe is drawn out. It is controversial whether this treatment should be used during pregnancy or only before conception. Talk to your doctor, an experienced midwife or lactation consultant about it. The Niplette is expensive and many lactation consultants use modified disposable syringes instead. They are used more often after birth when helping the baby to breastfeed.

It is sometimes suggested that pregnant women with flat/inverted nipples use breast shells (breast shields) which are usually made of plastic. These are saucer-shaped with a hole for the nipple on the inner surface. The shells are placed over the nipples to help shape them and are worn inside the bra. Some mothers continue, or begin, to use them while breastfeeding. Their use may make the nipple stand out and so help the baby to attach well to the breast. However, there is a danger that the pressure of the shell may obstruct the milk ducts and lead to engorgement. Also, within the shell the nipples can become moist and even swollen and predisposed to soreness and fissures. Many babies can learn to breastfeed well on such nipples without the use of breast shells. If your baby is finding it difficult to attach, seek experienced help.

Sometimes people want to relate alarming or unpleasant stories of pregnancy and birth to expectant mothers – either their own or someone else's experience. It is usually best to say 'I really feel I do not want to listen to that just now'. If you have worries or concerns you can discuss these with your health adviser.

# 3

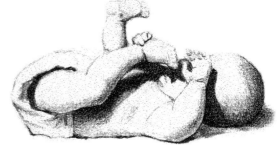

# The birth experience

The birth of a baby is a momentous life event. Remember that each mother's experience is unique. Regardless of your wishes, your body, in conjunction with your baby, will perform in its own way following its own programming. Be prepared to flow with nature. Avoid having expectations of what your body should do and you can lessen any disappointment and feeling of failure should it behave differently.

Generation follows generation for all living things on the planet, and humans are no different. A new generation will replace us and live its span before giving way to the next. Giving birth to a baby is part of the program that ensures the survival of our species. While this basic reproductive function has not changed, the cultural attitudes that surround reproduction have. There have been enormous cultural changes in the last 10 000 years or so. Initially people lived in small groups, hunting and gathering for their food. As people began growing crops and herding animals, villages, towns and cities became established. Complex societies developed in which lifestyles and behaviours became quite different.

It seems likely that reproducing women have always been cared for and supported by other women. Very recently men and the medical profession have become more involved. Increasingly, partners and expert healthcare are being depended upon. It is important for society and the individual to keep assessing the quality of care provided and ensure that it meets the needs of the mother and her baby. Too often rules and regulations have been used to make things easier for the maternity units and the caregivers. Unfortunately this can still occur and can compromise the experience of birth.

When a woman comes into labour feeling well prepared and flexible, and that she can rely on her chosen professionals for skilled care and possibly her partner or a friend for support, she is likely to be in the best frame of mind for the experience ahead. Cultural practices that alter the way our bodies naturally reproduce have to be approached carefully and adopted with discretion. At times they are appropriate and even life-saving – the natural program is not infallible. However, when used to suit fashion or convenience, it is likely that they are at best unnecessary or, at worst, damaging. Such practices include, for example, elective caesarean sections chosen without a medical reason. All surgery carries a degree of risk and should not be undertaken lightly. Surgical birth can also affect how a new mother feels. The unwanted separation of a healthy mother and baby in the hospital setting and ill-considered use of breastmilk substitutes also are unnecessary and possibly harmful.

Most women can give birth and provide the precise nourishment for their offspring that nature intends. If we respect nature's program and at the same time make use of new skills and technology when appropriate, we can have the best of both worlds. To make good choices, learn all you can about your options. Examine the advantages and disadvantages of each before you make your decision.

Each woman has different hopes and wishes for her experience of birth. Her choices will depend on the availability of options. Even in cities, but more so in country areas, choices can be restricted, so obtain the information you need to make the best decision within your reach.

Some women want to maximise personal control and involvement in all aspects of their pregnancy, labour, birth and in the postnatal care of their babies. They see their doctor and/or midwife as providers of skills, care and information, supporting them in their endeavours. Others want to depend totally on the decisions and direction of the professionals they have chosen, with little involvement themselves. Many choose a model of care somewhere between these two.

# Where to give birth

Women give birth in different environments – in hospitals, birthing centres or at home. Your choice of your professional caregiver will influence your decision. Doctors and midwives are often restricted in the areas where they can work. For example, some are not prepared to attend home births. You can learn about different options by talking to people, reading and visiting maternity units. It is probably best to keep an open mind. You do not know what the circumstances of your birth will be. If you come into labour very early or a medical emergency occurs, your needs will be quite different from a normal, full-term labour and birth. Sometimes compromise will be necessary. This is likely to be less stressful if you have accepted this possibility. If any aspect of your labour and/or the birth has disappointed or concerned you in any way, talk about this with your midwife or doctor. Doing so can be very helpful.

## *Hospitals*

Many hospital maternity units aim to meet the particular wishes of the mothers or couples concerned; some are less flexible because of administrative or staff attitudes. If you have a choice of hospitals, find out how midwives and the medical staff regard all aspects of birthing and postnatal care. Today there are hospitals which have been accredited as Baby Friendly: they meet the criteria which are considered to give mother and baby the best opportunity to establish successful breastfeeding. You might ask if the hospital has been accredited or if it is working towards accreditation.

**Some questions you could ask of a hospital include:**

- Can I have my own midwife?
- Do they offer continuity of midwifery care models? That is, will I be cared for by a midwife or team of midwives whom I can get to know and trust?
- What is available – private, shared or family rooms?
- What will be the total cost?
- What will be covered by health insurance?
- Does the hospital provide nappies, baby clothes, sanitary pads and other items?
- What is the hospital's policy on rooming-in? (Most hospitals now routinely keep healthy babies beside their mothers, unless either needs some special care.)
- Who may be present with me during labour and birth?
- What options are there for pain relief?
- Do they offer water birth?
- Is there an early-discharge scheme?
- Who will determine my length of stay in hospital?

Many hospitals provide printed information. They are likely to have brochures of government and community services available too. Most encourage you to visit their maternity unit to see the facilities and to meet staff members from the various areas. You may ask questions, discuss your views and explore possibilities. Hospitals can provide a list of the doctors and any independently practising midwives who are accredited and have visiting rights with that hospital.

The length of your stay in hospital after your baby's birth will depend on your labour and birth experience. Most hospitals with early

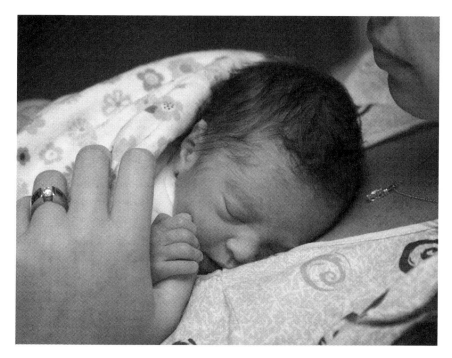

discharge programs will encourage you to go home after one or two days if all is well with you and your baby and your birth has been normal. If there have been complications, you may need to stay longer. During your postnatal stay midwives provide care for and advice about the body changes you will experience. Midwives also provide any post-operative care you may require. You will learn how to feed, settle and care for your baby. Staff will be there to answer your questions. Many hospitals offer talks, demonstrations and videos. Such information will increase your confidence in nurturing your baby when you return home. You should also be given information and advice about postnatal exercises, and larger hospitals will have a Women's Health physiotherapist available to help you.

## Birth centres

In Australia, birth centres are usually located within hospital precincts but separate from the delivery suites or labour wards. If problems arise the woman can quickly be transferred to wherever she needs to be for the birth of her baby. Birth centres aim to provide a family-oriented, home-like environment where woman-focused, midwife-led care encourages birth without unnecessary intervention. A team of midwives provides skilled care and education. Women are encouraged to make informed choices and to take an active part in their birthing experience supported by the people they have chosen.

Many women feel that a birth centre is a halfway house between a hospital birth and a home birth. They value the continuity of care provided by a team of experienced midwives throughout pregnancy, labour, the birth and the immediate postnatal period. These women value the care of midwives they have come to know well – in whom they have confidence. Nevertheless they like to know that there will be access to medical technology should the need arise. Medical appointments are made according to the policy of the birth centre or at any time if needed.

If the birth is trouble-free it is usual for mothers and their babies to go home within 24 hours of birth. Home visits by a midwife are arranged and usually continue for a week. If necessary, further visits may be arranged.

If you choose such a birth, you may need to book early because the birth centres are usually small. You can contact your nearest birth centre for detailed information. You will be given the chance to meet all the midwives in the team.

## Home births

In choosing a home birth an expectant mother decides to labour and give birth at home. Most often her health professional will be a midwife, or her midwife and doctor may share care. Women choosing home birth usually feel strongly that the birthing process is a normal physiological event which has no place in a hospital setting unless there are medical problems. These women wish to actively participate – to share responsibility and decision-making with their professional attendants. They look for a competent midwife or doctor who shares this view.

The Australian College of Midwives can provide a list of hospitals or health services that provide a home birth service and of eligible midwives in private practice in each state or territory. At present there remains an issue with insurance for midwives working with women birthing at home. The Australian College of Midwives is working with federal and state governments and insurance companies to find a solution. If your wish is for a home birth you can contact the college for information.

## Discharge from hospital

The length of stay following a normal birth varies and there is often a difference between public and private hospitals. Some mothers go home on day two or three. They may feel very anxious if they are discharged before their milk 'comes in' and breastfeeding is underway. When a mother is discharged early it is to be hoped that she can be part of an early discharge program in which a midwife visits daily for the first week and, if there is a need, arranges further visits. Both mother and baby are checked. Help, advice and information can be given and any questions answered. Provided the mother has home support and help this can be a happy arrangement for all concerned. Early discharge for mothers without support is strongly discouraged. Giving birth is demanding physically, mentally and emotionally and all mothers deserve and need someone on hand to care for them in the first days and weeks following birth. Information can be obtained from the hospital or birthing centre you are planning to attend. Some hospitals have weekly or monthly coffee mornings that many new or expectant parents find helpful and pleasant.

It is becoming more widely recognised that mothers need a restful environment together with emotional and practical help following birth, not only in the first few days while in hospital but also on returning home and preferably for as long as 30 to 40 days. Postnatal exercises are important and gentle walking is helpful – but do not underestimate the need for frequent rests, restriction of visitors and the opportunity to spend time focusing on the new baby. Mothers must not feel that they are being lazy but understand that this is best for their baby and for themselves as they regain their strength and adapt to their new circumstances.

If there is an early childhood centre near you, find out where and when you can visit. Here you can obtain ongoing help and support. Meeting other mothers with their babies can be an additional benefit. Many family doctors encourage a visit to their rooms as soon as possible after the birth. Mothers often find this visit very reassuring.

## Today's changing attitudes

In recent years ideas have changed. Not long ago rigid regimes and rules were imposed mostly for the convenience of hospitals and staff rather than for the total wellbeing of the family unit. Holistic care – the care of the feelings and wishes as well as of the physical needs of families – is now seen as important by the majority of health professionals. Many expectant parents see this care as a right and actively seek it.

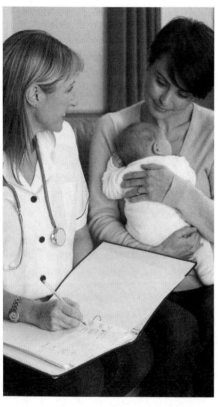

If you have a limited choice of maternity units and you are unhappy with any of the practices followed, you might enlist the support of your doctor and/or midwife and discuss your feelings with the staff. Make a list of your wishes, outlining the things that are important to you during your labour, birth and early postnatal time, and remember to remain flexible. Expect cooperation and offer it. Good communication can lessen misunderstanding. When goodwill and trust are established it is easier to accept a change in your birth plan should it be necessary for the safety of you or your baby.

# Parents have different needs and preferences

The following examples demonstrate the need for mothers to ask, read and visit. Discover the options available in your area and then make the choice you feel is right for you. Remember: you are the consumer and may need 'to shop around'.

When they were expecting their second child, Caitlin and Barry had a much clearer idea of what they wanted than when expecting their first.

**Caitlin:** *'We wanted a safe birth for our baby and for me and we chose our local hospital. We discussed with our doctor the things we felt strongly about. She was ready to support us but did advise us to remain flexible in case of difficulties. Together we made out a birth plan.*

*We talked with the midwife in charge in the maternity unit. She was happy with each point we made – most were hospital policy anyway.*

*I needed to be sure that our baby could room-in with me. I was told that rooming-in was usual but, if at any time I wanted a complete rest, the nursery staff would take baby into the nursery for a while. I asked about visitors. I remembered being exhausted by visitors last time and I really wanted them to go. The midwife then suggested that delaying the birth notice in the paper might simplify things.'*

Caitlin had a normal birth. As Emily arrived safely she was lifted onto her mother's abdomen. A little fluid drained from her mouth but she did not need any suction.

Caitlin was a little anxious about Emily's slightly elongated head and a bloodshot eye but she was reassured when told that both would gradually disappear. Emily was safe again on her mother's warm body – a light cover was placed over her, her mother's hands stroked and applied loving pressure. She could hear again the familiar heart beat and her mother's voice. She really did look relaxed and at rest after the upheaval of the last few hours. The cord was not cut until it had stopped pulsating. When Emily began to whimper Caitlin offered the breast. Emily licked a bit and then suddenly fixed, sucked for two or three sucks and then stopped. Caitlin worried a little and wondered if Emily was going to be difficult to breastfeed but the midwife explained that even a couple of sucks were fine and it was best to leave her to rest until she was ready to feed again.

Caitlin continues her story.

*'I guess it is a matter of luck, the rapport you establish with staff. Perhaps I was more relaxed the second time but I found that the midwife-in-charge was so considerate and encouraging. Her attitude seemed to rub off onto all the staff. I was much less tense and found the whole atmosphere supportive instead of intimidating. I couldn't have received more help.'*

Ainslie had different needs:

**Ainslie:** *'I told Landy that I wanted to find a highly regarded, competent obstetrician with very definite ideas of his or her own. Provided that we were on the same wavelength I wanted to put the whole business into the doctor's hands. After all, those who have been doing a job competently for years should know a lot better than I what decisions to make. I wanted to make use of whatever modern technology was appropriate.*

*I liked the thought of the monitoring gadgets, ultrasound, pain relief and an epidural. I wanted all the works for the safest and least painful birth for baby and me.'*

Kate didn't want Josh to be with her while she was in labour and when giving birth.

**Kate:** *'I didn't want Josh to feel that I did not want him there but I knew him too well to have any doubts about his reactions if I found the going tough. Then I'd be worrying about him worrying about me and I didn't expect to have any spare energy for that. He agreed that he would be better out of the delivery suite but would come in if I changed my mind. I think Josh felt bad that he did not want to be at the birth and it might have helped if the subject had been discussed at antenatal classes and he had been reassured that there was no 'must' about being present. I was relieved about our decision and felt that I could give a good yell if I wanted to. I would have tried not to if Josh had been there. However, I did feel that I wanted my close friend, Danielle, with me for support. She had already had two children and was a calm and sensible person to have around. She was just as good as I had expected her to be.'*

Lucy and Eli wanted a home birth.

**Lucy:** *'We really wanted a home birth but we met with all sorts of opposition from our GP, our own families and some of our friends, although we did get support from other parents, whom we contacted, who had had home births. We learnt all we could about home births.*

*We contacted Homebirth Australia and the local branch of the Australian College of Midwives. They provided us with a list of independently practising midwives. When we met Robyn we were happy. Robyn listened to our hopes and reasons for wanting our baby to be born at home and discussed the advantages of home births as she saw them and also some of the problems which could and did occur in some cases. She explained that I would have to qualify as a low-risk expectant mother according to Julie, the obstetrician she worked with. I would meet Julie once during my pregnancy and more often if necessary. Julie would expect to be available should I need specialist medical care at any time. We met Julie and liked her. Although it was my first pregnancy I was accepted.*

*Robyn persuaded us to visit the maternity wing of the hospital that she and Julie would use if there were any problems. I wasn't keen but we did visit and we were agreeably surprised. It was light and airy and there was no sign of all the equipment and monitors and things we expected to see. No doubt they were there in the large cupboards which lined one wall.*

*During my pregnancy Robyn became our friend as well as my midwife. She provided antenatal care and supplied information. Robyn was able to be with me during the whole of my labour and helped me birth Zac. I managed without drugs for pain relief. I was encouraged to move around in labour, to take hot showers (sitting on a plastic chair), and she used hot towels on my lower back to ease the pain. The massage she gave me was really helpful. Best of all I had confidence in her skill and judgement and it was her encouragement and praise and Eli's support that helped me through to a normal birth. It was wonderful to have Robyn with us for the pregnancy, the labour and birth as well as the postnatal period. She encouraged me to feed Zac myself, settle him and do things my way but was ready to answer questions and make suggestions where she felt they would be helpful. I needed some help as I sorted out breastfeeding.'*

The birth of your baby is a momentous event. Some mothers find it enormously helpful to talk about their experience with their midwife or doctor. If you wish, tell him or her that you would like to do this.

# 4

# Following birth

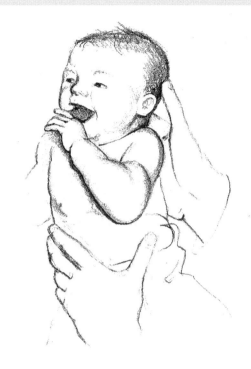

For new parents, the arrival of their baby brings a new and enormous change to their lives, but what of the new baby? We think that we have much to learn! Surely the change encountered by a baby at birth must be the greatest he or she will meet in a whole lifetime, and yet it is only a beginning. Babies cannot tell us how they feel about things; but how do we think about a newborn child? Firstly, this is a new individual unlike any other. Right now this baby can make no choices about ways of behaving – cannot be naughty, cannot be good, but can just be – a bundle of sensations and reactions (but still absorbing everything around him or her) which can vary from moment to moment as he or she learns to adapt to new impressions, events and inputs as this separate life begins.

# Baby's behaviour and caregivers' responses

Babies can survive and grow only if their survival needs are met so they must be cared for, as they cannot do this for themselves. They can and do ask for care, often in quite specific ways, which you can learn later. In this section some of these messages are described. They may be direct or subtle. The subtle messages will only be recognised if the caregivers are observant and as they become familiar with the baby they are nurturing. Learning to read the messages correctly is the first part of caregiving. It is an art acquired by loving, involved parents and other sensitive caregivers and takes time to develop.

Babies' immediate behaviours are concerned with their feelings of the moment and will be governed by their physical comfort or lack of it, by feelings of security and emotional wellbeing. They need to feel safe in their environment, which includes the caregivers, at all times. You will be very much aware that the way your baby behaves when feeling comfortable and relaxed differs from their behaviour when feeling uncomfortable or insecure.

## *You cannot spoil a young baby*

Your baby cannot decide to manipulate you. That is to say, babies cannot consciously or deliberately set out to annoy, irritate or bother anyone. When they feel secure and comfortable then everything is right. If anything is making them anxious or they are physically uncomfortable in any way then everything is wrong for them. Babies have only one sure way of telling you that help is needed. They cry. It will take a little time but you will learn to interpret your baby's cries better than anyone else.

During the first few weeks parents often feel that they are on an emotional roller-coaster. Mothers particularly are likely to feel exhausted. Immediately their hormonal balance changes as their breasts begin to produce milk – nipples may be tender and the breasts over-full and there may be pain and discomfort if there are stitches or a caesarean wound. At the same time the new mother is likely to experience waves of joy, which may be replaced by doubt in her ability to care for this new baby, and then she is surprised because she becomes euphoric again.

When women do not fall instantly in love with their new baby they can feel deeply distressed and guilty. They may not know that this is quite common and that they can expect love to grow through the days ahead as they both learn to know one another. During these early days, be ready to accept these changing feelings as your body recovers from the birth and you meet your baby's needs for food and comfort. Aim to avoid fatigue and you can expect to regain your physical strength. Your skills and confidence will grow and you can expect life to become increasingly easier for you all.

## Your new baby

When further healthy growth and development can no longer continue in the uterus, it is time for birth. So what happens? Contractions of the uterus bring the baby down through the birth canal, which must expand to allow the birth.

We have evolved to survive the incredible experience of birth but what then does nature intend for the newborn infant? Firstly the baby, though still totally dependent, must begin to exist separately. The stress which accompanies birth needs to be lessened. The simplest way is to provide something familiar, something associated with the previous security of the uterus. The mother's body can do this as she holds her naked newborn in skin-to-skin contact.

Body systems which sustain life must now function adequately – the most immediate need is for oxygen, which is obtained from the air by breathing. Soon the baby must take in food, digest and absorb it and then excrete the waste and must also start to use other body systems which have not been used before. The baby's sensory system will have to interact with vastly expanded and different stimuli. As the woman responds to her baby's signals she helps with the touching, stroking, caressing and holding which she instinctively applies. Her eye contact helps her baby to focus on her face. Her voice can soothe even as it stimulates her baby's hearing.

It is instinctive for a mother to gather the newborn to herself, to suckle her baby and interact as described. Genetically programmed bonding then begins as the pair spontaneously respond to each other.

It happens intuitively for most mother-baby pairs, and is the beginning of the emotional satisfaction each can be expected to find in the other. The importance of bonding is discussed later. Understandably women can become extremely anxious if their babies are removed from them. They certainly need a quiet time for this first interaction before the baby is weighed and clothed, preferably by the mother's bedside. Mostly, babies will not be bathed until the next day to allow for smells of the mother and baby to be part of the early connection between them. Fortunately, routine separation of mother and baby happens less and less in Australian maternity units today. If it must happen because of illness or prematurity, mothers and babies can 'recover' this delay quite quickly when they do get together.

During your pregnancy you may have heard of, read about or seen a video called *Kangaroo Mother Care* (KMC) by Dr Nils Bergman. Kangaroo mother care is defined by Dr Bergman as a universally available and biologically sound method of care for all newborns, but in particular for premature babies, with three components:

**1.** skin-to-skin contact
**2.** exclusive breastfeeding
**3.** support for mother-infant pair.

In the video, Dr Bergman describes this method of care and why it works. The video provides the latest up-to-date research and evidence to prove that the newborn thrives best in its original 'rightful place' – on its mother's chest. He discusses the advantage of skin-to-skin contact. This closeness avoids the possible release of hormones which would interfere with the baby's digestion and other bodily functions; improvement in heart rate and temperature can also occur. If you are interested you may be able to borrow the video from your local branch of the Australian Breastfeeding Association or from Lactation Consultants of Australia and New Zealand (LCANZ).

Undoubtedly we approach our babies with assumptions that we have acquired somewhere in the past. Some may not be applicable to this baby. We need to avoid expectations of how this baby should look and behave. We need to learn about this new person – an individual with unique qualities, quirks and potential. We need to be ready to nurture and assist in whichever way our baby's and our own needs lead us as this newcomer becomes part of our family life. As we interact together, respond to each other and share our lives, we can expect love to grow, but it is not enough to love without clear evidence that we do love; that is, we need to actively show our baby that we truly love him or her.

Given these clear signals, the baby's self-esteem will grow – self-esteem which is not conceit. Self-esteem is the basis of emotional health and the formation of a successful identity. Ideally the message from the parents is of unconditional love and acceptance which instills feelings of security and self-worth as they guide gently and consistently, according to the age, stage and development of their child.

It is important to recognise that we all have needs. The more adequately and easily our own needs are met, the more easily we can meet our baby's needs. The more adequately and easily we meet our baby's needs the more happily and comfortably we can live together as a family.

## The first breastfeed

Immediately following birth your baby will need to rest for a short time. Allow this in skin-to-skin contact as you hold him or her closely to allow your baby to touch, smell, hear and see you. Babies are born with a strong instinct to suck and it is thought to be very strong within the first half hour of birth so offer your breast as soon as possible.

You can expect your midwife to be there to offer assistance to position and attach your baby correctly. Touch your baby's cheek with the nipple so that the baby turns towards the breast. If your baby needs encouraging you can express a drop or two of colostrum as you begin. At the feel of your nipple your baby is likely to lick or nuzzle it for a moment or two, or may immediately open their mouth wide and fix onto your breast and feed for a few minutes. If your baby is simply too tired to feed, allow them to rest skin to skin with you before trying again. If you are both well you should give nothing but your breast. No other fluid is needed.

## Your baby's appearance

If you have not considered your baby's likely appearance at birth, you may be surprised. Many parents, although delighted and thankful for a safe birth, have not been prepared for the little person who arrives. Someone who has some bloody mucus on their skin from the birth and who may have greasy, greyish-white vernix on them too. (The vernix protected the baby's skin from the amniotic fluid in the uterus.)

### Head

At birth the head is a large part of your baby's mass, and about one quarter of the length. The head can be especially moulded by the birth canal because the bones of the skull are soft and not yet joined. This amazing design means your baby's head changes shape and size to fit through the birth canal. Do not worry if your baby's head is misshapen; this moulding helps to prevent injury and does not indicate damage. The head may appear lop-sided or elongated and there may be bumps or swellings as a result of the pressures exerted during birth. All of this is normal and will not need treatment. You can expect your baby's head to return to a normal shape within days and there can be a marked improvement within a couple of hours.

If forceps were used to assist the birth any marks on the cheeks usually fade within a week. If the birth was by vacuum extraction a lumpy bruise may be found on your baby's head. This too can be expected to disappear quite quickly. Babies born by caesarean section after labour can also have marks and bruises on their heads from the birth canal.

There are two soft spots, called fontanelles, between the bones of the skull. The larger is in front, on top of the skull and is diamond shaped. It varies in size and you may see it pulsating. The smaller soft spot is triangular in shape and at the back of the skull. You may not notice this one. It closes soon after birth while the larger one may not close until around eighteen months, although it may do so long before this. The skull is made up of several bones. The places where these bones meet each other are called sutures. Suture lines radiate from the corners of the fontanelles. These allow skull growth. The cartilage and skin which cover the fontanelles are tough. While you should avoid pressing on the fontanelles, you can wash the baby's head firmly but gently without fear of damage.

## *Hair*

Your baby's head may be bald or well covered with hair. This first growth of hair is likely to rub off or fall out. The new hair may be of a different colour and texture. At birth there may be some fine hair on parts of the body – it may be on the back, shoulders or forehead, particularly if the baby is born early. It is also more common in people from around the Mediterranean. This will fall out within a week or two.

## *Eyes*

The slatey-blue colour of the eyes that is common in the newborn can change. By six months you are likely to know what the permanent colour will be. It is usual for tears to be absent when a newborn baby cries and it may be days or weeks before they appear. The eyes may be puffy at birth and there may also be small reddened areas involving the white of the eyes due to blood leaking from tiny vessels; both are due to pressure on the head during birth. Treatment will not be necessary. Your baby will be able to see faces and objects most clearly at 20 to 25 centimetres, and the eyes will react to light. Newborn babies are often cross-eyed at times but as the eye muscles strengthen they are likely to outgrow this, usually within a few weeks.

## Ears

The cartilage in a newborn baby's ears is soft at birth and there may be times when the outside of the ear is folded forward or creased, particularly by the baby lying on it. Gradually, as the cartilage strengthens, the ears become less flexible. They do not need tapes or bands to hold them in place.

## Mouth

There may be a few whitish spots on the roof of your baby's mouth. These 'pearls' usually vanish within the first two months. Sometimes there are tiny cysts on the gums. These are not teeth and will also disappear within a week or two. Very occasionally a baby may actually have a tooth at birth. This is often loose and it is likely to be removed so that it is not inhaled or swallowed.

## Nose

The nose may be a little misshapen due to the birth. Your baby breathes through the nose and sometimes breathing may seem noisy. This is likely due to the small size of the nasal passages. There is often some mucus present in the nose, particularly in the first 24 hours after birth. The baby may sneeze often to clear the nose but this does not mean that your baby has a cold. Apart from wiping any mucus externally, do not try to clear inside the nose.

## Tongue

The under-surface of the tongue is joined to the floor of the mouth by a thin piece of skin called the frenulum. Parents sometimes worry about 'tongue tie' and are concerned that it might interfere with sucking or talking. This is unlikely but you can seek a medical opinion if you are anxious.

## Breasts

Both boy and girl babies can have enlarged breasts, which are often most noticeable on the second or third days after birth. Around the end of the first week there can even be a little milky fluid oozing from the nipples. This is due to maternal hormones passing from mother to baby before birth. The swelling will subside and milky fluid will stop in a few days. Do not try to express the fluid or massage or bind the breasts as this can result in infection.

## Umbilical cord

The umbilical cord begins to dry as soon as it is cut. It then darkens, shrivels and falls off – usually between seven and ten days, although it can take longer. The cord is cared for by washing with clean water as the baby is washed or bathed. If the cord becomes smelly or reddened or if there is a discharge you need to immediately see your health adviser.

A small bulge may appear at the umbilicus which mothers may find a little scary; this is called an umbilical hernia. It may enlarge as the baby cries. You can expect it to resolve spontaneously. If it does not, surgery may be necessary when the child is four or five years old.

## The genitals

There may be some temporary swelling of the genitals in both boys and girls. This is especially likely if yours was a breech birth. In boys the scrotum may be swollen and bruised; in girls the vulva may appear enlarged and puffy. Baby girls may have a white to pink vaginal discharge, containing blood, which will stop within a few days. This discharge is due to maternal hormones and needs no treatment.

## Circumcision

Sometimes the foreskin, covering the tip of the penis, is surgically removed. This is usually done for cultural or religious reasons. If performed on a baby without anaesthetic, this operation is painful and

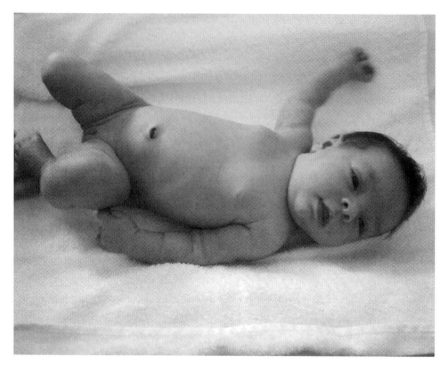

today it is actively discouraged by most doctors. Many paediatricians now recommend that if parents wish to have their baby circumcised they wait until he is approximately six months old and the operation can be done under anaesthetic. Circumcision is not without risk. The most common complications are infection or bleeding. If you are considering circumcision for your baby, read widely to gather information and ask your doctor for full information before making a decision.

## Skin

At birth your baby's skin is usually covered with *vernix caseosa*, a white, slippery, creamy substance. Vernix can be washed off but we don't encourage washing newborn babies for a day or two; it is preferable to let the vernix be absorbed into the baby's skin.

When bathing, water is all that is recommended for babies' skin or a water-based product such as aqueous cream if their skin is very dry. The skin may turn quite red but this 'boiled lobster' colour gradually fades. Hands and feet may be mottled or have a bluish tinge which may be marked for the first 24 hours. The skin may be dry and even peel a little. Do not be surprised if pimples and marks are present or soon develop. Usually these skin conditions are normal and clear up without any treatment. They can be explained by your health adviser.

## Milia

These are small whiteheads, often on the nose, chin or forehead. They will disappear in a week or two. Do not squeeze these as doing so could cause an infection.

## Mongolian spots

These spots are a temporary collection of bluish-grey pigment under the skin, often on the baby's buttocks and back. They are common in babies of African and Asian parents and may be present in babies of Greek or Italian parents, or any baby who has or will have dark skin. These areas of pigmentation are in no way connected with Down syndrome (or mongolism as it was previously known) nor are they due to bruising. They are harmless and can be expected to disappear in the first two years of life.

## Stork bites

These are pink or purplish-red marks on the eyelids, nape of the neck and back of the head. They nearly always fade without treatment within the first two years.

## Erythema toxicum

This usually occurs during the first days of life – red blotches which look rather like hives or insect bites on the trunk or buttocks. These are harmless and usually fade in a few days.

## Dry and flaky skin

The skin may peel a little, especially if the baby was a little overdue. You could warm a little aqueous cream or olive oil in your hands and smooth it gently over your baby.

## Measurements

Your baby's measurements (size and weight at birth) will be entered on the percentile charts in the personal record book which is usually handed to the parents. Your baby's growth can be plotted on these charts which are based on all Australian babies of recent times. For example, the average weight at birth of babies in Australia is around 3400 grams; the 10th and 90th percentiles are about 2600 grams and 3800 grams respectively; and nearly all babies at birth, it is expected, will weigh between these weights. If your baby's weight is outside these values, either more or less, your health adviser will investigate for the probable explanation. It may be that your baby is simply different from most, which is why a continuing record is kept as a later check on growth. The average length at birth is about 50 centimetres, and the head circumference about 35 centimetres. The chest is usually a little less than 35 centimetres, and the abdomen less again.

## Stools (faeces or poo)

After birth your baby's alimentary tract begins to process food – digesting, absorbing nutrients and eliminating waste. The waste appears in the stools.

The first bowel movement usually occurs within 24 hours of birth; the first stools, called meconium, are odourless, greenish-black, smooth, sticky and sterile. (Friendly bacteria will establish later.) The bowel becomes very active over the next days, with six or seven loose motions per day. Frequency then decreases and the consistency and appearance of the stools settle according to whether your baby is breast- or formula-fed.

Breastfed babies may not produce a stool each day; some will go a week or more between motions. They may show slight discomfort towards the end but the stools will be soft and normal, with no sign of constipation. The odour of the breastmilk stool is not offensive. The consistency after the early days is soft and mushy. The colour is variable: while meconium is still present it is dark, but then brown to yellow, even bright yellow. It may be greenish, especially if the motions are frequent, but diarrhoea is unlikely in breastfed babies so this is not of concern unless your baby appears ill and the odour of the stools has changed. Ask your health adviser if you are worried. Do not be concerned if you notice small, white solid curds in the stools.

The stools of formula-fed babies are different. The frequency will probably settle fairly soon on once per day. Some babies can produce soft stools every second day but, for most, constipation – hard stools which are difficult to pass – is likely if the stools stay too long in the rectum and dry out. (See 'Constipation' in Chapter 20.) If the formula is based on cow's milk the stools are usually a yellow paste. On soy formula they are a dark green to grey paste. The odour is slightly offensive. There may be soft white curds and a little mucus, which are unimportant. However, an increase in mucus together with an increase in frequency may indicate the onset of diarrhoea (see 'Diarrhoea' in Chapter 20).

When looking at the stools consider your baby's condition as a whole. If the baby is well with a good appetite, any concern you feel may be unnecessary. If in doubt, ask. If there is a sudden change to frequent, watery, greenish stools which are more offensive than usual, your baby may have diarrhoea or gastroenteritis. This will need immediate medical attention especially if the baby is feverish and/or vomiting (see 'Diarrhoea' and 'Dehydration' in Chapter 20).

## *Urine*

It is routine to take note of the time of the baby's first wet nappy. This is expected in the first 24 hours.

Immediately following birth the output of urine is usually comparatively low. The output of the first 24 hours then gradually increases, although there may be only two or three wet nappies until the mother's milk 'comes in' around day three or four after birth. A healthy baby comes with extra body fluid which, with the colostrum from its mother's breasts, is enough until the breasts fill.

By the end of the first week there may be six or more good wet nappies of very pale, straw-coloured urine in 24 hours. It is easy to recognise when a cloth nappy is quite wet. It is more difficult to know if a disposable nappy is just damp or really wet.

If dry when you pick up your baby for a feed, you can expect a wet nappy during or just after the feed. Dark, infrequently passed urine is usually due to insufficient fluid intake. Remember that there is a danger of dehydration if your baby is not taking enough fluid. Check for signs of this (see 'Dehydration' in Chapter 20). If there is any doubt consult your doctor at once. If your baby appears well, just offer extra breastfeeds or if formula feeding give some cooled, boiled water. You could offer 30 to 50 millilitres between feeds. Sometimes a substance in the urine called urates will stain the nappy pink but this should not be confused with blood. If you are doubtful show the nappy to your health adviser.

## Jaundice

Jaundice in the newborn is not uncommon. It may appear on the second or third day and may last for about a week. It is usually within normal limits and needs no treatment.

While in the uterus, the baby obtains oxygen from the placenta and needs more of a particular type of haemoglobin than is required after

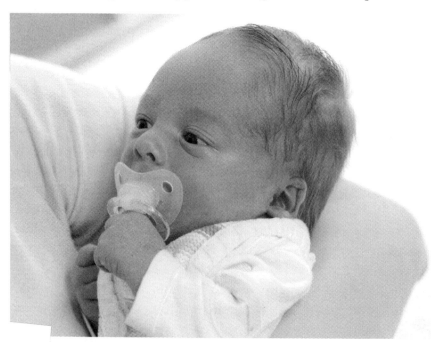

birth. Following birth the oxygen is obtained by breathing. The liver is responsible for breaking down much of this pre-birth haemoglobin. One by-product of this breakdown is bilirubin. It is yellow and when there is an accumulation of this in the body it causes varying degrees of staining of the skin and the whites of the eyes – so-called jaundice. If the bilirubin level in the blood exceeds safe limits the baby can become ill. It may appear after 24 hours and be highest between the third and fifth days, fading as the liver function increases. Bilirubin is excreted by the liver into the bile ducts and is then passed from the body in the stools.

At birth there is bilirubin in the meconium in the baby's intestinal tract. It is important that it is passed without delay to avoid reabsorption into the circulation. The best stimulation is short frequent breastfeeds starting as soon as your baby is ready following birth. Eight or more feeds in 24 hours are desirable. It is important to avoid giving any other fluids because it is the colostrum followed by the breastmilk that maximises bowel movement.

If the jaundice causes concern blood tests will be done to check the level of bilirubin. If necessary treatment will be started so that it does not exceed safe levels. There are some pathological causes for jaundice; medical personnel will investigate these if necessary.

Exposure to sunlight or fluorescent light causes a rapid decrease in the bilirubin in the skin. The bilirubin molecules, through the absorption of light, are broken down into a form easier for the baby to excrete. To give this phototherapy, a fibre-optic bili-blanket, bili-bed or bili-base may be used. This treatment might be needed for two or three days. Babies can be dressed and stay beside their mothers and be fed normally during treatment. The eyes will not need covering. If overhead fluorescent light is used great care must be taken to see that the baby does not become cold; as much of the body as possible is exposed to the light so temperature control is essential. With this treatment eyes are covered to protect them from any glare. Usually the baby continues to be fed and cared for by the mother, whether the baby is rooming beside her or receiving treatment in the nursery.

### *Breastmilk jaundice*

Occasionally babies develop breastmilk or late-onset jaundice. It is said that this jaundice is due to a substance in the mother's milk. Instead of beginning to drop around day three or four, the jaundice increases and may not peak until day seven to ten. If untreated it may continue to rise even up to day fifteen. It may persist for nine or ten weeks. Because mothers are often at home by the third day, jaundice may not develop until after discharge. It is important to contact your health adviser should you be worried about the colour of your baby's skin or eyes so that any treatment needed can be arranged.

# Screening tests, procedures and treatments

Following birth your baby will be assessed. Two Apgar scores are given to check condition and recovery. Later there will be more detailed examinations and tests on blood (see below).

Many maternity units routinely test blood from the umbilical cord following forceps or caesarean delivery: the level of acidity shows the baby's level of oxygen.

### *Apgar score*

Within one minute of birth the newborn's breathing, heart rate, colour, muscle tone and reflexes are observed. Each of these five aspects is scored 0, 1 or 2; the best total score is thus 10. A second scoring is made at five minutes after birth.

The size of the score is an indicator of overall condition. A perfect score of 10 is rare, if only because the lower limbs take time to become pink, thus lowering the score for colouring. Low scores do not necessarily mean there is a serious problem but do call for close monitoring of the baby. Comparison of the two scores shows any change: its direction is important.

### *The Newborn Screening Test*

Newborn Screening is a publicly funded system which tests for more than thirty rare but treatable diseases that babies can be born with.

Some of these conditions, often called 'inborn errors of metabolism', can cause physical or intellectual problems if not treated early. This is why blood will be collected (with your permission) from your baby on the third or fourth day after birth. Blood is taken from your baby's heel on special blotting paper and allowed to dry; it is then sent away for testing.

Some of the congenital diseases screened for are phenylketonuria, hypothyroidism, galactosaemia and cystic fibrosis. If you hear nothing back about the results, it means that all is well. Mothers can find it hard to think of their baby having a blood test so early but it only takes a few minutes and if you keep the baby close to you for comfort, or breastfeed at the time of the test, your baby, and you, will likely manage well.

## Phenylketonuria

In this metabolic condition the amino acid phenylalanine from protein in milk accumulates because the enzymes necessary to break it down are missing. Untreated, the baby will suffer severe mental retardation. However, if treated correctly the baby can have normal brain development. The treatment has been to give a formula – Lofenalac – which is low in phenylalanine. It is sometimes possible to partially breastfeed with careful monitoring of the serum phenylalanine levels.

## Hypothyroidism

This is a condition due to an absent or an inadequately functioning thyroid gland and can severely affect both physical and mental growth and development. Early treatment will provide the necessary hormone and the baby can be expected to grow and develop normally.

## Galactosaemia

This is a hereditary disorder of the metabolism of the milk sugar galactose and can cause brain and liver damage. Babies must be given a galactose-free formula; it is not possible to breastfeed these babies. They can then grow normally.

## Cystic fibrosis

This is an inherited disorder affecting the pancreas. There is a salt imbalance and an excessive secretion of thick, sticky mucus which lines the cavities and ducts in the body. This affects the lungs and causes breathing problems. Infections are common. There can be difficulties with digestion and the absorption of food. Appropriate treatment aims to provide sound nutrition and keep the lungs free from infection and so lessen the effects of the illness. Early diagnosis and treatment can reduce complications; parents whose babies have been screened appear to adjust better to their baby's condition and these babies may have better weight gains than those that have not been screened.

## *Vitamin K1 deficiency*

Parents are asked whether they wish their baby to be given vitamin K1 (Konakion) as a precaution against haemorrhagic disease of the newborn (HDN). If vitamin K1 is deficient the baby's blood cannot clot normally. A rare condition, HDN is marked by uncontrollable bleeding which can occur in various areas of the body such as the umbilicus. It most commonly occurs between four and six weeks of age and is not likely beyond the first six months. Your midwife or doctor will answer any questions you wish to ask about vitamin K1 before you consent to your baby being given it. The vitamin K1 can be given by intramuscular injection or by a series of oral doses.

## *Reflexes*

Your baby's reflexes will be checked. Among the reflexes checked are: the grasp reflex – the baby will grasp a finger placed on the palm of their hand; the startle (or Moro) reflex – sudden movement or a loud noise will cause your baby to fling their arms and legs out wide and then bring them back. (This reflex, with its jerky movements, can occur during sleep and waken the baby. Wrapping and swaddling can lessen these movements.) The walking reflex, which rarely lasts beyond the first five or six weeks, can be seen when the baby is held in an upright position and their feet touch a table surface. The feet are picked up and placed as if walking. Finally there is the rooting reflex. This ensures that your baby will turn towards anything which touches their cheek and will open their mouth wide ready to attach to the breast (or bottle) to feed.

## Multiple births

With the use of fertility drugs the number of multiple births has increased. Also today many women are delaying having babies until their thirties and forties and these women are more likely than younger women to have twins. Often these babies arrive early and if necessary they will spend time in a special nursery to grow and gain weight until ready to go home. The care they will then need is the same as for single babies.

However, there are additional challenges for parents who have multiple births. The major one is finding the time to complete all that must be done in each 24 hours without becoming fatigued. Careful planning can make life much easier. It helps to decide on priorities and to leave undone things which really do not matter. Both the Australian Multiple Births Association (AMBA) and the Australian Breastfeeding Association (ABA) in your region can provide support and information. You can often buy pre-owned equipment such as double prams and strollers through the AMBA. Many mothers successfully breastfeed twins and some have breastfed triplets (see 'Breastfeeding twins' in Chapter 13).

## When baby is born needing special care

Sometimes a baby is born with a short- or long-term problem and will need to be cared for in the special nursery where specially trained staff can constantly monitor the baby's condition and the required medical treatment can most readily be given. These babies are very often in an incubator. Such babies may have a low birth weight – sometimes the baby is just genetically small but healthy and will be kept in special care for only a day or two. Another may be small because he or she was not receiving enough nourishment from the placenta. Other conditions when babies may need special care include some types of jaundice, infections, disabilities – in fact, any baby with a medical problem may need it.

Then there are those who have arrived early – the premature babies. These are babies born before the 37th week of pregnancy. The majority of these babies grow to become normal, healthy children but the more premature the birth the greater the concern for the baby, and they are less likely to survive. If born before 32 weeks it is common for a baby to have breathing problems due to an immature respiratory system. However, with present-day technology and the skilled medical and nursing care available, many of these tiny babies now survive and thrive.

When a baby needs to be in the special nursery, the separation from the mother often causes distress. Women are likely to feel bereft and anxious. In special-care nurseries parents are encouraged to be involved with their baby as much as possible. Mothers provide their breastmilk – something no-one else can do. Parents are encouraged to touch and feel their babies and when possible to hold and cuddle them.

The mother or both the mother and partner can be so anxious and distressed that they can feel overwhelmed by the whole situation. Such parents can feel guilty, wondering if they did, or failed to do, something which caused or contributed to their baby's condition. They can feel grief for the loss of the dream of the way they expected their baby to be. They can feel anger: 'Why did this have to happen to me/us?' Then they worry about their ability to provide any ongoing special care their child may need, particularly if the disability will be permanent.

At this time, apart from information, the mother and usually the father need generous support and understanding, the opportunity to discuss their feelings with whomever and whenever they wish. Professionals and others with counselling skills, community groups – particularly those groups of parents who have a child with a disability – and caring family and friends can provide real help. The parents can expect to work through the shock and sadness they experience initially and as they learn to know their baby they can expect love to grow.

## Bonding

In recent years bonding between individuals has been discussed in depth. It means the development of a special attachment of one person to another or others. In the present context of family and a new arrival, it is the attachment which forms between parents, any other children and the newborn.

The purpose of bonding is to guarantee that the new person, the baby, will be cared for during the period of total dependency on others. Moreover, when satisfactory bonding occurs the caregivers freely give this care and derive great satisfaction from doing so. Adults, particularly the parents, respond instinctively to their infant's needs. The interaction between them flows back and forth in the day-to-day living they share.

It is believed that our ability in later life to form loving, stable relationships is affected by our first early experiences of bonding to a recognised loving nurturer. This loving caregiver is the baby's security and provides a 'safe place' from which to reach out to other people. As time passes the baby can feel safe and happy for longer periods with other friendly people before needing to return to the security of the initial constant nurturer, the first provider of a safe place – usually the mother. Boundaries and trust expand if new interactions with people and the environment are positive. The emotionally secure infant is free to begin to explore and find the world an interesting place. The baby has a firm foundation upon which independence can grow.

## When bonding is delayed

Sometimes parents, who have had no particular problems with the labour and birth and who had looked forward to their baby's arrival, worry that bonding isn't occurring if they do not experience instant maternal and paternal love. They need not be anxious if they are willing to provide loving care in their day-to-day nurturing of their baby. Attachment grows as you respond to and share experiences with your infant, as you lovingly talk to, look at, smile, touch, hold close and play together.

When there has been necessary separation of mother and baby and immediate time together was not possible for medical reasons, some women feel anxious. They may feel that they have not bonded with their baby as they would wish. However, they can look forward to developing a deep and loving attachment as the days pass. The more parents can be involved in the care of their baby, the more rapidly this is likely to happen. However, if there is a delay in this happening, parents need not despair; bonding can certainly occur even if there is a delay.

Staff caring for premature and other babies in special-care nurseries involve parents in the care of their baby and encourage maximum interaction between them. However, if you feel that you are not involved in the way you would like to be, find a sympathetic listener amongst the staff and say how you feel. It is often possible to increase your care and leadership role within the team.

At birth parents and their baby need space, privacy and time to interact and begin to know each other. It is normal for this to occur immediately after the baby is born provided that both mother and baby are well.

Even when mother and baby are physically well there may be other problems which might affect bonding. The pregnancy may have been unwanted, or it may have caused unexpected interruptions to a career. The birth may have caused financial difficulties. A baby of the 'wrong' sex may have arrived. For these parents, those early minutes following birth, of skin-to-skin and of eye-to-eye contact, can have a dramatically positive effect and lessen any possibility of the baby becoming a scapegoat for frustration or anxiety. For many of these anxious parents the actual arrival of their baby overcomes their initial dismay. Their priorities change as they begin to adapt to the new circumstances.

If for any reason you are feeling unable to respond lovingly to your baby discuss this with your midwife or doctor. If parents' problems are so great that either or both suffer feelings of rejection towards their baby with no wish to offer loving care, then get help. The earliest possible help is needed for all concerned. A disturbed relationship between parent and baby is a crisis situation. Talk to your health adviser or you can ring Lifeline's 24 hour service on 13 11 14 in any state or territory in Australia. And remember, having the courage to step forward and say 'I need help' is a very important gift to your child if this is how you are feeling.

## The effect of bereavement on bonding

If there has been the death of a loved one, especially of a close family member, partner, parent or child just before the birth of the baby, bonding may be difficult until the worst of the pain of bereavement is over. Just be willing to talk lovingly, cuddle, look at and play gently with your baby and you can expect bonding to take place naturally as time passes. Be prepared to talk about any anxieties you experience and get appropriate help if negative feelings persist.

## Partner and siblings

Parents generally agree that when the partner is closely involved, preferably before conception and throughout pregnancy and birth, the quality of family life is enhanced. Anxieties which come with problems are minimised and strong ties of affection can begin from the moment of birth as they interact together.

Bonding between siblings can be helped with wise handling. A toddler is likely to feel displaced by the new baby. Just before your baby is born, you can involve him or her in your preparations, visit the hospital you will go to and when the time comes tell your toddler

where you are going and that he or she can come to visit you there. A present from the new baby to the toddler can be helpful too. Siblings, even from an early age, can help with the new baby and feel that their contribution is important. This helps family attachments.

## Staying together: rooming-in for women and their newborns

The obvious benefits of having your baby with you at all times are:

- the mother relaxes because she has her baby with her
- breastfeeding is helped because she can feed whenever the baby is interested or hungry
- the baby is unlikely to be offered any unnecessary formula
- the mother begins to understand her baby's behaviour and can ask for explanations.

The mother is usually the main source of the newborn's security, food, comfort and sense of wellbeing. With the cot beside her bed, she can see and touch her infant. She is constantly learning how to interpret cries, how to recognise hunger and how to relieve discomfort, and she is able to offer the breast without delay. She can enjoy and share her baby's quiet, alert and wakeful moments. Her instinct to protect her infant is strong and she can feel that she is on hand to do this. She becomes more and more confident as she nurtures her newborn. Maternity units in hospitals today have a standard practice of keeping babies with their mothers (often called rooming-in). Rooming-in can be expected to provide the best environment for both mother and baby.

Nurseries, or at least an area where babies can be cared for apart from the mother, are sometimes necessary if a baby is unwell. Some babies require continued observation or special care. Mothers need to be clearly informed and their wishes for the care of their babies met where possible. It may be possible for the mother to nurse and cuddle her baby for short periods and even more likely that she can hold or stroke her baby's hand or head even if the baby is in a special crib. Any separation needs to be for as short a time as possible.

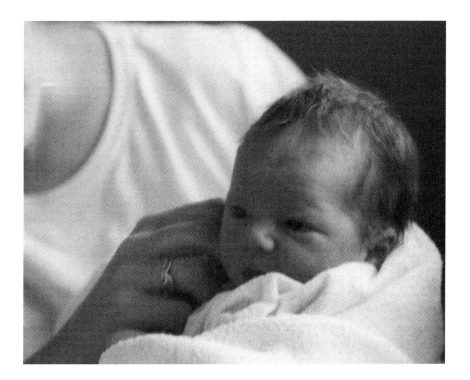

## Sucking needs

Both breast- and bottle-fed babies vary in the amount of sucking they need. Some obtain what they want from feeding time alone, others look for more and may obtain it by spending more time at the breast or, if bottle-fed, by being given a slower teat and lengthening the feeding time. Some babies find their fingers or thumbs to suck, others are given a dummy.

Usually a very young baby feeds for at least fifteen to twenty minutes. In this time, as well as satisfying the appetite, it is likely the baby's sucking needs are met too. There are babies who finish their feed much sooner. If breastfeeding they may continue at the breast, even when their tummies are full, because they are not ready to stop sucking. This is more likely when the mother has an abundant and/or a fast-flowing supply and her baby obtains the feed quickly. Bottle-fed babies who take their feed too fast can be slowed down by managing the teat and by tightening the screw top of the feeding bottle.

There are thriving babies who, even when they are not hungry, want to suck at the breast when they are awake. It is the warmth and comfort of the breast itself that they want. They may show signs of overfeeding (see 'Too much milk' in Chapter 21). You can try interesting your baby in the environment, talking, playing with, and moving the baby around so that they can can see and hear you. Babies often find a thumb or fingers to suck. This may be a time when a dummy will help although do not be surprised if your baby treats it as an insult and rejects it.

## A word about dummies (pacifiers)

A dummy or pacifier is a teat of soft rubber or silicone on a flat plastic shield. The shield may be round (which suits many babies) or shaped so that it does not rub against the nose as the baby sucks. Dummies come in different shapes and sizes. There are specially moulded 'orthodontic' dummies and teats. The advertisements claim that the action needed to suck these dummies or teats is similar to the action used in breastfeeding, but many babies are happy with non-orthodontic dummies. Their use is controversial but widespread.

### Some arguments against using dummies

Dummies have some disadvantages. Dummies may:

- cause less physical closeness between mother and baby
- cause sucking confusion if given to a very young baby who is learning to breastfeed
- use energy which a new or small baby may need for feeding
- mask some other need requiring attention such as hunger, loneliness, discomfort or boredom
- become contaminated (if you do use a dummy have two or three on hand so that there is a clean one available when needed)
- establish a pervasive habit which interferes with ordinary feeding, settling and sleeping.

## Some arguments in favour of using dummies

Dummies have some advantages, as they are under the control of parents and are less likely than thumbs to distort teeth or jaws. They may:

- provide extra sucking for a baby needing it
- soothe a miserable baby when all other means fail.

## Managing the use of dummies

- Do not dip dummies in sweeteners. Doing so can encourage a baby's taste for sweetness to develop and when teeth appear they will be at risk of decay.
- Avoid attaching a ribbon to the dummy; it could choke your baby or tangle in fingers.
- If your baby is crying, try to deal with other possible causes before reaching for the dummy.
- Replace an ageing dummy.
- Wash the dummies in hot soapy water, rinse, then sterilise by boiling in water or immersing in sterilising solution. Keep them in clean lidded jars. Use boiled water to rinse off solution.
- You can lessen dependence by minimising the time spent sucking the dummy. You can try removing it once the baby is asleep.

# 5

# On being a parent

**P**arenting brings change. Along with its infinite rewards there will be adjustments to make, continued learning, challenges to meet and problems to solve as you live together as a family.

With the birth of your first baby you become a family and your lives change forever. Initially there was the preparation for and then the excitement of the birth itself. It is likely that there were cards, flowers and visits. All of this changes when you arrive home. Now there are all the demands of the previous household *plus* the new baby. Where there are partners they often feel anxious about their ability to fill their new role. Sharing the parenting can begin in planning the birth and continue throughout the pregnancy and into caring for the new baby. When the health professionals say goodbye you take on the full responsibility for this new life and, wonderful as it can be, there are major adjustments to be made.

Stresses are inevitable and all parents will face upsets at some stage. Sometimes there are added difficulties – mothers may be physically unable to manage well if in pain or exhausted. Anxiety may increase if they previously have had little to do with babies or if their baby seems to be different from any they have known. As they face unfamiliar and unexpected situations they may discover that life at home is not the way they want or expected it to be. The continuing demands on energy, time and capacity may be overwhelming.

Where there are other children they will need extra understanding and help for their world has also changed. It is impractical to expect to be perfect parents – it is not possible. The learning curve is steep. It is acceptable to make mistakes. Learning that never involves mistakes is probably impossible. Mistakes understood make the difference between experience-based and book-based learning.

## What is good parenting?

Is it luck? Is it skill? Is it learning? Being a successful parent seems to be a combination of all three. One baby in a family may be relaxed and easy-going, feed well, be reasonably contented, interact happily and settle to sleep without difficulty, or have short restless episodes due to obvious causes. Parents feel competent and happy, reassured that they are achieving the right approach. Another baby in the same family may find life more difficult, often seeming to be distressed, tense and unsettled. This baby may be hard to soothe and parents may find it difficult to identify just what is causing the crying. This time, to achieve the right approach they will need different skills. Can you acquire these? I believe that, in most cases, you can.

You will find that you are continually learning about your baby and yourself as you look after this little being but you may doubt your own judgement and lack confidence. You will find that within a few weeks you will know your own baby's needs and moods better than anyone. As confidence increases decision-making becomes easier. As you watch, assess and respond you are learning what to expect and how to make the best choices according to the needs and circumstances of the moment. Some anxiety can be expected but it need not dominate. It is wise to seek help when feeling unsure in this new or different experience of parenting. Reluctance to do so may stem from unreal expectations of how you and/or your baby should be performing.

## *Seek help when you need it*

It may surprise you to find just how willing people are to help. Be prepared to ask for and accept it. It can come from your partner, family, friends, and the health professionals who provided care during pregnancy, birth and the immediate postnatal period. There are family doctors, and early childhood nurses at baby health centres who may be only a visit or a phone call away. There are child and youth health resources, postnatal hospitals and family-care centres. There are 24-hour help line phone services you can contact at any time.

## Grandparents

Grandparents often have a very special role within the family. Today, society is complex. The new grandchild will often have one parent with a different background and different family traditions, part of another culture or from a different country. Grandparents may be presented with a step-grandchild or grandchildren. However it comes about, there is an opportunity for happy and fulfilling years ahead, but with challenges at times.

Grandparents can be the lifeline when there is a family crisis. From the first days grandmothers are often there with hands-on help, while grandfathers tend to come into their own from the time the grandchild becomes a toddler. Both grandparents can continue as loved companions and counsellors throughout the years as they build on the trust which so often exists between their grandchildren and themselves. Today life is so often lived in the 'fast' lane, which results in increased strains and stresses. Grandparents can be the ones who pause awhile to spend leisurely moments with their grandchildren.

They can listen, share in activities, tell stories, provide comfort, can be peacemakers and harbours of unconditional love.

The happiest family relationships involving the three generations grow out of mutual respect for each other. Grandparents need to be sensitive to the parents' ideas and views of child rearing, accept the family rules and know how to be involved without being interfering. It is then likely that their wisdom, interest, generosity and help will be truly welcomed and will enrich the lives of their grandchildren. Parents need to avoid unrealistic demands on the grandparents' time and energy, as grandparents today are often still in full- or part-time paid employment when their first grandchildren are born, or may be off travelling or involved in community work now that their own children are grown. New parents often need to negotiate with their own parents their availability and take care that they do not take it for granted that grandma or grandpa will just drop everything to be at their beck and call without thought or any prior warning. Crisis situations are different and grandparents are usually more than willing to come to the rescue where they can, particularly when their response is appreciated.

Today many grandparents are part-time or even full-time carers of their grandchildren. They cannot be expected to have the strength and energy they had when they were parents and they often need support and understanding themselves. In various places group support is available. If you feel a need for such a group and none is available in your community, you might like to organise one yourself – arrange a monthly meeting or such to help one another. You could start by discussing the idea with a senior citizens' information centre near you.

There are a number of books on grandparenting full of common sense and helpful suggestions which can be bought or found in libraries. One well worth reading is *You and your Grandchild* by Joan Gomez, published by Bloomsbury.

## Take care of yourself

As you begin to care for your new baby, keep your own needs in mind too and work out ways to meet these. The early days can be daunting – you have much to learn but the rewards are great. You can expect your confidence to increase daily. Just remember that babies are not 'things' to be picked up and moved without a word or a smile. They are not possessions to be shaped to fulfill parental wishes and ambitions. They are individuals with their own inner drives and needs, and with the right to be themselves. Tune in sensitively, love and guide them – but respect them too as you live, love and learn together.

Good parenting also means taking care of yourself. You need nourishing food simply prepared, a balance of rest and activity, emotional support, some intellectual stimulation and enjoyable social interaction. These things help you to remain balanced – able to relax and see things in proportion.

You will find life much easier if you are ready to accept the unexpected, to see difficulties as challenges and 'go with the flow'. A sense of humour is a great asset, a real help in preventing us from taking ourselves too seriously. An example of my own experience can illustrate the need for this. Even midwives who have spent years working with mothers and babies can overreact to their own babies' upsets. My own six-week-old daughter had been trouble-free. She fed comfortably, smiled and gurgled and then settled easily, the ideal baby. So when we were asked to join in a 21st birthday celebration my husband encouraged me to go, saying he would care for our toddler Lachlan and baby Jill. 'They both sleep well when put down and Jill never wants to feed before 2 a.m.,' he reasoned. Off I went for my first night out since her birth. It was a great party – then at 9 p.m. the phone rang. There was one distraught father on the other end. 'Come home! Both of them are awake and Jill is cracking the walls with her screaming. I can't do a thing with her and now Lachlan is getting upset because I can't leave her and go to him.' Our poor baby was having her first severe attack of colic. When I arrived home my husband had toddler on one hip and the baby against his shoulder. Fortunately her attack was subsiding. When both were settled again we looked at each other and laughed. So much for our belief that we would have no problems with our small daughter!

On another occasion, when John came in from work, he found me mopping up vomit from the floor with a nappy, ready to weigh the amount on the kitchen scales. With tears running down my face I explained it was the third vomit that day. He looked intently at our baby with her chubby, rosy cheeks. She gave him a wide smile and waved her arms in excitement. 'Have you plenty of milk for her?' he asked me. I looked down at the damp patches on my shirt. We both looked at our roly-poly daughter. Her father raised his eyebrows. My worry was absurd and reason enough for a good laugh. When we feel tired and overwhelmed very minor upsets can seem calamitous.

Many new mothers feel very isolated if they are at home alone with a new baby. Women without partners or those with little or no support have even greater demands on their time and energy. To avoid this you can arrange meetings with other mothers, friends and family. Perhaps there is a community support group in the vicinity. You could look for one. It appears that unrelieved loneliness may contribute to postnatal depression.

The father, other partner or close person who lives nearby can provide support for the mother as she is contending with the adjustments that her body is making, as well as learning about and caring for the new baby. Ideally fathers can provide hands-on care with nappy changing, holding and comforting as they fit into this new interactive role. Many fathers now want to be equal partners in parenting and caregiving, and do so very successfully. There is so much that is new, so much to learn. Be content to take each day as it comes and know that you can expect it all to become easier with increasing experience.

A healthy full-term baby and a well mother can expect to adjust fairly easily to the new circumstances. Modern society, however, does not always help this adjustment. Many people are isolated from family and friends either in crowded cities or in country areas. Few are taught about parenting before the event.

It is not helpful to compare yourselves and your baby with 'model' parents and babies 'out there' in an idealised community. If your baby does not behave as you have been led to expect, you may feel that you are failing and that your baby must have a real problem. With the best will in the world you may just have inappropriate expectations. For example, you may have heard from Suzi Jones that her baby settled into a comfortable feeding routine and slept for long periods at night when only a few days old. It can happen – Suzi Jones may be truthful but she may also have forgotten the details of her baby's early weeks, leading to a rosy glow of inaccuracy. Whatever the case, if your baby is expected to but does not 'toe this line', the problem is not necessarily with your baby but in using Suzi Jones and her infant as the standard – *you do not need to try to keep up with the Joneses.*

Be patient and realistic in your expectations of yourself and of your baby; do not expect your baby to be like any other you have had or like your friends' babies. Each is an individual with a different personality and each grows in his or her own way. Relax and flow with this new experience as you and your baby grow to know and love each other.

# You may know more than you think

Following the birth of your baby it is likely that, for the first few days at least, you will have daily contact with your midwife or midwives, and perhaps with your doctor. There will be someone there to provide information and to help you learn.

It is likely that you will wish to discuss many things with your midwives – your baby's appearance and behaviour, for example, which will probably change daily. You will be learning how your baby responds to your voice, smiles and caresses; how they like to be held and cuddled, picked up and put down. You are discovering how to soothe and comfort and what your baby feels about bathing.

In these first few days you will learn much about feeding. You will know if your baby is a vigorous or a slow feeder, fixes on the breast easily or with difficulty. As your lactation becomes established and adapts to suit your baby's appetite, which can vary from feed to feed, you will find that you have more milk at different times of the day and the times on the breast will also vary. Relax and tune in to these changes and enjoy them. You are likely to realise when he or she wants a short rest or to pause to bring up a bubble of wind. If your baby is formula-fed you will know if the formula is taken happily and appears to be suitable for your baby. You can see that already you have learnt much. Much of the time you will be unaware that you are learning but it goes on continually through your own experience of caring.

Your baby's behaviour and abilities continue to change as each day passes. It may take time to fall in love with your baby; if so, you need not be concerned. Provided you are loving and gentle in your care you are unlikely to make any serious mistakes. Speak kindly, smile, cuddle and share eye-to-eye contact as you provide the nurturing your baby requires. Should you find negative feelings dominate, talk to your midwife, maternal and child health nurse or doctor who will listen and advise you. If necessary you can be referred on for further help. Appropriate support is likely to prevent damage to your relationship with your baby. Should you feel so angry that you want to hurt your baby *get help without delay*. In an emergency you can ring Lifeline on 13 11 14 from anywhere in Australia, day or night (see 'Red alert!' in Chapter 18).

## Coping with change

People change throughout life, pass through stages of growth and development and through changing social circumstances. Expanding experiences can alter the way we interpret and react to events. Common lifetime changes include being born, starting school, leaving school, entering the adult world, hopefully working, pairing, having children, retiring and becoming old. How successfully we adapt to changes affects our feelings of wellbeing and those of the people with whom we live and interact, including, ultimately, the community.

We draw on our own personal resources, moulded by our life experiences – the parenting we received, the conditioning, education and cultural attitudes to which we have been exposed. When there is a stress and demand on us for action, we decide what to do by drawing on our habitual methods of coping – those tried and true solutions that have worked for us in the past. When there is a major life change such as the birth of a baby, we face an unknown situation. We need new skills to meet the new demands.

We manage change by learning to behave differently. First we need to be aware that we need new skills, then we have to learn them. Anxiety occurs when we realise we are facing a new situation and don't know what to do. However, this motivates us to learn and then we find we can manage. We begin to relax, and the unknown becomes the known and familiar. Awareness and learning may occur simultaneously but it is convenient to consider them separately.

## Awareness – getting in touch

Being aware is being mindful of what is happening around and within us. Our senses register what is occurring. Only then can we think and interpret why it is happening, predict what could happen next and, if necessary, plan ways to alter the outcome.

For parents, awareness involves observation and interpretation of their baby's behaviour, facial expressions and body movements, whether the baby is happy or miserable, tense or relaxed. Awareness of our own and other family members' behaviour and feelings is also important if the family is to function well as a unit.

When under stress we may not be aware of certain things. For example if we are tense as we hold a crying baby we can unknowingly add to the baby's distress. By pausing to think – in this case to be aware of our own tension – we can consciously relax and so will be more likely to solve the problem we are facing.

## Learning

Fortunately parents are generally motivated to acquire the new skills needed for nurturing their babies. Information is the starting point and can come from life experiences, from family, friends, midwives, nurses and doctors. It can be found in parent magazines and books and on radio, television and the Internet. Community group sessions are useful as parents share similar experiences and learn much from each other. A good place to start is in an antenatal education program or an antenatal breastfeeding class. These are offered by hospitals and the community.

We can use our own knowledge to test and assess that which is new as we face different situations. Then we can accept those methods which produce positive results and discard those which do not.

Although tentative at first, we become more confident as we find new approaches that serve us well.

Observing and questioning can challenge previously held attitudes, and changes can be made. When health professionals realised that the routine imposition of rigid three- or four-hourly feeding schedules on mothers and babies was actually responsible for many feeding problems and produced many tense and unhappy mothers and babies, changes were made in the health system and flexibility was introduced.

In learning the new skills we need, we once more feel in control. Confidence grows and we increasingly trust our own judgement.

## Anxiety

Anxiety is a state of mind – an indication that we are reaching the limit of our resources and it is time to change our approach and possibly look for help. A little anxiety can be positive because it challenges and expands thinking. Unrelieved anxiety, however, is negative and can lead to severe stress.

Even if their first efforts to overcome a problem are unsuccessful, some mothers may still feel in control. They may be concerned, even mildly anxious, yet still able to try to discover what it is that their baby is trying to tell them. For others, anxiety may be so high that it prevents them from thinking of other approaches they might make. They simply become overwhelmed. For example bath time may be a misery – the overwhelmed mother will feel apprehensive and inadequate and not know what to do as her baby continues to scream. Another mother is able to think about possible reasons for the upset: perhaps her baby feels insecure when undressed and naked. She may try keeping the baby covered. Perhaps it is being lowered into the bath – the baby's natural fear of falling may be the problem. The mother may try wrapping firmly in a cloth nappy, then moving the baby very slowly and smoothly into the bath (still wrapped in the nappy). She might think of altering the temperature of the water. Would her baby be less miserable if the bath water were warmer or cooler? If nothing she does helps, this mother might confidently decide that she can keep her baby clean and comfortable without a bath. Her final decision will depend on her baby's reactions. However, when she has exhausted all the possibilities she can think of and her baby is still upset she will become anxious.

Being aware of anxiety can allow you to monitor your state of mind, using the first signs as an alert to change your direction. You will be able to decide when you need to implement a *fail-safe* plan before your level of stress becomes acute. Think about the steps you will take if this need arises (see 'Red alert!' in Chapter 18). And remember, too much fatigue is a very important risk factor for anxiety.

## *Unrealistic expectations*

Unrealistic expectations make for anxiety and disappointment. Think about and talk with your partner about both your expectations before the baby arrives, if you can. Be ready to question how you and your partner are expecting your baby and yourselves to behave. For example, when taking some views from the media parents need to beware: real people are not always well dressed, beautifully made-up, with freshly styled hair in an immaculate house with dinner simmering on a spotless stove, with a contented baby who smiles and gurgles between long and peaceful sleeps. Real women are also not usually back to their pre-baby weight and shape for many months. Be prepared for the 'straggly hair' days and the 'no shower until the afternoon' days. If you expect days like this, they will not be so bad when they arrive.

## *Relaxing to relieve anxiety*

There are times when you will feel anxious and it is necessary to try to relax. The following suggestions may help you to relax:

- Take slow, quiet, deep breaths.
- Relax your face: forehead, eyes, jaws; and then shoulders, arms, wrists and hands.
- Be aware of your self-talk – make it calming and positive.

If your anxiety or distress becomes severe it is important to seek professional help immediately.

### *Five basic principles for nurturing a baby*

These basic principles can guide you as you nurture your baby. Your baby needs to:

**1.** grow – if not growing you will want to know if there is a medical reason or if your baby is receiving insufficient or unsuitable food
**2.** receive an enormous amount of body contact – loving, holding and cuddling
**3.** be as comfortable as possible
**4.** feel safe and secure in the environment
**5.** enjoy appropriate interactions.

## Making adjustments to the changed lifestyle

In discussion groups I have learnt how quickly many mothers worked out ways to rearrange their lives after the birth of their babies.

**Carly:** *'No-one tells you what it is really like. I assumed I would be a bit tired because of feeding but I certainly wasn't prepared for the utter weariness that I felt, especially in the first couple of weeks. My nipples were a bit tender and I was leaking milk everywhere and my stitches were still sore. I wasn't sure that I was doing the right thing. It's that awful feeling of total responsibility. Will was good but he didn't know a thing about babies and relied on me to know everything. He was surprised if I couldn't comfort her at once and then he got uptight too and so I felt guilty and that I was a hopeless mother. Still, things improved and now Sienna is five weeks old and we are all managing much better. It is a case of learn as we go along.'*

**Rachael:** *'Even in this day and age babies are really seen as women's work. We are expected to know instinctively what's wrong and what to do – if your efforts don't work you feel guilty and a poor mother and self-esteem is zilch. My main problem was conflicting advice* *from all directions. One of the midwives suggested that I could listen and then do what suited us both – to imagine I was on a desert island and nobody was telling me what I should do or feel and that I'd probably get it right. I was to remember that there was help at the end of the phone if I needed it. That was good advice and I just make up my own mind what I will or will not do.'*

**Kirsty:** *'It really is hard being a single mum. In the first two or three weeks I was in an emotional whirlpool. I thought I was glad I had Cooper – there were times when I was sure I was and then I'd suddenly think hell, what have I got myself into? Sometimes he'd stop crying and look up at me and move his arms and legs and then I'd feel a bit motherly but it wasn't until he started smiling that I really felt good about having him. Now things are miles better. He is ten weeks old and in a fairly good routine and I belong to a mother's group. We meet and have morning tea once a week. We can share our feelings and ideas and this really helps.'*

**Amy:** *'One of the hardest things I had to cope with was the change in our relationships – with each other, our families and friends. Our early childhood nurse at the clinic was great. On our first visit she just smiled at little Ruby and then very seriously asked me how I was feeling. She was the first one to do this and I felt that she really wanted to know. I guess that opened the floodgates. It is amazing how much you can tell a sympathetic person in ten minutes. It was good to hear that my stresses were normal. We talked of ways of lessening them and I walked out of that clinic seeing light at the end of the tunnel, realising that there was someone there for me as well as for our baby. I felt I really would be able to cope and be a reasonably good mother.'*

**Shifa:** *'Aashir was ten days old when I went along to our GP. My main worry was my lack of sleep. She suggested that I take a nap while*

Aashir was sleeping. I told her that I could never sleep in the daytime. She just looked at me, smiled and said, "Maybe, maybe not, but try it." I did catnap for short snatches. I was surprised that I did. It did help.'

**Madeline:** 'What worried me most was trying to split myself into three parts. Baby took most of me then Ben needed his share and I still wanted a bit for me. Actually my doctor must know me rather well, he warned me that I would have to make an effort to plan things so that I had some time to myself. Having a sensible breakfast and lunch when on my own was a must as far as he was concerned.'

**Le:** 'I've always considered myself a very together person and I hated feeling unsure and dependent on others for support. I missed the office group and felt isolated. Then I started talking to the other women in the clinic waiting room – they had babies of all ages. On the whole they were a friendly lot who had had odd worries but were generally comfortable and friendly to be with. It was obvious that they had survived. Those who had other children too were often the reassuring ones. They told me that soon I'd get over these early days. By the time I've had a couple more (heaven forbid) I'd be far too busy to spend time worrying over minor things. I have made two really good friends through the clinic and I'm really enjoying Oliver now.'

**Lily:** 'I didn't have that choice. I had to go back to work when Ella was born to meet our mortgage repayments. That was three years ago. Now we have Charlie and I have taken maternity leave plus another three months without pay. When Ella was coming we planned it all so carefully. I was to be home for the first three months and then put her into a really good daycare centre nearby. I found it terrible. As the time came nearer I became so miserable. I dreaded leaving her. I worried that she would miss me. Would the staff have time to play with her and talk to her? They wouldn't know her little ways –

how she liked to be burped and oh, just everything. Actually it hasn't been as bad as I imagined and I was able to express my milk for her to have during the day and continue with breastfeeding when she was at home which was a comfort for us both. She is now a friendly toddler and loves the daycare staff, other children and the various activities.'

**Alice:** 'My worst feelings were that I felt abnormal because I didn't have instant maternal feelings for James. He was so often miserable and difficult to get to sleep and would work himself into a screaming state just so quickly. Whatever I did seemed useless and I'd feel so helpless and inadequate. You feel that mothers should love their babies regardless of anything they did. Actually I am very close to my Gran and she saved my sanity. I was able to talk to her about the way I really felt and she was so matter-of-fact about it, assured me that I was no monster and my feelings were quite normal. James was eight weeks and two days before he smiled and I was the favoured one. I flipped, and that was the first time I felt really maternal and loving towards him.

Things have just got better. He is much more settled and sleeps for several hours at night although he does still have his bad moments. Now I couldn't imagine life without him.'

**Greta:** 'What I found so hard was feeling so tired and that I wanted someone to fuss over me and coddle me. In fact, what I wanted more than anything was for Mum to come. Dad was ill and couldn't be left. My stitches were sore; they told me my haemorrhoids would settle down quickly and they didn't. Jack got a terrible nappy rash which made me feel guilty – in fact it was due to the laundry detergent I was using. When Ben came in I'd just burst into tears and he didn't know how to handle me, I'm not usually a weepy person. The third evening he led me to the lounge, tucked a cushion behind my head and said we had to work out some way of helping me. He offered to either *take Jack out for a walk in the possum pouch for an hour or so or cook the dinner. I chose getting dinner. I've always loved the cooking and it was excellent not to have to think of the baby at all for a time. I'm usually in bed by eight o'clock and fall asleep almost at once. Ben brings Jack in when he wakes then Ben goes to bed. I feed him and put him down again. I get up for his next meal around 3 or 4 a.m. That way we each get some longer sleeps. Ben gets up and makes breakfast and I sleep in. I'm feeling much more relaxed over everything now.'*

## How do you respond to advice?

Parents can encounter advice that is not based on the needs of their particular baby. Well-meaning friends, relatives or neighbours may be convinced that their ways are best. Although they do not know your baby as you do, they may urge you to follow their advice. Commercial interests offer magical solutions to parental difficulties. Cultures and religions can also impose constraints and expectations.

Advice that leads to confusion is to be questioned. Some advice may not benefit you and your baby. Be wary if it causes distress to either of you. You can ask your advisers for reasons and see if these reasons make sense to you. You may have been told to wrap the baby firmly for sleeping but you find that your baby becomes restless and struggles in the wrap. Many babies find firm wrapping very reassuring but maybe yours does not. Try loosening the wrapping: does it help?

Perhaps you have been told that complete demand feeding is the only way to feed a new baby. This is usually very good advice, but you have lots of milk – your baby cries every hour or so and immediately drinks vigorously each time you offer the breast (see 'Too much milk' in Chapter 21). Your baby is uncomfortable at the end of the feed and often spills. The baby may also be having large weight gains. You are likely to feel that the amount of milk taken from the breasts is too much and is causing discomfort but you may hesitate to lengthen the time between feeds. Listen to yourself and be prepared to try different approaches. If what you have chosen to do helps, you know you have chosen a way that works. However, the baby's behaviour may change. The right approach can depend on how the baby is feeling at the time, or on the time of day; it may even vary from day to day. Or maybe you have been told that daily routine is important. Babies, like us, tend to be comfortable with routine but it may take several weeks to find a routine that suits your baby. Furthermore, routines should never be inflexible.

Suppose you think your baby is tired and ready for sleep but crying either persists or begins. You have been advised to put your baby down when it is time for sleep but crying continues. What you do will depend on the baby's behaviour and your reaction to it and your confidence in yourself to decide. If the cry is merely complaining you might wait a while allowing time for the baby to fall asleep, recognising that some babies seem to unwind and relax by doing so. If the cry becomes a bout of screaming you may ignore the advice and try to find some way to comfort and soothe the distressed infant. You could not leave your baby in distress. You ignored advice which did not suit you and trusted your own judgement about your own baby's need.

## 'Everyone tells me something different!'

The more the advisers, the more confused and apprehensive the new parents may become: 'You must have the baby in hospital.' 'Don't go to the hospital for the birth.' 'Breastfeed your baby.' 'Use a milk formula.' 'Never use a dummy.' 'Get your baby used to using a bottle.' 'Give your baby this.' 'Do that.' 'No.' 'Yes.' 'Breastfeed through the night.' 'Just give boiled water through the night.' 'You need your rest, so let the baby yell.' 'Have him circumcised.' 'No, don't.' No wonder new parents so often feel confused and anxious.

Can you identify with the centipede who was out enjoying a walk when he was asked, 'Which leg comes after which?' He felt so confused he ended upside-down in the ditch.

In thinking about the conflicting advice you may receive, you can choose to make your own decisions on what you will try and so discover what works best for you.

During pregnancy you may have read and heard something about the care of the newborn. It can come from many different sources. Some advice made sense to you and some did not and with some you were just unsure. However, with the birth some time off in the future there was no hurry to work out which advice you would accept and which you would reject. This changes when your baby is born. From then on you will have to make immediate decisions on what to do. There will be little time to read a book when the baby is screaming and you are exhausted.

Advice may be offered from an interested neighbour, the experienced father at work or cousin Clara who has had six babies and should know. These people may be very helpful but they only have a hazy understanding of your situation and of your baby, so what they say may not apply to you. You can listen if you choose. If the advice is unwelcome or disturbing or visitors say, with implied criticism, 'We didn't do things that way', you can change the subject. Ask after their garden, their children, work or views on TV shows. You can start them on politics – anything will do, any topic other than your baby. If necessary you can also ask them politely to stop, telling them that you do not want to hear. Or just listen to them all, smile politely, take on board what sounds useful and throw away the rest.

It is confusing when you are given contradictory advice from various sources but it is worse when the advisers are unanimously opposed to your approach. Consistent advice need not be good advice if it only seeks to impose entrenched attitudes and the beliefs of the current society – thus in the 1940s and 1950s most new parents in Australia were advised to feed their babies strictly by the clock every three or four hours and then for ten minutes only on each breast. That was the way babies should be fed. Today such scheduled feeding for a well baby is considered most inappropriate. Routine advice also included leaving the baby to cry in the cot between feeds – to pick up the baby would be indulgent and create bad habits. This belief harks back to the Victorian era when, ideally, children were seen and not heard and the serious business of stern character-building began in the cradle. Most people today do not accept these attitudes. Generally our society is more compassionate. Even so there are still people whose advice it is to 'Let the baby scream it out; if you don't you are making a rod for your own back.' 'Let the infant know who is boss from the day you return home.' Responding to your baby's needs will not create problems, it can prevent them.

Parents need to confidently make their own decisions based on sound information and their knowledge of their own baby. There are times when they may disagree with each other on what to do. If the issue is discussed a compromise may be reached and/or they can talk it over with a health adviser. However, health professionals do not always agree with one another either and conflicting advice coming from midwives and doctors can be very disturbing. They too are influenced by personal values and beliefs based on experiences such as family memories. Also their professional education and experiences differ, so we need to look for those who are supportive, skilled, knowledgeable and flexible in their attitudes – people in whom we have confidence.

We need to feel free to ask for information and for the reasons behind the advice offered if they are not clear to us. We also need to feel confident to seek a second opinion at any time.

# Unrelieved tiredness and fatigue

Because your new baby is totally dependent 24 hours a day and needs to be fed frequently around the clock, it is normal to feel very tired at times. Mothers of new babies need to know that their previous sleep patterns will change. They need to find ways of obtaining needed sleep to avoid 'sleep deprivation'. In accepting this they can often arrange the day so that they can have some sleep while the baby sleeps (not so easy when there are other children). Mothers also have to cope with major bodily changes which follow birth and their associated strong emotional reactions. However, we humans are fairly resilient and mostly we manage to survive these challenges. Tiredness becomes a problem when it continues so long that it leads to fatigue. If you are one of the increasing number of women experiencing caesarean birth remember that you have also to recover from major surgery on top of baby-led tiredness and fatigue.

If you can make it possible, when the baby sleeps in the day lie down and sleep too. If you have housework to do but feel extremely tired, sleep first and do housework second. Do not be tempted to use baby's sleep time to get things done if you are very tired in the early weeks; rather, use this time to regain your strength and energy through sleep.

Tiredness is the signal for us to rest. Simple tiredness does not affect our health – it is the result of loss of energy, which is readily restored by adequate food and rest. Fatigue, however, will result from unrelieved tiredness. It does affect our health. It can lead to physical, emotional and mental exhaustion. It makes it difficult for us to respond, particularly if we are experiencing feelings of anxiety over our ability to care competently for our baby. Fatigue can be confused with postnatal depression but when it is relieved recovery is rapid, whereas a woman with postnatal depression will take longer to recover (see Chapter 9, 'Depression following birth'). However, mothers who are consistently unduly tired or exhausted need expert help.

Partners also need sleep. When they are working they cannot have a daytime nap so plan to maximise their sleep too. Just help each other. It may take time to work out a mutually helpful way of handling night feeds and fussy or miserable periods. Single parents are even more at risk of fatigue. Make a particular effort to have some time to yourself when you can rest knowing that the baby is being well cared for.

Aim to prevent fatigue. Plan your nutrition, some exercise, rest and relaxation. Prioritise the day's activities. Simplify household chores. A quick tidy of the house and basic cleaning are enough most of the time. Be ready to accept help if it is offered and to ask for it if necessary.

Often babies sleep soundly after their early feed and this can be an excellent chance for mothers to sleep too. So what about the baby's bath if you sleep until 9 or 10 a.m.? There are no 'shoulds' about bath time. When the baby wakens you could bath or 'top and tail' (sponge face and bottom) or feed the baby immediately depending on what suits you both. You may choose to leave the bath until the evening. Fathers often enjoy bathing their baby. Many babies are fussy or even miserable in the evening and a deep warm bath can soothe and relax them.

Partners and friends can do much to help conserve a woman's energy. The result is likely to be a more relaxed baby and a woman who is able to manage reasonably well. Here are some ways they might help. Don't expect them to read your mind: ask and give specific suggestions of what they could do. They may:

- help any other children start the day by giving them breakfast, dressing a toddler and/or organising older children in readiness for school
- undertake any of the household tasks such as shopping, cooking or tidying
- put the washing through the machine and, unless using a dryer, either hang it out on the line or, if the weather is wet or doubtful, hang it on a rack in the laundry
- share the hands-on care of the new baby
- let you sleep for an hour undisturbed by the baby.

More and more partners are sharing the responsibility for the care of their babies and most of them enjoy the current freedom to choose to be an active parent – whether it is in changing, bathing, carrying, comforting or playing. They feel that they are participating equally in nurturing their infant. Women benefit when they can hand over the responsibility to someone who loves the baby as they do, even if only for a short time.

There are times when women feel weary and pressured but a sleep is not possible. The next best thing is to take a few moments to relax. There are many ways of relaxing – you can sit in a comfortable chair or stretch out on a bed or lounge. By taking a few deep breaths and consciously relaxing you can let go of tension. Try to reduce emotional upsets and anxieties. It is also beneficial to spend some time enjoying an activity apart from the baby and household chores, both with partner and/or friends and on your own, even if only for very short periods.

---

Here's what some of the women from our discussion groups had to say about tiredness and fatigue.

**Lucy:** 'Before Noah was born I went to bed late so I planned to stay up and feed him around 10 p.m. I would try to waken him but he would have a few sucks and then fall asleep again. It was useless to persevere so I would put him down. Around 1 or 2 a.m. he would waken really hungry. I could hardly surface. Tim brought him in for me to feed. At first I sat up to feed him but then tried snuggling him down beside me in the bed. He drank happily while I dozed but he made it clear when he was ready for the other breast. Often I'd wake up later with him sound asleep beside me. We decided that it would be easier to bring the cot in beside me. We used a dim light and I fed him before he was fully awake so it remained a drowsy meal although he took a good feed. I didn't change him at that feed although he was wringing wet by morning but I used the inner nappy and snap-on flannels when I put him down for the night and being wet didn't worry him. He must have had pretty tough skin because he stayed free of nappy rash.

After the first few days at home I surprised myself by falling asleep easily when I went to bed early. I guess when we are tired enough we will sleep any time.'

**Sally:** 'Riley was not easy, he would sometimes sleep for two hours and other times for five after the evening feed so it was no good trying to plan the best time to go to bed. I would fall into bed after dinner and Peter, who never went to bed early, would bring Riley in to me when he wakened which was always before midnight. I enjoyed a mug of hot milk which Pete gave me after I'd fed Riley. I would get up to him for the next feed. Actually I rather liked that feed in the early hours. It was quiet and restful, just the two of us. We just enjoyed each other. In the first few weeks Riley would sometimes have another short feed before his 6 or 7 a.m. meal and, when he did this he was often fussy and difficult to settle and this was wearing. I used a CD of womb sounds which I would switch on and put beside him. Sometimes it worked and sometimes it didn't. Funnily, I could depend on him to settle into a comfortable and longish sleep after the 6 or 7 a.m. feed so I'd sleep too and not get up until after he wakened and fed around 10 a.m. I found I was a lot less tired. Pete got his own breakfast and, if I was awake, he'd give me mine. I felt a bit guilty at first, sleeping in like that. I changed Riley's bath time to the evening and just gave him a wash in the morning. It worked well. I was rarely disturbed by the phone or callers during the first part of the day. Riley was an erratic sleeper after that and tended to cat nap during the rest of the day so I appreciated that early morning sleep-in. Mum was horrified. She had visions of me in a dressing gown when Pete came in. She needn't have worried – a shower was a must straight after that next feed, my nightie was dripping milk.'

**Margot:** 'Well, after the first three weeks I couldn't handle Max's lack of routine. He was wanting a feed every couple of hours, sometimes even sooner. Billy was four and Joshua not quite two. I had gallons *of milk, probably baby was waking with a tummy ache rather than hunger. He put on 300 grams the first week and next week 340 grams. Nancy, my early childhood nurse, agreed that he must have milk coming out of his ears. I'd been giving him a few minutes on each side just to ease my breasts but she said that it was important to let him finish on the first side before changing over. That way he drained at least the first breast well. By staying on the breast longer he had more sucking time too. He was much better. I would offer the second breast but often he did not want it. Sometimes I had to express a little from the second breast if it was too full. For me it was great when she suggested that I try to ease him into longer periods between feeds provided that he did not become too upset with the wait. We decided I should begin this during the first part of the day when he was more likely to be relaxed.'*

While trying to do this Margot would divert him in various ways. She would put her baby on a rug in the middle of the playpen where he could watch the others playing. Sometimes she had him in the kitchen where she was busy and the radio was on but at least once a day all four of them went out to the park nearby – the baby loved outings in the pram and he would wait for a feed for quite a while when propped up so he could see. With the actual feeds she kept him on the first side for as long as he would suck. In the morning he was satisfied with one side only but after lunch he had a minute or two from the other breast. By evening he took much more from the second breast. Within a week he was sleeping for longer periods. His large gains reduced to around 200–250 grams a week. He was more contented and did appear to be more comfortable.

**Tess:** *'Charlotte needed lots of feeds. I tried to make her wait. Mum said she had us all on four hourly feeds as soon as she brought us home from hospital and that I was letting Charlotte get into bad* *habits. I stuck to feeding her whenever she wanted for the first two weeks just as they advised me to do when I was in hospital and then I switched and tried to keep her on four hourly feeds; I certainly never let her have anything under three hours. I kept at it for three days. It was hopeless – she cried and cried and then fell asleep half way through her feeding when she did get to the breast. I just hung in there until David came in from work and then I handed her over to him and told him to take her out of my hearing. It was tough on him coming in to a screaming baby and an exhausted and irritable wife but he just took her and I was able to turn my mind to the dinner and stop worrying about Charlotte for a while.*

*Anyway, that week she only gained 60 grams. I'd had more than enough, so we went back to feeding according to need. We were both happier. Next week she had a much better gain but more importantly she was much more content. Although she fed often through the day she slept much better at night and only needed two feeds and I felt my supply increasing. She was beginning to go for longer periods when, at seven weeks she went back to wanting extra feeds. I phoned Alison my community midwife who delivered her, and she said it was likely that Charlotte just needed a little more milk because she was growing – just to feed whenever she asked and I would soon increase my supply to satisfy her. She fed often but had a better week plus a good weight gain. Then she more or less settled back into her old routine and is now fairly predictable. She is just ten weeks now and having six or seven feeds each day. Mum was disgusted but thank goodness she didn't carry on about it.'*

Each woman altered her care according to her baby's response. She saw that what she was doing was not working. One recognised that neither her own nor her mother's expectations were appropriate. She tried something different, she trusted her own judgement and used her baby's response as a guide. This is really active learning. Each success, however small, increases confidence.

# Human needs

Why do we behave in certain ways? A useful way of explaining behaviour is to see it as a response to our needs. These include our physical needs for air, water, food, safety, warmth and shelter. Our feeling and social needs require that we have self-esteem, the opportunity to love and feel loved and to belong to a group or community where we have people we can relate to and depend on.

If our thinking needs are to be met we must have mental stimulation and the chance to learn, gain knowledge and satisfy our curiosity. We need to develop skills and understanding. We also have a need for beauty and the chance to develop our spiritual values and views which give meaning to our lives.

When our needs are being met we function best – we feel that it is 'good to be alive'. If some need is unsatisfied and particularly if our attempts to deal with it fail, then we feel anxious and stressed.

Needs affect one another. For example: if we are tired and in need of rest (a physical need) this affects the way we think – we find it harder to think clearly to handle difficult situations. This leads to anxiety and/ or irritability – another need we want to relieve. Further, our tiredness may result in our eating inadequately (not meeting a health need) and we can become unreasonable and impatient with other members of the family or friends (making us feel miserable and isolated). If we become aware of how we are feeling and can think about why we are behaving in a particular way, we can then understand and help ourselves and those around us.

Babies signal their needs by crying. If the first cry does not bring attention it will become louder and more urgent. If hungry, the need is for food; if lonely, it is for company and to be lovingly held and talked to. If uncomfortable or in pain the baby needs help to relieve it.

There are times when we all fail to meet some of our baby's needs. No-one can be perfect. We all, including our children, have some negative experiences as we pass through life. Were all our experiences in our young life positive then we would be ill-equipped to deal with the negative experiences in our adult lives.

If we generally manage to convey to our babies through careful, loving handling and tone of voice that they are lovable and valued, odd moments of irritation, frustration and weariness will do no lasting harm. At such times we need time out, to 'switch off' for a while – time to attend to our own needs and to regain balance.

Successful family life takes adequate account of the needs of all members of the family. We should not focus all our attention on the baby to the exclusion of ourselves and any other children.

## Mothers – some special needs

During pregnancy the woman's needs automatically encompass her baby. By providing for her own requirements, the baby's needs are also met. Birth brings the physical separation of the baby from the mother's body. For many women their immediate need is to hold and cuddle as they re-establish body contact with their infant.

Usually the mother becomes the chief caregiver and the strong link continues between her and her baby. She will begin to produce breastmilk and establish lactation. Because her baby will feed frequently she needs to adjust to new patterns of sleeping to obtain necessary rest.

As her body begins to return to the pre-pregnancy state she needs to find the time for rest and exercise. She will certainly benefit if she includes postnatal exercises in her daily routine. Altering hormonal levels can affect her.

All these changes can impact on her wellbeing, both emotional and physical, so she needs support, willingly given, as she regains her strength. If she is experiencing mood changes and heightened reactions which concern her, she needs to know they are usually normal and temporary. She may be helped if there is an opportunity for her to discuss her feelings with a sympathetic and supportive listener.

Further, a mother has a basic need (and so too does a father, but perhaps less urgently) to feel competent in caring for the baby. As mother and baby interact and begin life together she is finding and providing the needed care. As she does so, and her baby's responses reassure her, her need to feel competent is met and her confidence increases. Praise from other people is helpful because it supports her belief in herself. Sometimes a woman provides good care but her baby is miserable and hard to comfort. This will be worrying until she can find a way to help the baby. The mother needs encouragement and whatever help is required to overcome any persistent problem.

## Fathers – what special needs might they have?

Many men feel totally overwhelmed by the birth of their child and especially by witnessing the strength and power of the woman they love as she gives birth to their baby. It is a life-changing event for him, as well as her. Following the birth of his baby a father's most immediate need is to know that both his partner and baby are well. If there are any issues he will want these empathetically explained. He will need clear answers to any questions he asks. He is also likely to need to know that his partner is satisfied with the care she is receiving and that any mood swings are normal in the early days following birth. If he has concerns and doubts, he is likely to find it helpful if he can discuss these with her and perhaps with others as they arise. As he takes a share in helping and caring for their baby, he needs to know that his efforts are welcome and valuable, even while he is learning. As his competence grows so will his self-esteem as a father and the pleasure he gains from his achievements and interactions with their baby. This will encourage further involvement in the baby's care.

Given the closeness of the mother-baby relationship, the father may feel a little left out – particularly in the early weeks. He may need reassurance at this time that he is still valued and loved by his partner. There will be added pressure on him, too, and extra responsibilities. His own routines, rest, relaxation and exercise, not only those of his partner, are affected.

## Other children's needs

The arrival of a baby means fitting a new member into the family. This inevitably affects other children. It is wise to assume that all children will need reassurance about their place in the family and their relationship with their parents. Try to find time to give some undivided attention to each. Their feeling needs will probably be mixed, and will vary with age. Older children, according to individual personalities, may welcome the new addition with real pleasure or they may be a little distant or reserved. Often they become very involved and love to help with the new baby. With other established interests of their own, their period of adjustment can be short and painless.

Toddlers will almost certainly feel displaced, if only because there will be times when they have to wait for attention. They are unable to wait patiently and may demonstrate anxiety in a number of ways. Think of the toddler who brings in a caterpillar to show to his mother. She may be changing the baby but it takes only a moment to look at the caterpillar and make some comment. Imagine the effect on the toddler if told crossly to take it away at once or if brushed aside because mum is too busy to look. The child would probably feel rejected and then angry and it is likely that the baby would be blamed. Diversion can be an effective way of changing troublesome behaviour. A toddler does not want to change an activity to suit the baby – for example, if banging noisily on a drum just as the baby is settling to sleep, the toddler is unlikely to want to stop. A mother can comment on the lovely noise but then suggest that the child try playing it very softly while she is finding another quieter occupation of equal interest. A gift for each sibling from the new baby is usually very happily received. Toddlers often enjoy a baby doll to bath, feed and cuddle.

Children need to know that they have access to their parents who can and will find time to spend with them. They will function best if kept aware of their parents' unconditional love. They need guidance and the reinforcement of family expectations appropriate to their ages and stages of growth and development.

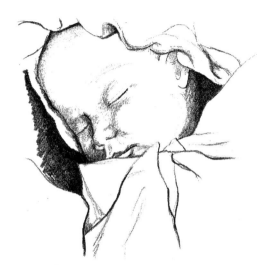

# Communicating

**W**hen we communicate with someone, we interact so that we are sharing thoughts, feelings and information. Our wellbeing depends on our ability to communicate with each other. This is a basic need. Our babies share this need to communicate. Their physical, mental and emotional wellbeing, as well as the parents' confidence, depends on the successful sending and receiving of countless messages. Babies must feel safe, loved and secure at all times and not be left to cry. Sleep and settling strategies are about the baby's cues being understood and the baby being continually comforted and reassured by her or his parents or caregivers.

Babies receive messages with each encounter – important feelings are generated and ongoing learning is initiated. Crying is a direct way of communicating and is certainly the most noticeable. It primarily summons care but it also carries shades of meaning which experience and careful observation on the part of the caregiver can distinguish. Body language, including facial expressions and the sounds the baby and we ourselves make, are the means of communicating. Communication is vital and ongoing in every situation, a two-way interaction between the baby and her or his mother/father or other caregiver. The Australian Association for Infant Mental Health states that research clearly suggests that babies who have early emotional security have long-term benefits: for example, they are more likely to be able to deal with stress, have a healthy self-esteem and manage satisfying relationships.

## Crying, vocalising and using body language

Immediately following birth there is often a period when your baby is quiet, alert and relaxed. Skin-to-skin contact at this time is vital as your baby takes in the smells, sounds and feel of you and the world on the outside. The baby's gaze fixes with interest on faces, usually on those of their mother and the father. Such eye-to-eye contact readily suggests that the baby is curious and interested. Usually the mother responds at once. Her voice soothes, her arms hold – preferably in skin-to-skin contact with her baby's body moulded to hers. She strokes and comforts with her hands. Her body language says, 'I'm here, here is something familiar, my heartbeat and other body sounds, my voice and familiar smell. You are safe.'

She is likely to offer the breast at once. Breastfeeding within that first hour is wonderful for the baby and for feeling close together. It is also vitally important for long-term breastfeeding. If the baby's cheek is stroked by a finger or a nipple the baby will instinctively turn towards it seeking the breast. If the baby finds the nipple the mouth may open ready to fix and suck. These actions say that the baby is interested in sucking. If too tired to try immediately the need will be to rest a while against the mother's warm body, perhaps licking the breast a little.

Body language will indicate if the baby feels safe and relaxed.

If your baby continues to cry and becomes distressed, the body language and crying say that the baby is overwhelmed by the incredible experience of birth or is in actual pain. When crying in a truly distressed way, the baby is signalling a need for immediate reassurance and relief. If this response is not forthcoming then the baby's anxiety can increase to extreme stress. Repeated episodes over a period of time can inhibit crying and lead to a state of hopelessness. No baby can bear to feel abandoned.

If there are bright lights in the room, the baby is likely to close, even screw up their eyes. This body language tells the observer that the lights are disturbing. If there is a loud noise the baby will probably flinch. If lowered suddenly without support for back and head the baby may stiffen and throw back their arms before flexing them again, and may cry. The body language says, 'I'm afraid of loud noises; I'm afraid of falling.' Crying reinforces these signals.

With your baby you may find that, as the baby's initial interest in faces, smells, touch and breast fades their eyes may close. The likely message is that your baby is tired and needs to sleep. What could be more comforting than being held in skin-to-skin contact cosily covered while you both relax and probably doze?

As time passes you may notice that your baby, when in the bassinet beside your bed, is a little restless although not distressed – their body language is telling you that something is not quite right, something is disturbing them. You can change the baby's position, give a gentle pat or tuck the cover firmly down. Perhaps your baby now relaxes and sleeps quietly again. But perhaps this contact is not effective and the baby becomes more restless and begins to cry miserably. You study their body language. You can check that their nappy is dry and clean. It is not long since you fed but perhaps your baby wants more food. Is your baby actively searching for the nipple? You offer the breast. If uninterested but still restless you wonder if a bubble of wind is the problem. Could the baby be too cold or too warm? You can feel their feet; if they are cold you can warm them with your hands then put woolly socks on them. If sweaty (feel under the chin and behind the neck) or you just think the baby is too warm then you can adjust the covers or clothing.

Perhaps none of these actions helps and crying continues. Could the baby be bored? Perhaps a change of scene may help. You remember that your baby could be lonely and simply need the comfort of your closeness, so cuddle the baby to you.

Think about the type of crying you are listening to. You are learning and communicating as you respond to the baby's behaviour and observe your baby's reactions to the procedures you are using. You do much of this instinctively without consciously thinking 'I'm learning all this'. It is most likely that you do not need books to tell you how to do this but there may be times when you find it hard to discover just

what is worrying or upsetting your baby. All the things you try do not seem to help. It is then that you might need more suggestions.

When quiet and alert and gazing around happily, the message is that your baby feels well, comfortable and interested in the surroundings. You pause in passing, smile and speak. The baby may respond with body movements or, if active, pause for a moment to fix their eyes on your face or look at an object you bring within the baby's focus. As you move away the baby may complain a little then look again at the coloured mobile or whatever is there to capture interest. In time the need will come for either another feed or simply another sleep. A change in behaviour will signal the need with or without crying.

You will learn the hunger messages, the sleepy signs and how much activity your baby can enjoy before needing to sleep again. Remember that the common routine is for baby to sleep, waken for a feed and then be ready to enjoy a play with a caregiver or interaction with other sights and sounds in the environment before sleeping again (see 'Recognising a sleepy baby' in Chapter 18).

Communication flows in both directions. The caregivers have a body language too. Facial expressions convey messages, and the face is a particular focus for babies. Your face can tell your baby if you are feeling happy, loving, involved, or rushed and preoccupied, irritated, resigned or 'absent' (that is, not involved in eye-to-eye contact).

Babies are very sensitive to manner and especially to tone of voice. Tone conveys feelings of sympathy, warmth and friendliness or irritability, impatience and anger. Even the absence of voice – changing the baby in silence – carries a strong message. As you handle your baby messages are received from your muscles: tense or relaxed, firm and confident or tentative and anxious. The baby registers whether they are jerky or smooth, gentle or rough, unhurried or rushed.

Gentle play and delight in the baby's responses communicate your feelings of pleasure, and if at ease your baby is likely to respond happily. However, caregivers are only human! There are times when we are rushed, tense, anxious or feeling angry – not necessarily with our baby, although that may be the case. This is most likely when nothing we do in trying to soothe loud persistent crying seems to help. We feel pressured by the baby. There may be other demands and others' needs clamouring to be met too.

When feeling tense or angry, it may be necessary to leave the baby safely in the cot and walk away for a short time and do something else to reduce increasing tension. It is usually better to do something active such as vacuuming the floors, watering the roses or even peeling the vegetables for dinner. One mother said her best relief for tension was to go for a brisk walk, and another said she scrubs the shower! Others find that they can sit for a few minutes breathing deeply, consciously relaxing. Usually such measures help to free us from our negative feelings. It will then be possible to try to help the baby again. Check your self-talk: instead of thinking 'I can't stand this', change it to 'I'm doing fine, this feeling will pass'. Changing your self-talk can be very effective.

When most of the wordless messages you convey to your baby are that she or he is loved and valued, then the occasional moments of parental irritation, frustration and weariness will do no lasting harm. However, if feelings of inadequacy, frustration and anger persist or frighten you or the negative feelings outweigh the good feelings, help is needed (see 'Red alert!' in Chapter 18). Given a particular set of circumstances anyone can reach desperation point so it is wise to have a fail-safe plan just in case it is needed. Parents sometimes need education about relaxation techniques or how to deal with aggressive thoughts or behaviours. It is good for both mothers and fathers to understand their own needs for self-care and professional support if necessary. If it feels as if you are not coping it might be useful to be referred to a counsellor or a psychologist. For a very small number of women who are unwell, referral to a psychiatrist may be useful.

## Crying

Babies signal their needs directly by crying. It is a highly effective means of attracting attention and then conveying a range of messages to a receptive hearer. Few people fail to respond to the cry of a baby but the exact reason for the crying may not be clear to them. Most parents are highly sensitive and soon become skilled in interpreting the cries of their own baby. When they are able to comfort and relieve their baby's misery they feel a sense of achievement. However, when the crying persists in spite of all their efforts parents can feel worried, burdened and helpless, particularly when well-meaning onlookers offer unwanted suggestions and advice.

There is always a reason for crying. It will continue until the cause is removed, usually by meeting a need, or until the baby falls asleep exhausted. If the need persists the lull may be brief and then the crying starts again. Crying represents a disturbance of the baby's wellbeing and caregiving aims at restoring calm so that there is no continuing reason to cry.

A baby can be left to cry for a few minutes but generally should not be left to become distressed. This is particularly true of the new or very young baby. Distress itself indicates a real need for rescue. When looking for a cause of the upset observe the baby's behaviour and consider how long it is since the last feed or sleep; or you might think of some other reason for the crying. You will need to provide comfort. When quietened you can try again to settle your baby to sleep. If unsuccessful maybe it is too soon and more time up and awake is the answer.

## Common causes of a baby's crying

The underlying need is often easily recognised and dealt with. The most common simple causes are hunger or thirst, minor bodily discomfort, tiredness (including overstimulation), the need to be held, frustration or boredom. However, crying may indicate real distress due to illness, pain, fright, insecurity or stress. Stress may be due to the baby's reaction to inappropriate handling or parental anxiety. Either may stem from lack of confidence, actual irritation or feelings of anger towards the baby or from worries due to other causes entirely.

Some babies seem to cry, not because they are directly affected by external or physical causes that are obvious, but because of internal causes that you cannot observe directly. Thus some babies regularly cry just before falling asleep. Others cry so much that we wonder whether they are still recovering from being born. We can easily believe that it is taking time for the baby to recover and adjust (see 'The unsettled baby' in Chapter 18). These babies will need all the patience and tender loving care that parents can find to help them. They will eventually come out of this difficult period.

It takes parents a little time to learn to interpret their baby's crying. Until they have the necessary experience they work on trial and error until they solve the particular problem.

As you gain experience you will interpret various types of crying and learn what steps you can take to help. The following are the principal causes of crying but the order in which they are discussed does not imply anything about frequency. However, it is true that hunger will cause all babies to cry at some time.

## Hunger and thirst

Thriving, young, fully breastfed babies need no other fluid than breastmilk, which supplies their food and satisfies their thirst. If you feel your baby may be thirsty, a moment or two on the breast will soon satisfy their thirst. Bottle-fed babies, if they are restless between feeds, may be thirsty and need drinks of cooled, boiled water.

The hunger cry usually comes some time after the last feed and starts as a request: 'I'm awake, Mum, when do we eat?' It is not really urgent at first. There could be a pause followed by another cry, then another pause. If your baby can see or hear you they may not fuss unduly, even if kept waiting. But soon the request for food will come again, this time more urgently. First a note of anxiety is added to the crying, then of frustration and finally of anger. Then the baby yells. Only in exceptional circumstances allow the baby to reach this stage because it is distressing, possibly to the point which makes it impossible for the baby to feed until comforted.

You can suspect hunger if it is some time since the last feed. Now it is likely that your baby is ready for another feed. Your baby will take the feed happily and be content when fed.

When the breastmilk supply is less plentiful there may be times when the baby is hungry at the end of a feed. It may be just after a particular feed or it may be after each feed. This sometimes occurs towards the end of the day. Often it is enough to just offer extra time on the breast or to give a couple of extra feeds in the late afternoon or evening. By doing so you may satisfy the baby's hunger and increase your supply. As supply increases the baby is likely to extend the period between feeds once more. If bottle-fed and still hungry at the end of the feed just give more of the prepared formula. Don't be tempted to add an extra scoop of the formula powder to the bottle; the formula must always be correctly made up.

## Discomfort

The discomfort cry varies. It may begin only as a grizzle, changing to a wail and, if the discomfort persists, ending as a disturbed noisy cry. Alternatively, it may be noisy from the beginning. There are various causes, usually easily dealt with, sometimes even by your baby. Babies can wriggle into a more comfortable position, at times they can bring up wind. They can satisfy a sucking need with a sucking action of their tongue or by sucking a finger or thumb. Then crying stops and the baby either lies awake contentedly or falls asleep again.

There might be continuing discomfort calls for help. After a feed your baby may need another few moments at the breast to 'top up'. You can help to relieve a troublesome bubble of wind, or if the baby obtained a feed too quickly extra sucking time might help. You can check the nappy and/or change position. Your baby could be feeling too hot or too cold, lying in a vomit, reacting to something in the feed or making involuntary, jerky movements. These movements often occur in very young babies and they may feel better if wrapped securely.

## Tired, over-tired or overstimulated

The tired cry is often fretful and accompanied by a heavy, sleepy look. Further sleepy signs can include grimacing or jerky limb movements. The cry may be only a whimper or become a miserable wail. The baby is not interested in people or things and does not focus on them – the baby is ready to be tucked down to sleep.

When overtired and/or overstimulated your baby can be much

more restless than usual – tense, possibly crying loudly and continually, and nothing you do seems to help. This can occur during or after a session of handling which has been too exciting or continued for too long. Your baby will cry if held, cry if put down and seem angry and distressed. It will take patience and understanding to help your baby to relax.

## The need to be held

This cry often begins as a complaining, intermittent cry, not particularly urgent, but if your baby is needing the reassurance of your arms and body-closeness the misery will increase until picked up and held closely and lovingly. If the baby seems to need to be held often, a baby carrier such as a sling or possum pouch can be really helpful.

## Fear

The cry of fear is one of distress. It is loud and has about it a sense of abandonment and panic. It is impossible to ignore and initiates your instant action. It is said that we are born with only two basic fears – of falling and of sudden, loud noise. Try to protect your baby from both. Whenever you lower the baby, support both the body and head and move your baby slowly and smoothly. As you pick up your baby speak quietly and move deliberately and firmly, again with your hand supporting the baby's back and head.

Fear can also be triggered by sudden stimuli such as noise, flashing of bright lights and sudden movement. Being naked in the early days may cause distress. Sometimes parents believe that their baby fears the bath when, in fact, it is the feeling of nakedness and/or of falling when being lowered into the bath which is the trouble (see 'Bathing' in Chapter 17).

## Pain

The cry of severe pain is not easily distinguished from that of fear. It is intense, shrill and urgent. Its aim is to alert and alarm anyone who hears it. You can check that there is no obvious cause such as an open pin, a wet or soiled nappy stinging a sore bottom, a burnt mouth

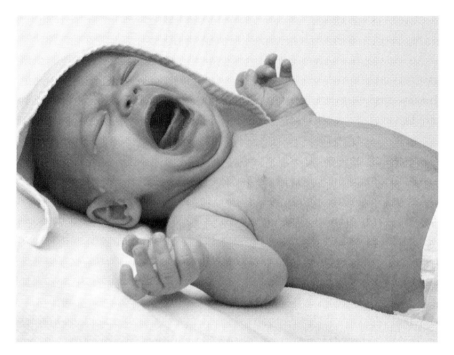

from an overheated bottle, or a poke or blow from an unhappy sibling, particularly a toddler who is feeling displaced. The most common acute pain in well young babies is colic – abdominal pain, which distresses many babies (see 'Colic' in Chapter 20). Colic attacks usually begin suddenly and occur most often in the late afternoon and evening, although there are babies who suffer from colic at any time.

Another cause of pain in babies can be due to oesophageal (gastric) reflux. This occurs when the valve between baby's oesophagus (food pipe) and stomach is lax and stomach contents flow back up the oesophagus. This can be mild or severe (see 'Gastro-oesophageal reflux' in Chapter 20). Reflux may still occur even though there is no vomiting or spillage from the baby's mouth. The baby is experiencing similar pain to that experienced by some mothers from heartburn in pregnancy.

## Illness

The cry varies with the type and stage of illness. A fretful, grizzly cry is likely with an illness that begins slowly and the baby is probably restless. As the illness develops the crying becomes more persistent and louder and the baby is likely to sleep even less.

With sudden illness, crying may begin abruptly and be loud and continuous. Common signs of illness may be present (see 'Recognising the sick baby' in Chapter 20). Continuing illness can lead to exhaustion and the crying can become weak and feeble.

### Boredom

Babies do become bored and are likely to cry fretfully. A change in the environment can help. Objects hanging across the pram or over the cot can be changed. Your baby may be moved from pram to floor and, depending on the weather and safety, from inside to outside in a sheltered spot beneath trees where leaves and shadows can provide interest. Keeping your baby near you to watch your activities, hear your voice and interact with you even while you are busy can solve the problem. You can carry your baby in a sling while you hang out the washing or vacuum the room. You can use a carry-chair or bouncer so that you can place the baby near you while you prepare a meal, wash up, etc. Remember to put the chair on the floor if you move away from the baby, even for a moment. By employing this simple safety measure you can prevent a fall caused by the baby moving the carry-chair with vigorous body movements.

## Crying for no apparent reason

As previously mentioned, some babies (particularly if new or very young) cry for long periods. It is not usually high intensity screaming, but there may be bouts of this. It is more likely to be low key, miserable and irritable. Nothing we do seems to help them (see 'The unsettled baby' in Chapter 18). No cause can be found even after medical checking. Although parents quickly learn to interpret their baby's ordinary crying and behaviour this persistent and unresponsive crying defeats them. They find it extremely trying and depressing. They can feel rejected and inadequate as parents. They are likely to become angry since it seems that the baby just will not stop crying. In fact, the baby just cannot stop. In the meantime, all they can do is accept it as they search for possible causes. They can expect the problem to improve as the baby grows older.

It helps to have a sympathetic support network, which may include an early childhood nurse, an understanding family doctor, helpful relatives, and friends including parent support groups. Of particular benefit is some regular time out when someone else takes care of your baby to give you a short break. If you have access to an occasional care centre you may be able to use it. Some mothers find it helpful to ring a support person or a parent support line just to talk to a calm, objective person.

Sometimes women are able to form a group in their area and meet together to socialise and babysit for each other. If there is an early childhood clinic you could ask there if there are mothers you might contact. If you feel that there are times when it is all 'just too much' and self-control is threatened, have a plan of action to fall back on (see 'Red alert!' in Chapter 18). It is not necessary to be constantly with your baby to be a good mother.

As parents it is good to both be involved in the baby's daily care, as this relieves the mother's burden of total responsibility for the baby. Also, try to arrange some time out to sleep, rest, relax and recharge your batteries. To do so is valuable for all parents, and their babies benefit too.

Older babies also may have varying episodes of unexplained crying within periods of a few days or even weeks. They are irritable and look for more body contact than usual. Soothing and cuddling are likely to help. Following research, van de Rijt and Plooij suggest that developmental leaps in the brain are associated with these episodes which can be considered normal (see 'Development' in Chapter 19).

# 7

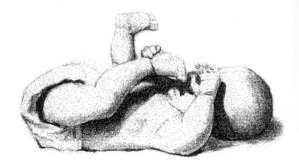

# Problems

**P**arents can expect to meet some upsets as they care for their babies. Fortunately most are minor and temporary. Be ready for the 'ups' and 'downs' that living with a new baby brings. Delight in the 'ups' and if 'downs' come along accept them as challenges as you look for the solution. Parenting brings its challenges but be aware of the fulfilling and rewarding experience it can be.

Apart from illness, the most likely cause of anxiety in mothers when caring for a young baby is a difficulty with feeding or in settling the baby to sleep, but with good luck, possible experience of previous babies – their own or other people's – and the support they need, few will have any major concerns.

It is hard to know how to prepare to manage such a new venture as parenting. For some women, to avoid needless anxiety it is wise to avoid reading about possible difficulties unless you are faced with one. Other women prefer to read a great deal, and that is what helps them get ready to become a mother. However, whether we read a lot or would rather wait to find things out, we often do not know exactly what we need for a particular parenting situation. For these reasons concerns about feeding, about breasts or nipples or about the baby's behaviour are placed in Chapter 21 at the back of the book. There they are discussed and suggestions and options offered which may help you find a solution. If you are looking for answers relating to settling and sleeping there are suggestions in Chapter 18, 'Settling, sleeping and wakefulness'. For other difficulties the index can guide you. Throughout the book you will find tables with problems and solutions as well.

Among other challenges parents may encounter are concerns and stresses of their own – stresses within the family or outside. The condition of the woman is particularly significant. She may be suffering pain, illness or anxiety, and because mothers and babies are interdependent, distress in one is likely to cause distress in the other. Until the upset in either is relieved, both will be disturbed.

Ask your midwife, maternal and child health nurse or general practitioner for help if you need it. Upsets with similar symptoms can have different causes and distinguishing them may be difficult. What is confusing to parents may be quite clear to competent health professionals. If they are experienced and supportive they can save you needless worry. They will have suggestions which have proven helpful for other parents who have faced similar difficulties. They can also refer you to other sources of help. For example, it may be possible to arrange for you (and your partner) to spend a day at a family-care centre. These exist in all Australian states and territories. There, during an extended visit, staff listen to your concerns and observe the baby's feeding and behaviour over a period of hours. They are then better able to offer constructive advice. Sometimes women and their babies are admitted to a postnatal hospital for a few days to help to resolve a problem.

# What is a problem?

Inexperienced parents may misinterpret unexpected, normal behaviour as abnormal. When parents, and mothers in particular, feel that they are not managing to care for their baby as they should, they are inclined to blame themselves unfairly.

How can you achieve a successful approach? You can seek information and help, accept the unexpected, and regard any challenge as a learning experience. You and you partner will then be less judgmental of yourselves and of your baby. It is best to trust your own instincts. Comments such as 'all parents worry needlessly' or 'just wait until you have two or three and you won't have time and energy to waste on anxiety' are not helpful. Most parents have all the necessary natural instincts to care for their own children, and this includes the ability to recognise when they need professional advice.

## Assessing your baby

If you have any doubts about your baby's health, here are some basic questions you can ask yourself. First, stand back and look at your baby. Are there any obvious signs of illness (see 'Recognising the sick baby' in Chapter 20)? If not, has there been a change in the crying pattern – unusual distress, or weakness, or fretfulness? And the other behaviours – is your baby:

- taking feeds with the usual appetite with no increased spilling or vomiting?
- gaining weight, growing and developing within normal limits?
- finishing feeds contentedly?
- having periods of peaceful sleep (even if the timing does not suit you)?
- wakening readily following restful sleep?
- enjoying moments of responsive interaction with you?
- enjoying quiet alert times and being happily aware of surrounding sights and sounds?

If you can answer 'yes' to these questions, then you can draw a breath and relax. The problem, real as it is to you, does not appear to be serious. On the other hand, if you have now recognised a real upset, think of possible causes and what you can do to overcome them. If you still have doubts, ask for professional advice.

## Assessing yourself

Could the problem lie with you? Mother and baby interact together. It can be difficult to maintain a sense of proportion and react in a balanced way if you are ill, under continued stress and/or suffering from fatigue or increasing anxiety. Are you:

*℘* in good health, well nourished and getting basic sleep and relaxation even if in totally different ways from your previous pattern?

*℘* able to arrange a little 'time out' separately and together with your partner or a friend?

*℘* able to manage any feelings of irritation, frustration and/or anger with positive feelings outweighing the negative?

If you are feeling overwhelmed and things are slipping out of control press your Red Alert button (see in Chapter 18) and act accordingly.

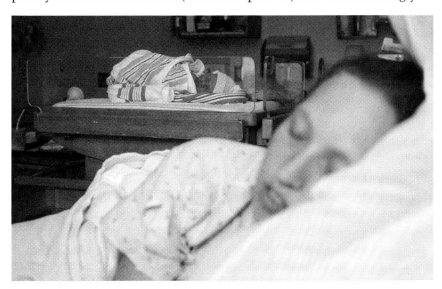

Women have related many of their own experiences of caring for a new or young baby and these can sometimes help other mothers.

**Megan:** '*I went home on the second day. A couple of days later I had a bit of trouble with engorged breasts but, although I still had a lot of milk, Isobel and I managed between us to keep me fairly comfortable. After about a week I noticed that my breasts were not nearly so full, in fact, by the afternoon they felt really soft. I panicked. I thought my milk was going. I rang Mary, the midwife in the postnatal ward who had helped me most. She asked me how Isobel was feeding and whether she was satisfied when she finished her feeds. When I said that she was, Mary told me that my milk was just settling down. I did not need to worry, just be sure to let her take all that she wanted and be prepared to let her have extra time at the breast if she looked for it.*

*Mary also suggested that I visit the early childhood clinic as soon as possible, so that Isobel could be weighed to check her progress. When we went, she had gained well. Now I'm relaxed about my supply and a lot more comfortable too.*'

**Laura:** '*At seven weeks Thomas was an easy baby until around 4.30 in the afternoon when he became restless. I'd bring him out into the kitchen with me and he'd be happy for a while and then start crying again. I felt he was hungry but, as he had had a good feed a couple of hours earlier, I wasn't ready to believe he needed more so soon, but because he was miserable I would feed him again. He would only stay on each breast for two or three minutes and then come off and cry. It was difficult to get on with preparing the meal and try to manage Bobby, who was then only just two years old. We checked Thomas's weight gains at the clinic and Judy, our early childhood nurse, said he was doing really well. She thought my supply was a bit light-on in the afternoon and asked if I thought I could express a little milk earlier* *in the day, to use later. Thomas was still having a feed at 2 a.m. My breasts were very full then, so while he fed on one, I expressed about 60 millilitres from the other. There was still enough for him to take what he wanted and settle easily. At around 6 a.m., when he next fed, I took a little more of my milk and had another 20 to 30 millilitres to add to the jar in the fridge for top ups. It certainly made a difference. He was still wakeful at those times but not continually grizzly. I gave him half my expressed milk after that late afternoon feed and the other half after the next, around 7 p.m. I used a small cup and was surprised at how well he took the expressed milk from it. Around 9 or 10 p.m. he would take a good breastfeed and settle for six or seven hours. I was lucky, he slept well at night. I was sorry that I had not expressed and stored some breastmilk when I first went home. I had a great deal too much in the first couple of weeks.'*

**Amal:** *'Mia was like Laura's Thomas, restless and hungry around much the same times of the day. I didn't really mind how often she went to the breast. Provided I let her suck for five minutes or so whenever she cried, she'd doze off for a short while and then want some more. At around three months Mia was a lot easier. I don't know why but she did not need to be at the breast so much. Maybe I just produced more for her, or she was so much stronger she sucked harder and took more.'*

Celia was bottle feeding had problems getting her baby to accept the teat.

**Celia:** *'I had to wean Lachlan when he was only two weeks old. I was ill and the medication I needed would have harmed him. I had to continue with it so my doctor said that I needed to bottle feed. Together we were readmitted to the maternity ward.*

*We had an awful struggle to get Lachlan to accept the teat. He just screamed when we put it in his mouth. My midwife Trish was so calm. She said that we would not fight with him but use a medicine measure to feed him. I could not believe that he would be able to take a full feed from one. I was amazed that he could actually do it. Lachlan slept by me and I had to call Trish when he first stirred waking for his next feed. She said it would be better if she tried with the bottle – he associated me with the breast. At the first sign of his waking I let her know and she came with the feed in the bottle, picked him up while still drowsy and walked with him. She didn't change his nappy until after the feed. With a little of the warm formula on the teat she slipped it into his mouth, still walking with him. He took a few sucks then wakened fully and screamed. She was satisfied with those few sucks and cheerfully said that he would soon learn but that we would finish the feed with the medicine measure. He took that. At each feed he was offered the bottle first and then allowed to finish with the measure. It took a couple of days before he settled down with a teat. I was so glad that I was still in hospital and had Trish to help me.'*

## Small weight gains in a thriving baby

Sometimes mothers believe that their babies are not gaining enough weight, and hence are not getting enough milk, although they are clearly healthy. It is important to remember that normal growth rate is different for each baby and partly dependent on individual genetics. The expected weight gains quoted in books are an average for all types and sizes of babies. Some babies' weight gains, while still normal, will be below the average and others above. When assessing a baby's nutrition, the weight, length, type of body and age, as well as the height and weight of his or her parents, must all be taken into account. A well baby whose length is greater than the average is likely to weigh more, just as one whose length is less than average will weigh less. Weight in thriving babies may also be affected by the level of activity – a placid, quiet baby may gain more than a wakeful, excitable one of the same age even though they had the same birth weight and length, and both are healthy. Visits to the early childhood centre or your family doctor to check that the baby's growth and development are satisfactory will help to reassure you.

**Pia:** 'Our Emily was only having small weekly gains and we were really worried. We believed that she should have been putting on between 150 and 200 grams each week. She was a contented baby, fed well and had lovely rosy cheeks. She had her miserable moments but they never lasted long and she was easily comforted. She did not look thin. Anyway, off we went to see our doctor and he asked us to take a look at me. I'm much shorter than average and my build is light too, although Brett is average height and weight. Doctor showed us a percentile chart and where Emily came on it. He explained it to us and said she was in proportion, well covered and obviously a healthy normal baby, but smaller than average, and there was no need to worry. She is getting plenty of milk from me so I guess she will have a smaller build too, like mine.'

# 8

# Sex following birth

**W**ith the physical and emotional changes which occur at the birth of the baby, your sex life is likely to alter, at least at first. Do allow yourselves time to find again the fulfilment that loving sex can bring. If you wish to be sure of avoiding another pregnancy (although it is very unlikely that this will happen within the first four to six weeks) you will need to discuss contraception with each other and possibly your health adviser.

## Sexual relations

There is no 'right' time for resuming sexual intercourse after birth. However, most couples have resumed some form of sexual activity together within the first eight to twelve weeks after the birth of their baby.

Parents' feelings differ. For men, there can be anxiety about hurting the mother of their new baby. For women, loss of interest at first is not uncommon considering she is usually physically and emotionally drained and may be concerned about her baby's wellbeing. Initially, there is also vaginal blood loss and there may be pain from perineal trauma or a caesarean wound. Following birth a woman's hormone levels change and her breasts will start to produce milk. The low oestrogen levels required to allow the breasts to produce milk can lessen her desire for sex and affect her vagina, making it dry. (When sexual intercourse is resumed a lubricating cream or jelly can make it easier.) Some women feel overloaded by touch at this time as breastfeeding and caring for their baby seems to take so much of this energy and need there is little leftover in the early weeks or even months.

Be patient as you both adjust to the changes which you are experiencing and remember that expressions of love can take many forms. Loving cuddling can be comforting and reassuring, gentle caressing and touching can fulfill the need for intimacy and even lead to orgasm. This is a time for understanding, communicating and delighting in your baby. Your mutual pleasure in sex will return in its own good time if you nurture your relationship through this transition.

# Contraception

Parents today are more fortunate than many of our forebears, who had few means of planning the number and spacing of their children. Now, through family planning thought can be given to the health, the economic circumstances, the careers and wishes of the couple concerned. Babies make huge demands on parents' physical and emotional resources. Planning your family allows you to regain strength and energy and provide the best environment you can for each of your children.

Following birth there are at least a few weeks before a mother's body will return to ovulation and menstruation. For women who are not breastfeeding, ovulation is likely to be delayed for four to six weeks after birth. Fully breastfeeding mothers are unlikely to ovulate or resume menstruation for several months.

After the birth of the baby you may wish to change your usual method of contraception, particularly if you are breastfeeding. Sources of advice about family planning include your obstetrician, family doctor, midwife or a family planning clinic. You will be able to ask for any information you need. In spite of the effectiveness of many methods of contraception, abstinence is the only one considered 100 per cent effective.

## The condom

The condom, made of thin rubber (latex), is a barrier method of contraception. It is rolled onto an erect penis before intercourse and holds the semen (and sperm) after ejaculation. The condom has a safety range of around 96 to 99.6 per cent, with the main reasons for failure being due to incorrect or inconsistent use or a condom that is punctured, perished or beyond its expiry date. The only reported side effect is latex allergy in some people. Condoms may be used as soon as you feel ready to resume sexual relations and are a suitable choice regardless of whether or not you are breastfeeding.

There is also a female condom which looks like a large, loose male condom and fits inside the vagina. Unlike the male condom, the female condom is made of polyurethane (a soft, clear plastic) which is stronger, does not have the associated risk of allergy that accompanies male latex condoms and is not prone to deterioration over long periods of time in storage. The female condom can be placed in the vagina up to eight hours prior to intercourse and is up to 95 per cent effective. Failure rates associated with the female condom are related to the same issues as male condom failure.

## The diaphragm

The diaphragm is another barrier method of contraception and is a reusable rubber cap with a firm rim that fits into the upper part of the vagina and covers the cervix. The only reported side effect is latex allergy or urinary tract infection in some people, and with correct care and storage a diaphragm will last up to two years. You can insert the diaphragm any time prior to intercourse but it must remain in place for a minimum of six hours after intercourse. Diaphragms are 84 to 94 per cent effective with the main reasons for failure relating to incorrect placement, a diaphragm containing a hole or one that is perished or an incorrect fit. For this reason, a diaphragm must be correctly fitted by a health practitioner and instructions given in its correct use, cleaning and storing. Women who used a diaphragm prior to their pregnancy need to have it checked before use after birth because a different size may be necessary.

If you haven't used a diaphragm before you can be fitted for one by an experienced sexual health or family planning practitioner approximately six weeks after the birth of your baby or once your bleeding settles. Like the condom, the diaphragm is a suitable choice regardless of whether or not you are breastfeeding.

## The intra-uterine device (IUD)

This small t-shaped contraceptive device is made of plastic and copper and can be inserted into the uterus eight to ten weeks after a vaginal birth or twelve weeks after a caesarean birth. An IUD needs to be inserted by a competent practitioner and is immediately effective. It may stay in place for at least five years and sometimes up to ten years but can be removed earlier if desired.

An IUD works by interfering with a sperm's ability to swim through the uterus and by changing the lining inside of the uterus to make it difficult should a fertilised egg try to implant. The IUD is more than 98 per cent effective but carries with it potential side effects such as cramps and heavier menstrual bleeding, although these usually resolve after a few months. Complications can also occur at the time of insertion and occasionally an IUD will 'fall out' unnoticed, leaving you at risk of an unplanned pregnancy. Like the condom and the diaphragm, an IUD is a suitable choice regardless of whether or not you are breastfeeding.

## The hormonal intra-uterine system

This is an IUD as discussed above but with the addition of the synthetic hormone progestogen (synthetic progesterone) which is gradually released into the body over five years. Due to the hormonal effects of the progestogen this IUD is not usually associated with heavier menstrual bleeding as mentioned above and many women end up not having a period at all after several months of having the progestogen IUD in place. Other progestogen-related side effects such as acne, breast tenderness, headaches and changes in mood are mild and improve over time as only a small amount of the hormone enters the bloodstream. Like the non-hormonal IUD the contraceptive effect of the hormonal IUD is immediate once inserted into the uterus.

## The contraceptive implant

This is a small, flexible plastic rod approximately the size of a matchstick that is inserted by a competent practitioner just under the skin of the inside of the upper arm. The implant contains progestogen (as in the above mentioned IUD) that is released steadily over three years, after which it must be removed and replaced (although it may be removed earlier if desired). The contraceptive implant is considered to be at least 99 per cent effective and works by inhibiting ovulation, thinning the lining of the uterus and thickening cervical mucus. It is advisable to use an alternative method of contraception for the first week following insertion of the implant. Progestogen contraceptives most commonly cause the side effect of irregular bleeding or spotting. Other side effects include acne, weight gain, breast tenderness, headaches and changes in mood. The contraceptive implant is considered safe if breastfeeding and is thought to have little impact on milk supply.

## The vaginal ring

This is a soft plastic ring which is self-inserted into the vagina. It is left in place for three weeks and taken out for a week. Once inserted it slowly releases low doses of two hormones, oestrogen and a progestogen, into the bloodstream. These hormones are the same as those used in the combined oral contraceptive discussed below and the way it works is also primarily through prevention of ovulation. Used correctly, this form of contraception is 99 per cent effective and side effects such as vaginal irritation and discharge, breast tenderness, nausea, spotting, headache, decreased libido or irritability often settle after a few months. Also, like the combined oral contraceptive pill, there are some serious health considerations with the vaginal ring. A prescription is required to obtain the vaginal ring so you will be able to discuss your needs and obtain professional advice before deciding if this form of contraception is safe for you to use. Breastfeeding mothers are advised not to use this form of contraception because oestrogen suppresses prolactin and therefore milk production is reduced.

## The combined oral contraceptive pill

The combined oral contraceptive pill (often called 'the pill') contains two hormones, oestrogen and progestogen, which work primarily to suppress ovulation. The pill comes in a 28-day pack and you take one every day. Taken as directed, the pill is considered 99 per cent effective. There is a large variety of combined oral contraceptive pills and although all are based on the same method of action, timing of commencement and immediacy of contraceptive effect is dependent on the individual pill type. However, because there is such a wide variety of oral contraceptive pills available, side effects such as breast tenderness, nausea, spotting, headache, decreased libido or irritability can often be managed by simply changing to a different type of pill.

There are some serious health considerations with this form of contraceptive and there are some women who cannot take any form of these pills at all. A prescription is required to obtain the combined oral contraceptive pill so you will be able to discuss your needs and obtain professional advice before deciding if this form of contraception is safe for you to use. Breastfeeding mothers are advised not to use this form of contraception because oestrogen inhibits milk production by suppressing prolactin. If you are not breastfeeding it is advisable to wait several weeks prior to commencing the combined oral contraceptive pill.

## The progestogen-only oral contraceptive pill (mini-pill)

Unlike the combined oral contraceptive pill, the mini-pill contains only one hormone – progestogen – and at a much lower dose than in the combined oral contraceptive pill. The main action of this pill is to affect the mucus at the entrance to the uterus, changing its composition and blocking the entry of sperm into the uterus. It also affects the lining of the uterus and the fallopian tubes. Like the combined oral contraceptive pill above, a prescription is required to obtain the mini-pill so you will be able to discuss your needs with a health professional before deciding if this form of contraception is suited to you and the best way to go about commencing it.

For maximum reliability the mini-pill should be taken strictly at the same time of day every day. The mini-pill is thought to be about 92 to 96 per cent effective in preventing pregnancy and is considered a suitable contraceptive option when breastfeeding due to the absence of oestrogen, which is known to interfere with milk production. However, there are some mothers who use the mini-pill and find that their babies become fussy at the breast, although it should not decrease milk supply (although there are mothers who believe that it does). Irregular bleeding or spotting is a common side effect of the progestogen-only contraceptive methods but the other progestogen-related side effects – such as headache, breast tenderness and weight gain – do not tend to cause a significant problem with the mini-pill as the hormone dose is quite low.

### *Injectable hormonal contraception (Depo-Provera)*

Depo-Provera is a long-acting hormonal contraceptive containing progestogen. It is given every twelve weeks as an injection, provides contraception for the full twelve weeks and has an efficacy rate greater than 97 to 99.7 per cent. It works mainly by stopping or delaying ovulation and also thickens the mucus in the cervix and thins the lining of the uterus. Depo-Provera takes approximately one week after the first injection to be effective so you will need to use an alternative form of contraception during this time. Depo-Provera can be given very soon after birth but it is often advised to wait approximately six weeks as its use may increase postnatal bleeding.

As with several of the contraception methods mentioned above, there are several health precautions to consider prior to commencing this contraceptive. Likewise, a prescription is required to obtain Depo-Provera so you can discuss your needs with a health professional before deciding if this form of contraception is suited to you. The most commonly reported side effect of Depo-Provera is irregular spotting or bleeding. Other possible side effects include weight gain (usually only a small amount – a large increase in weight is uncommon), headaches, abdominal bloating, breast tenderness, mood changes, acne and decreased libido. In addition, there can be a delay in the return of fertility of up to twelve months. Because Depo-Provera is progestogen only, it is thought to have no effect on breastfeeding.

## The 'natural' methods

Natural family planning (sometimes called fertility awareness) depends on periodic abstinence and includes the rhythm (or calendar) method, the temperature method and the Billings method. These are based on abstaining from sexual intercourse around the time of ovulation and are considered less reliable, particularly if you have not had extensive previous experience and especially in the first six months after birth until hormonal levels have returned to normal. You can discuss these methods in detail with a knowledgeable health adviser such as your GP or a sexual health and family planning practitioner.

Withdrawal and lactational amenorrhoea have been used by people from many different cultures over many generations.

## The withdrawal method

This method depends on the withdrawal of the penis from the vagina before ejaculation and can be considered another form of natural family planning. The risk of some seminal fluid escaping before ejaculation and the discipline and accurate timing required (mostly on the part of the man) makes this form of contraception unreliable without extensive practice.

## The lactational amenorrhoea method (LAM)

Most women who are exclusively breastfeeding (including during the night) are unlikely to ovulate for the first ten weeks and often not for the first six months following the birth of their baby. However, relying on breastfeeding for contraception is not 100 per cent dependable so further care must be taken.

Lactational amenorrhoea refers to the suppression of menstruation due to lactation, which results in inability to become pregnant. The lactational amenorrhoea method depends on exclusive breastfeeding with frequent suckling. There are women in many parts of the world who rely totally on this method of contraception and they usually have their children about two years apart. However, they usually breastfeed their babies far more frequently than we tend to do (twenty to thirty times over 24 hours). It seems that the total time the baby spends suckling on the breast is the major factor in reducing fertility.

If you are exclusively breastfeeding and the baby feeds vigorously at least six times daily and continues with night feeds and you have not started giving the baby any other food (including formula) and have not had a period, you are unlikely to become pregnant in the first six months after the birth. In the presence of these three factors LAM is considered to be approximately 98 per cent effective. However, the contraceptive effect of the LAM method is limited after six months, hence alternative methods should be considered.

## Emergency contraception

This is not for routine contraception but can be used occasionally following unprotected sex. The emergency contraceptive pill or ECP (sometimes inaccurately called the 'morning-after pill') is a special dose of the oral contraceptive hormone progestogen. The emergency pill can work in several ways depending on when it is taken in the menstrual cycle: it can delay ovulation or, if ovulation has already taken place, it may stop a fertilised egg from implanting in the womb. It also affects the fallopian tubes and cervical mucus. If a fertilised egg is already implanted in the womb and a pregnancy has started the ECP will have no effect; it cannot cause an abortion. It is about 85 per cent effective if taken within three days of unprotected intercourse and may be effective up to five days after unprotected sex. A prescription is not generally required to obtain emergency contraception and it is available at sexual health and family planning clinics and some pharmacies. Before you take it, the health professional will give you detailed information on suitability, side effects and precautions. If you are breastfeeding ensure you obtain a progestogen-only ECP.

A copper IUD (as discussed earlier) can also be used as emergency contraception and is more than 98 per cent effective if inserted within five days of unprotected intercourse.

## Permanent birth control

It is often not the best time to decide on sterilisation immediately after having your baby. It is usually a good idea to wait for about twelve months, making sure that your baby is healthy and that you would not want another child under any circumstances. Although sterilisation can sometimes be reversed, there is no guarantee that pregnancy will happen after reversal.

Counselling is advised before proceeding with any method of permanent contraception. You will be able to discuss the procedure with your doctor. Sexual function and libido are not affected by sterilisation.

## Micro-inserts

This procedure can be performed without general anaesthetic and there is no surgery involved. A small flexible device – a micro-insert – is placed in each fallopian tube. Body tissue grows into the inserts, blocking the fallopian tubes and physically preventing sperm and egg being able to meet up and thus preventing pregnancy. Micro-inserts are 99.9 per cent effective but there is a three-month delay in the effectiveness of this method of permanent contraception while the tissue grows into the inserts to block the tubes. You will need to use another form of contraception during this time.

## Surgical sterilisation

Both men and women can be surgically sterilised. This procedure in a woman is known as tubal ligation. The fallopian tubes are cut, tied, clamped or occluded so that an egg released at ovulation is unable to make its way down to the uterus and sperm are unable to travel up the fallopian tubes to meet an egg released at ovulation. A general anaesthetic is needed for this procedure and, as such, the procedure carries with it the same risks as any surgical procedure and anaesthetic. A tubal ligation has a failure rate of less than 1 per cent and is effective immediately. Tubal ligation can be done at the time of a caesarean section but there is an increase in failure rate when done at that time.

For men there is a simple surgical procedure – a vasectomy, which can be done without a general anaesthetic. The tubes which would normally carry sperm from the testes to the penis are cut and tied. This does not interfere with ejaculation but prevents sperm being in the semen. A vasectomy has a failure rate of less than 1 per cent but, unlike female surgical sterilisation, there is approximately an eight-week window where pregnancy is still very possible as there is sperm still stored in front of the blocked tubes which will still be in the semen for several ejaculations after the procedure. For this reason, you will need to use another form of contraception during this time.

When choosing a method of contraception there are many things to consider. Take your time to read and think about which method might suit you. When trying to narrow down the options consider things such as whether the method is easy to obtain, convenient to use and affordable for you. If you are not in a long-term relationship it may also be important to consider whether the option provides any protection against sexually transmitted infections. Consider also the effect the method of contraception might have if you are breastfeeding and how your choice affects the return of fertility once you stop using it should your future plans include further pregnancies. Finally, it is very important that you feel happy with the choice you and your partner, make. If you are not comfortable with a particular method it could make you anxious or tense about having sex, which is not the goal. Choosing a method of contraception is about making the best choice for your future, your lifestyle, your health and your peace of mind.

# 9

# Depression following birth

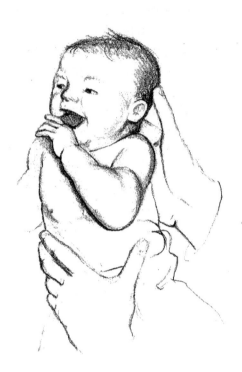

There are three commonly recognised states of mood disorder that can follow birth: the 'new baby' blues; postnatal depression; and, much less commonly, puerperal psychosis.

## New baby blues

The new baby blues are relatively common and the proportion of mothers affected is thought to be in the range of 50 to 80 per cent. They often occur around days three, four or five after the birth and last from one to ten days. The condition is usually mild and is usually seen as normal. Typically there are mood swings, usually short-lived and thought to be mainly due to the changing levels of hormones in the mother's body occurring after birth. However, that does not lessen their importance and their impact on the mother. Severe blues are a risk factor for postnatal depression.

We often hear of the new baby blues when mothers feel really miserable but less often do we hear of the highs when the mother's mood is euphoric, probably because it is seen as natural for a mother to be ecstatic over the birth of her baby. However, no-one can continue in a state of bliss indefinitely. Her moods will change and very often she can swing from one state to the other fairly frequently. The degree of highs and lows can vary from day to day and from mother to mother. During this time most mothers simply need reassurance, acceptance and plenty of rest.

An attack of the baby blues can be triggered by an event that would usually be of no concern. Mothers become tearful and overwhelmed, often wondering how they are going to cope. Sometimes they feel angry with themselves because they are unable to control their emotions. If they can accept that the blues are normal they are likely to be able to flow with them for the few days that they last. With support and acceptance from those close to them and reassurance and encouragement from their health caregivers, they will recover without any special treatment. Sometimes the blues will continue and lead on to postnatal depression. Recovery will then take longer.

Mothers who discussed their experience of the baby blues spoke of their feelings of misery, anger, anxiety and self-doubt. Because the blues so often occur within a day or so of birth, most mothers have experienced helpers on hand to reassure them that they are not collapsing in a heap, and that the feelings can be expected to rapidly disappear. From the discussion groups:

**Sarah:** 'At 3 a.m. on the third morning after Grace was born I sat up in bed ready to feed her and I felt the tears start. They just rolled down my cheeks and I had no idea why. When the midwife came in to see how I was managing the feeding she took one look at me, sat on the bed and asked, "Now, what is troubling you?" That was enough to set me off but I couldn't explain why I had the miseries. I told her that I didn't know and that I felt such a fool, that I felt wretchedly miserable, that I probably would not be a good mother and that my baby needed something better from life than I was likely to be able to give her. My midwife Tracy took my hand and asked if I could think of some possible reason for my feelings. I looked at her and then gave a watery laugh and said, "Perhaps I've just been attacked by the baby blues." Tracy smiled and said that she thought that I was very likely right. She suggested that I allow myself to feel the feelings, to swim along with them and tell myself that they will pass. She said that they would be likely to come and go for the next day or so and gradually lessen and then I would feel more or less normal again. She said that feeling normal does not mean being happy 24 hours of the day, it just means that you can take your ups and downs as they come without being overwhelmed by the downs.'

**Emily:** 'Liam's birth had been straightforward, he was a beautiful baby. He took to the breast with no trouble. Mike, my husband, was just so proud and happy and so was I until after visiting on the third day when he said goodbye and walked out of my room. I felt wretched and then angry with him for going off and leaving me, which really was absurd. I felt he should have known that I wanted him to stay. That was my first attack of the blues. Fortunately I soon felt better again but I ranged up and down between feeling on cloud nine and in the pits for the next three or four days. I felt a lot of anger with myself too for carrying on like a wimp, as well as anger towards others, and then I slowly came out somewhere in the middle – neither so high nor so low.'

# Postnatal depression

Postnatal depression is probably no different from depression suffered at any other time throughout life – the same symptoms appear – although in mothers suffering postnatal depression, anxiety and excessive concern about the baby may dominate their thinking.

Within the first twelve months following birth some mothers become depressed. They can be tearful and lose their capacity to care for themselves and their families. The condition is common and not restricted to mothers with their first babies – in fact, it is more common in women who already have one or more children. The severity varies. Recovery is usual, but if unresolved the depression can persist for years.

The term *postnatal depression* is used to describe a mother's condition of persisting depression after the birth of her baby. Postnatal depression may not appear until a few weeks after birth, but it may occur earlier or at any time during the first twelve months. It varies in severity, with feelings of depression ranging from mild to severe. Mothers can experience varying symptoms and different combinations of them from day to day. In order to minimise the longevity of the symptoms, help and treatment must be effective.

More women than men are likely to suffer depression in their lifetime. It is during their reproductive years that women are at greatest risk. For a woman, having a baby is a life event ranking even above puberty and menopause. Men may also experience depression following the birth of their baby.

Rates of postnatal depression internationally are approximately 10 to 20 per cent, and research in Australia supports these findings. For example, research undertaken by beyond blue suggests that up to 10 per cent of pregnant women develop antenatal depression and this increases to around 16 per cent after the birth (Postnatal depression).

Postnatal depression is not new – Hippocrates described a case of postnatal depression in ancient Greece over two and a half thousand years ago. It was mentioned in the Middle Ages, and occurs throughout the world. However, the increased attention it attracted in the nineteenth century was not maintained and the topic was neglected. Women were left to suffer in silence and labelled as 'crazy'. During

the 1980s interest was revived and there is now increased awareness, knowledge and understanding among health professionals and in the community.

Groups of women, who have often had painful experiences themselves, have worked to support mothers with depression. It is now much less likely that depression is seen as a personal failure or immaturity. However, women themselves often feel guilty and ashamed and are mindful of the stigma attached to their condition.

## Causes of depression

Pregnancy alters the ordinary functioning of the body. After birth it begins its return to the pre-pregnancy state and the process is virtually completed when the breastfeeding mother weans. Obvious changes include an alteration in the levels of hormones (notably reproductive and thyroid) circulating in the body, the commencement and establishment of lactation (and its ending if the baby is not breastfed or is weaned), the healing of any wound and the establishment of new sleep patterns. All mothers of new babies undergo these changes and some degree of postnatal stress, but only some develop depression. It is not known why. Many factors have been implicated and they may contribute in varying degrees.

**Although not yet proven, possible causes include:**
- a previous (or family) psychiatric history
- depression during pregnancy
- continuous nausea during pregnancy
- an unhappy birth experience
- being either considerably younger or older than the average mother
- being a single mother
- past or present poor relationship with parents
- difficult relationship with partner
- an unplanned or unwanted pregnancy
- the physiological changes which occur at birth and continue for some time
- grief due to termination of a previous pregnancy, a miscarriage or stillbirth, or a traumatic, abusive childhood.

Her birth experience may strongly affect a woman. She may have felt that her wishes were of no account – that she was 'out of control' or that she was expected to be a passive recipient of decisions taken by other people. In those circumstances she may have felt that she was without support. She may have felt distressed because the birth differed from her expectations. Perhaps she had planned a completely natural birth and then felt acutely disappointed in her professional carers or herself because she had needed assistance.

Pain relief can be a major issue, particularly if the woman had decided against using any and then found that she needed it. Was she given a choice of different forms of pain relief? (This is an issue that needs to be discussed before labour begins – it is hard to ask questions and understand explanations when in strong labour.) Perhaps the woman needed an assisted birth using forceps, a vacuum extraction, or a caesarean birth. She may have suffered a loss of self-esteem if her own performance during labour, while giving birth and postnatally, had failed to reach her expectations. A feeling of having failed may result.

**The following postnatal circumstances may contribute to depression:**

- negative reactions to the birth in herself or others
- early discharge from hospital – if feeling anxious, unsure and lacking in confidence
- a pre-existing or new health problem in herself or her baby, who may be premature, sick or with a disability, any of which can increase the pressures she is under
- the arrival of a baby of the undesired sex
- a continually miserable baby
- breast- or formula-feeding problems
- sleeping problems
- an emotionally stressful event, or a series of them, during pregnancy and the early postnatal period such as grievous loss – the death or loss of a partner, child or parent
- low self-esteem and lack of confidence in caring for her baby
- a major loss of income resulting in hardship
- adverse environmental conditions – these may include lack of family and community support, isolation, financial hardship, death in the family or loss of a job.

Again, not all mothers experiencing one or more of such factors will develop depression. There are also those who do not experience any of these circumstances yet develop postnatal depression.

## Helping to prevent depression

There are a number of activities that may help to prevent depression. Aim to be in the best possible health before and after the birth. From the beginning, if you have a partner plan to share parenting, including hands-on care. You can attend antenatal classes and it is particularly beneficial when partners attend too. Here you will receive information.

There will be opportunities to talk with the educator and share views and reactions with other expectant parents. These classes can help to increase understanding of the whole process of parenting.

If you remember that your own birth experience will be unique and avoid having rigid expectations you can prevent or at least reduce disappointment. By having the baby room-in beside you, you can learn much about your new baby's feeding and behaviour before returning home so increasing your confidence. If you can't have the baby room-in, do not feel a failure. Your learning will commence in earnest when the baby is back with you.

When you do return home set realistic goals for each day and beyond. As one grandmother said, 'Have your house clean enough to be healthy and just tidy enough to be happy' and forget about being 'house proud'; but if there is one room in the house that everyone keeps tidy it can be a wonderful place to rest. If the rest of the house is messy it does not matter so much. Find a trustworthy baby-sitter so that you can have time out with partner, family or friends and do something for yourself when there is an opportunity.

Mothers are often reluctant to admit that they could do with some help. Do not hesitate to accept it and be prepared to ask for it if you need it. Believe that people who offer to help mean it and, when asked, be ready to tell them exactly what would be helpful. For example you could ask: 'Would you please hang out the washing/make a casserole/ pick up a particular item or items from the shops/hold the baby while I make a cup of tea/baby-sit for a short time.'

You can help to prevent feelings of isolation and loneliness by spending time with people whose company you enjoy. These may be family members, local friends or other mothers or parents in the community. They may have also been at the antenatal classes, in the maternity ward or they may attend the same early childhood centre. Lone parents may need to make a special effort to prevent isolation.

## Experiences of depression

Depression is more severe and much longer lasting than the baby blues. One mother described her worst feelings during postnatal depression as those of guilt, of total helplessness and powerlessness and the belief that things would never be better. These miserable feelings were accompanied by a heavy, dark cloud of depression.

It is most often family members who become aware that the mother is 'not herself' but they may not understand what is happening and may feel unable to do anything about the situation. Sometimes other people feel impatient and angry with the mother because of her 'unreasonable' behaviour. Once the condition is recognised professional help can be sought and those involved given guidelines and suggestions for supporting and encouraging the mother as they aid her recovery.

**A woman suffering postnatal depression may experience the following:**

- She may suffer guilt because she is aware that she is behaving in uncharacteristic and regrettable ways; guilt because she is unable to cope and is quite sure every other mother out there in the community is coping well and only she is a failure.

- Irritability and resentment – 'Why me?' She is quick to anger, then despondent and miserable, often tearful because of her outbursts of anger.

- Isolation and loneliness – 'There is no-one there for me.' These feelings can be there in spite of caring support from her partner and others.

- Loss, which may include loss of identity – 'I'm no longer me, Julie. I'm this new baby's mother, I'm Jerry's wife but who am I, myself?' Other feelings involve loss of self-esteem with a poor body image, loss of concentration and memory, loss of ability to make decisions, loss of any motivation to plan or carry out anything including household chores.

- Low energy – she is lethargic and may be slow to face a new day, to get up, shower and dress. She feels exhausted. Her appetite may be poor, her libido low and she may be suffering from lack of sleep. She may become obsessed by this.

- Shame – she resists any attempt to encourage her to discuss her feelings, particularly if she feels no maternal love for her baby. She may withdraw from family and/or friends and even from her partner. In fact, it is often towards those closest to her that she shows irritability, anger and resentment. Often she resents visitors and phone calls.

🖋 Fear – she may fear that she is going insane, have a vague fear of something calamitous happening, of not being able to care for the baby or other family members, or of actually harming the baby, another child or herself.

Outside the home many of these mothers are able to present a false front of managing well and may appear at ease and in control of their lives. They may actually straighten their shoulders and find a smile as they walk in to the office of their early childhood nurse or visit their doctor. Sometimes the alert health professional will notice the 'slump and dragging steps' as they leave and recognise a possible problem. Then help and treatment can be offered.

## *Treatment of depression*

Look for skilled medical help and understanding. If medication is advisable and you are breastfeeding, your doctor will choose medication which is compatible with breastfeeding.

Accept support and encouragement from other sources. Even severely depressed mothers have found themselves able to take some positive steps to help themselves.

## *Self-help*

- Eat sufficient, balanced nutritious food. It could help to have some simple meals prepared and in the freezer and some wholesome snacks and sandwiches in the fridge. This is something a willing partner could do for you.
- Lessen tiredness and reduce fatigue. Don't stand when you can sit. Whenever possible sleep when the baby sleeps. Remember that a walk in the fresh air can benefit both you and the baby.
- Reduce expectations of yourself. Your baby will be a baby for such a very short time, so decide that this will be a happy time. Prioritise the things you must do each day.
- Ask for and accept help. Most people are willing to help a friend in need, so do believe that you are deserving of such help and entitled to ask for it, and happily accept it.
- Recognise and enjoy the moments when you are feeling better and anticipate more of them.
- Banish feelings of guilt by knowing that no mother can be perfect and accept that you only have to be 'good enough'.
- Arrange time out when someone else can care for the baby. Do something just for you, however simple – take a walk, go out and window-shop for a while, have a hot drink, spend half an hour in the garden, play some relaxing music or sleep.
- Complementary therapies for which there is good scientific evidence of their effectiveness include exercise, bright sunlight, omega 3 fatty acid supplementation and massage (for both mother and baby).

## Help from family and friends

Mothers are usually the main suppliers of nurture and care for their families. Now they are in need of help. Those who offer help need to take care not to come in and just take over, as to do so could unknowingly add to a mother's feelings of inadequacy. It is better to ask her what she would find most helpful right now or at a later time. Should she have no particular request then they could make suggestions.

There could be a plan to allow the mother to have a sleep-in at the weekend when other members of family can take the baby for a walk. They may bath the baby while she has her own shower or just care for the baby while she prepares dinner or is busy with some other activity. On the other hand the woman may prefer to care for her baby while others relieve her of some of the household responsibilities. It will benefit her most if they just discover sensitively what she would find most helpful.

A willing and caring partner can provide the best care and sympathetic support when he understands what is happening. It will help him to talk with the doctor who is caring for the depressed woman. Suggestions can be offered. It is easier to remain calm in a difficult situation when there is the opportunity to talk about it and know that someone outside of the home is aware of the difficulties. It may be hard to communicate with a partner while she is suffering postnatal depression but it is worth every effort to do so.

Women suffering from postnatal depression benefit from non-judgemental, skilled and sympathetic support. They need to feel that they are accepted and loved in spite of their own low self-esteem. If they are concerned because they are not feeling maternal and loving towards their baby, they need to know that love for their baby can grow slowly. Relationships can return to normal given time. They need help in developing coping skills. Acquisition of skills may lead to feelings of empowerment and renewed self-esteem. This can lead to recovery.

## *Other sources of help*

In addition to family and friends, mothers can turn for help to:

- 🖋 the family doctor, an obstetrician, a psychologist or a psychiatrist
- 🖋 the midwives who cared for or are caring for her and her baby
- 🖋 the early childhood nurse at the clinic or community health centre
- 🖋 family care centres which offer mothers day-stay help or admission as well as a 24-hour phone counselling service
- 🖋 occasional care centres, where babies can be left for a short period to give mothers a little 'time out'
- 🖋 community groups, either professionally run or 'self-help'. Some mothers find such groups very reassuring as they share their experiences with other mothers suffering from postnatal depression.

If medication is involved, the doctor will consider whether it is safe for the baby to continue with breastfeeding.

For one in ten women postnatal depression is a reality, so do not be ashamed or embarrassed if you happen to be one of them. Mothers can have a harrowing time while suffering from it but they can expect a full recovery.

## Puerperal psychosis

This affects only one or two mothers in a thousand. This is a severe illness requiring urgent medical help and hospitalisation. The onset is usually sudden and the mother is clearly out of touch with reality and she may suffer hallucinations. Her behaviour is so strange and unpredictable that it is quickly seen as odd by those around her. Her baby may be at risk of harm and professional help is required immediately. With good medical care and adequate support most women fully recover.

# 10

# Feeding
# your baby

**T**he choice of how you feed your baby needs to be an informed decision and it's good to be supported in your choice. Returning to work may require planning and additional support for your choice of feeding.

Breastmilk is recognised as being the perfect food for babies, except in very rare circumstances. However, whether by choice or if a woman is unable to breastfeed, there are babies who are bottle-fed. Some mothers choose to bottle-feed breastmilk to their babies. Although manufactured formulas cannot match breastmilk, formula-fed babies can be expected to grow and develop well as long as the formula is prepared correctly and made with a clean water supply. If you are bottle-feeding your baby you are encouraged to mimic breastfeeding behaviours to encourage bonding between you and your baby. In this section, formula feeding refers to bottle-feeding with formula only. The following table distinguishes many differences between breast- and formula-feeding.

## Comparison of breast- and formula-feeding

| Breastfeeding | Formula-feeding |
| --- | --- |
| A natural part of reproduction. Breastmilk usually suits the baby. Breast milk supplies all the necessary ingredients in proper balance for optimum growth and development | An artificial procedure. Formulas continue to improve and babies can be expected to grow and develop normally. Adverse reactions can occur |
| Breastmilk is free | Formulas cost money. Good quality water must be available for reconstitution |
| Breastmilk contains human protein which delays or lessens the onset of sensitivities and/or allergies | Breastmilk substitutes contain animal and/or plant ingredients which may cause sensitivities and/or allergies |
| No special equipment needed | Equipment needed for sterilising, storing and giving the bottle |
| The mother must breastfeed the baby or express breastmilk which others can feed to her baby | Others can feed the baby formula |
| The amount the baby takes is not known – it varies at different feeds according to the baby's appetite at the time | The baby is given a predetermined amount, often without regard for his or her appetite |
| Mother's health and wellbeing affect milk supply | Supply is independent of mother's wellbeing |
| The composition of breastmilk changes during a feed and over time, matching the baby's changing needs | The composition of the formula does not change during a feed or as the baby grows. Mixing errors can lead to inappropriate feeds |
| Breastmilk is easily digested, with little waste and inoffensive stools | Digestion is incomplete and stools are offensive |

| Breastfeeding | Formula-feeding |
|---|---|
| Breastmilk contains living cells and antibodies which protect against infection | No built-in protection against infection |
| Breastfeeding provides benefits for the mother | No direct physical effect |
| After birth, breastfeeding helps contract the uterus and lessens bleeding | No effect |
| Helps mother to return to normal weight | No effect |
| Prolactin possibly helps mothers to fall asleep again easily after night feeds | No effect |
| Automatic close body contact between mother and baby | Close body contact certainly can be given but it is not automatic |
| Breastfeeding is usually a pleasurable, shared, physical and emotional experience for mother and baby | Formula feeding, too, can allow loving interaction |

Establishing breastfeeding can be challenging for some mothers and so accessing correct support is very important. Midwives are your main support in the early days, whether in hospital or at home. Breastfeeding is important, so seek help from someone knowledgeable in breastfeeding. This may be your mother or friends who have had positive breastfeeding experiences; or your primary healthcare providers such as your midwife, a maternal and child health nurse, lactation consultant or GP. Peer support groups are an excellent source of support and you can obtain 24-hour direct telephone advice from parenting support centres or the Australian Breastfeeding Association (ABA). There are advisory services available in many communities from the ABA counsellors, and also from private lactation consultants who work on a fee-for-service basis. Seeking advice from pharmacies may not provide you with expert breastfeeding advice.

# Breastfeeding – an overview

Breastfeeding is the perfect way to feed your baby with benefits for both mother and baby.

**For the mother, breastfeeding:**

- provides the best nourishment for her baby
- naturally brings the mother into frequent contact with her baby
- contracts the uterus after birth and so lessens bleeding
- helps her return to her normal weight more quickly
- reduces her possibility of developing breast and ovarian cancers in later life.

**For the baby:**

- Breastmilk will supply all the nourishment needed for at least the first six months of life.
- Skin-to-skin contact with the mother is enjoyed by the baby from birth, supporting baby's transition from the uterus to life beyond.
- Living cells (antibodies) in the breastmilk protect the baby from infection, particularly during the early months until the baby's own immune system matures.

Research into breastfeeding continues. An ongoing joint study conducted by Brisbane's Mater Hospital and the University of Queensland examined the cognitive development of 3880 children and their experience of breastfeeding. It was found that the longer the duration of breastfeeding the greater the child's skill with language at age five years.

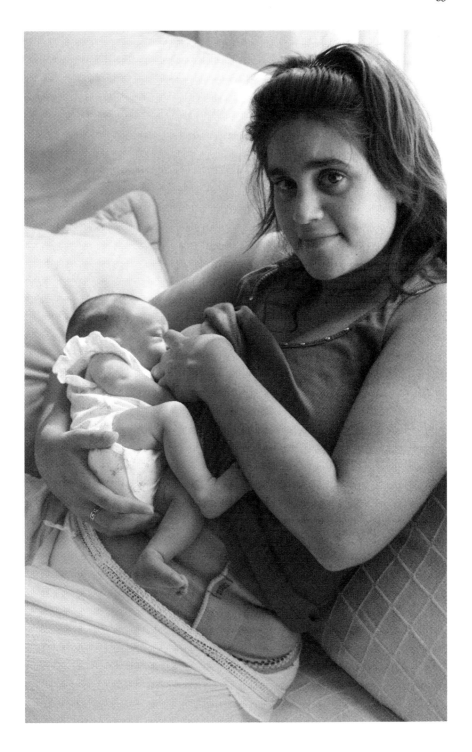

# Mobile phones: a warning

When feeding or interacting with your baby, beware of using your mobile phone. It is wise to switch it off.

This is Mary's story.

*Mary: 'Gerry was three days old – I was still in hospital and loving the cards and phone calls coming in. I was breastfeeding him when my midwife came into my room to see that all was well with us both – it was. A moment or two after she left my room my mobile rang; it was Gran. I was happy to speak with her. She was so excited because she had become a great granny. Gerry seemed to be feeding well. I did not notice that he had stopped sucking. Suddenly Alicia, my midwife, came back in again. (She said later that she had a strong feeling that she needed to do so.) She looked down at Gerry and she went white. Gerry had stopped feeding, was an ashen colour and floppy. My breast was pressing against his nose, his breathing had stopped – he looked dead.*

*Alicia grabbed Gerry and was able to revive him. I shudder to think that we could have lost him so easily simply because I was using my phone instead of being focused on Gerry. It was the worst experience of my life. I guess it could happen to any mother and her baby if she is talking on her phone or is distracted in some other way and does not notice something wrong.*

*I will never leave my phone switched on while feeding or doing anything with Gerry again.'*

Feeding your baby – whether you are breastfeeding or bottle-feeding – is a very special time for you both to enjoy each other. It is important to focus exclusively on your baby and avoid distractions as this is time your baby uses not just to gain nourishment and comfort but also to learn about you and the world.

11

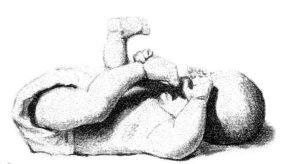

# Breastfeeding

**D**uring pregnancy mothers' bodies are preparing for breastfeeding, and after birth – with rare exceptions – they will go on to produce milk. It is nature's way of ensuring the baby's wellbeing. Understanding breastfeeding can help you to breastfeed successfully.

In this chapter and the next the various processes of breastfeeding are explained and then in Chapters 13 – 15 ways of managing the feedings are suggested. You may prefer to skip over the processes and move on to the management of feeding.

For many women the drive to breastfeed is a natural and instinctive one. But not all women feel this way. For every mother and every different baby there is also learning involved. Don't be surprised if it is not instantaneous – a little like learning to dance. When larger families were common many women learnt by watching their own mothers breastfeeding their siblings or by observing other women breastfeeding their babies. Because this happens less frequently today, many women do not have this knowledge when their first baby is born. They will need to learn it. This could be from knowledgeable health professionals or from other breastfeeding mothers, or counsellors in the community who have the special knowledge needed to instruct, support and help with breastfeeding. Research shows that being part of a group of breastfeeding mothers can be a great source of information and support and very helpful. If you need help, ask for it.

The pregnant mother supplies the nutrients and protective properties from her circulating blood via the placenta to her developing baby. After birth, for many months, her breastmilk supplies all the nourishment her baby needs, together with antibodies against many diseases. In time the baby will be ready to digest food from outside sources and the undeveloped immune system of the newborn will mature and become functional.

Following birth, mother and baby become separate individuals but can come together again in breastfeeding. Loving breastfeeding can also strongly influence the baby's emotional development and foster deep attachment between mother and baby. When held close the baby feels the mother's warmth and is reassured by her known smell and body noises, and very many mothers feel the satisfaction of nurturing this new being who was for so long a part of themselves.

# Your food while breastfeeding

When breastfeeding you have to meet your needs as well as those of the baby. Have a little more of the healthy food and drink that you had during pregnancy. Perhaps you will need considerably more. On the other hand an extra glass of milk may be all the extra nourishment you need. Your appetite and thirst will guide you. You do not need to drink great quantities of fluid – drinking to satisfy thirst is usually enough. Women are advised not to 'diet' while breastfeeding – eating less than you need in an attempt to lose weight is unwise. Breastfeeding helps you to reduce your weight when you are eating sensibly. Appropriate exercise will also help.

# Your clothes while breastfeeding

As well as looking after your nutritional needs, you may find you need some specific clothing for easier access during the months you will be breastfeeding your baby.

## Shirts

Front-opening blouses or shirts, or those which can just be lifted for feeding, such as T-shirts, are easy. Some purpose-made clothes are available with flaps and folds for a discreet approach. If they are patterned they are less likely to show any moist patches if there is some leaking of milk from the breasts between feeds.

## Bras and breast pads

Some women are happy without bras, some find crop tops comfortable. Your breasts will enlarge during pregnancy and particularly while lactating (most mothers will go up at least one bra size and two cup sizes). Select a bra for comfort and support to minimise stretching of the breast tissue. You may find you are more comfortable wearing one for sleeping. You are likely to need at least two during pregnancy, and three or more while breastfeeding.

### Check that the bra is:
- comfortable with wide shoulder straps that support the breasts well
- easily opened with one hand – some have cups which unhook from the shoulders, others are front-opening
- made of a cotton or cotton-blend material which breathes; these are usually more comfortable to wear than those made of just synthetic material
- exerting no pressure on, or constriction of, breast tissue which can lead to blocked ducts. 'Porthole' or wired bras may cause pressure problems.

You may find an experienced shop assistant helpful when you are choosing your bras. They know what is available and what mothers are finding most comfortable.

Many women are surprised when they seem to leak breastmilk continually and yet have ample to satisfy their baby. You may need plenty of breast pads. You can buy these but you might choose to make your own from terry towelling or to use men's handkerchiefs; both such types of pads can be laundered and reused. Change them often to avoid soggy breast pads.

## Some reasons why mothers do not breastfeed

For various reasons some women are unable or do not wish to breastfeed their babies.

When a woman wishes to breastfeed and is unable to do so she can feel deeply distressed, but she can look forward to making feed time a close and loving experience shared with her baby and she can expect her baby to grow and develop well.

Other women may not wish to breastfeed: they may be misinformed about breastfeeding or have strong feelings that they do not wish to breastfeed. They too can form a loving relationship with their baby and expect healthy growth and development.

Almost every well woman can expect to make enough milk for her baby. There is clearly unused capacity in reserve – after all, many mothers breastfeed twins (and even triplets). There is also help available from qualified breastfeeding advisers – other experienced mothers, midwives, counsellors in the Australian Breastfeeding Association (ABA), maternal and child health nurses and qualified lactation consultants.

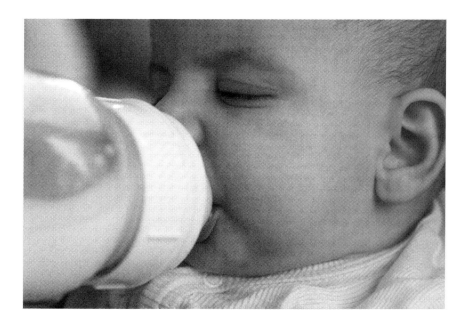

# Contra-indications: when not to breastfeed

Breastmilk is the best food for babies. However, although rare, there are a few medical conditions in either mother or baby in which the mother is advised not to breastfeed, including those listed below.

## In the baby

Babies with some metabolic disorders, such as galactosaemia and phenylketonuria, are bottle-fed. In the latter, the baby may be allowed some breastmilk under carefully monitored medical supervision. Both of these metabolic disorders can be diagnosed by the newborn screening tests which are offered routinely in Australia for newborns during the first days of life.

## In the mother

Women with malignant tumours, untreated tuberculosis and some life-threatening illnesses are advised not to breastfeed. Each mother will be assessed and her doctor will discuss the options with her.

### Malignancy

Women who are diagnosed with breast cancer are advised not to breastfeed. High prolactin levels in lactation may accelerate tumour growth and there are adverse effects if the mother is being treated with chemotherapy. Also breastfeeding takes energy and strength which the mother will need as she strives to overcome her illness. Treatment for the condition will begin at once, so her baby will need to be bottle-fed a formula.

### Tuberculosis

A woman who is diagnosed as having active tuberculosis, which has not been treated, will be advised against breastfeeding. A temporary separation from her baby will be necessary until treatment ensures contact with her baby is safe. When the mother is no longer considered to be infectious, contact with her baby can be resumed (this can be within one or two weeks). She may have been able to express her milk to establish her lactation and maintain her supply of breastmilk in readiness for her baby when tests show the milk to be free of infection and fit to use.

## Breastmilk jaundice

Breastmilk jaundice is rarely a reason for formula feeding (see 'Breastmilk jaundice' in Chapter 4).

# Medications: effect on breastmilk

Medications can travel to the baby through your breastmilk. It is wise to avoid all drugs if possible but if medication is necessary tell your health adviser or pharmacist that you are breastfeeding and check any possible effect on the baby. Discuss the timing of dosage with your doctor (see next page).

## *Prescription and over-the-counter medications*

These are prescribed to treat illness or are bought over the counter for self-treatment. Most drugs are considered safe and unlikely to harm babies even if the concentration in the breastmilk is high. Other drugs present in the milk, even in very small quantities, may be harmful so your doctor will carefully select your medication. *Always tell your doctor that you are breastfeeding* and discuss side effects. Ask about the possible effects on the baby. Your doctor can be expected to minimise drugs and choose medication least likely to affect the baby – long-acting forms are better avoided where possible. Also you can expect to be advised on the best time to take your medication. The impact on the baby of severe, untreated postnatal depression in the mother will probably outweigh the risk of taking antidepressants. Reactions in adults and babies differ. When possible, take medicine immediately after feeding so that there is the longest possible interval before the next feed.

Occasionally a woman will be advised to take her baby off the breast for the course of a medication. A store of previously expressed, frozen breastmilk would allow the baby to continue with the mother's milk. If there is no stored expressed breastmilk available, the baby will need to be given a formula until it is safe to breastfeed again. The mother can maintain her supply of breastmilk by expressing regularly. In this case the expressed breastmilk will be discarded. The baby will be able to return to the breast when the course of medication is completed.

Over-the-counter medicines may also affect the baby. Discuss any you buy with the pharmacist. Avoid their use where you can. For example, if you are constipated you can try eating prunes, other dried fruits and extra fibre and drinking ample water instead of taking medicine.

### Herbal medications/preparations

Always use herbal medications with caution while breastfeeding. There is very little research on the effects of some herbal medications on breastfeeding. They can affect your milk supply and the taste of the milk.

## Socially acceptable drugs

Sometimes referred to as social drugs, items such as caffeine and alcohol as well as nicotine can pass into breastmilk. They can affect lactation and the baby. They are taken as part of social rituals and therefore considered by many people to be acceptable, although nicotine is now almost universally recognised as harmful. Small quantities of caffeine and alcohol are said not to be harmful, but nicotine is not considered acceptable at all.

### Caffeine

Caffeine accumulates in babies and is difficult for them to metabolise. It can overstimulate them. Wakeful, overactive infants who find it difficult to settle, who sleep for short periods and who are often irritable may be reacting to caffeine. If this describes your baby, try four or five days without caffeine. There may be a marked improvement. Caffeine is present in coffee, tea and cocoa as well as in some carbonated soft drinks and cola. If you do have these drinks it is wise to limit them to two or three a day. Preferably keep tea and coffee weak. Restrict the chocolate you eat as it may cause rashes and other upsets in some babies.

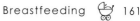

## *Alcohol*

Alcohol does reach the baby through the breastmilk. Alcohol in excess is harmful and can inhibit the let-down. Some mothers choose to avoid it totally. However, there are many doctors who feel that a glass of wine with your dinner should do no harm. You could try to have your drink soon after a breastfeed rather than just before.

## *Nicotine*

Make every effort not to smoke. Many women manage to stop smoking completely while they are pregnant but then resume after their baby is born, mistakenly thinking that it really does not matter too much – it does.

*Don't allow anyone else to smoke in your home and avoid taking the baby into any smoke-laden environment.* Don't smoke in the car if the baby is with you; and smoke on clothing can also be a problem. Nicotine can pass into breastmilk and can reduce breastmilk supply. It can cause nausea and vomiting in babies. If the baby is exposed to passive smoking the effect may be even worse than the uptake of nicotine from breastmilk: it is a serious risk factor for SIDS (see 'SIDS' in Chapter 18) and is implicated in respiratory diseases including asthma.

# Illicit or 'recreational' drugs

These are taken to produce changes in mood and perception. Among these it is known that heroin, morphine, marijuana and cocaine appear in breastmilk if taken by the mother and affect her baby. So take no so-called recreational drugs, to avoid any risk of harming the baby and/or your lactation in any way.

# 12

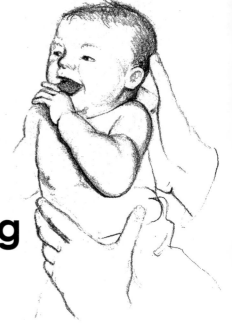

# How breastfeeding works

**F**ollowing birth there is a change in the hormonal balance and your body moves into the next stage – milk production or lactation. Lactation is the production and release of breastmilk to nourish and protect your new baby and is a programmed part of reproduction.

**Note:** this detailed description of how breastfeeding works is for your information but you may prefer to leave this and go straight to Chapter 13, 'How to breastfeed'.

# Milk production: lactation

As lactation begins the process can be sensitive to anything which interferes with the baby's access to the breasts when hungry. This is why imposed schedules or the use of bottle feeds instead of, or to supplement, a breastfeed can disrupt it. Milk production can be expected to run normally if the baby is able to feed effectively whenever hungry – this can be frequently at first. Later, well-established lactation is more resilient.

The two main hormones controlling lactation are prolactin and oxytocin. Both of these hormones are secreted in the pituitary gland in the brain – prolactin from the front of the gland stimulates milk production and oxytocin from the back of the gland triggers the release of the milk, also known as the let-down reflex, from the alveoli – milk glands. It is as the baby feeds at the breast that nervous impulses from the nipple and areola are sent to the pituitary gland so that there is a continuous release of these two hormones into the bloodstream. They travel to the breasts to enable them to function.

The breasts become larger as they fill with milk. When they are full, the hormones present in the milk inhibit further production. As the milk is removed these hormones are removed with it and milk production is stimulated again. The breasts soften and become smaller at the end of a feed or when milk is expressed.

# The breasts

The breasts are the visible external organs of lactation. Each breast is made up of fifteen to twenty lobes of milk-producing glands – the alveoli. These glands take water, nutrients and protective elements from the mother's circulation to make milk. They can be likened to a bunch of grapes: the alveoli are the 'grapes' and the ducts are the 'stalks'. Each gland is surrounded by fine muscle cells which contract under the influence of oxytocin and force the milk into the lactiferous ducts. Following the let-down the ducts dilate and carry the milk through to the nipple. Until recently, it was believed that when the baby stopped feeding, milk in the ducts then collected in widened areas in the ducts called sinuses, just behind the areola. At the University of Western Australia's Department of Biochemistry, research showed that the dilated duct returned to its smaller diameter when the milk was not removed from the breast at let-down. The milk flowed back into the smaller ducts and alveoli.

The milk is delivered through the nipple, which has a number of fine openings. If you express you will see thin sprays of milk coming from these openings.

It is important to know that the hard, over-full breasts of the first days and weeks will lessen and your breasts will become softer. This does not mean that you are not making enough milk: your supply is simply adapting to the baby's needs.

There are women whose breasts have low storage capacity, but they can fully breastfeed, provided they do so frequently.

## Milk production

During pregnancy the placenta, with its high levels of oestrogen and progesterone, prevents prolactin from acting to fill the breasts with milk. When the placenta is expelled after birth the hormonal balance shifts and the prolactin is then free to act upon the milk-producing cells to begin milk production. Your milk may come gradually or your breasts may fill suddenly with an abundant quantity. The levels of prolactin vary over the 24 hours and are highest at night.

When breastfeeding begins the baby's effective feeding ensures that the supply of prolactin will increase and continue. When lactation is well established the prolactin becomes less important in the production of the breastmilk and the baby's efficient feeding becomes the main stimulus for continued supply.

The hormonal balance in lactation may be upset if oral contraceptives are taken while breastfeeding (see the information on contraception in Chapter 8).

Milk production is governed by demand, i.e. by the amount taken from the breasts. If they are emptied regularly and efficiently milk production will be assured. For some mothers the milk may 'come in' as early as day two after birth, particularly when they have breastfed previously. For others it comes in on day three or four, but it can take longer. You can expect to change the cup size of your bras from smaller to larger.

If your breasts are very full you may need to express some milk. You can just hand express enough for the baby to attach well to the breast or to relieve painful fullness (see Chapter 15). This may not be necessary at all feeds. Within a day or two you may be able to reduce the amount you express. Keep in mind that what you remove from your breasts will be replaced.

In the first days following birth babies may feed every one or two hours but the number of feeds the baby wants may vary. Take care that from the first feeds the baby is correctly attached to the breast and is not nipple sucking (see 'Positioning and attaching your baby' in Chapter 13). As the weeks pass you can expect the feeds to become less frequent.

# Milk delivery

Between feeds most of the milk produced remains in the alveoli until the let-down occurs, but some collects in the milk ducts and is there as the baby begins to feed. There is usually enough to keep the baby interested until the let-down occurs, which constitutes the greater part of the feed. Remember that your breasts are never empty; milk is always available for your baby.

## The let-down or milk-ejection reflex

'Let-down' is the actual physical *release* of breastmilk from the milk-producing cells.

When the baby starts to suckle, the contact with your nipple and areola triggers nervous impulses which travel to the pituitary gland where oxytocin is released for the let-down. It travels in the bloodstream to the breasts where it causes the fine muscles which surround the alveoli to contract and so squeeze the milk from the cells. The milk which flows following let-down supplies about two-thirds of the feed. Without the let-down a baby has to work hard for little milk. Throughout the feed there is a succession of these contractions with a pause between them. A fast or forceful let-down may cause gagging and spluttering for a moment or two but it usually settles as the rush eases. Some babies seem to be able to control the flow themselves using their gums. This is easier for older babies. (For other ways to control the flow see Chapter 21.)

## *Changes in composition of milk*

The levels of the constituents in the breastmilk vary from feed to feed and also throughout a feed. There is least fat in the morning feed and most around midday and then it decreases again in the evening. The total in 24 hours varies little so a baby breastfeeding comfortably and finishing on one breast before taking the other gets a perfect balance over 24 hours. As a feed continues the levels of protein and fat, especially fat, increase. There is four to five times as much fat towards the end of the feed, particularly as a breast is emptying. It is probable that the higher fat level present towards the end of the feed helps to satisfy the baby's appetite *so do not change to the second side until the baby loses interest in the first side*. In this way the first breast is drained well and at the same time the baby obtains maximum hind milk. Milk not taken from the second breast tracks back to be stored again in the alveoli.

Let-down occurs in both breasts from the stimulation of either. After the baby begins sucking, the time it takes for the let-down to occur can vary from mother to mother and from feed to feed. It is usually between one and two minutes before the milk is in full flow although it can come more quickly or take longer. However, let-down can happen simply when a mother is just thinking about or looking at her baby, particularly if the baby is crying and/or it is nearing a feed time; it can even sometimes occur when a mother simply hears any baby cry, such as in a supermarket. At such times nursing pads are essential.

Women often describe the let-down feeling as one of warmth in the breasts and/or of tingling or of having pins and needles for a moment or two. Briefly there may be slight pain but this soon passes. Do not be concerned if you do not feel your let-down at all. Not all mothers are aware of it. Some women with their first baby first feel their let-down at around six weeks. Milk can jet from one or both nipples as let-down occurs. If it leaks from the second breast firm pressure on the nipple (the forearm can be used) usually stops the flow.

### *Another effect of oxytocin*

Oxytocin is also responsible for the contractions of the uterus during labour and often in the early days after birth, and can cause cramp-like 'after-pains' as the baby feeds. If severe, an analgesic may help you. These contractions reduce bleeding from the placental site and help the uterus to return to its former size. You may find that you have an increase in vaginal blood loss after a feed. This is normal.

## Establishing lactation

Lactation begins when breastfeeding begins. It is preferably within the first half hour of birth, when the baby's instinct to suck is particularly strong, but if this is not possible do not be distressed, you will still be able to breastfeed successfully.

If you have the baby rooming-in you can begin to manage the feeds yourself and offer the breast whenever the baby wants it. When you return home, continue to allow the same free access to the breasts. Soon a feeding pattern is likely to emerge, which makes life easier. It is most likely that the frequent feeding of the first few weeks will lessen, so be patient.

**The following guidelines will ensure good management of lactation:**

- Start each feed with the breast you offered second at the previous feed. To do so helps ensure the continued stimulation of your milk supply, effective let-down and good breast drainage, lessening the risk of problems such as engorgement, blocked ducts or mastitis.
- Allow unrestricted feeding.
- Position and attach the baby well (see 'Positioning and attaching your baby' in Chapter 13).
- Allow the baby to 'empty' the first breast before offering the second side.
- Give the baby breastmilk only – any other fluid can interfere with the appetite for the breast and reduce the baby's interest in feeding from it. A baby can develop allergies to some of the components in formula.
- Avoid giving a bottle or dummy before breastfeeding is well established – some experienced people believe this can cause sucking confusion in the newborn because of having to switch sucking technique.

If your breasts are very full it may seem reasonable to give a half feed from each but it is not recommended because the baby will not 'empty' at least one breast at each feed or even reach the higher-fat milk which increases as the breast empties. With very full breasts the baby may appear satisfied with the milk from the first side. Even so, offer the second breast – the baby may want to take some milk from it. If not and the second breast is uncomfortably full you can express enough to relieve it. You might choose to store the expressed milk if this is possible (see Chapter 15, 'Expressing, using and storing breastmilk').

## Continuing lactation

Procedures which result in good establishment of breastfeeding will result in reliable, continuing lactation. It can continue for many months, even years. Well-established lactation often survives quite severe upsets. Even so, aim for good health, relieve anxieties where possible and plan a balance of rest and exercise.

Provided your baby feeds effectively and the appetite is satisfied, breastmilk alone will supply all the nourishment that your baby needs until ready for the addition of solid food at around six months of age. Solids are often introduced too early. Even after six months when you have started on solids, the baby is advantaged if breastmilk continues as the main source of nutrition for the first twelve months. When your baby no longer feeds regularly and your breasts are not emptied, lactation will decrease and then cease.

It can be seen, therefore, just how perfectly adapted breastmilk is for the wellbeing of babies. If you choose to breastfeed your baby it is your right to receive whatever support and skilled help you need to enable you to do so. Remember that there are experienced breastfeeding advisers who can help you either by appointment or over the telephone, so do not hesitate to contact them if you need help.

## Breastmilk: the best food for your baby

Breastmilk consists mostly of water, but it contains many substances – soluble nutrients, fat and body cells. It is designed to supply all the water and nourishment that the baby needs. It is the only source of antibodies and living white blood cells which provide protection during the time that the baby's own immune system is maturing. Research also claims breastmilk helps in maximising the development of the brain (see Chapter 10).

Breastmilk changes over time in both appearance and composition. There are differences during a single feed and throughout the day. The hormones active during pregnancy are so cleverly synchronised that the breasts can even provide milk of different composition for a premature baby.

Lactation commences with the increased production of colostrum. This is followed two to three days later by the transitional milk and then by the mature milk. The fluid that is in the breast towards the end of weaning once more resembles the composition of colostrum.

## Colostrum

This is present in your breasts in the later months of pregnancy in readiness for your baby at birth when the volume increases rapidly. It is a thick, yellowish fluid high in protein and low in carbohydrate and fat compared with the mature milk. It is especially adapted to supply the first food in an easily digestible form. Colostrum supplies enough water for your baby's needs. It also contains a high concentration of immunoglobulins, which are antibodies effective against bacterial and viral diseases. There is a special enzyme present in the colostrum which prevents the breakdown of the antibodies by digestion. It helps to establish colonies of the desirable bacteria (*Lactobacillus bifidus*) in the intestines and these inhibit the development of disease-producing bacteria, such as those causing diarrhoea. Colostrum stimulates the baby's first bowel movement of meconium (see 'Stools' in Chapter 4).

Breastmilk contains many different live white cells. These leucocytes, which are also present in the blood, help prevent infection. One group of these cells lodges in the mucous membranes of the nose, throat, lungs and intestines – the surfaces where bacteria and viruses are most likely to enter the body. These leucocytes secrete new antibodies, coating these mucous membranes. This protective layer resists the entry of disease-producing organisms and foreign proteins which can cause allergies.

There is another important group of protective leucocytes – the macrophages. These circulate freely in the body. They are scavengers which simply engulf bacteria and combine with the enzyme lysozyme to destroy the disease-producing organisms. There are also specific leucocytes in breastmilk which help to fight any virus they encounter by producing the anti-viral factor, interferon. These are the main known protective mechanisms of breastmilk. Further research may reveal more. The protective properties of breastmilk do not lessen your baby's need for immunisation.

Gradually your colostrum thins and whitens as it mixes with the newly produced milk. This early mixture is referred to as transitional milk. As this gradual change continues the levels of protein fall but the levels of sugar and fat rise to suit the baby's increasing ability to digest them. There are more of the water-soluble vitamins and less of the fat-soluble vitamins. There is also an increase in volume so that the total amount of the various constituents, including water, actually increases. The changes progressively lead to the mature milk.

## Mature milk

Your mature breastmilk is white or bluish-white and is often described as 'watery looking'. This does not mean that the milk is weak or of poor quality: looks are deceptive. For example, creamy-looking cow's milk is unsuited for human babies although ideal for calves. Mature human milk continues to be produced until the baby is weaned.

## Breastmilk at weaning

As your supply decreases the milk becomes more concentrated and some mothers describe it as yellowy and looking like colostrum. Amongst the changing constituents the immunoglobulins increase and probably help to protect the baby in the final change to a different diet.

# 13

# How to breastfeed

**T**here is no one right way to breastfeed your baby. If your breasts and nipples are healthy and you are comfortable as the baby feeds, and the baby takes the breast happily and is thriving, you can be confident that you both have it right even if you are upside-down as you do it.

I remember one young woman whom I offered to help with her first feed after her first baby was born. She looked puzzled; she shook her head, thanking me, but could not see why she might need help. She cuddled her baby against her. Her baby was awake and ready to suckle. She smiled as the baby opened wide and fixed on the breast like a little limpet and sucked vigorously, obeying the strong instinct to do so. Both mother and baby were relaxed and happy. She had naturally placed her baby in a comfortable position where the baby was able to attach perfectly. As the feed finished on the first breast she held her baby against her shoulder hoping for a bubble of wind. Then her baby went to the second breast and in a moment or two fell asleep, so she tucked her baby down in the bassinet beside her. Almost at once she was asleep too. This woman was one of a large family. She learnt about breastfeeding by observing her siblings being fed.

Sometimes the first breastfeed is not so easy – each birth and each baby are different and we have to adapt the method accordingly. It can take some time to establish comfortable, relaxed breastfeeding. Support and knowledgeable help during this time can be invaluable.

When breastfeeding, try to arrange the environment to suit you. Have a glass of water to drink (you may feel thirsty as you are feeding) and a towel to mop up any spills of breastmilk. You might like to have music playing quietly. You can avoid telephone interruptions – set the answering machine or unhook the phone. Do your best to make feed-time a rest time and a time for close, loving contact. It is easy to advise you to relax and rest quietly as you feed but it may not always be easy for you to do so, particularly if you have a toddler as well. With thought you can often find ways to keep a toddler occupied for much of the time while you are breastfeeding. Some mothers have found the 'cot box' very successful: you can have a small carton with some toys or other items to place in the cot with the toddler while you sit close by to feed the baby. It is important that these items (not too many) are only used in the cot while you are feeding the baby, as they need to remain special and not be part of the other toys.

# Positioning and attaching your baby

Positioning refers to the way you hold the baby at the breast. Attaching is the actual fixing of the baby to the breast. Successful breastfeeding begins with good positioning so that the attachment is correct. The success of each feed will depend on good attachment (see the diagram below).

## Understanding attachment

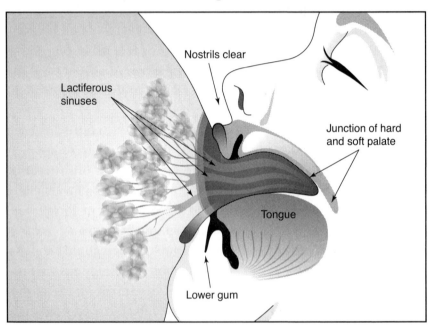

Lactiferous sinuses · Nostrils clear · Junction of hard and soft palate · Tongue · Lower gum

## *Positioning baby*

When you have control of your baby's body, tuck baby into your body underneath your breasts.

Your nipple as well as a good part of the breast is taken into the baby's mouth. The nipple sits well back on the tongue and sucking is stimulated. In this position your nipple is safe from damaging friction from tongue and gums. Your baby's contact with your nipple and areola triggers the let-down and your milk flows. In the first few days, even when correctly attached, the nipples may be tender, particularly at the beginning of the feed. This tenderness usually eases when the let-down

## Positioning baby

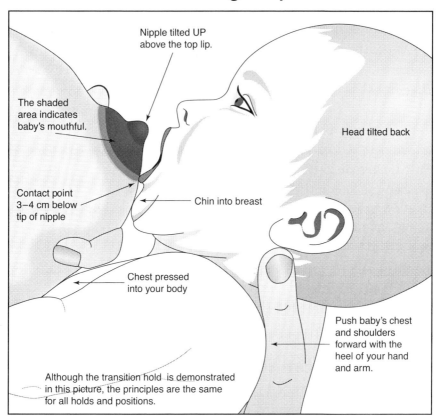

Nipple tilted UP above the top lip.

The shaded area indicates baby's mouthful.

Head tilted back

Contact point 3–4 cm below tip of nipple

Chin into breast

Chest pressed into your body

Push baby's chest and shoulders forward with the heel of your hand and arm.

Although the transition hold is demonstrated in this picture, the principles are the same for all holds and positions.

occurs. If the feeding is causing you pain, such as squashing, stinging or burning, gently take the baby off the nipple. Do not pull baby off quickly; break the suction by inserting your little finger between the baby's gums and reattach again (see 'Tender or sore nipples' in Chapter 21).

As the baby feeds, the baby's hold on the breast and the rhythmic movement of the jaw and tongue enables your milk to flow. The baby's sucking, swallowing and breathing are coordinated during feeding. Your baby feeds in cycles of sucking and pausing. You can expect the baby to breastfeed instinctively and very effectively if well attached and positioned at the breast.

If offered a bottle, a breastfeeding baby attempts similar actions but must learn a different way of sucking. It is clearly very demanding to expect a new baby to switch sucking technique between breast- and bottle-feeding and is better avoided.

As you breastfeed your breasts will adjust the supply of milk to match the baby's appetite. This adjustment may take a few weeks. There may be feeds when the baby wants very little or even no milk at all from the second breast, but do offer it when the baby loses interest in the first side. Begin the next feed with this second breast so it can be emptied in turn. In this way each breast should be well drained at least at alternate feeds. To assist your memory you can fix a safety pin or ribbon to alternate sides of your bra as a marker.

As your milk supply adapts to your baby's appetite you are likely to find that both breasts are emptied and the feeds are shorter. If given free access to your breasts and they are 'emptied' regularly they will automatically increase your supply to satisfy your growing baby. (A breast is never truly emptied. One can usually express at least a few drops from an 'empty' breast but, as far as your baby is concerned, it is empty.)

## Managing a breastfeed

Before starting have all that you might need close by – a glass of water, a cloth to mop up any spills, and pillows or cushions to support your arms and back. Have your lap level – you can use a footstool or a pile of books to raise your feet if needed. A pillow on your lap may help you to position the baby comfortably. See that your breast is free from clothing so that your baby can attach easily. At some feeds you might like to remove your top and bra to increase skin-to-skin contact.

Arrange yourself comfortably so that you both happily share this time together. You take cues from each other. For example, while feeding the baby may like to hold your finger or rest a hand on your breast. The baby may need to pause for a rest or to bring up a bubble of wind or to simply stop for a moment or two to look up and study your face with delight as you smile, talk and interact with each other before continuing with the feed.

# How to begin a feed

Here are two methods of attaching (or fixing) a baby to the breast when in a sitting position. In the first method the underside of your breast is supported with your fingers, while in the second it is supported by your baby's upper body.

## *First method of attaching*

- Unwrap and then hold your baby closely to you – chest to chest or tummy to tummy, supporting the baby's back and shoulders with the palm of your hand.
- Tuck the legs under your other arm. An easy rhyme to remember is 'chest to chest and chin to breast'. If any encouragement is needed, express a few drops of milk onto the nipple.
- Hold your baby on your wrist and forearm, with their head a little higher than their body.
- Have her or his head free to move, slightly tilted back so that the tongue can reach well under the breast. Hold your baby beneath and facing your breast. There should be no twist in the baby's neck. The nose should be clear of the breast as the chin pushes into it, since baby needs to continue to breathe through the nose during the feed. If the nose is pushing into the breast move the baby a little so that the legs which are under your arm move further around your side towards your back. This can free the nose while still keeping your baby's chin against the breast.
- Have your fingers under the breast supporting it but well back from the nipple. Rest your thumb on top of the breast behind the nipple. Now, press with the thumb so that the nipple tilts up above the baby's top lip opposite the nose and the chin points at the breast.
- Brush the bottom lip with the underside of your breast and areola to urge your baby to open their mouth; when it is open wide with the tongue down, bring your baby swiftly to the breast. If the mouth is wide open the baby should fix well onto your breast.

# How to begin a feed

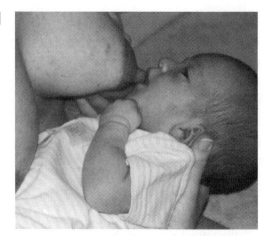

**Brush lips or cheek with nipple**

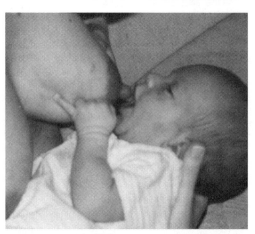

**Wait for the open mouth**

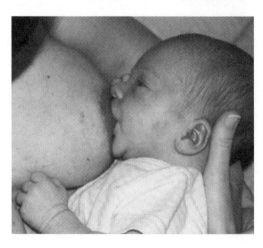

**Attach directly onto the breast, not just the nipple**

### Second method of attaching

Many women find this second method easy and effective. When using this method you keep your fingers well away from the underside of the breast. Place your finger or thumb-tip on the top of the breast close to the nipple. Press slightly so that the nipple tilts up. As the baby opens wide, offer the nipple and areola together with the soft underside of the breast. This allows your baby to take a generous mouthful of the breast. Hold your baby close with the shoulders and chin forward so that the body/chest supports the underside of your breast. Follow the other steps as listed on the previous page.

When well attached (see diagram earlier on page 174) your baby has taken into the mouth much more of the areola and breast below the nipple – about 2 to 4 centimetres – than above it. The chin presses into the underside of the breast, and the milk reservoirs lie over the tongue. The top gum and lip fix over the top of your nipple and onto the breast, forming a seal. The bottom lip is curled out down towards the chin; if not, turn it out with your little finger, or reattach (see below).

## Sucking action

As your baby sucks, a vacuum is created so that the whole mouth is filled with the breast and nipple. The nipple is drawn well back on the tongue, deep in the mouth where it is protected from squashing or chafing. There should be no nipple pain. If it is hurting, insert your finger between the gums to break the suction and then re-attach the baby (see 'Nipple problems' in Chapter 21).

**When your baby feeds, remember the following points:**

- The feed will begin with quick, short sucks. When the let-down is triggered the baby's jaw movements will be stronger and there will be movement of the ears as the sucking becomes deeper and rhythmical. Now there is a suck-swallow pattern and regular resting pauses.
- The action of the lower jaw and the undulating movement of your baby's tongue push the milk sacs against the roof of the mouth so that the milk flows to and out from the nipple and is swallowed.

- There should be no movement of the breast in and out of your baby's mouth and it should not hurt.
- Allow your baby to 'empty' the first breast by staying on it while still interested, before moving onto the second side.
- If the baby seems uncomfortable try for a bubble of wind. If the baby is tired allow time for a short rest; however, breastfed babies if well attached will not swallow air or require burping.
- At the end of the feed check that your nipples are undamaged – there should be no change in their appearance at the end of the feed, no flattening or stripe across either and your breasts should be comfortable with no lumps, blocked ducts or tender areas. If there is a lumpy spot encourage the baby to take a little more milk as you gently massage the lump towards the nipple (see 'Blockages in ducts' in Chapter 21).
- If your baby wants none or very little from a full second breast you can express enough for comfort.

## Breastfeeding twins

Mothers' breasts can produce enough milk to feed twins and even triplets. Care for your own health to meet the extra demands on your time and energy. Planning your day so that you obtain maximum nutrition and rest with minimum effort will help your supply of breastmilk. You can also talk with the Multiple Birth Association in your home state or territory who can support you or look on the Internet for chat rooms and information for parents with multiples.

If you are breastfeeding twins you can decide whether to feed the babies together or separately. Feeding both at once can save you time but if you prefer to feed each separately you can do so. This is a good idea in the early days as you learn to know each baby as an individual. If you are feeding both at once there will be times when you will need to waken the second baby. Take a little time to make sure that the baby is well awake before starting the feed or you are likely to find that this twin will doze off to sleep at the breast.

The most frequently used position is the twin or football hold: the babies' legs will be tucked beneath your arms pointing back. Use pillows to support their heads or to support your forearms and hands as you hold their heads to the breasts. Other positions sometimes used are: both babies in the cradle position or one baby in the football and the other in the cradle (see later in this chapter, 'Different positions for breastfeeding'). The usual principles of attaching the babies well to the breasts apply.

**Twin feeding**

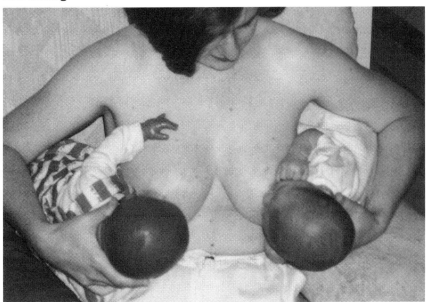

## *Should you alternate the breasts you give each baby?*

There is no rule. If one baby sucks more strongly than the other, alternating the breasts at each feed or daily should give both breasts equal stimulation. However, you may find that the babies feed more contentedly if they each have their 'own' breast and if each is obtaining enough milk you can continue this way. You could feed both together at most feeds but now and then you may enjoy feeding each baby separately.

If the babies are born early and are small they may still be able to breastfeed at once. Some low birth-weight or premature twins are very vigorous but they will need to feed more often. You will receive help and advice following their birth. If at first they are unable to go to the breast at all, you can still express to establish your lactation and provide the milk they need. When they have grown enough they will then be able to directly breastfeed.

If you have triplets it is good to know that mothers have managed to fully breastfeed all three. Look for special help from those skilled and experienced in breastfeeding. There is an increasing number of lactation consultants available today, many of whom are midwives.

# Different positions for breastfeeding

Below are listed a number of positions in which you can breastfeed your baby. Try them and see which one suits you and your baby best.

## The sitting position

Most breastfeeds are given with the mother sitting, cradling her baby in an arm. Sitting is usually convenient, whether done at home or when out. Attaching the baby in the sitting position has been described above.

**Sitting feeding**

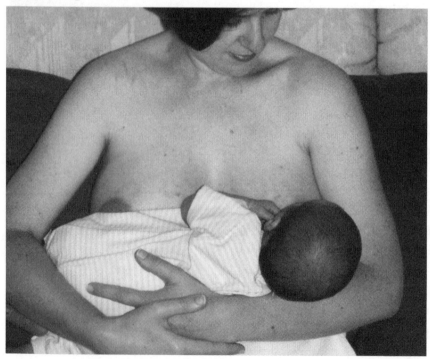

**Here are some guidelines for sitting to breastfeed:**

- You can sit up on a chair, the lounge, the bed or even on the floor. Ensure you are comfortable. Your back needs to be straight or even leaning a little forward. As you lean forward the breast falls towards the baby and fixing to the breast will be easier. If you are leaning back the baby has to try to fix to the slightly flattened breast. Once attached if you lean too far back you could pull the breast away from the baby's mouth. Have your lap flat – to do this you may need a support to raise your feet a little.

- Feed from the right breast by cradling the baby in your right arm with face and shoulders facing the breast and with the head free to move. When feeding from your left breast use the left arm. If you prefer to use the opposite arm to the breast the baby is feeding from then your lower arm will support the back and shoulders and the palm of your hand and spread fingers will support the head.

- Attach the baby when correctly positioned (follow the steps outlined on page 178 in 'How to begin a feed'). The baby can rest their upper arm on your breast or against your sternum, and you can tuck the lower arm beneath your breast.

## *The twin or football hold*

This position can be used at any time if you wish. It is the usual, but not the only, position used when a mother is feeding twins. It can help when nipples are tender or sore as it allows you to change the baby's

position on the breast during a feed. The baby's body can be supported on a pillow tucked in against your side and beneath your arm.

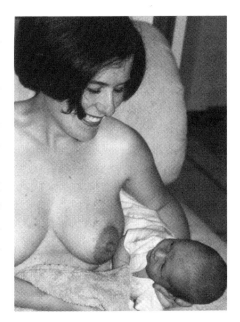

## *Feeding lying down*

Place pillows so they will support your head or head and shoulders and have one which will support the small of your back. To begin with you may need assistance from your partner or support person. If you do start as you lie on your side, use your free hand to bring the baby onto the breast rather than using it to put the breast into the baby's mouth.

**Lying down feeding**

## *Feeding following a caesarean section*

It is important to avoid any pressure on any stitches for at least the first few days following a caesarean section. Many mothers find that feeding lying down is the most comfortable way to avoid such pressure. Ask for any help you need to arrange yourself and the baby for the feed and when you change sides. You will have to lie on the other side when you give the second breast. Alternatively you may prefer to sit up. To reduce pressure on any stitches have a soft pillow on your lap. It can raise the baby to the right height for easy attachment. You may prefer the football or twin hold; this lessens the chance of any pressure on the wound.

# Burping: bringing up wind

Take care not to attach too much importance to wind. It may sometimes cause a little discomfort but is rarely a real problem. Discomfort from wind is very different from abdominal colic.

Babies vary in the amount of air they swallow as they feed. Some swallow very little, others swallow more. If the baby is held with the head higher than the tummy while feeding, the milk lies below the air and you can expect the baby to bring up wind if there is pressure causing discomfort. They often do this themselves when lying in the cot or when being moved. What air remains will pass, usually easily, from the stomach and out through the bowel as flatus.

Whether breast- or bottle-fed, the baby will stop feeding if the pressure of milk and wind in the tummy becomes uncomfortable. Just give him or her the opportunity to burp. Hold the baby upright, firmly against your chest and shoulder. You can have a little pressure on the tummy. Now pat the back gently or rub up the spine. *Do not thump.* Do not spend more than a couple of minutes trying to burp your baby. Continue with the feed when the baby is willing.

At the end of the feed, if the baby is asleep do not try for a burp, just put him or her down in the cot. If awake, you can again give your baby a chance to burp. If no bubble of wind comes up do not worry – put the baby to bed when he or she is ready for sleep.

If you feel that wind really is making the baby uncomfortable, just altering the position may help. Hold him or her upright again – often, like a spirit level, the bubble comes up. If not, put the baby down in the cot for a sleep. If the baby is still restless wind may not be the cause. You can consider the possibility that a little more milk may help or that the baby is not yet ready for another sleep.

Flatus passed from the bowel can also be produced during digestion. It may or may not be accompanied by bowel motions. Large amounts may be due to undigested lactose (see 'Diarrhoea due to lactose overload or lactose intolerance' in Chapter 20).

The baby may or may not spill some milk with a burp. You can have a small towel or cloth nappy over your shoulder to protect your clothes. Sometimes the amount brought up may concern you but a

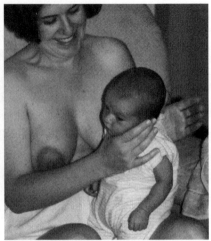

small spill can be misleading and is unimportant. If the baby complains because the tummy no longer feels full, offer a little more milk.

If you still feel that wind is causing discomfort, your baby may be able to burp more easily by him or herself with the head of the cot raised, either by putting it on steady blocks or by putting a large pillow *under* the head of the mattress (pillows for babies to sleep on are best avoided because of the risk of suffocation). If the discomfort continues you could try carrying the baby upright in a possum pouch. This is a material baby carrier which you wear in front of you. Babies usually love to spend some time being carried in these. They can be obtained from nursery outlets and the Australian Breastfeeding Association.

When it seems that wind is continuing to make the baby miserable you can offer another few minutes on the breast. The troublesome burp may then come up. If bottle-fed, just give a couple of teaspoons of warm boiled water. If you are considering using a 'wind mixture', discuss this with an experienced baby health adviser.

## After the feed

During the day if the baby is awake and alert at the end of a feed it is a good time for talk and play. Time on the floor might be enjoyable or ten to twenty minutes in a bouncinette as it allows the baby to see much more of the surrounding environment. Do not leave the baby unattended as it is unsafe to do so. (As well as the restraining strap across the tummy, see that there is also a crotch strap so that the baby cannot slip down; without a crotch strap this can happen and a baby can be strangled.)

If well supported, babies can be propped in the pram where they can enjoy looking at colourful items within focus range. When they show signs of becoming tired (see 'Recognising a sleepy baby' in Chapter 18) they can be settled to sleep again. At night just speak very softly and move the baby slowly, keeping the feed restful. In the early hours, if baby's skin is good and there is no sign of nappy rash and you have put on a woollen nappy cover for warmth, you need not change the nappy. You can both get back to sleep as soon as possible.

## Successful breastfeeding: a summary

Your baby:
- thrives and is bright-eyed
- attaches comfortably, feeds efficiently
- has five or six good wet cloth nappies daily; the urine is pale and odourless (it is harder to judge the quantity of urine in a disposable nappy)
- develops and grows well.

You:
- manage the feeding in simple and flexible ways which suit you both
- feed your baby whenever hungry
- alternate the breast you offer first
- hold and position your baby so that your baby gets the milk easily and your breasts are comfortable during and after the feed
- allow your baby to 'empty' the first breast before changing to the second and allow your baby to stop feeding when satisfied or to continue for longer if interested
- plan to eat wisely and obtain some exercise, extra rest when possible and some time out for yourself.

# 14

# Breastfeeding: Frequently asked questions

**A**s you begin breastfeeding you will wonder about various things. You may want to know how often you should feed, how long the baby should have on each breast and how you will know when the baby has had enough. There may be questions about night feeding – you may want to know if you can ease the baby into more regular feed times and why your obviously well baby has suddenly become wakeful and unsettled and appears hungry. The following may help you.

## What happens when my baby is just born?

The first three days are very important, not just in beginning but in maintaining breastfeeding. Straight after birth your baby should be put on your chest and not removed until after the first breastfeed. This imprinting (or bonding) is called skin-to-skin contact. During this special and lovely time thousands of messages are exchanged between mother and baby. Once your baby has fed quite soon after birth, he or she will probably not need another feed for about ten hours. Your baby will often have a big sleep, resting after the big day. After birth there is usually lots of amniotic fluid and mucus in the baby's gut which is very nutritious and hydrating. Your baby will either digest this or vomit it up and either is acceptable. For a well baby just one to two feeds in the first 24 hours is fine.

Going into days two and three your baby will start wanting to suck very frequently. This is what makes your colostrum (first milk) change to breastmilk. It might seem that baby is very hungry but it is nature's way of making milk. So don't worry, just keep feeding.

Once your milk comes in your baby may stop wanting to feed so frequently. During this time it is important to continue lots of skin-to-skin contact as this promotes continued milk production and attracts baby to your breast.

If you are worried about your supply of milk, 'switch feeding' is a *short-term* measure that may be helpful. Switch feeding means the baby is alternately fed from each breast with frequent side-to-side changes during the one feed. Ask your midwife for help.

## How often should I breastfeed?

The simple rule is to feed your baby when hungry. You will soon recognise the signs. Hungry babies will cry, possibly suck on their fingers and become restless. When held the baby is likely to turn towards the breast actively seeking a feed and when given the breast will latch on and feed with vigour. Babies are not hungry every time they cry but hunger is the most common reason, particularly in newborn and very young babies.

Let the baby be your guide. As you begin breastfeeding expect frequent feeding – at least every two or three hours for the first week or two, although some babies will sleep longer between feeds. The stomach is small, the milk is digested rapidly and soon another feed is needed. However, intervals between feeds may vary. Remember that frequent feeding is important as you establish lactation.

As time passes you will find that the baby is feeding less often. During the first three months many babies take six to eight feeds over most 24 hour periods: if they are well, allow the baby to decide. As babies grow they need more milk. Many babies stimulate the supply by feeding for a little longer and perhaps more vigorously than usual and mothers may not be aware as they do this. Other babies have a period when suddenly they are clearly more hungry and certainly let you know that they need more frequent feeding and it is said that they are having a 'growth spurt' (see 'How do I manage when baby suddenly asks to feed more often?' later in this chapter).

**Some points to remember about more frequent feeding:**

- Accept that frequent feeding is important as you establish breastfeeding. It is best for both of you, so continue this as long as necessary.
- Be easy – relax, and feed the baby when hungry. Offer the breast when the baby cries unless it is obvious that hunger is not the cause.
- Do not make the baby wait. When babies have to wait they quickly become upset.
- Hope that the baby sleeps longer at night but the new baby will still need at least two feeds. Gradually the time between feeds will lengthen and it is likely that between four and six weeks there will be a predictable and easier pattern for you to live with.

Babies who are breastfed do not need burping unless they are clearly windy. You don't have to wake your baby to burp him or her when they have blissfully fallen asleep at the breast.

## *How long does a feed last?*

Let your baby stay on the breast until satisfied. It is important that your breasts become soft and comfortable too. It was once commonly believed that allowing a new baby to feed for as long as the baby wanted would lead to sore and/or damaged nipples. Now we know that the common cause of sore nipples is poor attachment. Also, poor positioning and/or attaching can result in a lengthy, inefficient feed because the baby will have difficulty obtaining the milk. A baby who drinks vigorously will obtain the milk more quickly than a slower feeder. Remember: 'chest to chest, chin to breast with a wide mouth'.

Once lactation is comfortably established it is common for babies to feed for around ten minutes on each breast, but there are no rules. Feeds vary from a few minutes to around 30 to 45 minutes. Watch that a long feed is not making the baby too tired. Sometimes the baby may need a brief feed because of thirst rather than hunger.

Sometimes babies may continue to suck at the breast just for comfort. Mothers quickly learn the difference between their babies' active feeding and comfort sucking. Firm rhythmic jaw movements followed by swallowing and a pause – this is the feeding pattern. A comfort suck will be gentler and less concentrated. Your baby may nuzzle and play with the nipple or just drowsily and contentedly suck intermittently. However, comfort sucking can trigger another let-down, not that this matters.

If the nipples are sore do not allow comfort sucking but if they are comfortable and you are both happy there is no need to stop it.

**When you feed, aim to relax and be comfortable. In addition:**

- don't restrict your baby's access to or time at the breast while actively feeding
- let your baby decide how long the feed should last
- allow your baby to finish on the first breast before offering the second.

## *When has the baby had enough?*

You can judge that the feed is sufficient if:

*C* the baby comes off the breast relaxed and content, showing no further interest in continuing the feed, or even strongly resisting the breast if you persist in offering it. If baby is awake and alert, this is a time when you can interact happily together. A good time to socialise until you see the tired signs (see 'Recognising a sleepy baby' in Chapter 18);

*C* your baby falls asleep at the breast after feeding well;

*C* your breasts feel empty after the feed.

These signs will be quite clear to you so do not be concerned that you cannot measure or see the quantity of milk that has been taken. We do not weigh and measure everything that goes into our mouths. Our appetite is our guide and our general health and wellbeing over time reflect an adequate diet. These principles also apply to our babies. Just observe and be aware of the baby's condition and behaviour to assess adequate feeding. As long as your baby is having wet nappies all is

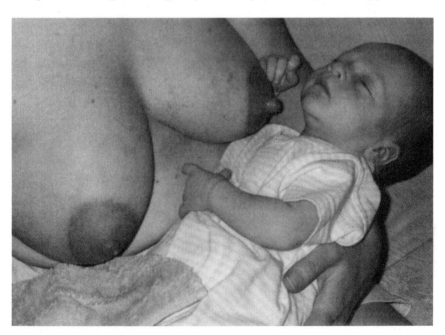

well. Breastfed babies can have a pooey nappy every change or less than one a day and both are normal. Check your baby's progress if you are able to visit a baby health centre. If not, and you feel unsure, arrange a visit to your family doctor.

## *What about night feeding?*

Unrestricted breastfeeding applies to night as well as day. Your breasts produce milk throughout the 24 hours. The newborn and very young baby is likely to take as much milk through the night as in the day. You may find yourself short of sleep so try to get extra rest during the day. It is believed that oxytocin, one of the hormones involved in the let-down of your milk, among other things, helps you to fall asleep again easily when the baby finishes a night feed.

To maximise your rest you could have the baby rooming-in beside your bed and perhaps you could give the feed with the baby lying beside you in your own bed. Remember that it is unnecessary to change the baby at each night feed if the skin is in good condition with no sign of a nappy rash. The idea is to disturb the baby as little as possible. If using cloth nappies an inner 'one-way' nappy, which allows the urine to flow through is likely to keep the baby comfortable. A woollen or flannel nappy cover will provide warmth. (See 'Nappies' in Chapter 1.) It is feeling cold rather than wet that makes babies wakeful. Some mothers who prefer cloth nappies use disposables at night as they are very absorbent.

Another aid to settling the baby easily after that early morning feed (especially when the weather is cold) is to put the baby back into a warm bed. A hot water bottle can be placed in the baby's bed while you are feeding. Of course, remove the hot water bottle before settling the baby back again. The baby's bed will be warm and comforting.

You may find that it is only a few weeks before the intervals between feeds lengthen. However, most babies need at least one night feed for months. Night feeding helps to maintain the breastmilk supply at its best. Eventually the pattern of feeding will be kinder and a little careful management may speed the day, or rather the night, of your first blissful long sleep.

**To repeat, your healthy, well-fed baby will:**

- look well
- feed vigorously
- have good skin tone with a firm body and well-rounded limbs
- have periods of quiet sleep and periods of being bright-eyed, alert and reasonably contented
- have five or six wet nappies daily (if using cloth nappies it is easier to judge than if you are using disposable nappies: the urine will be pale and clear)
- continue to grow.

Don't mistake lethargy for contentment. Babies underfed to the point of lethargy (see 'Recognising underfeeding' in Chapter 21) may seem contented but their overall condition will be poor. If so, check with your health adviser.

# What about a routine?

You may wonder when you can expect a predictable routine, possibly feeding three or four hourly, and when the baby will sleep through the night. It is wise to have no firm expectations. Regular feeding patterns appear gradually as babies grow. The baby may establish a routine within the first week or two; other babies feed erratically for much longer and the pattern which does develop is not necessarily one of feeding every three or four hours and sleeping soundly in between. It means that the baby's routine, whatever it may be, usually becomes regular and predictable and further changes occur only slowly. Expect any pattern the baby develops to change over time. Accept the baby's pattern and timing. Do not compare yours with other babies as each baby is unique.

## How can I ease my baby into a different pattern?

Most babies adopt a recognisable pattern as they follow roughly the same timetable of feeding, sleeping and being awake within two or three weeks. The individual pattern for a particular baby reflects age, size, metabolism and personality. Perhaps your baby may take the longest sleep in the daytime or may sleep through late evening but insist on feeding in the early hours of the morning. Babies sometimes snack, taking frequent short feeds rather than longer ones – there are many variations.

As the weeks pass you can expect intervals between feeds to lengthen. After the first six weeks, if you find that the baby is sleeping for long periods during the day rather than at night you can alter the pattern. Four hours after beginning the last feed, waken the baby. Although it can be difficult to waken a baby who is sleeping soundly, you can turn on the radio, loosen the bed covers, then change the nappy. The baby needs to be fully awake before the feed or he or she will simply fall asleep again. If the baby feeds well then you may be lucky and find that the long sleep shifts to the night.

Persevere for a few days if not immediately successful. If the baby cannot waken enough to feed well but regularly falls asleep again after taking a small amount, you may have to accept this for the time being. You are likely to find it is easier to change your own pattern for at least another week or so before you try again. Time your sleeping to match some of the baby's. Many babies fall into a deep sleep after their 6 or 7 p.m. feed and can be really difficult to rouse a few hours later if the mother wants to feed her baby so that she can go to bed. If you find that this is happening you may be able to go to bed early and take a longer sleep during the first part of the night.

The thriving older baby who continues to take frequent short feeds is often one who loves breastfeeding. With such a baby it is reasonable to try to lengthen the intervals between feeds if you wish. A really hungry baby will not be diverted for more than a few minutes. Just try; you will soon know what is reasonable. You can have the baby near you to hear you and watch what you are doing. You can provide things of interest, play games together, go for a walk with the baby propped up on pillows in the pram so that it is possible to see out of it. Sucking a dummy may help to lengthen the interval between snacks. With longer intervals between feeds the baby is likely to be hungrier and so feed more vigorously and take more milk, and then is likely to sleep for a longer period before looking for the next feed.

# What do I do when my baby is hungry in the evening?

The thriving baby may be reasonably contented for three or four hours between feeds in the morning but look for more frequent feeds later in the afternoon and evening, just 'cat napping' – that is, just dozing off for a few minutes before waking again. The baby may simply have had enough sleep. Some babies show signs of hunger because it seems that their mothers have less milk later in the day, particularly around early evening. A baby may be fretful or even frustrated and stay at the breast for shorter times than usual but then will want to feed again very soon. Babies who are growing and gaining weight well but are behaving in this way are taking enough milk over 24 hours but not quite enough to satisfy the appetite at the later feeds. This behaviour may continue for many days or even weeks. Many mothers give their babies frequent short 'snacks' at the breast throughout the late afternoon and evening. This can lessen their baby's distress while stimulating the breasts.

At a late afternoon or evening feed some mothers find that a 'top up' of their expressed breastmilk (taken earlier on the same day or from a store of expressed milk) can be a lifesaver for both. It can settle the baby and so make life more peaceful. If you feel that tiredness is affecting your evening supply, try to have an afternoon rest.

# How do I manage when baby suddenly asks to feed more often?

When there is a sudden demand for more frequent feeding in a previously contented baby it is most likely due to increase in appetite due to continued growth.

At these times your baby's previously predictable feeding pattern may change. The baby is more frequently asking for more milk, and may be fretful, frustrated, fussy at the breast and hard to settle. Your baby may stay at the breast for much shorter times or may want to stay on for much longer than usual. This behaviour is usually temporary – you just need to increase the supply of your milk by feeding more often and sometimes feeding for longer. When your supply increases you can expect your baby to settle again and feed less often, returning to the more predictable pattern. As mentioned earlier there are babies who increase the breastmilk by sucking a little harder and for a little longer without a noticeable change in their feeding routine – they do not have a sudden need for increased feeding.

**Managing a growth spurt involves:**

✓ giving unrestricted access and offering breastfeeds as often as the baby wants them

✓ persevering patiently while increasing the supply

✓ allowing both breasts to be 'emptied' at each feed

✓ not giving supplementary feeds, which lessen the stimulation that the breasts need to increase production although a 'top up' of your expressed milk at an early evening feed, particularly if you have managed to express it earlier in the day, can be given

✓ believing in your body's ability to provide the breastmilk the baby needs

✓ avoiding the trap of reaching for a formula.

Misunderstanding the cause of a baby's increased appetite and believing it is due to a low supply of breastmilk is possibly the commonest cause of unnecessary and unwanted weaning during the first three months.

# How can I continue breastfeeding after I return to work?

This section is about women whose work outside the home separates them from their babies during working hours. Lactation and exclusive breastfeeding can be maintained by working mothers. You can combine expressing with natural feeding. If possible, take maternity leave for at least three months. It will be even better if you can prolong this period. The baby in childcare has to take at least some feeds from the bottle unless you are fortunate enough to have the baby close enough to your workplace to breastfeed, plus the flexibility to do this. Once breastfeeding is well established you can expect the baby to manage both breast and bottle easily. Mothers provide expressed milk for the feeds when they are absent and breastfeed at home before and after work and so both enjoy the warmth and closeness which help compensate for the separation during the working day. Mothers with premature or sick babies in hospital face the same need to express regularly. They will be encouraged to spend time with their babies.

Breastfeeding and working call for careful planning and organisation of daily routines. On your maternity leave you will be able to establish lactation, settle the baby into a general routine and accustom yourself mentally to the timetabling of your day.

Have a supply of expressed milk, stored at the correct temperature (see Chapter 15, 'Expressing, using and storing breastmilk') ready for your return to work. This store can be built up gradually by expressing whenever there is a surplus – commonly at the morning feeds, although there may be a little extra at other times. By making this new demand on

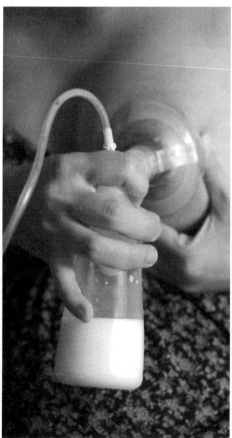

the breasts one or two weeks before returning to work there should be ample to freeze. You could begin storing your breastmilk earlier if you choose. The supply is increased simply by increasing the removal of milk.

You can prepare yourselves for separation by leaving the baby with another carer. It can be most helpful if you both to get to know the carer or carers by visiting the centre or home the baby will be attending. If the carer is to come to your own home, have the carer visit and handle the baby a few times before you return to work. Most babies, especially young babies, will readily accept separation if they are lovingly cared for. It is the mother who may be surprised and overwhelmed by her feelings when the time comes for her to leave her baby in another's care.

Arrange what help you can and accept any that is offered. Support and practical help from a partner in the daily routine and care of the baby will be invaluable. The Australian Breastfeeding Association (ABA) has booklets which provide valuable information and suggestions for the working mother: 'Breastfeeding, Women and Work' and 'A Mother-friendly Workplace' (an information sheet for employers). Among many items discussed in detail are childcare options and choosing a caregiver. You could ask your local branch of the ABA for the booklets and whether they can introduce you to other local mothers who are working and breastfeeding if you would like to meet some.

**To express and maintain a good supply of breastmilk you will need:**

- confidence that the baby is receiving good care and that the caregiver knows how to handle expressed breastmilk;
- at least a day's supply of stored milk (preferably much more) before returning to work;
- the opportunity to express your milk during the working day. You may need sessions of about twenty minutes approximately four hourly. The milk expressed has then to be stored safely until needed;
- a clean container and a refrigerator at work (or your own small portable ice box) and possibly a pump; it is best to sterilise the containers once in 24 hours for the first three weeks – after that, hot soapy water and air drying is all that is needed;
- a place and time to express without interruption;
- ways to minimise tiredness and fatigue and maintain your health and nutrition.

Prepare your baby for the changes coming at least a week or so before you return to work. After the first few days most babies can manage both breast and bottle successfully. If at first your baby is unwilling to take the bottle you will need to be patient while the baby learns. It often helps if someone else gives the bottle.

Remember to use a teat that is closest to the natural shape of your nipples. The teat should be round and symmetrical.

You will need to decide how to feed at the weekends. Many mothers express their milk on Friday and store it for daycare on Monday then fully breastfeed over Saturday and Sunday. Other mothers continue with the weekday routine: the baby receives the usual breastfeeds and then bottles of expressed milk at the usual daycare times. The mother continues to express at home at the same time as she would express at work. Do what suits you best. There are a few mothers who choose to express exclusively. They give their baby all the feeds of their expressed milk from the bottle and provide loving closeness as they do so.

## Does it matter if I wean my baby early?

Weaning, particularly during the first three months, should not be undertaken lightly because breastmilk suits the baby's digestion in a way that no substitute can match and provides antibodies to some diseases which the young baby is not yet able to make. In addition, weaning may be emotionally upsetting for both the mother and her baby. Breastfeeding for at least six months is a worthy health goal. When weaning occurs later it is likely to be less disruptive for both the mother and her baby if it is done gradually. The older baby may or may not be weaned onto a bottle – your baby may manage a cup but it is usually easier to use a bottle. However, the young baby will need to be bottle-fed. Abrupt weaning is to be avoided if at all possible – however, it may be necessary in the event of severe illness in a mother or baby, or if there is lengthy separation of the mother and her baby for some other reason. Usually a baby who suddenly becomes ill has a particular need to continue with breastmilk.

Unwanted weaning can distress mothers. They may suffer feelings of disappointment and failure. It has been suggested by Ruth Lawrence in her book *Breastfeeding* that the effect in emergency weaning of a sudden drop in prolactin levels in the mother (prolactin is thought to contribute to a feeling of wellbeing) may cause hormone withdrawal syndrome and that this may be associated with depression. If so the mother will be in need of help and sympathetic support.

If abrupt weaning is unavoidable look for experienced advice and support. Observe your baby's behaviour. Particular care must be taken of your breasts to prevent engorgement and to avoid mastitis. Although there may be compelling reasons for some mothers to wean early, others do so because they lack correct information and doubt their capability to continue breastfeeding.

The following table may help to dispel some false beliefs which can lead to unnecessary weaning.

| False beliefs | Reality |
|---|---|
| Because mature breastmilk is bluish-white and looks 'weak and watery' it must be 'no good' for babies | The change in appearance from yellow and creamy (colostrum) to thin bluish-white (mature breastmilk) is normal; the composition is always fully suited to the baby |
| Unexpected signs of hunger in the baby mean that the mother is 'losing her milk' | Most likely increased hunger is due to the baby's continuing growth. An increase of the supply by frequent feeding is all that is needed |
| Bottle feeding with formula is easier and trouble free, and breastfeeding is time-consuming | Formula is a substitute which may bring problems. It is costly and takes time and effort to prepare, store and give |
| It is not possible to continue and hold down a job | Expressed breastmilk can provide food for a breastfeeding baby while mother is at work |

## *Managing gradual weaning*

If circumstances are such that you must wean early, try to do this gradually over two weeks at least. Even taking a week would be much less traumatic than an immediate or abrupt weaning. The more time that you can allow, the easier the change is likely to be for your baby and for you. Approached slowly and carefully, weaning is usually trouble free, but the aim of management is to minimise any disturbances while substituting formula for breastmilk.

If upsets do occur, the mother may feel emotionally upset, especially if the weaning is unwanted or unplanned; the mother may also have problems with over-full breasts.

**The baby may:**
- find separation from the breast upsetting
- reject the teat, disliking the feel of it instead of the nipple
- have difficulty learning to use the teat – a different sucking technique is needed, with no help from let-down
- have some digestive upset with the formula.

**You can practise with the teat before introducing the formula using the following guidelines.**
- Choose a time when the baby is relaxed and happy, preferably a little hungry, two or three days before starting to wean, and offer your baby some expressed breastmilk in the bottle.
- Relax yourself and make a game of it – let the baby set the pace.
- Have around 30 millilitres of breastmilk already expressed. Start with 10 or 15 millilitres in the bottle in case the baby refuses to suck on the teat.
- Put a few drops of breastmilk on the teat and let the baby lick and mouth it.
- Offer more if the baby takes it.
- Now offer the ordinary breastfeed.
- Repeat at other times.

If you have any problems seek professional help. If you feel that the formula you are using does not suit the baby, talk again to your early childhood nurse or doctor before changing the formula. It may also help to share your feelings with others. Try to have someone known to the baby give the bottle-feed if the baby resists taking it from you. Do not re-use any formula left in the bottle at the next feed.

## Preparing for the actual changeover

(See Chapter 16 for information on bottle-feeding and the equipment you will want.)

**You can discuss the following with your health adviser:**

- a formula appropriate for the baby's age – many paediatricians advise against any unmodified cow's milk before babies are twelve months of age
- the amount of formula the baby is likely to need each 24 hours; the amount to offer at each feeding will depend on the number of feeds you usually give, and the baby's age, weight and condition
- the checks to be made on the baby's growth and condition
- proper care for yourself, your breasts and also your emotions.

## A possible program

Here is a possible timetable for a baby having five feeds, substituting an additional bottle-feed for a breastfeed after every second day. The 6 p.m. feed on day one and again on day two, then the other feeds successively on days three, five, seven and nine.

| Days | 6 a.m. | 10 a.m. | 2 p.m. | 6 p.m. | 10 p.m. |
|------|--------|---------|--------|--------|---------|
| 1 and 2 | Breast | Breast | Breast | Bottle | Breast |
| 3 and 4 | Breast | Bottle | Breast | Bottle | Breast |
| 5 and 6 | Breast | Bottle | Bottle | Bottle | Breast |
| 7 and 8 | Breast | Bottle | Bottle | Bottle | Bottle |
| 9 | Bottle | Bottle | Bottle | Bottle | Bottle |

If you can allow the time and wish to do so you can make the changes even more gradual – you could have each stage above taking four days instead of two. If you must wean within a week you can replace another breastfeed with the bottle on each successive day. If the baby is taking more than five feeds each day, simply extend the timetable to complete the changes.

If you have some stored breastmilk you need not waste it. It is quite acceptable to give mixed feeds of formula and breastmilk in the same bottle. For example, in a 180-millilitre feed you could mix together 90 millilitres of each.

As you are changing to the formula you will notice a change in the stools. The soft yellowish stools from breastmilk become firmer, change colour and their smell becomes more offensive. It is usually necessary for a baby to have at least one daily bowel motion once formula is introduced, to prevent stools from becoming hard.

Watch for signs of sensitivity or allergy (see 'Food sensitivity (allergy and intolerance)' in Chapter 21). If you are able to visit an early childhood clinic you can have the baby's weight and general condition checked and will be able to discuss any concerns you may have.

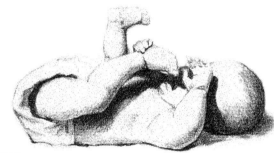

15

# Expressing, using and storing breastmilk

**T**here may be times when you will want to give your baby some of your expressed breastmilk. You can remove milk from your breasts by expressing it either by hand or by using a breast pump (manual or electric). It is wise to learn how to do it. You could learn from your midwife, preferably after the birth of the baby or later from a health adviser experienced in breastfeeding.

As your milk 'comes in' you can ask for information about expressing and have the techniques demonstrated by the midwives who attend you. You can express one breast at a time or both simultaneously. When hand expressing it is easier to catch the milk if you use a wide-necked container. It is better to use a plastic container as some valuable components of the breastmilk can be lost if you use glass since they stick to it. You will need to refrigerate or chill the expressed breastmilk, although breastmilk can be kept at room temperature for six hours for a well baby if necessary. If you express at work and there is no refrigerator you could place it in an ice box. As soon as you return home label the container with the date and time of expression. There is detailed information about storing breastmilk in this chapter.

**You may wish to express breastmilk for any of the following reasons:**

- to make it easier for the baby to attach to a very full breast
- to relieve discomfort from over-full breasts or to free a blocked duct
- to rest very sore or cracked nipples
- to increase your milk supply
- to feed a low birth-weight or sick baby who is in hospital or at home. It may help to have a photo of the baby beside you as you express. Some women find it helps to have an item of their baby's clothing that smells like the baby near them. Sometimes, too, having your partner give you a neck massage while you express or looking at the milk and visualising giving this milk to the baby can help trigger let-downs to while expressing.
- to store milk ahead of any separation from your baby so that breastmilk continues to be given
- to continue regular removal of milk from your breasts, if you are separated from your baby, so that you maintain your lactation
- to take a medication that may mean you cannot breastfeed during that time. That is, use previously stored expressed milk during the period when you require medication. Continue to express to maintain supply but discard the milk as advised by your doctor.

When, how much and how often you express will depend on the reason for doing so and on your supply. There are babies who are fully fed with their mothers' expressed milk for many months.

# When to express

If possible use fresh breastmilk for the baby (see below, 'Storing expressed breastmilk').

If you wish to leave one feed of breastmilk for someone to give the baby, express about 20 millilitres before each feed during the 24 hours prior to the outing. If you feel that you are taking too much you can express around 20 millilitres in the early hours of the morning and at the following morning feed when you usually have most milk. Then express at the end of the later feeds. If there is very little left at these later feeds then express an hour later. Usually there is still time for the breasts to supply more milk ready for the baby's next feed.

If you are expressing all your milk – perhaps for a premature or sick baby at home or in hospital – you will need to do so frequently, particularly as you begin, possibly two to three hourly during the day. As lactation is established you can expect to manage with three hourly expressing during the day and four hourly at night. It is important to express at least once in the night. If you are resting cracked nipples, three to four hourly will probably be enough. Be guided by the midwives caring for you and the baby.

# How to express

You can express either by hand or breast pump. Remember that cleanliness is most important. Remember these guidelines:

- Wash hands well.
- Wash everything which will come in contact with the breastmilk thoroughly in hot soapy water and then rinse well.
- Prevent any contamination of the expressed milk and store it safely.
- Handle breasts and nipples gently to avoid any damage.
- If stimulating let-down use finger and thumb to gently stroke the breast and 'roll' the nipple. It may take five to seven minutes before the let-down occurs, especially if you are away from your baby. Some mothers stimulate both sides at once. When the let-down occurs express either by hand or pump.

- Having someone doing gentle neck massage while you express aids your let-down reflex.
- Move to the other breast as the flow slows. Repeat the nipple rolling if necessary. You can keep moving from one breast to the other while you express milk.

## Expressing by hand

Don't be put off or dissuaded from expressing by hand. It is a learnt skill and takes practice, but once mastered hand expressing is reliable and easy to do. If you do use a breast pump be sure that it is comfortable and does not cause or increase soreness.

As you practise you will soon learn to coordinate the gentle pressing and relaxing action needed to express breastmilk. The muscles in your fingers will strengthen and expressing will become less tiring. It is very helpful to watch another mother expressing by hand. If you can attend an ABA group while you are pregnant someone may be willing to demonstrate. After your baby is born the midwives will help you.

At first you may find that you are able to express a few millilitres only at a time – do not become discouraged. As you become skilled it will become easier. When learning to express you may find it helpful to do some expressing under the shower, particularly if you are expressing to relieve over-full breasts or a blocked duct.

You may find it easiest if you rest the container either on a pillow, on your lap, or on a table. Lean over as you express. Be prepared to stimulate a let-down unless it comes readily.

**Steps to take as you hand express:**
- Use either hand to express breasts.
- Place the index finger beneath the nipple and 2 or 3 centimetres back. Rest the thumb just behind or on the outer edge of the areola above the nipple. Support the breast with the other fingers.
- Press the thumb and forefinger back into the breast towards your ribs, and rhythmically squeeze finger and thumb together, milking the sinuses beneath the areola.

✐ Repeat, moving your hand around the areola so you are not always pressing on the same area – continue gentle, rhythmic squeezing and releasing. Don't chafe the skin. You can change from breast to breast several times in order to express the milk from both. Swap hands or pause for a rest if your hands tire. Always have a small towel to dry the hands if they become slippery as you are expressing.

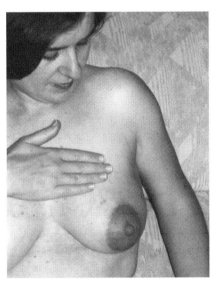
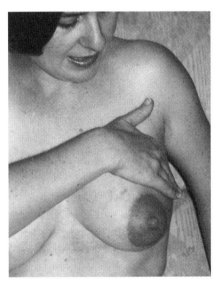
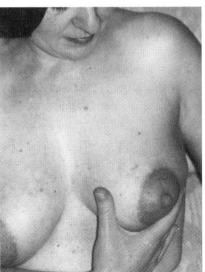
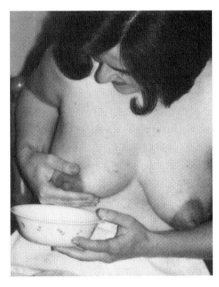

Choose the method you will use to express your milk. If you have a copious supply then, at a feed when the breasts feel full, you can express one breast while the baby feeds on the other. Using this technique the milk flow is automatically stimulated by the baby feeding. It does take some practice.

As the baby finishes on the first breast, stop expressing. Offer the baby what is left in the one you have been expressing. If still hungry offer the first breast again and then if necessary, give the baby what is needed from the milk you have taken. Within an hour there will be more milk there for you to express.

### Breast pumps

If you can, visit a pharmacy and look at and discuss the properties of the various models of breast pumps or talk to your midwife or child health nurse. It is important to learn the skill of hand expressing early, so ask your midwife to teach you before you leave hospital or before you are discharged from your midwifery service.

The electric pumps are either mains or battery driven. The container and any part of the pump which is in contact with the milk must be washed thoroughly in hot soapy water. With some larger electrical pumps it is possible to express both breasts together. The funnel fits over the nipple and the areola onto the breast. The milk is removed by the alternating pressures. Take care that you do not press the funnel too firmly onto the breasts compressing the ducts and/or sinuses. Most mothers find using a pump less tiring than hand expressing. There will be breast pumps in the maternity unit – probably electric. As your milk 'comes in' you can ask for a demonstration of both the mechanical and the hand-operated pumps.

A hand-operated pump has two plastic tubes, one fitted within the other. It works by creating a vacuum. The inner tube with a rubber flange on the end (to tighten the fit) opens into a funnel which is placed over the nipple and areola. You gently pull the outer tube in and out rhythmically to extract the milk, which collects in this outer tube. These are comparatively inexpensive, easy to clean and simple to operate but can tire the hands as you use them. More popular are the small, battery-operated hand pumps. These can be useful for a mother who is lactating well and who needs to supply some expressed milk only occasionally or who may sometimes need to express where there is no handy power supply. They are very low powered and may not provide enough stimulation if used exclusively. Don't forget: you do not need to use the teat and bottle provided with the pump to feed your baby. It is better to give your baby your milk from a cup or spoon if they are breastfeeding.

More costly at present are the small electric pumps which have a hole at the base of the flange. You close this hole with a finger to create the suction. By rhythmically opening and closing this you can control the pressure. Following let-down you can expect a good flow of milk.

The larger electric pumps are usually very efficient. The timing is fixed but you set the pressure at something lower than 200 mmHg (pumps now prevent pressure exceeding 200 mmHg). Follow the instructions carefully. As you start expressing, begin with low pressure. As the flow of milk increases you can slowly increase the pressure. Aim for the maximum level at which you feel comfortable – this is best for milk ejection and optimal pumping. The foremilk is soon removed from the breasts and obtaining the rest will depend on strong and reliable let-down (or let-downs). You may need to stop pumping while you stimulate a let-down by rolling the nipple. Look for experienced help as you learn to use it.

The advantage of the electric pumps is that they can leave you with one hand free to massage the breast as the pump expresses, to hold a book or a drink. These pumps are often hired because they are expensive to buy. The Australian Breastfeeding Association (ABA) and many pharmacies offer them for hire. If you choose to buy, it is worth inspecting the various pumps available. New models keep coming onto the market. An advertisement in the 'Wanted to buy' section in the ABA newsletter or in your local paper or posted on the Internet may result in a good bargain-priced electric pump but make sure that the pump is electrically sound.

The let-down may or may not occur easily when you begin to use the pump. It may be slow because the funnel of the breast pump fits over the nipple and areola onto the breast and the nipple and the nerve endings in it are not stimulated by direct contact as they are when the baby starts to feed or as you hand express. Do not increase the pressure since this will not help and can be harmful. You can use any of the methods discussed to help a slow let-down (see 'Difficulties with let-down' in Chapter 21). The nipple-rolling technique is simple to use and many mothers find it works well. As the milk lets down and starts to flow you can hand express the first few millilitres before attaching the pump. Now the pump, with its alternating pressure together with the suction, can be expected to remove the milk.

If you are using an electric pump which can express both breasts simultaneously it will save you time (this is known as doing a 'double pump'). When expressing each breast separately, as the flow slows to a few drops repeat the nipple rolling to obtain another flow then move to the other breast and repeat this. Your breasts may feel soft but there may still be milk to express. Stop when you can stimulate no further flow. Ask for help if you need it.

When you have finished using the pump it is a good idea to see if you can express any more milk by hand as this helps to fully drain the breasts.

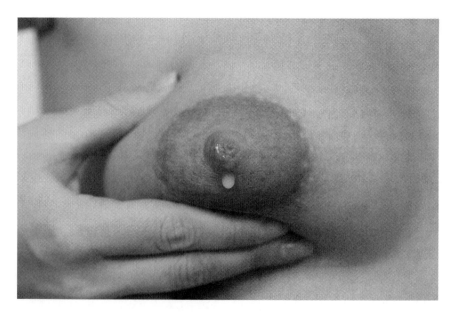

## How often should you express?

This will depend on your reason for doing so. You will discover what is necessary. If the baby needs to be fully fed on expressed breastmilk – the baby may be premature, in hospital or unable to breastfeed for some other reason – then routine expressing will be necessary. As you start expressing you will get more milk by expressing every two to three hours through the day. When the breasts are used to it, three to four hourly expressing may be enough. More frequent and longer sessions can increase supply.

One night expression is recommended as it is known that night-time pumping is good for maintaining supply. It is unlikely that you will need to express more often at night but be guided by your individual experience and the baby's needs. Breast tissue becomes distended if more than six hours elapses between expressing, and lactational amenorrhoea will be affected if more than four to six hours lapses between expressing.

## Expressing and your milk supply

The breasts replace whatever milk is removed, whether by your baby or by expressing. This means that you can maintain your established supply even if you and your baby are separated, by expressing to match the recent pattern of removal by your baby. Furthermore, you can increase your supply by expressing to empty the breasts more often than is occurring at present, either by baby's efforts or by expressing (see 'Low milk supply' in Chapter 21).

Both these abilities – to maintain and to increase supply – enable you to provide breastmilk for a carer to give your baby during separations from you. If the baby is premature or ill the separation may be long with no direct breastfeeding; if you are working, the separation is usually for two or three feeds at a time (see 'How can I continue breastfeeding after I return to work?' in Chapter 14). Careful planning is needed for expressing, storage and transport of the breastmilk to be done over several months.

Discuss with your employer the need to express and store your milk. It is best for you to have the use of a quiet, private, comfortable area and access to a refrigerator. If there is no fridge you will need an insulated container with ice bricks. Some workplaces are very supportive of breastfeeding mothers and arrange for the necessary breaks. Some workplaces are less so but no woman should have to use the toilet for expressing. If there is a staff room you may be able to use a small screen for privacy when expressing and then store the screen in a corner. It is useful to check your workplace agreement for your entitlements in relation to breastfeeding.

## How much milk will be needed for each feed?

Most women produce about 800 millilitres to 1 litre of milk each day once their lactation is established. The approximate volume of milk to be offered at each feed can be worked out from the total intake over 24 hours. It is accepted currently that all babies up to six months of age need approximately 150 millilitres of breastmilk daily per kilogram of body weight. So take your baby's weight, multiply it by 150 and divide this total intake by the number of feeds the baby is having in each 24 hours. This is the volume of the average feed; it is what to offer to begin with. Feeds should still be on demand so some feeds will be larger and some smaller and more frequent. **Example:** if your baby weighs 4 kilograms and is having six feeds daily then offer 4 x 150 ÷ 6 = 100 ml.

You will soon discover whether this is the right amount for your baby. To be on the safe side have some extra on hand (in a smaller pack to avoid waste). As your baby grows and needs more milk, you will have to provide more, by increasing your supply. How to do this is described in detail in 'How to increase your supply' in Chapter 21.

## Storing expressed breastmilk

To prevent changes in the composition of the milk and a loss of some of its immune properties, use sterile feeding bottles or containers made of hard plastic. If glass is used fat globules adhere to the surface and fat-soluble vitamins can be lost. The containers need screw-on tops. Avoid tops or lids with fixed washers or pads in the lid which may be hard to clean. You can freeze the milk in a sterile plastic ice cube tray which is placed in a refrigerator storage bag, or you can use special polyethylene bags manufactured for the purpose. These are available at pharmacies. Bags and containers should be no more than three-quarters full because the fluid expands as it freezes.

Mark the time of expression on any chilled milk you plan to use within 24 hours. Mark the date on any container you freeze.

The following is the advice offered by the National Health and Medical Research Council (NHMRC) in 'Dietary Guidelines for Children and Adolescents in Australia incorporating the Infant Feeding Guidelines for Health Workers' 2003.

| | | |
|---|---|---|
| Room temperature less than 26°C | Store in the coolest position available | 6–8 hours |
| Refrigerator less than 4°C | Store in the back where the temperature is most stable | 3–5 days |
| Freezer compartment (no separate door to main refrigerator) | Store in the back where the temperature is most stable | 2 weeks |
| Freezer compartment (separate door) | Store in the back where the temperature is most stable | 3 months |
| Deep freeze less than –18°C | | 6–12 months |

## Using stored breastmilk

✐ Thaw frozen breastmilk quickly. Start by using cold running water which you make warmer as the milk is thawing. Shake the container and stand it in a jug with warmer water until the milk is warmed.

✐ It is not recommended to use a microwave oven to thaw or warm breastmilk for two reasons. Firstly the baby is at risk of scalding as it can heat unevenly and the bottle will feel cooler than the milk within it. Secondly the microwave may alter the composition of the milk.

✐ Before using expressed milk which has been standing, shake it well – it separates into layers but remixes easily.

✐ If you think the baby may take only a little, offer small quantities separately so that there is minimum waste. You can give more if necessary. Store some 60 millilitre lots for this purpose. It is disheartening to have to discard precious breastmilk that the baby does not drink. It is necessary to throw out any expressed breastmilk which is left in the bottle.

## Giving the expressed milk

Decide how you will give the expressed milk. The method you use can depend on the reason for giving it and the amount to be given. You can choose between a supply line, a small cup, a medicine measure (even very young babies can learn to drink from a small cup or medicine measure), spoon, dropper or bottle (see 'Complementary feeding' in Chapter 21).

If breastfeeding is well established you might choose to use a bottle and teat but remember that a different technique is used when sucking from a teat than when breastfeeding and the baby might fuss when put back to the breast – there is information on giving a bottle feed in Chapter 16.

In any of these ways you can top up an inadequate feed, replace an occasional whole feed or replace several feeds routinely when you are separated from your baby.

# Care of breasts and nipples

| Remember | Why |
|---|---|
| To examine the breasts for lumps, blocked ducts or tender spots. If found check 'Blockages in Ducts' in Chapter 21 | Areas of poor drainage may predispose the breasts to infection |
| That breast tissue bruises easily | Bumps or pressure can be damaging. Watch for knocks from active toddlers |
| To correctly position and attach the baby and allow unrestricted feeding | Protects nipples from injury and helps good drainage |
| To alternate the breast with which you start each feed | Ensures regular complete drainage and stimulation of both breasts |
| To keep breasts and nipples clean with a daily shower, but avoid soap on the nipples. Dry with a soft towel | Soap removes the natural protective oils and keratin on nipples |
| To change breast pads as needed. Men's handkerchiefs, which must be very well washed, work well as pads | Sogginess predisposes to infection |
| You can express some hind milk at the end of a feed. Allow it to dry on the nipples | Protects and helps healing if necessary |
| To avoid creams or ointments. If your nipples are dry or not supple you could try purified lanolin. Check that you are not sensitive to it | Some ointments retain moisture leading to sogginess. You or the baby may be sensitive to some creams |

# 16

# Formula (bottle) feeding

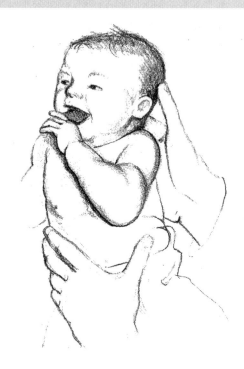

**B**reastfeeding is best for your baby, but if for some medical reason you have been advised to discontinue breastfeeding, you will need to formula-feed your baby. Some women may choose not to establish breastfeeding. Artificial baby milks are commercially produced foods, usually a powder with a cow's milk base that requires a safe water source for reconstitution. To ensure the baby's proper development the bottle should be given with close contact and interaction between baby and mother. This will also help to overcome the sadness and sense of loss that may be felt by a mother who for some compelling reason has had to forgo breastfeeding.

Some women may have an undersupply despite all efforts to increase their supply and may need to supplement their babies with formula.

If formula-feeding from birth your health advisers will be available to answer questions and help you. If you are planning to bottle-feed from birth you will need to choose the formula and have this ready with feeding equipment for when your baby is born. Full bottle-feeding may begin immediately after birth or you may take a few days giving both bottle and some breast, progressively decreasing time on the breast until the baby is fully formula-fed. In this way the baby has the protection of the colostrum, which is high in immune factors and stimulates the passage of the meconium. Sucking at the breast will also help your uterus to contract, which will minimise your bleeding after birth – an advantage of breastfeeding.

If you change your mind during those first few days and decide that you do want to breastfeed, it is likely to be easier if the baby has started with the breast. If you are changing to bottle-feeding after returning home, you can talk with an early childhood nurse or speak to your midwife. Weaning during the first three months is discussed in Chapter 14.

If your baby is being established on full formula-feeding it is important that your breasts are cared for while you are suppressing your lactation. Your breasts will become engorged if undertaking a quick suppression. You may need to express for comfort; however, do not remove more milk than necessary as the breasts will replace that which is removed. It is safer to undertake a slow suppression if your lactation is already established, to minimise your risk of mastitis (see 'Breast problems' in Chapter 21).

## Infant formulas

If you are not breastfeeding your baby, commercially produced cow's milk baby formula is recommended. Most formulas can be purchased as dried formula powder to be reconstituted with a clean, safe water supply. If travelling, pre-mixed formulas are available. As the baby grows your maternal and child health nurse will advise you on volumes per feed to ensure adequate growth. From birth, one tin of formula will last approximately six days, which will increase with the baby's increasing needs.

In Australia all infant formulas must comply with the Australian Food Standards Code which uses human milk as the reference. It regulates the composition, the quality and labelling of infant formulas sold in Australia. A baby's formula must provide sufficient kilojoules of energy, the food constituents needed and enough water and be digestible.

It is important to remember to mimic breastfeeding behaviours while formula-feeding to maintain the mother-baby relationship; this can be done by the mother holding her baby close while bottle feeding and switching from side to side to allow baby to see both sides of mother's face while feeding. Babies should never be left alone while bottle feeding. Do not ever prop up a baby's bottle – always hold it yourself.

# Different formulas

When deciding on the formula you wish to use, obtain the information you need from your healthcare adviser before making a choice. It is vital that the formula is reconstituted according to the manufacturer's directions, and all equipment used for formula must be sterilised before use.

## Cow's milk formulas

Most healthy bottle-fed babies are fed formulas based on cow's milk. The proteins whey and casein occur in both human milk and cow's milk, but in different proportions: more whey than casein in breastmilk, but less in cow's milk. The whey protein forms a softer, lighter curd than the thicker, heavier casein curd so it is considered easier for babies to digest.

## Whey-dominant formula

The most frequently used cow's milk formulas for babies are the whey-dominant formulas.

## Soya bean formula

Unless there is a special reason why the baby needs to have a soy milk feeding there is no advantage in giving this. The soy infant formulas contain protein from the soya bean – a vegetable rather than an animal protein. These formulas are more expensive and babies can develop sensitivity or allergy to the soy protein just as they can to cow's milk protein. If you have reason to think that the baby is having problems and needs a soy formula it is important to obtain professional advice before changing.

## Goat's milk formula

Goat's milk formula is sometimes used successfully when a baby is having difficulty tolerating both cow's milk and soy formulas.

## Prescription formula

Babies who are unable to tolerate over-the-counter formulas must be seen urgently by a medical officer. There are several specialised formulas available by prescription which may be required for these babies under medical supervision.

## Formula for older babies

There are 'follow-on' formulas produced for babies over six months of age; they are expensive and unnecessary. You can continue past six months with your usual formula while gradually introducing solid foods. At twelve months you can introduce whole cow's milk. Ask your maternal and child health nurse about the change-over.

# What about extra vitamins?

The vitamins your baby needs are added to the marketed formula when it is produced. You will not need to add more, unless advised by your medical officer.

# Preparing to formula-feed

You will need bottles, teats, one or two measuring jugs, a scoop (which comes in the tin of dried formula), a knife, a funnel, a container with a screw top for teats after they have been sterilised, and a bottle brush.

## Bottles

Heat-tolerant plastic and glass baby feeding bottles are available. If choosing plastic it is recommended you choose BPA-free bottles.

It is recommended to make up each feed as you use it.

## Teats

Baby teats are available in silicone and latex; silicone is considered the safest choice. Teats can be purchased with varying sizes, shapes and flow speeds, from slow to medium to fast. It is important that your baby is able to enjoy the feeds at a pace that enables them to swallow and breathe comfortably. Choose a teat that suits your baby for their age. Have at least three teats in current use.

## Cleaning and sterilising equipment

Equipment used for formula preparation should be kept separate and used for this purpose only. Any items used to formula-feed your baby must be washed well in hot soapy water before sterilising.

Rinse bottles in cold water immediately after feeding. Use hot soapy water and the bottle brush to clean the bottle and carefully clean the ridges that take the screw top. Rinse in clear boiled water. Rinse teats under the cold water tap, turn inside out and rub well. Force water through the hole in the teat to be sure that it is not blocked.

Your equipment is now ready to be sterilised, either by boiling or using a steam steriliser, or using a cold sterilising solution.

### Sterilising by boiling

Immerse all feeding items (except teats) in a large saucepan of cold water, bring to the boil and simmer for five minutes, and then add the washed teats and continue to boil everything for another two or three minutes. Use clean kitchen tongs to remove teats and other items. Keep sterilised feeding equipment in a clean, dry, separate area in your kitchen.

### Steam sterilisers

You can purchase these and you need to follow the manufacturer's instructions to sterilise equipment.

### Sterilising using a cold sterilising solution

This method of sterilising does not destroy some bacteria and yeast spores. You will need a container for the antibacterial solution. Follow the manufacturer's instructions.

## Making up a powdered formula

Your choice of formula will need to be readily available. You can expect to find it at the chemist or the supermarket. Costs vary.

When purchasing the formula check the expiry date on the tin and again when you open it. Write the date of opening on the tin. You can usually then use it for the next 30 days after which you must discard any remaining formula. It is recommended and safest to make up the formula at each feed. Hand hygiene must be attended to. Carefully follow the manufacturer's instructions when making your baby's formula.

**Alert:** adding too much or too little powder will be detrimental to your baby's health.

## Giving the bottle

Never allow your baby to feed from a propped bottle. It is dangerous to prop a bottle, allowing the baby to take the feed without help and while lying down. This can result in the baby inhaling some of the formula, which could choke the baby or lead to a respiratory illness. Formula can also flow through the baby's Eustachian tube and into the middle ear, resulting in an ear infection.

For feelings of security and emotional wellbeing your baby needs to be nursed comfortably and lovingly, mimicking breastfeeding behaviours, with the head higher than the tummy, and to be able to feel the warmth of your body and enjoy suitable stimulation and interaction while looking at their mother's face at feed time.

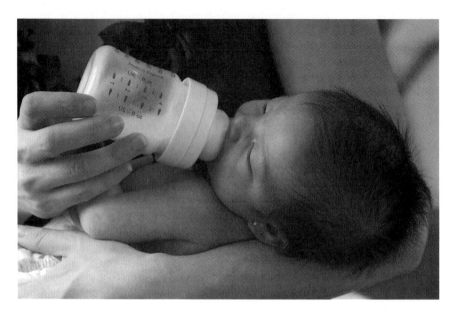

Choose a comfortable chair. As you feed, cuddle your baby. To feed, the baby sucks on the teat to obtain the formula, which is then swallowed. Swallowing and breathing are coordinated. To feed from the teat may take a little practice and when starting bottle-feeding babies sometimes need help and encouragement to learn.

Warm the bottle so that it is lukewarm by standing it in a jug of hot water then test by dropping a little onto your wrist. It is not advised to use a microwave oven to warm the feed as the bottle may feel cooler than the formula within it – it might be hot enough to burn the baby's mouth. Next, follow these steps:

- Check that the rate of flow is suitable – about a drop per second. You can usually adjust the speed of the flow by loosening or tightening the screw top. As your baby sucks, the air must be able to flow in to replace the formula removed; otherwise the teat will flatten, a vacuum will form and the formula will not flow. A slightly loosened screw top will prevent this.
- Touch your baby's cheek next to you so the baby turns to take the bottle.
- As you begin the feed let your baby take the teat well into the mouth.

- Hold the bottle so that the teat is full of formula to prevent your baby sucking in air.
- If your baby seems uncomfortable or starts to lose interest before taking most of the feed, pause and allow the baby to rest for a moment or two. You could try to get up a bubble of wind then offer the bottle again.
- You can change your baby onto your other arm mid-feed – this will allow the baby to see the other side of your face and allows the baby freedom to move the other side of their body around.
- It is important to feed your baby to appetite, however it is essential to ensure your baby is growing and developing adequately.

Feed time can give so much more than food. Enjoy this time together. From the security of your closeness your baby is learning to trust and enjoy the wider world around him or her. As hunger is satisfied the sucking will become slower and the baby may doze off to sleep with the teat still in the mouth; remove it at this time. If not sleepy the baby will simply lose interest in the bottle and push the teat out with the tongue. Once again you can try to bring up any wind.

At the end of the feed, if the baby is awake and alert, have fun together. Babies love the sound of their mother's gentle voice, her smiles and loving touching and stroking. Fathers can support mothers by making some of the formula and settling the baby after feeds. You will very quickly recognise those signs which tell you when the baby has had enough (see 'Recognising a sleepy baby' in Chapter 18). Then it is time to settle the baby to sleep.

While night feeds continue, try to keep the feed as quiet and peaceful as you can (see 'What about night feeding?' in Chapter 14).

## How often, how much?

As with breastfed babies, bottle-fed babies are individuals with their own variable appetites. They too will be happier if strict feeding schedules are not imposed. The new and very young baby may also want frequent feeds. There may be times when your baby will not wish to finish the bottle and others when he or she is clearly hungry at the end of the feed and needs to be offered a little more. Remember: what is more significant is the *total taken over 24 hours,* not what is taken at each feed.

You will soon discover how often your baby needs to feed and how much to give at any particular time. It is usual to start your baby on small but increasing feeds of full strength formula. Amounts to give will be calculated by your midwife. A placid baby who enjoys lengthy sleeps may need less than an active, wakeful baby. A baby who grows quickly in weight and length may need more food. Babies can be affected by the weather and may need more food in cold than in hot weather. Babies can become thirsty in hot weather and may need some cooled, boiled water to quench their thirst. It is good policy to feed according to appetite. It is tempting to try to persuade the baby to empty the bottle at a feed but it is important to allow your baby to be the judge of how much to take at any one time.

When you are at home and the baby takes considerably more or less than the expected quantity, consider the baby's general condition, contentment and growth. Then discuss these observations with your early childhood nurse or doctor so that they can check that the baby is neither overfed nor underfed.

## How do I know my baby is hungry?

Feeding cues in a newborn baby include starting to wake, putting hand to mouth, licking their lips, reaching and searching for their mother, opening their eyes. If not responded to quickly, your baby will cry.

## How will I know that the formula is suitable?

Your baby will:

- take the feeds willingly
- be gaining weight, growing and developing well; body and limbs will be firm and the baby's colour will be good
- have six or more wet nappies of pale urine daily

- have normal stools (faeces or poo) – they can be expected to be of toothpaste consistency and passed at least once daily; the colour will vary according to the formula (see 'Stools' in Chapter 4)
- look well, be bright eyed and contented at the end of the feed.

Your baby can be expected to have periods of crying, to have relaxed and happy, wakeful times too, and to settle to sleep easily when ready to do so. However, thriving babies vary: some may be demanding for no obvious reason, particularly in the early weeks just as breastfed babies can be (see 'The unsettled baby' in Chapter 18).

If you feel that your baby has a problem with bottle-feeding, there is information in Chapter 21. However, discuss it with your maternal and child health nurse or your GP and continue with the same formula until you have done so.

# 17

# Daily care

In your everyday care you will be meeting your baby's needs for: enough suitable food for energy and growth; relief from discomfort; being touched, held and cuddled in close and loving body contact; feelings of safety and security in the environment; and appropriate interaction with people.

Our babies are born helpless and the daily care we provide nurtures them. This care changes to meet the needs of the moment. There is a primary need for enough suitable food for growth and development. Mother's milk can meet all the requirements for at least the first six months (see Chapter 10, 'Feeding your baby').

Babies respond to being touched, held and cuddled in a loving way. Skin-to-skin contact is part of breastfeeding and can be given in bottle-feeding as well. You can hold baby's bare body or cheek against your own and your hands can massage.

Such contact readily gives feelings of security but abrupt handling and sudden loud noises are alarming. Do not leave your baby to cry for long periods (unless 'Red alert!' applies – see Chapter 18) – it is distressing. You will soon know when he or she can wait a little or when instant attention is needed.

Finally there is interaction with you, your partner and other caregivers which begins at birth. It occurs as you touch, hold, share eye-to-eye contact and talk to your baby. As you talk you are laying the foundation for speech. Interaction changes according to the way the baby is feeling and to the age and stage of development. Much will depend on your baby's personality. Your interaction with a placid baby will differ from your interaction with an excitable baby (see Chapter 18) and you will soon be able to recognise what is appropriate at the time. When your baby is uncomfortable you will do your best to ease the discomfort as promptly as possible.

## Handling your baby

New parents often feel anxious about handling their babies. Babies do not break easily and will feel more secure if your gentle touch is firm. Speak before moving your baby, look relaxed and confident. Babies learn to read facial expressions within days. A worried, anxious face may make the baby anxious too.

Remember the baby's in-built fear of falling and the need for firm support of head and body as you move your baby smoothly and slowly. Hold your baby against you for a moment before putting them down again. This can be reassuring.

## Wrapping and swaddling

Some babies don't like to be firmly wrapped. You will soon know what your baby likes. However, wrapping can bring comfort, warmth and a sense of security to many babies and reduces the small, jerky movements that may disturb and waken them. You can use either a

## Wrapping baby with arms out

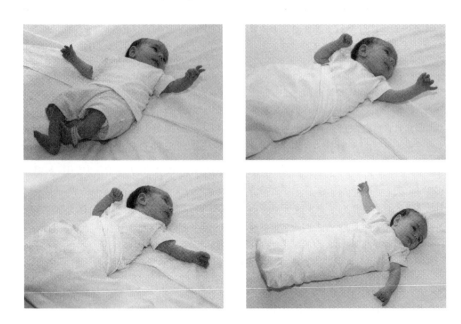

## Wrapping baby with arms in

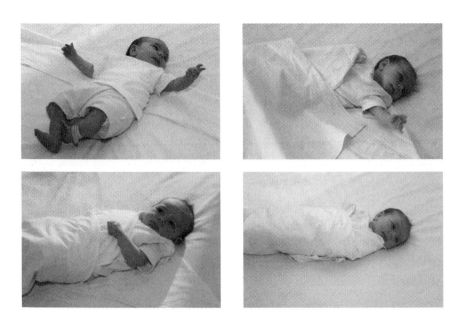

cotton wrap or a light bunny rug. If the weather is warm you can use a cotton sheet or a large gauze nappy. Watch for overheating. (See 'Keeping your baby cool' later in this chapter.)

There is no one right way to wrap a baby. The following description and the illustrations opposite may help. Lay your baby in the centre of the baby blanket with the shoulders just above the top edge of the baby blanket; take one top corner and bring it down diagonally across the body to the knees and tuck under; take the other top corner and fold straight across below the arms and tuck under. You can then fold up the bottom of the wrap over the feet. Put the baby down on his or her back. This lessens the risk of SIDS (see 'SIDS' in Chapter 18).

## Nappy changing

You could have ready:

- a stack of nappies and a tray with nappy pins or other fastenings if using cloth nappies
- packets of disposable nappies
- nappy wipes (you can make washable wipes by cutting up old towels), a small bowl for warm water, soap, washer and towel
- optional items such as cotton wool, powder or cornflour, a jar of baby cream, nappy liners, a box of tissues and a container for used disposable nappies, tissues or wipes
- a nappy bucket with a lid for cloth nappies if you are using those. If you use nappy sanitisers for soaking, follow the instructions carefully. It is not necessary to use these solutions provided you can wash nappies in soap and really hot water (see 'Nappies' in Chapter 1).

While you have the help of your midwife following the birth of your baby it is likely that you will be shown how to fold and put on a nappy. However, many hospitals have only disposable nappies.

When changing or bathing an uncircumcised baby boy, don't pull back the foreskin on the penis as it is attached for the first three or four years. When changing a baby girl wipe her vulva from the top down towards the bottom to lessen the risk of infection.

Your breastfed baby's motion is semi-liquid but you can still rinse most of it off the nappy under the laundry tap or you can purchase a tap squirter which will provide a stronger jet of water. It is usually easy to scrape motions off the nappies of a formula-fed baby into the toilet before rinsing under running water.

Keep your baby comfortable and the skin healthy. If the baby wakens ready for a feed, has healthy skin and only a damp nappy, you can wait until after the feed before changing the nappy. The baby will probably pass urine during or straight after the feed. If your baby's nappy is soiled you can use wipes and/or you may need to use a little soap with the warm water. Rinse and dry well. Check that the skin creases are dry and if you do use powder, use very little. Powder is easy to apply with a cotton ball and less likely to cake in the creases. Mothers who use cornflour find it very soft and silky.

If your baby is unsettled and fretful, changing the nappy might help. A wet nappy, especially cloth, can feel cold and clammy and can be uncomfortable or even painful if the skin is reddened or if there is a nappy rash. Flannel or woollen nappy pants help to keep the baby warm. Changing the nappy brings you into contact with your baby which the baby is likely to find reassuring and comforting. Babies enjoy some time kicking without a nappy – perhaps on a rug on the floor. Be sure there is no draught and that the room is warm. Remember to always wash your hands well after nappy changing.

## Bathing

The bath and bench need to be at a comfortable height for you to prevent back strain. Although many babies love bath time, some do not. Babies do not have to be bathed daily. Also it can be very taxing for the mother/carer to bath the infant daily. New babies in particular may be distressed by nakedness and the bath. They can be kept clean and comfortable if washed carefully with a cloth and warm water.

Bath time should be a happy time for you both so don't be in a hurry. Let your baby learn to enjoy it. Choose the right time to bath the baby. Some babies are happy to be bathed before a feed but if they are hungry they may protest angrily, a misery for you both. If bathed immediately after a feed the baby may be too sleepy to enjoy it or may spill a little or vomit. Some babies love a bath after feeding. They feel sociable and ready to play and may not spill a drop of their feed. The baby may be happier bathed between feeds or in the evening. Often fathers like to share this time in the evening. Remember that babies are creatures of habit so it is wise to generally give the bath around the same time on a regular basis. However, there may be times when you wish to bath your baby at a different time.

**There are many different ways of bathing a baby. This is a description of one way:**

- Avoid draughts – close the window and door and do not let your baby become cold.
- Do not leave your baby alone on a bench or in the bath. If you are interrupted, wrap the baby in the towel and take with you or place in the cot.
- Always put the cold water into the bath first. If you are using your bath, a large sink or a laundry tub, run some cold water through the hot

tap after the hot water has been added. Make the water quite warm, not just tepid. Make it deep enough for your baby to float and move in. You can test the temperature of the water with your wrist before placing the baby in the bath.

*C* Place your baby on a large towel and remove clothes. To remove the outer garment first gently take out the arms. If you need to take it over the head, gather up the front of it and lift it cleanly over the head without touching face and eyes. Talk to your baby quietly, handle gently but firmly. Keep your voice soft and reassuring and your expression calm and smiling. The baby will be quick to pick up signs of anxiety in you and likewise will feel safe if your body language is confident. If the baby shows any signs of becoming upset, wrap the towel firmly around the body.

*C* Leave nappy and bootees on and wrap the baby firmly in the towel.

*C* Wipe baby's eyes with a piece of cotton gauze moistened with clear water. Wipe from the inside corner out – if you need to wipe again use another moist piece and repeat. Use a clean piece for the second eye.

*C* Now wipe your baby's face gently with a damp face cloth and pat dry with the face towel.

*C* Avoid cleaning inside the mouth. Don't use cotton buds to clean ears because cotton buds can push wax deeper into the ears and can damage the ear if inserted too far or the baby moves suddenly. Wait until the wax comes out far enough to simply wipe it away. If there is mucus in the nose, it is likely to be sneezed out, but if it appears to be troublesome you can twist a little dampened cotton wool to a point then gently insert this a short distance and twist it to pick up and lift out the mucus.

*C* Provided your baby's skin is not sensitive to soap, you can wash the head using a good lather on your hands. (As an alternative you can use aqueous cream.) Massage and wash the scalp well using the palms of your hands. Do this firmly unless the head is tender following birth. Don't avoid the fontanelles (the soft spots). They are covered by strong membrane which has already protected the baby's brain during birth. If the whole scalp is not washed thoroughly cradle cap – greasy, yellow-brown scales – can develop and spread (see 'Cradle cap' in Chapter 20). It is likely that the baby will enjoy having their head washed.

- Avoid getting soap in the eyes or if you do, rinse freely with clear water.

- Rinse the soap off the scalp with the baby still firmly wrapped in the large towel. Support the whole body on your arm and hold the head in your hand and tuck the body under your armpit, holding the baby close to your body. With the head held over the bath rinse the scalp thoroughly. Return the baby to the table and dry their head with a small towel.

- Loosen the large towel and remove nappy and bootees. Re-soap your hands making sure that they do not feel cold, and smooth them over the whole body in a flowing movement, first the chest and tummy and then the back, legs and arms.

- Cover your baby with the towel while you wipe your hands before lifting the baby into the bath. Soap on the hands makes them slippery.

- If you are right-handed support the head on your left wrist and with your left hand grasp the left armpit firmly. Slip the other hand under the bottom, grasping the left thigh with finger and thumb and move the baby gently and slowly into the bath, remembering babies' very real fear of falling. If you are left-handed reverse the procedure and support the head with the right hand – you can practise this while in hospital.

- Don't splash a young or timid baby. If happy, allow the baby time to enjoy the bath. Babies often move their hands and arms and kick their legs as they enjoy the buoyancy of the water as you rinse the soap off. Some babies become tense. They can be covered with a large washer or even a cloth nappy. They may be more relaxed if turned onto their tummies. In this position the chin is held in the palm of the hand to keep the face clear of the water. *Be sure to keep the mouth clear of the bath water.* Many anxious babies relax when they are bathed this way.

- Lift the baby out smoothly onto the large towel. Gather up the towel and pat dry, paying special attention to the creases. Turn the baby onto the side and dry the back.

✐ Remove the damp towel and dress – singlet first followed by the nappy. Avoid dragging garments over the baby's face. Gather them up and lift them clear. Talk happily to your baby as you do this. You will quickly work out a bathing routine which suits you both.

# Cutting the nails

Do not cut the baby's nails until they have grown to the stage where they can scratch their face. When necessary it is best done when your baby is relaxed and sleepy or even asleep.

Hold the hand or foot firmly; curl the fingers into the fist and extend one finger at a time. Use small scissors with round-tipped blades (which can be bought) and cut straight across. Take care not to cut the quick, which grows to the top of the finger. You may find it easier if another person helps with the holding.

# Keeping your baby comfortable

Babies have only a limited ability to regulate their own body temperature. Therefore, during fluctuations in weather it is necessary to be aware of your baby's needs and adapt as necessary.

## *Keeping your baby warm*

Babies need to be kept warm, but not hot. The younger they are the less they are able to regulate their own body temperature. It is important that they are not exposed to chilling. Unless warm they will not be relaxed and comfortable. We know ourselves how restless we feel when we are cold at night – our sleep is disturbed. Like ours, a baby's body will take whatever energy it has to keep warm and then use what is left for other bodily activities.

A room temperature of around 20°C is usually best for babies provided they are dressed and covered. There will be individual differences in the clothing and covering that each baby needs. You will alter these depending on the temperature and season. Usually babies need a singlet, nappy, gown or stretch suit and bootees. Some like to be wrapped in a bunny rug. You can cover with a sheet and light blanket.

If it is cold, it is generally better to add additional clothing such as a woollen cardigan rather than use extra blankets and wrappings. This is less likely to lead to overheating, but check regularly. Make up the bed so your baby's feet almost touch the end and the baby can't slip down beneath the covers and become too hot.

The first signs that a baby is not warm enough are usually restlessness and crying. Breathing is likely to become faster and the skin may begin to feel cool or cold to touch. To test if your baby is too cool or too hot, touch the skin at the back of the neck. The hands, often uncovered, may often feel cool and are not the best indication of the body temperature. When we know what to check and are aware of changes in behaviour and appearance, we are likely to recognise when extra warmth is needed.

If you are out with your baby when it is cold or windy, you will need to put on a warm hat as babies lose heat rapidly through their heads. Dress and cover appropriately. Woollen garments and covers are warmer than synthetics. If you are putting the baby outside in the pram, choose a spot protected from a cold wind.

When the environment is so cold that the body's ability to produce heat fails, babies become quiet and still; the whole body becomes colder to the touch. The chilling becomes a medical emergency if it progresses to the point where the baby is not just cool but so cold that limbs become soft and floppy and the baby lethargic. Feet and hands may look reddened and they may swell. The baby is unlikely to have enough energy to feed. At this stage babies need more than extra covers to help them. The best and quickest way to warm a chilled baby is to take the baby into bed with you and hold the naked body against yours in skin-to-skin contact with a warmed cover over you both. Get medical help.

## *Keeping your baby cool*

Babies seem to take longer than adults to feel uncomfortable in rising temperatures but they can become distressed if they become too hot. As previously mentioned, overheating is a risk factor for SIDS. Well babies become overheated if wearing more clothing than they need, if

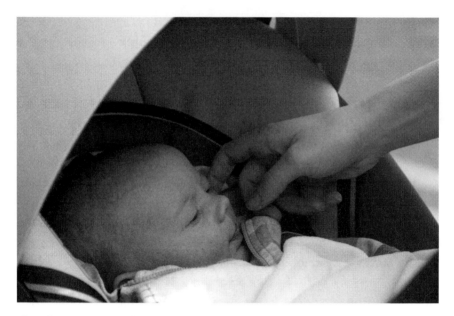

they have too much cover, if they are exposed to very hot weather or an overheated room or car.

It is best not to have hot sun shining directly on a stationary pram, bassinet or stroller. If you are pushing a pram or stroller, always be aware of the sun's direction. It is distressing to see babies with the full sun on their faces when they are being pushed in a pram or stroller. Those with handles which can move from front to back are ideal as they can change the way the baby is facing. Never leave the baby unattended in the car. Don't allow the baby to sleep on an electric blanket because of the risk of overheating, dehydration, burns or electrocution. Hot water bottles are also dangerous. Quilts are not recommended as babies and infants can readily overheat beneath them or even suffocate.

It is generally unwise to have young babies on the beach in the middle of a hot day, even under an umbrella or beach shelter. In addition to the direct sun, rays are reflected off the white sand and the water and a baby can easily become overheated and sunburnt. It is safer and more comfortable for them to be taken onto the beach in the early morning or evening. Keep in mind the possibility of sand fly and/or mosquito bites. Insect repellents may irritate the baby's skin. A mosquito net is preferable but not fine enough to protect from sand flies.

In heatwave conditions you need to take steps to maintain the baby's comfort in whatever way you can. Remember to provide extra fluid – breastmilk if breastfed or cool, boiled water if bottle-fed. If you do not have air-conditioning, a fan in the room will keep air circulating and if the fan is directed onto a wet towel draped over a chair it will further cool the room. Re-wet the towel as it dries. However, don't direct the fan onto the baby. Waterproof mattress protectors are hot. The baby will be more comfortable if you cover the mattress with a woolly blanket and then a sheet. They allow greater air circulation and can be washed when necessary.

If your baby looks and feels hot or is fretful, sponge or bath with tepid water. If the baby has already had a bath do not use soap again as this may be too drying for the skin. You can dress the baby in just a nappy and perhaps a singlet. If it is safe you can put the baby on a mattress on the floor as there will be more air circulating there than there will be in a bassinet or pram. If the baby is in a woven cane bassinet with a lining you can remove the lining. The hallway or the bathroom may be the coolest part of the house.

## Suitable clothing

Adapt the clothing to the temperature in the house or to the weather if you are taking the baby outside. Often it is necessary to start the day with extra garments and then, as it becomes warmer, to remove a jumper or cardigan. Try feeling your baby's body and feet with your hand. If just warm the baby is probably comfortably dressed. Unless it is hot you may need to use bootees. Babies' feet can become cold easily.

In heatwave conditions you might use a cotton singlet or shirt. Remember that synthetic clothing can be very hot. Just a nappy may be enough but be ready to add more if the temperature begins to fall. Gauze nappies are the coolest. Avoid plastic pants as they will make the baby hotter and may cause nappy rash. Watch for a decrease in the number of wet nappies. Urine should be clear and pale.

## *Breastfeeding in very hot weather*

- Breastfeed the baby more frequently.
- Choose the coolest part of the house in which to breastfeed – mothers have sometimes successfully fed an uninterested baby in the bath.
- Reduce heat by lessening skin-to-skin contact. Have the baby on a pillow on your lap. You can place a thin sheet over your arm and between the baby's body and yours during a feed. This will reduce the transfer of heat between you. You might prefer to feed with the baby lying beside but not against you.
- Offer the breast if the baby is fretful between feeds. Small extra drinks can ease thirst. It is not usually necessary to give boiled water to the fully breastfed baby, particularly in the first few weeks while you are establishing breastfeeding. However, if you feel that the baby is not content with a few moments at the breast between regular feeds, you could offer a little tepid boiled water, preferably from a cup or spoon.

## *Bottle-feeding in the heat*

As with breastfeeding, choose the coolest part of the house when giving the feed. You can try feeding the baby on a pillow on your lap, the floor or lounge. Bottle-fed babies often need drinks of tepid, boiled water between their regular feeds. You can offer 30 to 60 millilitres or a little more if the baby wants it. It is important not to give so much that it decreases the appetite for the next feed.

# Baby massage

Baby massage has been practised in many cultures since ancient times. It can stimulate a baby but also soothe and relieve stress by relaxing muscles, easing pain and providing comfort. Massage allows skin-to-skin contact and loving interaction. We instinctively lovingly stroke and pat our babies and it is likely that we do this often. Baby's physical and emotional health requires such touch. You could include in your daily or weekly routine an all-over body massage, which is likely to provide a pleasurable experience for you both.

For some parents the time for massage is just not available. As long as your baby is cuddled, loved and interacted with no parents should feel guilty if they don't do this. Other parents enjoy massaging their babies and often find that, through massaging, they become much more confident in handling their babies.

Massage can help a baby to uncurl, stretch muscles and joints and coordinate movements. Fathers often enjoy massaging their baby; it is a great way of being involved and expressing love.

Never massage if you feel disinclined, tense or rushed or if the baby is not in a state to welcome it. You might spend about ten to fifteen minutes massaging. Be ready to stop if your baby shows signs of restlessness or a lack of enjoyment. Some babies enjoy a massage before their bath and feed but young babies cannot wait long once they feel hungry. Because they become comfortable with routine, you can try to massage around the same time each day and yet remain flexible. Other babies enjoy a massage after a feed if they are quiet and alert and ready to socialise before settling to sleep. These babies need to be able to lie on their tummies without spilling and the tummy massage must be very gentle. Just choose a time for massage which suits you both. If during the massage the baby becomes too tired, stop.

## *Preparing to massage*

There is no one right way or set of techniques to be used but here are some guidelines you might follow.

- Have the room really warm with no draughts. Use a heater if necessary.
- When massaging try to avoid interruptions. Perhaps take the phone off the hook.
- You can massage with the baby on your lap, on the change table, on your bed or on a rug on the floor.
- Have a towel or nappy beneath the baby.
- Remove rings or jewellery, and warm and relax your hands. A rinse under hot water will warm them, then shake your fingers and allow them to fall loosely to relax them.
- Slowly undress your baby.

- *ℓ* Although not necessary, it is very soothing and pleasant to use a natural gel or oil. Check that it is suitable to use on the baby's skin before doing so. The natural oils include olive, almond, apricot and avocado. You can rub a drop on the inside of the baby's wrist a few hours before using it on the whole body to check for sensitivity.
- *ℓ* Check your hands again, rub your palms together till they feel really warm, use a generous amount of the gel or oil and smooth over the baby's body.
- *ℓ* Aim to make all movements smooth, flowing, rhythmical with gentle, slightly firm pressure. Use both hands and work on both sides of the body where appropriate. Repeat each stroke three or four times if the baby is happy.
- *ℓ* Maintain eye contact, talk or sing softly during this shared experience.
- *ℓ* Be sensitive to the baby's responses. You do not have to begin and follow through in a strict order. If the baby does not seem to enjoy any particular part of the body being massaged, leave it. New babies' heads may be very sensitive following birth. Some can accept an extremely light and gentle touch. This may apply just to the head or to the whole body. Other babies may enjoy firmer pressure. You will discover what your baby finds pleasurable.

## Massaging body parts

Following is a brief guide to ways you might like to massage your baby's various body parts.

### The head

Place thumbs together in the centre of the forehead, and smoothly stroke across the forehead to the temples. Then using alternate hands, stroke smoothly from the brows up the forehead and then over the head.

### The chest

Place both hands thumbs together on the chest, and move smoothly from the centre out to each side of the body.

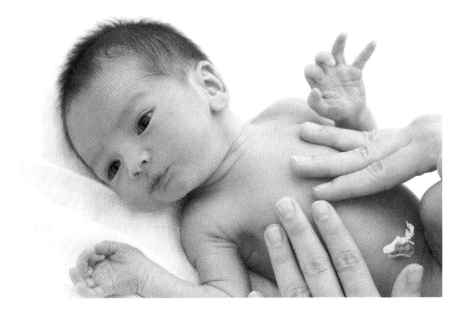

## The arms

Because of the direction of the circulation in the veins (flowing up the arms and legs towards the heart) it is wise to massage from the wrists and the ankles up the limbs. You can start at the wrist and massage up the arm and finish by stroking around the shoulders. Then encircle the wrists with your fingers and, exerting very gentle pressure, move up the arms to the shoulders.

When using an oil or a gel leave the baby's fingers until you have finished the other parts of the body so that there is no risk of the baby getting any gel in the eyes or mouth. When you return to the hands, stroke the back of them and the fingers too. Your baby will probably uncurl their fingers. Babies do seem to enjoy having both limbs massaged symmetrically.

## The legs and feet

Start at the ankles and move up the legs to the top of the thighs, first stroking and then encircling, squeezing gently as you move up. Hold the feet firmly, massage the soles with thumb and fingers and use the thumbs to stroke the toes.

## The abdomen

Using both hands, one following the other, stroke down from the chest and over the abdomen and around the abdomen in a clockwise direction; this follows the bowel. Try using a little gentle pressure on the abdomen with the palm of the hand.

Move your fingers in small circles as you move up the bowel from the baby's lower right-hand side to the ribs then continue across just above the umbilicus and on down the left side. If there are times when the baby has a windy, uncomfortable tummy you might like to try gently 'kneading' it. This may help colic too, especially if used between spasms of pain. It may increase the pain if used during an actual spasm.

## The back

With your baby on their tummy or side, massage down the back with long firm strokes using the whole of the flat of your hand and fingers.

Now dress the baby, who may now be ready to sleep. If just alert and wakeful you can play together or place the baby where there is something of interest to watch.

# 18

# Settling, sleeping and wakefulness

**N**ew parents are often concerned about their baby's sleeping. How many hours' sleep in the 24 should their baby need? If awake, when should they try to settle the baby to sleep again? How can they help their baby to settle to sleep?

## Sleep

Sleep slows down all the baby's body functions. The breathing slows. Visible activity and movements decrease. The brain has a rest from the continuous input it receives from the senses when awake. It may be deep and sound sleep from which it can be very difficult to rouse the baby; or lighter sleep in which the baby may twitch and make little noises such as snorts, snuffles, whimpers and even an odd cry; or mere dozing, in which the baby drifts between sleeping and waking.

# Being awake

Young babies spend their time sleeping interrupted by periods of being awake. Whilst awake they feed and interact with their environment before falling asleep again, which they do most easily when they are feeling sleepy, comfortable and neither hungry nor thirsty. Sleep can also be preceded by exhaustion if a baby has been crying for a long time.

Babies differ in the amount of sleep they need. It can be as little as nine or ten hours or as much as eighteen or more over 24 hours. It is not possible to persuade them to sleep more than they need and it is very difficult to keep them awake for longer than their body dictates. In time you may be able to encourage the baby to alter sleeping patterns (see later in this chapter) but the total amount of time the baby sleeps will still be determined by need.

# Sleeping issues

When trying to resolve sleeping issues it is first important to become familiar with your baby's tired signs, and with how best to settle your baby.

## Settling the baby to sleep

When relaxed, newborn babies usually fall asleep quickly and easily following a feed. Later, their behaviour changes. Many times older babies also settle without a fuss. However, it is not uncommon for them to go through periods in which they are difficult to settle. What to do with an unsettled baby is a common concern for new parents. Here are some options and choices of procedures which have helped on many occasions.

Remember that what works today may not work tomorrow, what works in the morning or after a particular feed may not work later in the day or after another feed. What works for one baby in a family may be inappropriate for another. Parents need to have faith in their judgement of what works and when.

There is normal unsettled behaviour that may not last long and is not too difficult to manage. On the other hand a baby may have much longer, really miserable periods and become distressed along with the parents. The baby will need help to settle again. It is our growing knowledge of our baby which helps us to recognise the need of the moment. This knowledge increases daily. As you provide food and comfort, love and closeness and tune in as you interact together, you will become aware of your baby's responses. Unexpected changes in the baby's behaviour and/or appearance alert you to consider possible causes that may be trivial or important. If you have other children you need to remember that you are starting again with this new baby – a different little person altogether.

Deciding whether or not a wakeful period is due to a real difficulty is not easy. Try to discover if there is something preventing the baby from falling into a relaxed sleep. When suffering pain there is usually no doubt.

A baby's sleep needs are individual. Many babies sleep reasonably well at night, settling again fairly easily after a feed and often at certain times during the day. Babies are often more difficult to settle in the afternoon and evening. They often just 'cat-nap' – sleep for five or ten minutes or so and then waken again, fussing, only to doze off for another short nap. This pattern of short naps is normal newborn behavior.

## Recognising a sleepy baby

It is important to learn to recognise your baby's tired signs. Some babies fall asleep while they are finishing a feed. As days pass they are more likely to be awake and alert and looking for some pleasant interaction and play before they are ready to sleep again.

**When becoming tired your baby may:**
- look sleepy
- lose interest in activity and in the surroundings
- grimace and frown
- become tense
- possibly start to cry
- move limbs in a restless way.

Your baby needs to be settled. Babies who become over-tired can become distressed, cry and become difficult to comfort. Walking with the baby held firmly against your body and using a soft voice may soothe and relax an upset baby.

It can be helpful to make a clear distinction between times awake and times asleep. When you recognise signs of sleepiness you can change the nappy, swaddle the baby (if this is what you usually do) and then tuck the baby down to sleep.

Do not ignore a true cry of distress. Nevertheless, some babies do need to unwind before they fall asleep and they may do this by crying a little – this crying can be noisy or grizzly which becomes more intermittent and soon stops. If this is the usual pattern don't rush to pick up the baby during this process. Perhaps there is time for you to shower, hang out the nappies or attend to some other matter. Very often the baby will have fallen asleep in that short while. If not, consider that the baby may not yet be ready for sleep.

How you react to the crying will depend on whether you feel it is just a normal period of crying which is likely to stop soon, or whether you feel there is some other reason. It will depend on the baby's age, the type of crying, the time of day (or night) and your own feelings and the immediate pressures facing you.

Parents don't usually worry if their baby is awake and quiet even when they believe that the baby 'should' be asleep. It is continued crying that is distressing.

Having recognised that the baby is sleepy, using a settling routine can establish a pattern leading to a restful sleep. You may vary the routine a little depending on whether you are settling the baby for a daytime sleep or for the night.

## *Helping the baby to fall asleep*

At settling time your baby will probably appear comfortable and will be showing signs of becoming sleepy. As you get to know your baby better you will learn what she likes best. Here are some suggestions for what you can do to help your baby fall asleep.

- Check the nappy.
- Wrap the baby in a bunny rug or light cot sheet if you feel this is helpful (see 'Wrapping and swaddling' in Chapter 17). Now just murmur a soft 'have a lovely sleep' or 'goodnight' or some other gentle message as you tuck your baby down.
- If crying begins as you leave the baby be prepared to wait a short time. A cross, tired cry lasting a few minutes will do no harm. The baby may be one who often needs to cry for a few minutes before falling asleep.
- If the crying continues, try gentle patting rather than picking up the baby again.
- If the baby is over-tired or overstimulated and the crying is noisy and angry you may need to cuddle the baby until relaxed and then tuck down with a sheet or blanket firmly across the body, holding it close to the cot.
- Playing a tape of womb and heartbeat sounds or some peaceful music may help the baby to relax and so fall asleep more easily.

If the baby, although tired, is really miserable, tense and restless it is probable that you will need to soothe and comfort before the baby will settle to sleep. Now it may help to provide different sensations.

- Add movement. Parents instinctively do this when they pace the floor. Try holding your baby firmly against your body, upright against your shoulder with the baby's bottom in one hand while you support the head with the other. Rhythmic pacing can soothe. You can accompany the movement with sound; use your own voice to sing or talk in a repetitive, low tone, perhaps repeating, 'there, there, there'.
- Rock in a rocking chair if you have one.
- Use the pram – push it back and forth, perhaps bumping over a coat hanger or two. This may provide the extra sensations that will allow the baby to fall asleep.

Perhaps right now you are having difficulty in settling the baby, who you feel is really tired and needs to sleep. Nothing you have tried has worked. The baby is still awake and crying. What more can you do? Think about the type of cry:

- Is it a tired, sleepy cry, more of a grizzle than a strong cry, and are there sleepy signs? If so the baby may fall asleep any minute.
- Maybe hunger is the problem. Consider the last feed. Could the baby have stopped feeding because of being tired rather than satisfied? Offer the breast or a further feed. Does the baby have hiccoughs? These are common in new babies but they are rarely troublesome; if they are, you can offer the breast for a moment or two, or offer a little cooled, boiled water if you are bottle-feeding.
- Between feeds the baby may be unsettled because of thirst, particularly in the summer or if the house is well heated when it is cold. The breastfed baby can take a little from the breast to quench thirst or, if bottle-fed, you can give a little cooled, boiled water.
- If neither thirsty nor hungry, check to see that the baby is comfortable. Simple discomfort can prevent the baby from settling. There may be a troublesome bubble of wind. Place the baby up against your shoulder, firmly pressed against you, and rub the back. Sometimes simply lifting the baby into an upright position is enough to release a bubble of wind. Maybe the baby is just in need of comfort. If still uncomfortable you can try using different positions. Try sitting the baby on your left thigh with the side of the body leaning against you as you hold the chin in your right hand and then, with the baby's back straight, rub it gently but firmly. Another position worth trying is lying the baby across your left thigh, supporting the forehead with your left hand. Use your right inner thigh to press against the baby's bottom while you rub the back. It seems that the pressure on the tummy can help. Another technique which might help is lying baby on his or her back and gently moving the legs in the bicycle motion, especially if the tummy feels tight. Avoid spending more than five minutes or so trying to get up wind. It is easy to blame wind when it really is not the cause of the crying.

## STILL awake!

Would the baby like to be wrapped or have wrapping loosened? Is the baby too hot, too cold or in need of a nappy change? If it is company that the baby wants the fussing will stop as you hold and cuddle, or it may be enough if you bring the baby to be near you to watch what you are doing.

If the baby is not ready to sleep you can provide changes in the environment such as music or voices on the radio, mobiles or other items of different shapes and colours. Although the television may readily capture interest, the effect of the flickering light on the baby's eyes and nervous system may be harmful and many health advisers strongly caution against it. If there is a warm, draught-free place on the floor where the baby will be safe you can try that.

Weather permitting, you could put the baby outside or take the baby for a walk in the pram. Babies often love to see moving leaves and shadows. Sometimes desperate parents take their baby for a drive in the car; this can settle the baby but he or she may wake again when the car stops.

Perhaps some of the procedures you have tried have worked for a time; perhaps they haven't worked at all. What now? You can try the pram again. If your baby dozes reduce the movement very slowly. To stop suddenly could wake baby again.

If your baby is still awake, be prepared once more to leave the baby to cry for a short time. This time the baby may fall asleep. If the baby is becoming distressed try the tucking down, stroking and/or patting method again.

Still your baby cries – what next? A really distressed baby may be helped by a deep, warm bath. This can be relaxing if bath time is usually enjoyed. This is most effective when the baby is held on their tummy in the bath in deep, warm water. Tepid bath water is not relaxing unless the weather is hot. Support the chin on your hand to keep the face clear of the water. If very distressed, wrap the baby in a clean cloth nappy and support the body well as you slowly lower the baby – still tummy down – into the water. If the crying stops you can loosen the nappy and slowly turn the baby over onto their back so that arms and legs are free to move. If the baby becomes anxious again replace the nappy over the body.

You might like to use a warmed towel for drying. Just pat dry. Keep the towel tucked closely against the body so that the baby does not become alarmed by the feeling of nakedness. Being dressed in warm clothes can be comforting in cold weather. Now put the baby down to sleep and wheel the pram only if necessary.

A variation of the warm bath method that can be relaxing and soothing is to take the baby into the large bath with you. Again, the water needs to be deep enough to cover both bodies and warm enough to be relaxing. It is necessary to have another adult to take the baby from you so that there is no risk of you slipping with the baby as you get in and out of the bath.

When you have tried all you can and the crying persists you may have to leave the baby safely in the cot or pram to cry him or herself to sleep, particularly if you find yourself becoming tense and angry. If there is someone else who can care for the baby for a while, get that help and have a little time out for yourself.

Finally you may simply have a wakeful baby. If you feel this is the case, perhaps the most helpful thing you can do for yourself is not to judge this as a bad thing. Accept that you have a baby who loves to interact with the world and then take steps to manage this.

Do not be hard on yourself. This can happen when you are feeling tired and discouraged – just be ready to use the fall-back plan suggested in 'Red alert!' below. At this time you need to walk away from the baby until you feel the tension leave you. You will decide just how soon you can go back. Remember that you do need to have some time out and make every effort to arrange this. Through the day you may be able to have a sleep yourself while the baby is sleeping. At night, if you have a partner, try to share the care of the baby in a way that best suits you all.

# Settling for the night

At night you could bath and put your baby into night clothes before the feed. It is better to keep night feeds calm and quiet. Speak with a low, soothing voice and handle the baby slowly and deliberately, and then you may have a relaxed baby to put down to sleep.

At night you may not need to change the nappy if it is only wet and there is no nappy rash. Some mothers who use cloth nappies during the day choose to use 'disposables' at night because they are very absorbent and appear to be comfortable.

## Night feeds

Here are some suggestions for when you are giving a night feed.

- Keep any disturbance to a minimum. A dim night light is helpful.
- Avoid putting your baby back into a cold bed by using a flannelette sheet or a woollen under-blanket rather than a thin cotton sheet. If you feed the baby in your bed you could take the baby's under-blanket in beside you; it will then be warm to put back in the cot at the end of the feed.
- At the end of the feed try briefly for any wind and then tuck the baby down again.

- *If a little soothing is needed use a very soft voice. A gentle pat might help.*
- *Use a rocking chair to soothe an unsettled baby.*
- *Try to lessen your own frustration at slow settling by picturing all the other parents in the same predicament; connecting in this way can be very reassuring and can lessen your feeling of isolation.*

During the night there may be times when the baby wakens between feeds – you may hear a whimper or little cry. Wait a moment or two to see if the baby can drop off to sleep again without waking fully. If not, you will need to check.

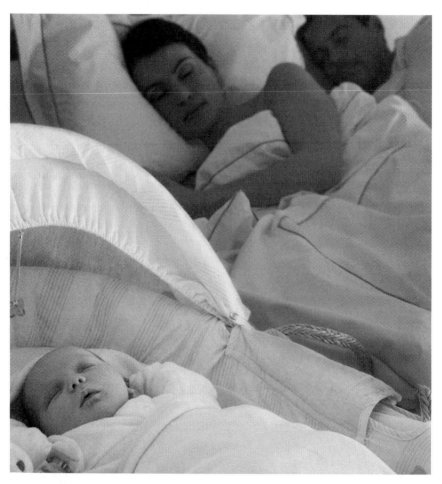

# Where to sleep

Babies fall asleep anywhere at any time regardless of where they are, but we need to provide sleeping places which are safe and comfortable.

During the day you may like to have your baby sleep where there is mild activity and many babies prefer this to sleeping in a silent room. Having the baby in a cot next to the parents' bed for the first six to twelve months is a popular option for night sleeping.

Research in New Zealand and the United Kingdom has shown that sleeping the baby in the same room, but not in the same bed, with the parents in the first six to twelve months of life is protective. This is thought to be because parents can see the baby and easily check to see that baby is safe. This protective effect does not work if the baby is in a room with other children, probably because the children do not know if the baby is safe or not. Recent evidence from the United Kingdom indicates that sharing the same room during baby's daytime sleeps is also protective (for more information see SIDS and Kids: http://www.sidsandkids.org/faq/).

Many women, whether breast- or bottle-feeding, sleep more peacefully with their baby in the bassinet or cot beside them. This can make breastfeeding at night much easier and less disturbing for you both. You may find that you can feed the baby snuggled in beside you and hardly wake yourself. Although not recommended in the safe sleeping guidelines from SIDS and Kids, some parents choose to make theirs a 'family bed' and have their baby sleep with them (also known as co-sleeping). If you choose this option you will need to ensure your baby is safe by following these guidelines:

- Do not swaddle the baby.
- Do not allow the baby to be covered by a doona (use a baby blanket).
- Ensure the baby's head and face remain uncovered.
- Do not allow the baby to become overheated.
- Do not use electric blankets.
- Do not co-sleep if you or your partner smoke, or are affected by alcohol or drugs/medications.
- Do not co-sleep if you or your partner are unwell.

All babies make noises while sleeping, and parents quickly become accustomed to them and waken easily when a feed is needed or there is some other need to be met. Having your baby sleeping in your room in their own bed is not only the safest place for a baby but the most convenient for you as you can respond more quickly.

The baby who sleeps in another room needs to be close enough to be heard. A reliable baby intercom which can be used to relay crying or other sounds may be useful. After the first week or two you might try settling the baby outside for daytime sleeps in good weather, but do not leave the baby outside unattended. Protect the baby from insects and cats with a strong cat net which, should a cat try to jump into the pram or bassinet, will not sag with the cat's weight onto the baby. In summer a period outside after the early feed at 6 a.m. or 7 a.m. can be very pleasant and after the evening feed around sundown. It can be too hot during the heat of the day. In winter you may be able to find a warm, sheltered place. In both summer and winter watch the sun's movement and protect the baby's eyes and face. Be aware of changes in temperature and adjust clothing and covers accordingly.

## Sleeping during transport

When you are out with the baby, a sling or baby carrier can make walking easier. In the early weeks your baby's head will need to be supported. You will be more comfortable if the carrier has wide, adjustable straps. The baby can be very comfortable, feel secure and sleep readily when held close to your body in a carrier.

If you use a stroller it must be possible to lower the back so that the baby can lie flat while sleeping. Babies may sleep very awkwardly if left in a propped-up position. The head may loll forward or twist too far to one side or the other and the spine may be crooked. You will need to be able to protect the baby from the weather.

### Travelling in the car

When travelling in the car, babies must be in a correctly installed and approved baby capsule or baby car seat (see 'Cars and children' in Chapter 23). Approved restraints are essential for the baby's safety and there are legal requirements to be met.

**You need to:**

- prevent slipping, so avoid wrapping your baby before fastening straps
- put covers over the straps, but remember that the capsule and covers reduce air circulation
- check that the sun is not shining directly on face or eyes
- use the capsule only during travelling to lessen the risk of discomfort
- stop in a safe place to check and comfort if your baby is crying in distress
- avoid leaving your baby alone in the car even for short periods; it is dangerous (see 'Cars and children' in Chapter 23).

# Sleeping-waking-feeding patterns

Now your day revolves around your baby's day. It is helpful when a pattern emerges; if it is a difficult one you may be able to alter it.

Some babies develop a routine within a few days of birth but this is unusual and it may not happen for a number of weeks. The pattern established is not necessarily one we would choose but it is clearly helpful when wakeful times become predictable. There are likely to be some sleep periods longer than others and the first to lengthen usually occurs at night. 'Sleeping through the night' can mean five to six hours of uninterrupted sleep. This can happen in the first six months but often takes longer.

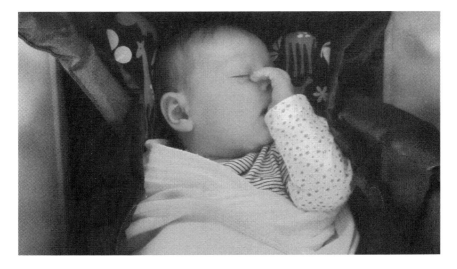

Although your baby may want to socialise and play with you after night feeds, discourage this. Settle the baby back to sleep as quickly as possible – night is not for play time. If comfort and reassurance are needed, provide these where the baby sleeps. Keep your voice and the lights low and minimise interaction and activity.

During the day babies often settle and sleep well after morning feeds. Following the next feed a baby may be more wakeful and even stay awake until fed again. There may be a shorter unbroken sleep or the baby may just 'cat nap' – have a number of short dozes, perhaps with grizzly intervals. This tends to happen around the same time each day, usually later in the afternoon or early evening. This can be a trying time for mothers who are preparing the evening meal and possibly coping with other children. (It can help if you can prepare the dinner earlier in the day.) Your partner can comfort the baby, prepare the meal and/or cope with other children, leaving you to care for the baby.

You cannot alter your baby's requirements for sleep, but as time passes you may be able to alter the actual times when your baby feeds and sleeps to establish a routine that is easier to live with. Remember, babies can only do things within their own limits, so while they are very young it is usually easier to adapt to their patterns. If it is at all possible, mothers are wise to sleep when their babies take their longest sleep.

## *Awkward sleeping patterns which you might be able to change*

These are:

- *𝒪* the frequent feeds that are common in the first few weeks and continue through habit – they may be two-hourly, perhaps even hourly
- *𝒪* waking frequently at night and having longer daytime sleeps
- *𝒪* sleeping through the late evening feed and waking for a middle-of-the-night feed.

Sympathetic handling may enable you to adjust these patterns. Here are some suggestions.

## Waking to feed frequently

Sometimes thriving babies continue to feed frequently, as they began just after birth. Although relaxed and contented, they take only small feeds. They sleep only an hour or so after each feed before wanting another one. Remember, babies have very small stomachs and are feeding on a very easily and quickly digested food. Most breastfed babies will feed eight to twelve times per day but as they grow they will be able to feed more effectively, so feeds will take less time. The emptier your breasts feel the higher the fat content of your milk, so frequent feeds in the evening will lead to longer sleeps in the night and increased weight gain.

## Short night sleeps, and long day sleeps

The aim is to move the longer sleeps from day to night. During the day try waking the baby gently after a sleep of no more than four hours. You can turn the baby over, loosen the covers and bring the pram out where there is activity and some extra noise. You can slightly turn up the radio. If your baby continues to sleep you can change the nappy and talk or sing to help the baby waken. Babies need to be fully awake before they feed or they will just doze off again. Do not try too hard in your attempts to wake the baby: by six or seven weeks of age the baby will start to learn the difference between night and day and their sleep patterns will change.

## Cutting out the 'wrong' feed at night

At some time the baby will want to cut out a night feed – this is unlikely during the first three months. Many babies start to sleep through the late evening feed. They fall into a really deep sleep in the late evening and are almost impossible to rouse. The baby may wake enough to take a small feed but will still want a good feed in the early hours. If you find this a problem you may wish to persevere in encouraging the baby to wake and feed well before you go to bed. Work out what the baby can do. If you are not successful just accept that, at this time, your baby needs the early morning feed. Within another week or two you can try again.

An easier way to cope with this pattern is to go to bed early so you can have a longer sleep when the baby is doing so.

# Waking

Being awake means that the baby is actively using his or her senses. Babies need an environment in which they can see, hear, feel, touch and smell different things. Ordinary household living can easily provide stimulation. Lying gazing at blank walls and the ceiling is not enough for babies.

As your baby feeds, all the baby's senses are naturally stimulated as you hold, speak and cuddle. At other times the baby will be absorbed while using one particular sense above the others. For example, your baby will use sight to watch a mobile, sunlight on a wall or while studying a face. Hearing will be used when listening to a voice, music, a household or outside noise. The baby will feel textures, will smell and taste.

Babies actively move too. When awake, the extent of activity and the state a baby is in varies – relaxed or restless, alert or drowsy, quiet or noisy, peaceful or distressed. When awake there will be times of crying, signalling feelings that range from vague disquiet to urgent need.

A baby will wake either slowly and quietly or abruptly and noisily. The former could mean that the baby has simply had enough sleep, is waking for a feed or is uncomfortable. The latter can be due to pain, the shock of a loud noise, or of sudden and unexpected movement (particularly of rapid and unsupported lifting or putting down).

When your baby is awake there will be more emphasis on the baby's needs than when asleep. As needs become more pressing to the baby they become more obvious to caregivers. Keep trying to help until the baby's reaction lets you know that you have got it right.

Clearly it is a help if wakeful times are predictable but do not be surprised if this is not so. You can expect this to happen as time passes. A comfortable, very young infant is most commonly awake before feeds and briefly after them although many babies fall asleep as they are finishing a feed and their appetite is satisfied. As the days pass babies begin to stay awake longer and become more active.

## Waking for a feed

When waking for a feed, the baby will need prompt attention. Young babies are unable to tolerate a lengthy wait. If crying, the baby may quieten for a moment or two when picked up but if not fed promptly will soon become frustrated and then distressed and, although hungry, may not be able to feed at all until soothed. If awake, satisfied and comfortable at the end of the feed the baby is likely to be quiet and alert, ready to enjoy socialising before sleeping again.

Some babies who are obviously tired remain awake, noisy and miserable simply because they find it really difficult to relax. They may doze only fitfully until it is time for the next feed and then they may be weary, have little energy and suck poorly. They need sympathetic, patient, gentle handling until they are able to cope with this bewildering new experience of life following birth. Remember that most babies are likely to have some restless, wakeful periods for no clear reason.

After the first three or four weeks babies may be able to wait a little longer for attention or a feed, particularly if they are aware of activity around them or have something interesting to divert them. The time will come when they may awaken, especially in the early morning, and lie quietly making their own noises and entertaining themselves for a time – parental bliss.

As babies grow and develop they want much more attention when awake. A change of scene may keep a baby happy for a short time. Between feeds some babies want a small snack at the breast or, if bottle-fed, a drink of cooled, boiled water.

It is wise to allow your baby to enjoy time alone for a while when content and happy to do so. Babies often look at or suck fingers, watch mobiles or reach out to toys or rattles within their grasp. Anything may catch their attention for a short time. They often enjoy a music box or music from another source. However, they soon let you know when they need you again.

Babies generally love to be carried so that they can see more of the world around them. A baby carrier or sling (possum pouch) is worth using. It can make you less tired and you can have your hands free to do other things. To allow your baby unrestricted vision you can use a carry-chair or a bouncinette for short periods. Be sure that the bouncinette has a five-point harness. Place the carry-chair or bouncinette on the floor because babies can bounce themselves off tables or benches. Don't leave your baby in a room alone in these; take the baby with you.

If just needing your closeness and movement, your baby may be satisfied with a cuddle, a turn in a rocking chair orsome time on the floor in a draught-free spot. You can place a stand with a few colourful toys strung above the baby. These do not have to be expensive toys, and you can change the items from time to time. Your baby can look at and reach out to them or you might join in for a time and play together. You can also try a little tummy time on the floor.

## Interacting with sleepy babies

Even after the initial days following birth some babies continue to be very sleepy. If you have been reassured by your doctor that the baby is well but just sleepy, accept that the baby may simply have a placid nature and may enjoy lots of sleep – think about the variations in the sleeping needs of the adults you know. If you enjoy happy times together when your baby is awake, feeds are taken willingly without difficulty and the baby is gaining weight, you can expect wakeful times to increase as the days pass. Such babies often benefit from stimulating interaction, so tune in and provide what the baby enjoys and, meanwhile, count your blessings.

Some babies seem to switch off rather than interact with their new environment. When they are awake these babies need gentle stimulation, plenty of eye-to-eye contact, smiling and stroking. They need to be talked to and carried around to see things in the house and garden so that they use their eyes and ears. From the security of loving warmth and closeness they will begin to learn that they can trust this new world in which they find themselves. Slowly your baby will begin to accept and enjoy interacting with you and respond to your patient nurturing.

However, some of these sleepy young babies may fail to thrive because they are not taking enough milk. Instead of five or six really wet nappies in each 24 hours, there are likely to be fewer, some barely damp.

The urine will be dark rather than pale in colour (see 'Urine' in Chapter 4). The weekly weight gains will be inadequate. Steps to increase the intake of milk are set out in 'Feeding the sleepy baby' in Chapter 21.

## Interacting with wakeful babies

Just as there are some new babies who are sleepy, there are some who spend much more of their time awake than you would expect. These are not the difficult-to-settle, sometimes jumpy and irritable babies, or the continually unhappy, wakeful babies. These are babies who can be easily entertained, but while very young they cannot amuse themselves for any length of time. Wakeful babies love playing and sharing all manner of activity with you. It is quite a challenge to provide change and an interesting environment for these alert, curious infants. It is

wise to guard against overstimulating them – handle them smoothly and slowly and interact in a quiet, gentle way, avoiding play which is too exciting.

Where many young babies will have daytime sleeps of between two and four hours at a stretch, the very wakeful infant may do very well to sleep between one and two hours or less, and then waken ready for more fun. They often make do with short 'cat naps' but usually sleep for longer periods at night. It may help to put your baby in a pram and move the pram around the house so that you can chat or sing to the baby as you attend to other matters. Encourage the baby to enjoy things apart from you.

Allow the baby time alone to appreciate variety. Bright, strongly-coloured toys or objects of different shapes strung within the baby's range of vision, music, time on a rug on the floor or a short period in a carry-chair or bouncinette can all be tried. Most babies love to be carried about in a sling or possum pouch, although some struggle if they cannot see out especially after the first three or four weeks when their ability to focus increases and vision is sharper.

It is a matter of providing a changing scene as the need arises – an environment that allows the baby to both enjoy their time awake without overstimulation and to fall asleep when tired. It is a matter of accepting that you have an alert, wakeful baby who needs less sleep than many others.

## The unsettled baby

Perhaps there were difficulties during pregnancy, labour or birth but, for whatever reason, your baby is difficult to settle. Having been reassured by your doctor that there is no medical problem, know that this will pass. Treat this time as a challenge, a time when you should muster all the sympathy and gentle patience you can. Parents can support each other. If you are on your own look for help from someone or from supportive groups. Try to arrange some time out.

Don't see the baby's unsettled behaviour as due to some inadequacy on your part or to some rejection of you by the baby. The baby has no other way to communicate with those who know and love him or her best that, at present he or she is adjusting to life outside the uterus. Accept the temporary difficulties you are both facing while the baby's nervous system is settling down and the baby matures to the point where it is possible to accept the new environment without feeling fretful and troubled by even low-grade stimuli.

Perhaps the greatest comfort and help you can give the baby is frequent skin-to-skin contact. All the baby's senses are soothed while snuggled close against your warm skin – one mother said that, whenever possible, she carried her baby between her breasts, held there by a sling. She was amazed how well she was able to do all manner of things. Both here and overseas many premature or low birth-weight babies spend their whole time in this skin-to-skin contact. It is appropriately called 'kangaroo mother care' (see 'Your new baby' in Chapter 4).

You can try the settling techniques suggested earlier in 'Helping the baby to fall asleep'. There are a few other aspects of this situation which we can look at further. The typical behaviour of such a baby is likely to include any of the following:

- The baby might be often distressed by almost any stimulus, whether severe or mild, whether from outside or within (for example, sudden jerky movements of their own limbs). The baby cries often and this can vary from a grizzly, low-key complaining cry, through the range to bouts of screaming.
- The baby might also be jumpy, irritable and unhappy looking. If you wrap your baby she or he struggles to be free. When the wrap is loosened the baby is still unhappy.
- Perhaps the baby is uninterested in feeds, possibly because of tiredness. Your baby might fall asleep a few minutes after starting the feed, before having taken an adequate amount, then soon wake and cry again. The baby may or may not be willing to take more food and although tired may be unable to relax enough to fall asleep.
- Your baby might become upset when put down but unhappy when being held for more than a minute or two. Your baby does not feel sociable and interaction is minimal. Frequent night waking can be a tiring part of the whole problem.

If available, look for a supportive early childhood nurse so you can discuss your worries and feelings with a sympathetic listener. Your baby's progress will be checked and it's likely you will be offered helpful suggestions.

Use whatever means you can to find time to relax yourself. If you are relaxed you can convey calm, reassuring messages to your baby. You will quickly learn what interaction you can share. Handle slowly and deliberately, and carefully support the baby whenever you lift or put down. Use eye-to-eye contact and smile to engage the baby's attention and speak softly and gently. Do not push or persist for long. You will soon know just what is possible. Give whatever loving touching or cuddling suits the baby. It will vary from time to time. Avoid shocks and sudden loud noises; protect the baby from enthusiastic visitors. Keep new experiences to a minimum. Daily routine can prove very helpful for some of these babies. As you lovingly handle, move, change, feed and cuddle in much the same way each time, your baby will begin to feel that there is something familiar, something predictable and stable in this new and confusing world and that there is someone there to kindly meet his or her needs.

Back in 1979, Doctor Kerry Callaghan of South Australia wrote of the factors experienced by the infant while still in the uterus just before labour commences – factors which, if we can reproduce them as closely as possible, can help to recreate feelings of security. Those mentioned are:

- constant movement
- continual body sounds
- constant skin stimulation; skin-to-skin contact can readily supply this
- a flexed body posture; in this position the knees are bent and drawn up against the body
- a continuous supply of food.

From the time the developing baby is first aware of movement the baby is accustomed to feeling the effect of the mother's moving body. Her baby is also accustomed to her voice and her body sounds. Surrounded by fluid, the baby is held within the uterus by its strong muscular walls. There is constant skin stimulation.

Following birth, your baby may miss these sensations and find the quiet, still bed disturbing. Being carried in your arms, in a sling or a possum pouch may provide again that sense of movement which may assist the baby to relax and fall asleep. If you tire from wearing the pouch you can sit and rock the pram, or push it around the house or garden if unable to go for a walk.

Allow your baby to feed whenever ready to do so, even when you feel that the previous feed was a good one. If crying persists or begins again look for other causes. You will develop an inner feeling for the best procedure to try at different times.

There are CDs available with some household noises which mothers find very successful in soothing their babies. The radio or a tape of womb sounds may also be better than silence. Talk and sing to your baby. Some babies find massage helpful while others do not. Babies' reactions can vary according to the way they are feeling when it is done.

Time passes and the continually unsettled baby outgrows this period. Accept or ask for help when you need it. If you find that you are beginning to feel desperate, take time out. Leave your baby safely in the cot while you do something else for a short break. Look for another trusted adult to take over the care of the baby for a longer time. Act before your 'red alert' button needs to be pushed (see below).

## *Red alert!*

**Note:** If you feel that you really are falling to pieces or you are in danger of hurting your baby you can ring Lifeline. The telephone number in all states and territories is 13 11 14 – this is a 24-hour service – or you can ring child abuse prevention services units; see your local phone directory for the relevant numbers.

When you have tried everything and you are beginning to feel desperate, your next step is to take time out.

An unbroken and unsuccessful struggle to settle a crying baby can lead to resentment and anger. If this happens, get help. Talk to your health adviser about your feelings. Of particular concern is the risk that a parent who is out of control may become so frustrated and angry with a continually crying baby that he or she may shake or hurt the baby in some other way. Shaking can cause brain damage which can be permanent or even fatal – never shake your baby.

Stop and do something else. If your partner is also at home or there is another adult in the house, take a break. If you are on your own with the baby put the baby down safely in the cot and stop for a cup of tea or coffee or go out into the garden. Perhaps you can wash the dishes, hang out or bring in the washing or start to prepare a meal, or get on the phone and talk to a trusted person.

You can try sitting quietly for a few minutes and using whatever method of relaxation works for you: deep breathing, consciously relaxing your muscles or listening to a favourite piece of music, the radio or television. It is necessary to give yourself some space and time to break the build-up of tension. When you have done so you are likely to be able to go back to try to comfort the baby. Always know that the baby has no other way to communicate distress other than crying; do not take it personally.

If these simple methods are not enough to help you cope with distressed and angry feelings or you are feeling powerless and resentful too often, talk to your family doctor or early childhood nurse; they are likely to be able to help you. Can you arrange for a relative or friend to take the baby so that you can be free for a while to do something for yourself? You might go out for a walk, have your hair done or just window-shop or have a leisurely cup of tea or coffee.

Anyone can reach breaking point. Have in mind a plan of action. You can relieve the situation before it gets out of hand and you lose control. Through trial and error and in learning about your baby day by day, you will become increasingly able to soothe and comfort the baby. Be patient with both the baby and yourself. This difficult time will pass.

**Remember:** You do not have to be perfect. Ask for help if you need it. Have a plan of action to use for any time that you feel you are not coping. In getting help you will know that you are taking a positive step. Take care of yourself as well as your baby.

# Sudden Infant Death Syndrome (SIDS)

A SIDS death is said to have occurred when a baby is put to bed apparently well and later is found dead. Autopsy examinations (a legal requirement) are performed to exclude other causes of death. As yet no specific causes of the syndrome have been identified. A great deal of research continues in this area.

Much of the material in this book was included because of the questions asked of me and my fellow health advisers by parents. Time and again one mother would mention her worries over the possibility of a SIDS death. Invariably, the other mothers would then be eager to talk about it too, thankful that someone had brought up the subject. Their greatest fear was that they might do something to cause, or not do something to prevent, SIDS.

So, what is known about SIDS today? There is a pamphlet available printed by SIDS and Kids Australia. There are also help and support services available for parents who have suffered a cot death. The pamphlet discusses some possible risks which may contribute to a cot death. By reducing the risk factors, the number of Australian babies who die of SIDS each year has been dramatically reduced. Equipped with this information, parents feel they are able to do something to reduce the possibility of a SIDS death.

The following information about safe sleeping for babies is from the SIDS and Kids website, which you may wish to access to find out more information about safe sleeping and SIDS prevention (go to http://www.sidsandkids.org/safe-sleeping/).

## How to safely position your baby for sleep

- Position your baby on their back from birth, not on the tummy or side.
- Place your baby with their face uncovered (do not use a doona, pillows, lambs wool underlay, bumpers or soft toys in the cot or bassinet).
- Avoid exposing babies to tobacco smoke both before birth and afterwards.
- Provide a safe sleeping environment (safe cot, safe mattress, safe bedding).

- Place your baby in their own safe sleeping environment next to your bed for the first six to twelve months.

**In addition:**
- Don't let your baby become too hot.
- Avoid medication to help the baby sleep. If the baby needs any medication use only that which is prescribed/recommended by your doctor.
- Breastfeed if possible.

Tummy play (or tummy time as it is sometimes known) is safe and very important for babies from birth, but only when they are awake and an adult is present. Tummy play helps muscle development in the arms, neck and back and prepares babies for crawling. Tummy play is also very good for helping prevent a misshapen head, but remember not to put your baby on their tummy to sleep.

If bed-sharing (see 'Where to sleep' earlier in this chapter) you need to be sure that the baby is not swaddled, can't slip under the covers, or contact pillows, thus overheating.

Major studies have shown that immunising your baby does not increase the risk of SIDS.

From one of the discussion groups I have been involved in, the question arose: 'Is it appropriate to discuss cot death or might it cause needless anxiety to talk about it?' The group was quite definite. They wanted the chance to discuss the topic.

**Michelle:** '*Maybe our parents never gave SIDS a thought although I can remember my mother often going to look at her sleeping babies (there were six of us) to make sure that they were still breathing, especially in the first few weeks.*

*Jim and I live with this anxiety. One of Jim's friends at work went through this while I was pregnant so I expect that has made us very aware that it can happen. Now that Sophie is nine weeks old we are not quite so paranoid about it all.*'

**Bethany:** '*Well, I don't know anyone who has had a cot death but there has been much in the media about it. Ken and I planned to have our baby sleep in his own room but we were too worried so we have kept Michael in beside us. I'm such a worrywart that I would have been up and down all night just checking to see that he was okay. I'm much better with him beside me. I'm sure that my subconscious hears him breathing and I'm able to sleep. It's funny how quickly we learnt to ignore the baby noises that are part of his normal sleeping. I think new parents need all the accurate information that is available about cot deaths.*'

**James:** '*Bernadette and I had similar worries. The worst part was our believing that there was nothing we could do to try to lessen the risk of SIDS for Jack. We decided to talk to our doctor. He was reassuring and took our worries seriously and gave us one of his journals to read. The most helpful part of our talk with him was to learn that there are things we can do to lessen the risk.*'

**Tim:** *'Yes, it's all very well to say that parents should never have guilty feelings if they lose a baby through SIDS. It would be impossible not to ask oneself what we did that might have contributed to it, or failed to do that might have prevented it. Now we have information that can lessen risks and we can take precautions.'*

**Sophie:** *'You can't put a lid on anxiety and hope that it will go away. It needs to be faced and when we have the available information we can decide what we can or cannot do about it and so cut the worry back to size.'*

Parents who have had a baby die of SIDS may need counselling and ongoing support. Each state and territory has an association affiliated with SIDS and Kids Australia. There are parents who have also lost a baby through SIDS and have trained as counsellors so that they can help other parents. Contacting such an association can be enormously helpful. Ask your early childhood nurse or staff at the community health centre, women's health centre, the local library or the council office, or there may be a local citizens' advice bureau for information in your area. You can also look up the Internet or check the phone book.

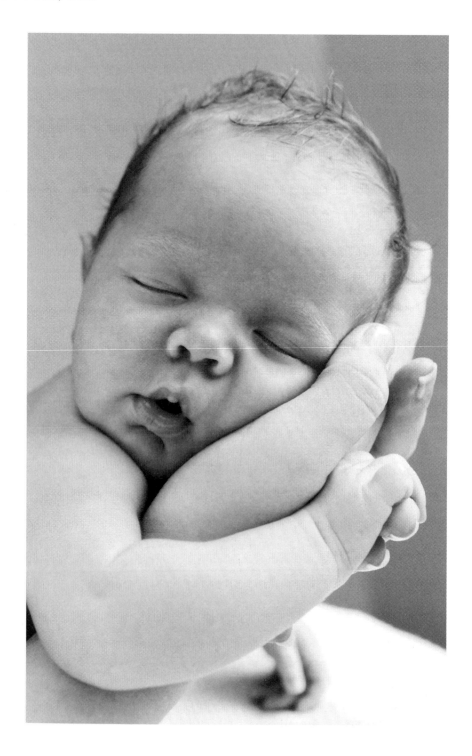

# 19

# Growth and development

**E**very human being begins life as a single cell. After nine months of intensive growth and development inside the mother's body the fertilised egg becomes a baby, a separate individual but still immature and dependent. At birth the baby's body cannot yet function in an adult way. Growth is the term used when referring to the increasing size of the body. Development is the term used for progressive change from the simpler to the more complex form of the individual. Growth and development go on together in much the same way for all humans. There will be subtle differences for every baby, determined by their genetic inheritance and the environment in which they live. In this chapter, various aspects of growth and development are discussed.

The baby's continued growth and development will be stimulated through the senses and by interaction with caregivers. This stimulation needs to suit the baby's temperament and their current stage of growth and development.

We help our babies to adapt to their new environment and harmonise with it. To do this successfully we need to lovingly nurture our babies. Many studies have shown the need for loving nurturing and its importance for brain development and adjustment well beyond the early years. The impact of brain development goes on for a baby's entire life, affecting schooling, qualifications, job prospects and earning capacity. Mothers in particular organise most of the care. They cuddle, soothe and encourage. Babies involve themselves with others around them and directly with their environment through their senses. Giving the right sort of care is largely intuitive for many parents. As they do this, parents further their own development as they gain new skills, awareness and understanding.

Every baby is unique and will grow and develop in their own way. *Babies will reach their milestones at their own pace.* The timeframe for normal development varies among babies although they follow the same pattern: they will learn to sit before they crawl; they will stand before they walk and they will walk before they run. Sometimes a baby may seem to be a little slow in reaching one particular milestone; equally, the baby may move quickly to another one. If your baby is bright and well, enjoy the baby's uniqueness and do not compare him or her competitively with other babies. If you are anxious consult your maternal and child health nurse or your general practitioner.

Growth and development are often spoken of together but, although they are continually affecting each other, they are different, as will be discussed.

## Growth

Growth refers to increases in size, of the length (height) and the mass (weight) of the whole body. Heredity, nutrition and the environment will determine a baby's size. Large parents are likely to have large babies while smaller parents can be expected to have smaller babies. The rate at which babies grow and gain weight varies. Most babies will lose some weight following birth and regain it within ten to fourteen days. They can be expected to grow rapidly in the first few months of life and many will double their birth weight (or weigh even more) by the time they are five months of age. They are likely to have trebled it by twelve months. They then tend to gain more slowly. In the first three months, many will consistently gain around 150 to 200 grams weekly; others may have a large gain one week and a smaller gain the next. There need be no concern about smaller or larger gains in a healthy baby. Provided the baby is well, their body and limbs are well rounded, they are fed according to their appetite, they are reasonably contented and their overall progress is satisfactory, parents can relax and enjoy their baby. In the event of sickness, babies often lose weight but as they recover, their appetite increases and if they are fed accordingly, they soon regain the lost weight.

Usually the baby's measurements are recorded at birth. The baby may be measured at intervals by an early childhood nurse or family doctor during the next few months. The average length at birth is about 50 centimetres, some being a little more and others a little less. The length can be expected to increase by 25 to 30 centimetres during the first year. Head circumference is about 34 to 35 centimetres at birth and will usually reach 47 to 48 centimetres by twelve months. Most of this increase is added in the first six months then the growth rate slows. The head grows as much in the first year as it does during the rest of life. After the first twelve months head circumference is less likely to be recorded.

## Development

In contrast to growth, development refers to the ongoing process of maturing: acquiring the physical, mental and social functioning we need in life. We speak of the milestones of development – the ages at which individuals are able to do 'certain things'. We see this progress as babies demonstrate new skills. In babies the first simple, jerky movements become more complex and skilful as muscular control increases. Mental and social development continues as they interact with and respond to stimuli provided by the environment and caregivers. The first limited sounds babies make increase in range and variety as they learn to speak.

Research by van de Rijt and Plooij found that all babies appear to take seven major leaps in development during their first year. In the babies studied, these observable increases in mental development seemed to occur at much the same time: around five, eight, twelve, nineteen, 26, 37 and 46 weeks of age during the first year. Following each leap in mental development new learning occurs and the baby then perceives the world differently. There is often an accompanying increase in the baby's physical skills too. At first these major mental changes can bring periods of varying upset. The baby often becomes anxious, fretful and clingy. Crying periods increase, and during this time you will find the baby harder to settle. Patience, quick response and extra tender loving care will lessen tension and help to soothe him or her. Always check the common causes of crying before considering that it may be due to one of these developmental leaps. Next the behaviour alters – now the baby may respond in different ways, acquire some new physical skills and become happier and more relaxed. The authors say that these clingy periods seem to occur just as the baby is about to undergo a developmental leap and that, when parents know that they can expect such reactions, they can manage these difficulties more easily.

## The senses

During the first weeks of life, your baby may appear to do little more than eat, sleep and cry. But in reality all senses are functioning and your baby is taking in the sights, sounds, smells, tastes and touch of this new world.

### Vision

Babies can see at birth but vision is not fully developed. Bright lights can trouble a new baby. Visual stimulation occurs whenever babies fix their sight on people or things. New babies focus best at 20 to 25 centimetres from the object of interest. This is just about the distance that a baby's eyes are from their mother's face when breastfeeding. Think of it as the usual distance between you and your baby as you hold, talk to and show the baby different things.

It is said that babies love to look at things that are black and white, hence the number of black and white toys on the market. Colour preference for yellow and red develops in babies from about four months. Don't use the television for visual stimulation. The American Academy of Paediatrics recommends that children are not exposed to the television before the age of two years.

It is common for babies to go cross-eyed at times (where both eyes are not looking in the same direction). This will become less frequent as the muscles around the eyes strengthen. A 'squint' is the name given to persistent or regularly occurring misalignment of the eyes; a squint will need correction. Early treatment is important and usually very successful. If you are worried or in doubt, ask your general practitioner or maternal and child health nurse.

**Here are some suggestions for stimulating the baby's sight:**

𝒞 Allow the baby to study your face. Babies are born with an in-built interest in faces and will study one (or even a picture of a face) showing special interest in the eyes.

𝒞 Hold an object about 25 centimetres from your baby's face. When the baby has focused on it you can move it slowly to suit the baby's ability to follow it. Soon the baby will be able to follow it with their eyes and even turn their head. Babies like bright primary colours, particularly red. You can expect the baby to be more interested in a complex pattern rather than in a simple one.

**When your baby is awake and alert, make sure that there are items of interest to look at:**

𝒞 String a few colourful items of different shapes and sizes across the pram or bassinet which are within your baby's focus and reach.

𝒞 Suspend mobiles, balloons, streamers or coloured pages from magazines on a string across a corner of the room or from the ceiling above the cot.

𝒞 When possible, have your baby near you to watch your activities.

𝒞 Place your baby near a window to look at moving leaves, clouds or rain but take care that the sun does not shine onto the baby's face and ensure they do not get hot.

Your baby is likely to enjoy short periods on a bouncinette or in a carry-chair. Check that vision is not restricted at the sides.

At five or six weeks many babies will begin to smile at any kindly human face and at around three months of age comes that special smile of recognition for you. Your baby is now recognising the familiar and showing an increased interest in the new. Eye muscles are strengthening, eye movements are becoming smooth, the focal range is increasing and the baby will spend longer studying whatever happens to be of interest.

## *Hearing*

Babies can hear clearly at birth; in fact they can hear noises while in the uterus. Once more we see nature's programming – the baby's attention is primarily focused on the human voice although the baby responds to other sounds too. The baby is extremely sensitive to tones of voice and seems to recognise their mother's and father's voices very soon after birth. Babies prefer high-pitched (but not loud) sounds to low-pitched. Have you noticed how natural it is to speak to a baby in a high-pitched voice? The baby can be soothed by quiet, gentle sounds, excited by bright, stimulating chatter, and distressed by an irritable or angry tone.

The baby will respond to your voice. While you talk or sing the baby will often move their arms and legs in a rhythmic motion. Before birth the baby was accustomed to your body sounds – your voice, heartbeat and digestive gurgles. Now, as you hold the baby, those familiar noises will be welcome.

Other auditory stimulation will come from noises around the baby: from music, appliances and household activities as well as outside sources. Rhythmic sounds can be very soothing. This is understandable given that the baby has been used to your heartbeat for so long before birth. Some babies are disturbed if they are put to sleep in a very quiet room – they seem to need some sounds around them and are better sleeping where they can hear the household noises. A sudden loud noise such as a door slamming can be very frightening and distressing. Babies become increasingly interested as mothers chat and/or sing to them. They love to hear other sounds and become aware of the differences – a musical toy, a rattle, the scrunchy sound of noisy crumpling paper, a bell ringing or a squeaky toy.

## *Speech*

The baby's hearing and listening lead to the development of new sounds and gurgles, and the baby is likely to repeat these sounds as you copy them. They will be used to attract your attention. By three months of age listening has enabled the baby to make many new sounds, with a range in pitch. Now your baby can 'talk' to you and enjoy gurgling, babbling and laughing as you play together. By 28 to 30 weeks the baby may be making repetitive vowel sounds and you can expect repetitive consonant sounds at around 35 to 36 weeks. As early as ten or eleven months of age, the baby is learning that certain sounds have special meaning, and so they will learn to speak through imitation. Talk to your baby often and about anything. At this early age their brains are absorbing it all in readiness for the development of speech.

## Smell

A new baby reacts to smells. The baby can distinguish between your breastmilk and that of other mothers. Snuggling into a well-worn jumper or some other article of clothing you have worn can be very comforting and reassuring. You will notice the baby turn away from some aromatic or acid smells. As the weeks pass you can interest your baby in different smells – a flower, a freshly baked cake, herbs, different perfumes. The list is endless. You will be interested in the baby's reactions and preferences. Allow the baby to explore one smell thoroughly before moving to another. Be aware when the baby has had enough stimulation.

## Taste

At birth a baby can recognise different tastes and will, for example, be distressed by anything sour and very quickly show a liking for sweet tastes. The baby receives all the sugar needed in breastmilk or formula so avoid giving additional sweetened drinks.

## Touch

From birth your baby reacts to touch and temperature, and will respond to heat and cold. The lips and tongue are very sensitive and the baby is aware of different textures. Skin-to-skin contact can bring warm feelings of comfort and security. Babies love to be soothed, patted and lovingly touched by their mothers and fathers. Many babies enjoy being massaged too.

# Acquiring body control

A newborn baby tends to lie in a flexed position: knees and elbows bent with fingers curled into a fist. Babies are without complete muscular control and it is necessary to support your baby carefully when you pick up him or her, particularly the head. The head is large in proportion to the rest of the body but as the baby grows this difference lessens and soon the baby will start to develop the use of neck muscles. This control gradually moves down through the body.

**Between one and two months you can expect your baby to:**

- start to lift and hold their head still as you hold the baby upright against yourself, and if lying on their tummy the baby will lift their chin for a moment or two; support for the head will still be needed as you move, pick up or put your baby down
- move more smoothly.

**At around six to nine weeks of age your baby is likely to:**

- smile and begin to squeal with pleasure
- open and shut the fingers and accidentally find one hand with the other; he or she she may soon after be able to grasp a rattle although the movements with it will be quite uncoordinated
- discover hands and feet
- grasp at objects strung in front of him or her
- start to look for and follow the sound that a rattle makes; the baby learns that the hands have something to do with producing the noise when they move, hit, hold or shake the rattle
- have some neck control; if your baby can hold up the head allow some time lying on the tummy on the floor, which will help to strengthen neck muscles (though do not let your baby become tired in this position)
- love action rhymes such as 'Pat-a-cake', 'Can you keep a secret', and 'This little piggy'. As you sing or recite, the baby will soon anticipate actions and respond with rhythmic movements of his or her own.

**Around six weeks to two months the baby is likely to:**

- lift their head for a moment or two and even turn it from side to side when placed on the tummy on a flat surface
- stretch their legs out when lying on the tummy; your baby will enjoy lying on the back kicking and waving arms
- be able to roll from their side onto their tummy or onto their back
- want to try to sit as you nurse them and will lean forward
- want to be pulled into a sitting or even standing position.

**Between three and five months the baby may:**

- be able to take some of their body weight on their forearms and be able to lift their shoulders
- be able to hold up their head with very little help
- have smooth control over many movements including the eyes
- start to roll from their back to their sides (at about four months they roll from back to sides, at five months they roll from tummy to back and at six months from back to tummy)
- sit up straight while supported
- pull themself into a sitting or standing position while holding your fingers
- show signs of becoming clingy or shy with strangers, and might object to being put down to sleep. A fear of strangers starts after five months, which is when they begin to discriminate strangers from family. The clingy behaviour is very likely a sign of this developmental leap and may last a few days or a week or two.

Once the skill of rolling is mastered the baby will roll back and forth with obvious pleasure, although there will be an odd bump of the nose or on the back of the head. A soft blanket covered with a sheet on the floor allows your baby to enjoy rolling and doing push-ups. Be ready to help with this rolling.

You can vary your baby's positions on the change table, on your lap or on a rug on the floor. You can provide times for the baby without clothes in a warm room. Remember to avoid any draught. Try rolling the baby gently from side to side while supporting the heavy head as you do this. You can move your baby's legs and arms smoothly in towards their body and away again.

## Skills and responses

At around three to four months of age, the baby's energy and interest in all manner of things increase. More skills are acquired, facial expressions are studied intently and the baby enjoys new activities. Babies can now concentrate longer.

At this time your baby is likely to enjoy different sounds such as those from rattles, bells, and musical toys, as well as being interested in the sounds he or she can produce, trying to repeat them if encouraged to do so. Watch for and enjoy your baby's responses to your smiles, laughter and the games that you play. Your baby may blow bubbles,

cry out happily and let you know that this is fun and can go on for longer. Your baby will also enjoy looking in a mirror at this age. They will look for variety in the activities you share. Your baby will really enjoy and deliberately play with hands and feet. Also, your baby might love to examine and play with your fingers. The baby might grasp at things with both hands and actually play with a rattle. Lastly, you will find that your baby will try to put anything and everything (including fingers) into the mouth.

## Play

Play is the normal, instinctive pursuit of the child and it is natural for you to respond to your baby's cues and also to initiate play yourself. Play provides many opportunities for communicating and socialising. You and the baby are constantly interacting and it is likely that you will intuitively suit the type of play to your baby's mood and ability to respond to and enjoy it. When the baby begins to take a real interest in examining different objects, walk around, point out things and talk to the baby about them. Through play the baby learns more about the world and about him or herself.

It is often after a feed, when relaxed and comfortable but not yet ready for sleep, that you both can enjoy active play. The baby is likely to be in a quiet, alert state with eyes wide open and fixed on you ready for fun. In the first month or two it is you who will initiate the play and look for your baby's response. The baby will watch your eyes and facial expressions and may try to imitate them and will become aware of different tones as you speak and sing. From around four weeks there may be coos and chuckles when playing.

You will quickly learn when there has been enough play. The baby may just lose interest in what you are doing, show signs of becoming overexcited or be too tired to continue. Respect the message. Some of the other tired signs include: yawning, fretting, grimacing and making jerky movements. Be ready to put your baby down for a sleep. If not ready to sleep the baby might just need to be able to look around quietly and rest, might suck on fingers or a toy – at the same time perhaps seeing, hearing, tasting, smelling and feeling, quietly absorbing impressions in a relaxed, low-key way. The length of time for which a baby can do this depends on how the baby is feeling and on age and temperament. Be aware and you will know when the baby becomes tired, bored, hungry, uncomfortable or lonely.

Play is a wonderful way to help your baby's growth and development and is recognised as an important and ongoing part of the infant's and child's world.

# 20

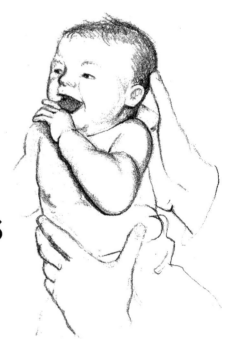

# Health and illness

There are times when all babies become ill. Parents worry. They are anxious not to underestimate a serious illness but they do not want to fuss over a minor upset. This chapter might help you in assessing your baby's condition by discussing some common ailments. However, if you are doubtful and uncertain get medical help. Immunisation is discussed in this Chapter 22.

## Recognising the sick baby

You are worried about your baby. Something is different and you have the feeling that the baby might be sick. Do not ignore your feeling. Parents are usually very sensitive to the onset of illness in their baby and may need to discuss their anxiety with their doctor. You will be asked what your baby's temperature is so it is wise to have a thermometer in your cupboard to use when your baby appears sick. A body temperature between 36.4°C and 37.2°C is considered normal. A temperature of 37.5°C or above is elevated and you will want to know why.

## Taking your baby's temperature

There are different thermometers for taking body temperature. You can ask your pharmacist to show you those available. Parents often prefer the reusable strip thermometer which is placed on the baby's forehead for two minutes and then read. Another thermometer that is very sensitive and rapid in registering the temperature is the one placed within the ear. It can be read within a minute but is expensive to buy.

Then there is the glass mercury thermometer which you may already have in the medicine cupboard. Some tips for using a mercury thermometer:

- Remember that it is glass and quite thin; dispose of the mercury properly if it breaks.
- If there is mercury in the stem shake it down into the bulb.
- Place the bulb of the thermometer in your baby's armpit, making sure that it is not in contact with any clothing. Do not place the thermometer either in the baby's mouth or anus, as you risk injury in doing so.
- Keep the thermometer in position for at least two minutes. Cuddle the baby against you as you hold the upper arm gently against the thermometer.
- Wash the thermometer in cold soapy water after you have read it and before returning it to its container.

## Observing your baby

What can you see or feel that is different?

Has your baby's appearance changed? Is there any rash, is your baby flushed and hot to touch or unusually pale? Does your baby feel cold?

Is the baby's temperature raised? This is the most common sign that a baby is sick. Take the temperature, preferably while the baby is quiet, and not immediately after a bath or sponge bath. Your doctor will be interested in the reading and the time the temperature was taken. A high fever can lead to convulsions so a baby with a high temperature needs to be cooled (see 'Keeping your baby cool' in Chapter 17).

## Baby's behaviour: is it different?

Have you noticed any of the following changes in your baby?

- Is your baby restless and irritable, sleeping more or less than usual, lethargic or difficult to rouse?
- Is your baby's crying different in some way from the crying you are accustomed to hearing? Is the crying continuous or intermittent, is the baby becoming increasingly miserable and distressed, difficult to comfort?
- Does your baby appear to be in pain?
- Has the feeding pattern altered? What about the appetite: how is your baby sucking?
- Is your baby uninterested in interacting with you?
- Is there redness or a rash, or a swelling on any part of the body?
- Is there any sign of thrush (see later in this chapter)? If there is thrush in the mouth, also check the area around the anus. Oral thrush can be very painful and interfere with feeding but is unlikely to make your baby acutely sick.
- Has your baby a nasal discharge which is blocking the nose, making breathing difficult? Is the discharge clear and thin or thick and perhaps greenish-yellow? These are signs of a cold.
- Has your baby a cough? Has breathing altered: is it rapid and shallow or slow and laboured? Is the baby wheezing?
- Is there a change in the bowel motions? Is your baby suffering from constipation, causing pain? If your baby has diarrhoea, especially if there is vomiting too, there is a serious risk of dehydration. Get immediate medical advice. (See 'Diarrhoea' later in this chapter.)
- Has your baby vomited? Continual, frequent or forceful vomits need investigating.

✎ Is your baby passing less urine? Is it darker than usual? Does it smell 'fishy'? Does there seem to be pain as the urine is passed?

If you make a note of your concerns and observations before you ring or visit your doctor you can then remember to describe them all. He or she will then be in a better position to advise you.

# Common ailments

The following is a list of ailments common to babies, along with steps you can take to manage each.

## Bronchiolitis

Bronchiolitis is caused by a specific virus. It can cause distress in a young baby very rapidly. The very small air tubes in the lungs become blocked and interfere with the transfer of oxygen to the bloodstream. Babies often need hospitalisation to be given oxygen. So far no vaccine is available but trials are about to start in the United States. Baby may have a runny nose, laboured breathing and wheezing, severe coughing, difficulty feeding, and vomiting. Consult your doctor, maintain fluid intake and watch the breathing (see 'The common cold and coughs' later in this chapter). A humidifier may help but don't add eucalyptus as it could irritate the airways.

## Chafing (see 'Nappy rash and chafing' later in this chapter)

## Colic

Cases of infant colic have been recorded for centuries but there is still no one accepted cause of the problem, probably because there are several causes, possibly in combination.

Babies suffering colic are usually found to be thriving and growing well although they have periods of acute distress from abdominal pain. These spasms of severe abdominal pain occur suddenly, then pass, only to start again. This repeating misery can continue for three or four hours and the baby is inconsolable while the spasm lasts. Colic is one of the most distressing conditions for babies and parents alike.

Both breast- and formula-fed babies can suffer from it. The consolation is that with time the colic will pass. If you think that your baby is suffering from colic talk to your health adviser.

Two probable causes are gas in the bowel and an immature nervous system. The baby might not be able to fully digest the feeds, or might be reacting to some substance that has passed from the mother's food into the breastmilk. Some ingredient in the formula may be responsible for colic in the formula-fed baby.

Babies who may at first have been relaxed and sleepy become increasingly alert as they respond to the sensory input from their new environment. Overstimulation or over-tiredness may increase attacks of colic.

The attacks of colic commonly (but not always) occur between three weeks and three months of age, although they may begin earlier and finish later. Although babies can suffer colic at any time of the day or night, most often it seems to occur between 6 p.m. and 10 p.m. This is often referred to as 'evening colic' and it commonly begins shortly after the feed taken around 6 p.m. However, it may start at any time between 4 p.m. and 8 p.m. It may last three to four hours, even longer at times.

The baby may wake suddenly with a loud, shrill scream and draw up the legs; the face may become red, the abdomen tight like a drum and the baby may suck desperately on anything available. There will be no relief until the spasm of pain passes. This relief often follows the passing of a stool or of flatus. As the pain eases your baby will flop against you exhausted as the screaming subsides. If there is time before the next spasm the baby may doze, only to be wakened again by another attack of the same acute pain. The screams leave you in no doubt that your baby is in very real need of any help you can give.

Are there any adults – the baby's father or maybe a friend or relative – willing and able to help through your baby's colicky time? You can take it in turns to hold and comfort the baby. While accepting that it is likely to take time before your baby outgrows the colic, there are things you can try that may help.

## Managing colic

First, observe how your baby is feeding.

- Is your baby swallowing large gulps of air? This could be due to poor attachment so check that attachment is correct. If your baby pulls off the breast or stops taking the bottle you can try to bring up wind but do not interfere with comfortable feeding. Wind may contribute to colic but it is by no means the whole or only cause.

- Is your baby taking a very large feed? This is more likely in the early hours of the morning and/or at the first feeding of the day after your baby has had a long sleep, and/or when your breasts are very full. Your baby may wake and feed ravenously, gulping and overfilling the tummy. The baby may not be able to fully digest this overload and ten or twelve hours later there may be a build-up of gas in the colon, which triggers the colic. Some women find it helpful to give smaller, slower feeds at these times. If your breasts are very full you can express a little milk until they soften. This may ease the flow. If not, you can try compressing the areola with two fingers until your baby can feed more easily (see 'Too much milk' in Chapter 21).

- Are you changing your baby to the second breast before the first breast is 'emptied'? It is tempting to do this when both breasts are very full. In taking just some from each full breast the baby is likely to take extra lactose that may not be fully digested and contribute to colic attacks.

- Perhaps your baby is reacting to something in your breastmilk. Breastfeeding women can consider their own diet. Some find that dairy products appear to cause or increase their baby's colic. You could try eliminating for a few days any foods containing milk products. If you decide that the colic has lessened and wish to continue to omit these dairy products, you will need to increase your calcium intake from other sources or by taking a calcium supplement. If you suspect other foods may be causing problems you can check in a similar manner. Be sure you have an adequate diet. Most major hospitals and community health centres have a dietitian whom you can visit or phone for advice.

## Three ways to hold a baby to ease colic pain

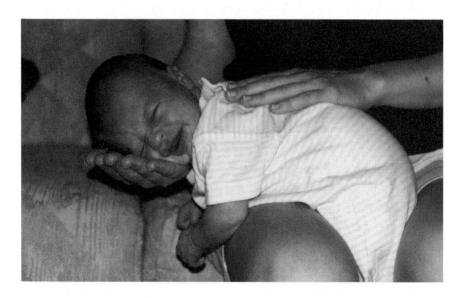

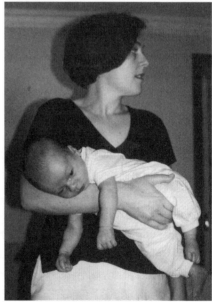

- Is your baby formula-fed and reacting to something in the formula? If you feel that this could be a problem discuss it with your health adviser.
- Is your formula-fed baby taking the feed too fast? Usually, young babies are most comfortable taking fifteen to twenty minutes to feed. If necessary you can try tightening the bottle top or using a teat with a smaller hole so that the flow is restricted and the feed takes longer. Trial and error will tell you what helps.

**Things you can do to help include the following:**

- Work together as partners so you do not become so fatigued. You and your partner can take turns at walking, rocking and soothing your baby.
- Arrange your day to lessen demands on your time during the likely colicky period. Your baby will need your help during the attacks of colic and to feel that there is loving care even when it can't relieve the acute pain of the actual spasms. Try not to leave your baby to suffer colic alone. Tell yourself, as each attack passes, that there is now one less you both will have to suffer. Some women find it helps to cross off each day on the calendar as they wait for their baby to reach three months – the time of hoped-for relief (even though it cannot be guaranteed).
- When trying to soothe your baby, look for any procedure that you find helps. Sometimes one approach works; at another time you may need a different method. If breastfeeding, do not be tempted to wean – formula-fed babies can suffer from colic too.

**In addition you can try the following:**

- Offer your baby the breast for a moment or two or, if formula-fed, some warm, boiled water.
- Hold your baby against your shoulder, with firm but gentle pressure on the back so that the tummy is pressed against you.
- Wrap your baby firmly.

- Place your baby tummy down across your thigh, with or without a warm hot water bottle which is well covered, or a flat, well warmed wheat pack beneath the tummy and firmly rubbing the back (see that your baby does not become too hot).
- Carry your baby lying across your arm, face towards the floor with the bottom supported against your hip.
- Give your baby a deep, warm, relaxing bath.
- Hold your baby with pressure on the tummy as you rock together quite fast in a rocking chair.
- Use a hammock or swinging cradle (check the safety features of the cradle) to provide rhythmic movement.
- Gently swing the baby back and forth in a light hand-carrier in which your baby can lie down. This can be awkward and become heavy so it is helpful if there is someone else to take a turn. (The 'back and forth' movement seems to be more effective than the 'side to side' movement provided by a cradle.) Movement apparently creates different sensations that may help.
- Wheel your baby in the pram or stroller. A slightly bumpy ride is better than a smooth one and you can push the pram back and forth over a coathanger or such on the floor.

You might combine some of these measures with warmth. You could, for example, warm the cot. If using a hot water bottle remember to remove it before you put your baby down.

Colic attacks do pass and babies outgrow them but they need sensitive, sympathetic help while they last. Mothers especially often need support too, from other family members or friends and from health professionals who understand their problem. Fathers also can of course become fatigued by a colicky baby. Do not give anti-colic mixtures without advice from your doctor.

## The common cold and coughs

Babies usually recover easily from simple colds. Colds are viral infections and readily spread – they do not occur because you have had your baby 'out in the cold'. However, if the baby becomes really chilled, their resistance can be lowered and the baby is then more likely to succumb to a viral attack. Babies may have as many as six to twelve colds in a year, especially if they are in contact with many people, particularly other children. To lessen the risk, visitors with colds can be kept away from your baby. However, the viruses are usually airborne and it is difficult to keep your baby away from other family members who are suffering from a cold.

At the onset of a cold your baby may be restless and irritable. The eyes may be reddened and the baby may suffer a fever – a temperature above 37.5°C – and there may be a decrease in the appetite. There may be sneezes and splutters, a nasal discharge may develop and possibly a cough. This nasal discharge from the lining of the nose begins as a clear, runny liquid. It may then alter and, although still clear, become a thick discharge.

If the nasal discharge is running down the back of the nose rather than out it can irritate the baby's throat and cause a cough. If enough is swallowed and collects in the stomach the baby may have spills or actual vomits containing mucus. Mucus may also appear in the stools. A simple cold is more than a nuisance to a young baby; it can be upsetting because a baby finds it so difficult to breathe through the mouth. A blocked nose causes constant interruption while feeding and may make the baby unwilling to feed regardless of hunger. You will need to be patient. Your baby may manage smaller, more frequent feeds more easily.

**Contact your doctor without delay if you feel anxious or if:**
- your baby's breathing becomes rapid, noisy, laboured or wheezy
- a cough has developed and is becoming worse
- your baby is refusing to feed
- your baby is vomiting.

Sometimes a cold leads to other infections, some of which, like bronchitis or pneumonia, are caused by bacteria. A fever may develop after the cold has appeared. The nasal discharge may become yellowy-green and thick. There may be an increasing lack of interest in feeding, distress from a sore throat or an earache due to a middle ear infection and/or the baby might have a worsening or distressing cough.

The onset of quite different, other infections can be mistaken for a cold because they develop with similar symptoms: for example, bronchiolitis (see earlier in this chapter).

Antibiotics do not help viral infections but are used if a bacterial infection develops. If your baby is prescribed antibiotics follow the instructions carefully and finish the course even if your baby seems to have recovered before the medication is finished. If you do not finish the course some of the stronger bacteria may survive and the infection may recur and resistance to the antibiotic could develop.

## Managing a cold

Some mothers do as many of our grandmothers did: they express a little breastmilk and, using a dropper, put a few drops into each nostril if the baby is troubled by a blocked nose. It will certainly do no harm. Today we usually use a few drops of normal saline solution in the same way. You can buy normal saline and a dropper from the pharmacist. Put your baby down on his or her back and place one or two drops in each nostril and then sit your baby up. There will probably be a

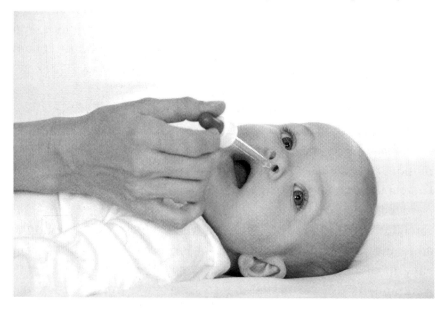

splutter and sneeze, which will help to clear the mucus. If you feel that the drops you are using are not clearing the nose and your baby is having difficulty feeding, discuss this with your health adviser. Avoid using medicinal nasal drops without medical advice – they are rarely necessary and may be harmful.

Sleeping can be more comfortable if the head of the cot is raised on stable blocks or a pillow is placed *under* the head of the mattress. Moist air is soothing; you can use a humidifier but don't add eucalyptus to it as this can irritate the lining of the nose. Care must be taken that neither the baby nor any other children can be scalded by the boiling water in a humidifier. You need to air the room well following the use of a humidifier or mould may grow on the walls.

It is best to avoid chest vapour rubs as they can irritate your baby's tender skin.

## Constipation

Constipation occurs when the stool becomes dry and hard and is passed with difficulty. Because water is absorbed rapidly by the bowel it is important that stools are passed while they are still soft.

This problem is usually restricted to formula-fed babies who need to have a bowel motion daily or every second day. More often constipation occurs when there has been no bowel action for 48 hours or more. Sometimes, even though a baby does have a bowel action daily, the quantity passed is insufficient and the baby becomes constipated.

It may be only the beginning of the motion that is hard and then the baby may be able to push it out with only minor discomfort and no damage. As the hard plug or 'marble' is passed the normal salve-like motion, typical of the formula-fed baby, follows. If the hard motion is larger and there is more hard, dry, perhaps crumbly stool to come the baby will suffer severe pain and scream while straining to pass it. It can break the skin and/or some of the small blood vessels around the anus and there may be fresh blood on the motion. Do not give your baby aperients (laxatives). Consult your doctor or maternal and child health nurse.

Breastfed babies may not pass a stool for four or five days and often even longer, and yet have a soft bowel movement when they do. This is normal and they are not constipated. However, they can become uncomfortable after four or five days. If you feel that your baby is uncomfortable and is well established on breastfeeding you could offer about 30 millilitres of cooled, boiled water between feeds. This could help your baby to pass a stool.

## Signs and causes of constipation

If constipated, your baby may:

- find it difficult to pass faeces, which have become hard
- have a loss of appetite
- become restless and have abdominal discomfort or pain
- vomit during feeding or just after while straining to pass a stool.

**Causes of constipation may be:**

- an incorrectly prepared formula, particularly if it is too strong – that is, too much powdered formula and too little water
- an unsuitable formula
- insufficient fluid
- insufficient food
- a 'sluggish' bowel where the peristalsis (the muscular action that pushes the food and waste along the bowel) is slow
- illness.

## Managing constipation

The cause needs to be identified and rectified. If the problem persists your baby may resist passing the stool for fear of the pain associated with this.

It is unwise to use any aperient (laxative) or suppository or to change the formula without discussion with your health adviser.

You may be able to help your baby to pass a hard plug of stool by making it slippery by pressing cotton wool dipped in olive oil against the anus.

Check the use-by date of any formula you are using and that it has been correctly made up. You can give extra cooled, boiled water between feeds, which can help to soften the stools. If your baby is more than one month old you can try giving a little prune juice. You can buy this from the pharmacy or the supermarket or prepare it yourself by taking four or five prunes and covering them with 300 millilitres of cold water. Slowly bring to simmering point and cook gently for about twenty minutes, then squash lightly with a spoon and strain the liquid into a jug. (You do not push the prunes through the sieve for a very young baby.) Start by offering only one teaspoon of this juice and, if your baby is comfortable, you can give another teaspoon or two. The juice may produce the desired effect.

If constipation persists consult your health adviser.

## Convulsions

Convulsions are fits involving an involuntary contraction of muscles that interferes with normal function. There are different causes of convulsions. Most often a convulsion is a sign of the onset of illness and due to a fever (febrile convulsion), particularly if the temperature rises rapidly. During a convulsion your baby will suddenly lose consciousness and become rigid; the eyes may roll back. Breathing may be irregular and difficult. Your baby will have jerky movements of the limbs, and the body may jerk and twitch as muscles contract and relax. Breath might be held for a moment or two, skin colour might change but your baby will then take a deep breath. Do not leave your baby during the convulsion. When it stops, ring your doctor. After the fit your baby is likely to fall asleep.

Although it can be very alarming for you it is important that you *do not leave your baby during the convulsion to get help*. The convulsion is likely to be brief and do no harm, but obtain medical advice so any appropriate treatment can be given and its cause determined.

## Managing a convulsion

🖊 Do not try to restrain your baby's movements.

🖊 Prevent any injury to your baby. Remove any objects that might injure your baby; clear the area of furniture and sharp objects; move the baby only if they are in a dangerous location (e.g. could fall off a change table); loosen any tight clothing, especially around the neck.

🖊 When you are able, place your baby on one side in the coma position (this helps to keep the airway clear).

🖊 If the convulsion continues beyond five minutes call an ambulance.

🖊 When the convulsion stops check your baby's temperature and contact your doctor.

🖊 If the temperature is raised, give your baby a full tepid sponge bath. Don't use cold water.

## *Cradle cap*

Cradle cap (seborrhoeic dermatitis) is the name given to the greasy, yellowish-brown scales or flakes that may form on the surface of the scalp of babies or older children. It often appears first on the fontanelle. The skin may be reddened or more severely inflamed beneath the scales or crusts. It is associated with the sebum from the sebaecous glands in

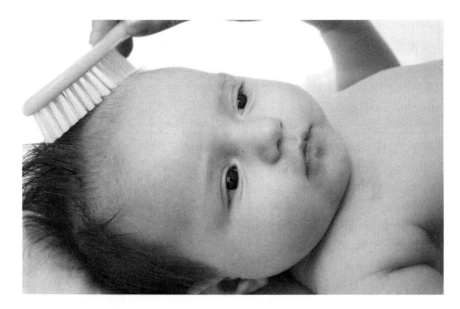

the skin, but the actual cause is not known. However, in the early stages if not treated it may spread beyond the scalp onto the face and body, particularly behind the ears and in other creases of the skin. If it has spread beyond the scalp see your health adviser.

## Managing cradle cap

𝒞 To soften the scales, gently massage the scalp with warm olive oil or sorbolene and glycerine cream and leave overnight.

𝒞 At bath time wash the scalp and massage well with a mild soap or baby shampoo and rinse carefully.

𝒞 Brush your baby's scalp morning and night. This will help to loosen and remove the scales. Wash the brush daily too.

𝒞 If the cradle cap is difficult to remove you can use a bicarbonate of soda paste. Mix enough bicarbonate of soda with water to make a paste which you can spread over the scalp. Allow this to dry and then brush gently before washing the scalp. Commercial preparations are also available.

## *Dehydration*

Dehydration is defined as loss of fluid to the extent that there is insufficient for the body's basic needs. It occurs when body fluid is lost faster than it can be replaced. This is a serious condition in a baby and is considered a medical emergency. Contact your doctor at once or go to the hospital emergency department day or night.

Dehydration can be due to inadequate fluid intake. This can occur if your baby has diarrhoea and/or vomiting (the risk is greater if your baby has both diarrhoea and vomiting), and persistent crying and excessive sweating. It can also be caused by fever and/or heat exhaustion.

A well baby who is not receiving enough fluid can also become dehydrated. Heatwave conditions can be a cause if precautions are not taken. Never leave a baby alone in a car. Apart from other dangers the sun can heat up a closed car and lead to heat exhaustion, and even death, very rapidly. Heat exhaustion and dehydration can result if a baby is left anywhere in the hot sun. Remember that the sun moves: if you have put your baby outside in the pram in the shade, in a short time the sun could move to shine directly onto and even into the pram. You will need to watch carefully. Over-wrapped babies and those left in overheated rooms can also become dehydrated.

## Signs of dehydration

Your baby may:

- become frantically thirsty
- start by being disturbed, restless and miserable and then become listless and 'flat' with cold hands and feet
- have a fever
- look pale and sick
- have a dry mouth
- pass little or no urine for eight to twelve hours; any passed will be dark
- have dry, loose and wrinkly skin, no longer elastic
- have sunken eyes and fontanelle (the soft spot on top of the head).

## Managing dehydration

- Obtain immediate medical help.
- Until seen by a doctor give your baby cool, boiled water with sugar. Mix one heaped teaspoon in a cup of boiled water; when cool, offer small quantities by spoon or bottle (try 30 to 40 millilitres at a time). Vomiting is less likely when small quantities of fluid are given. You can offer more every ten or fifteen minutes.
- Follow the steps listed below in 'Managing diarrhoea' if your baby has diarrhoea.

## *Dermatitis*

For seborrhoeic dermatitis see 'Cradle cap' earlier in this chapter.

Mothers can suffer breast dermatitis from thrush infection: see 'Thrush' later in this chapter.

## Diarrhoea

Diarrhoea is one of the most common illnesses in infants and young children. Mild cases of diarrhoea rarely need medication but more severe cases will. A baby is said to have diarrhoea when the bowels act with abnormal frequency – say, three or more bowel actions a day above the normal number – for 48 hours or more.

The frequent stools change in consistency and are usually watery. They may become green, contain mucus and sometimes blood. These stools are usually very offensive and may be passed explosively. The baby's buttocks may become red and raw.

Diarrhoea must be taken seriously. It can lead to dehydration and electrolyte imbalance, particularly if the baby is also vomiting, is feverish and/or refusing to drink. The loss of body fluid can occur very rapidly and medical treatment is urgent. Talk to your doctor without delay or go to the hospital emergency department.

### Causes of diarrhoea

The most common cause is an infection caused by bacteria or viruses. Other causes include:

- an association with other illnesses, such as an infection of the respiratory tract, urinary tract or middle ear
- incorrect feeding: formula incorrectly prepared, or one unsuitable for the baby's digestion or simply too much
- reaction to something in the mother's diet if breastfeeding (e.g. excessive fat), or in the formula if formula-fed (e.g. excessive fat or sucrose); such reactions may be temporary or allergic: consult your health adviser to identify the cause and to plan what to do
- lack of an enzyme in the intestinal tract (e.g. the lactase needed to digest the lactose in the feed) may be temporarily deficient following a bowel upset.

## Infective diarrhoea

This is is more common in formula-fed babies, rarely occuring in fully breastfed babies. Don't mistake the 'mushy' breastmilk stool for diarrhoea (see 'Stools' in Chapter 4).

The incubation period can vary from a few hours to several days, depending on the organisms responsible, but the onset of the symptoms is usually sudden. It is highly contagious. The type of stool and the baby's condition will depend on the severity of the illness. The number of bowel motions will vary between four or five up to a dozen or more in 24 hours. (See description of stools above.)

**Observe the changes in your baby and inform your doctor. Take note of:**

- the appearance and character of the stools, the frequency and number of bowel actions and when they occur;
- signs of dehydration (above), any fever, pain, vomiting, loss of appetite, and even refusal to drink or coughing;
- altered behaviour such as continual distressed crying, disturbed sleep or lethargy.

## Managing diarrhoea

- Obtain medical advice.
- If you are breastfeeding, continue with small frequent breastfeeds. If your baby refuses to breastfeed you can offer the boiled water and sugar mix (see 'Dehydration' earlier in this chapter) while waiting to see your doctor. Express and save your milk.
- If your baby is formula-fed, stop the formula and give the boiled water and sugar mix (see 'Dehydration' earlier in this chapter); if vomiting, offer 5 to 10 millilitres every five minutes. If there is no vomiting, give what your baby will take. Your doctor will advise you about your baby's feeding and decide whether there is a need for special rehydration fluid. In severe cases intravenous fluid may be necessary.
- Avoid contact with others, particularly other babies and young children.
- Wash your hands after handling your baby, particularly after nappy changing. Some mothers use disposable gloves to change nappies at this time.

- Rinse faeces off cloth nappies. Store nappies in a lidded bucket until washed in very hot water. Keep apart from other laundry. Remove the stool from disposable nappies before putting them out with the rubbish.
- Change your baby frequently. Wash gently with warm water and pure, unperfumed soap and dab dry or use warm olive oil on cotton wool if the stools are sticking to the skin. If the bottom is raw, spread zinc and castor oil ointment on a piece of cotton material and place it against the affected area. This will be both soothing and healing.

## Prevention of infective diarrhoea

- Do not knowingly expose your baby to anyone with diarrhoea and take precautions to prevent diarrhoea spreading from you or your baby to others by avoiding contact and by careful hygiene.
- Breastfeed if possible. Breastmilk contains cells and antibodies that protect against and help overcome infection; milk taken directly from the breast has not been exposed to contamination.
- When formula-feeding, be sure that the equipment you use in the preparation of any feed is scrupulously clean.
- Wash your hands thoroughly before preparing the formula and after nappy changing and using the toilet. Again, you might choose to use disposable gloves.
- Prepare formula feeds carefully and check the mixture is within its 'use-by' date.
- Store the made-up formula in the refrigerator or make up each feed as your baby needs it.
- Do not leave made-up formula standing at room temperature or carry unchilled or warmed feeds when visiting or travelling. If your baby will need a feed while you are out you can carry the boiled water in the bottle and then add the formula powder when you are about to give the feed.
- Throw out any leftover formula or thawed, expressed breastmilk.
- Protect your baby and the formula from flies.

## Diarrhoea due to lactose overload or lactose intolerance

Lactose is the main carbohydrate in both breastmilk and cow's milk-based formula. It is digested by the enzyme lactase. It is normal for some undigested lactose to pass through the bowel but too much can cause diarrhoea, ranging from mild to severe. Unless managed, it can affect the baby's growth. If there is insufficient lactase available, diarrhoea can result. This may be a temporary upset in very young babies. It may follow an attack of gastroenteritis or bowel surgery. Expect the temporary decrease in lactase production to improve as your baby recovers. Premature babies may have difficulty digesting lactose until their digestive system matures. Rarely are babies born with a true lactose intolerance but when it does occur the baby can be given a special formula to prevent chronic diarrhoea and failure to thrive. These babies need regular medical supervision.

Diarrhoea due to undigested lactose can produce explosive, acidic, green motions that can scald the baby's bottom. The undigested lactose draws water from the lining of the bowel, fermentation occurs, gas is produced and diarrhoea results.

If breastfeeding, do not wean your baby but get professional help. It is likely that the problem can be managed simply. A formula-fed baby with a temporary upset will be given a lactose-free formula if necessary. In both cases your health adviser can be expected to advise you.

A well, breastfed baby may suffer lactose overload if the tummy is over-filled. This overload can easily happen when the mother's breasts are very full and the baby drinks hungrily. There may not be enough of the enzyme lactase to digest the feeding. This is likely if, instead of 'emptying' the first breast the baby is given a short time on each breast to relieve the fullness of both. With a longer time at the first breast the baby is likely to be satisfied with a smaller feed which can more easily be digested. (You can ease an uncomfortably full breast by expressing a little of the milk.)

## Signs of upset due to undigested lactose

- The baby may be miserable with bouts of distressed crying.
- The stomach may be distended by the gas produced and this will probably cause pain as it passes on down through the bowel.
- Stools may be watery, frothy, often greenish and usually explosively passed.
- Skin in the nappy area may be burnt, i.e. made red and raw by the stool.
- In the healthy breastfed baby with undigested lactose, the symptoms are often worst approximately seven to ten hours after the 'offending' feed.

## Managing lactose overload in a breastfed baby

- Allow your baby to empty the first breast before you offer the second. If you have very full breasts and cannot empty even the first, express approximately 20 to 30 millilitres before starting the feed. This may allow your baby to 'empty' the first side before you offer the second. You will soon know how much to express.
- If possible, space the feeds so that your baby has time to digest them. Try to allow at least three hours between feeds.
- If a lactose upset is distressing your baby and does not improve rapidly, consult your doctor. You will need advice until the condition improves.
- Protect your baby's bottom with a barrier cream such as zinc and castor oil and change soiled nappies promptly.

## Managing lactose overload in a formula-fed baby

- Obtain medical advice. Your baby will be given a lactose-free formula if it is necessary.
- Protect your baby's bottom as above.

## Diarrhoea due to metabolic disorders

Diarrhoea can be the presenting symptom in some congenital metabolic disorders such as coeliac disease and cystic fibrosis (a disease of the pancreas). The onset is usually slow and if unrecognised the baby's condition deteriorates. These babies need ongoing medical treatment.

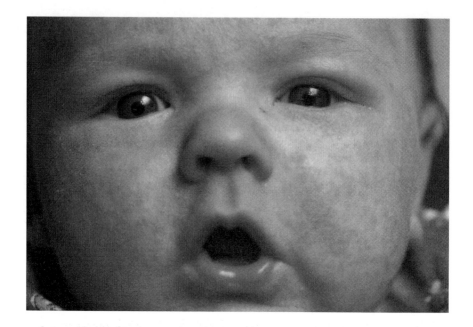

## *Eczema*

Eczema occurs as an inflammatory reaction that involves the skin in a characteristic rash. Some babies are predisposed to eczema and this is more likely if the parents have a history of allergies. Triggers include substances in the diet, particular substances that come in contact with the skin, infection, stress and becoming too hot.

An eczema rash may be rough to touch, scaly and dry but it can become red, raw and weeping. Patches of it may appear as early as six weeks and most often it appears on the forehead and cheeks of young babies who are affected. Older babies and toddlers may have it in the elbow creases and on the skin behind the knees. Wrists, ankles and the trunk may also become involved. Many of these babies continue with eczema while their milk teeth are coming. When these teeth have erupted the eczema may lessen or remain around wrists, elbows and knees. It may disappear completely. Babies with eczema usually need medical help.

As eczema tends to occur in allergic families, make every effort to breastfeed these babies as this may lessen the likelihood or severity of eczema and other allergies.

## Managing eczema

- Breastfeed if possible. Remove items in your diet that may be affecting your baby (see 'Food sensitivity' in Chapter 21).
- If your baby is formula-fed, discuss the formula with your doctor.
- Prevent your baby becoming overheated, but avoid chilling. Consider the weather. When possible do not have your baby out in the heat, direct sunlight or a hot wind.
- Strive to avoid irritants: laundry detergents, water softeners and nappy antiseptics can cause problems. Even the pure laundry soaps, which may be the best to use, need to be rinsed out thoroughly.
- Try softening the bath water with oats. Tie two or three tablespoons of oatmeal or rolled oats in the end of a sock or pantyhose and soak in water for half an hour or so; squeeze out the fluid and then add this to the bath water or you can just swirl the sock with its oats directly around in the bath and squeeze it. This can be very soothing.
- You may need to avoid soap (even the pure and unperfumed soaps) and instead use oil in the bath, a pine-tar solution or sorbolene and glycerine cream. You can discuss this with your doctor.
- Protect your baby's skin from direct contact with wool and synthetic materials. Use cotton socks and soft cotton clothing next to the skin. Woollen caps need a cotton liner. If a jumper or cardigan is needed have a long-sleeved cotton garment under it.
- If your baby scratches you will need to use cotton mittens. Remember to keep both fingernails and toenails short.

Many babies outgrow these sensitivities but it is not possible to predict which ones will cease or when.

## *Eyes: blocked tear duct*

A duct drains the fluid from the eye and runs from the tear sac in the inner corner of the eye down into the nose. Normally, babies produce very few tears for the first five or six weeks after birth. However, if you notice a watery leak from the corner of the eye you can suspect that the duct is blocked. This condition may occur in one or both eyes. It may lead to conjunctivitis in which case your baby will need medical treatment.

### Managing a blocked tear duct

✐ Using your clean little finger, gently massage with a circular motion the inner corner of the eye, over the region of the tear duct. Ask for a demonstration from your health adviser.

✐ Watch for signs of infection (conjunctivitis) and obtain medical advice should it occur.

✐ The massage may clear a blockage but if not, the duct may need to be cleared by an eye specialist.

## Eyes: sticky eyes

These occur most often in the early days following birth. The eyelids may simply be a little crusty. You can express and put in the baby's eye a few drops of breastmilk. You can make up a saline solution using ¼ teaspoon of salt in 150 millilitres of cooled, boiled water. Keep it in a sterile container which is clearly labelled. Make this up daily. Every few hours, gently wipe from the inside corner of the eye to the outside with a sterile cotton gauze dampened in the saline solution. If it is necessary to wipe the eye a second time take a fresh, moistened cotton ball and repeat the process. If the eye itself seems to be affected in any way – bloodshot or discharging pus – your baby will need medical treatment; meanwhile, you can express and put in the eye a few drops of breastmilk as it can help to fight infection.

## Eyes: conjunctivitis

This is an inflammation of the eye and can be due to a bacterial or viral infection, to an allergy or to any substance or foreign body that has reached the eye. The eyes are usually reddened, may be puffy and there is often a discharge of pus. Your baby will need immediate medical assessment and appropriate treatment; meanwhile, express and put in the baby's eye a few drops of breastmilk.

## Fever

This is an abnormal rise in body temperature. There will be an increased pulse rate and body functions can be upset depending on the rise in temperature and how long it persists. If your baby feels hot you can check the temperature. Take it under the arm as described earlier in this chapter ('Recognising the sick baby'). A baby's temperature is usually around 37°C. A raised temperature indicates a fever.

A fever does not necessarily mean that a baby or young child has a serious illness, although it is often the first sign that your baby is not well. It is one way the body responds to infection and fights it. But it must not be ignored.

## Managing a fever

*✎* If your baby has a raised temperature obtain medical advice. Your doctor will advise you and may wish to see your baby.

*✎* You can dress your baby in a nappy and cotton singlet if the environment is warm. Avoid even light synthetic materials. You may need a light cotton sheet as a cover.

*✎* You can give your baby a tepid sponge bath or a lukewarm bath.

*✎* Aim to keep the room cool – around 19 or 20°C.

## Gastroenteritis (infection of the gut)

This is the most common cause of diarrhoea (see 'Diarrhoea' earlier in this chapter).

## Gastro-oesophageal reflux

This occurs when the valve muscle between the oesophagus (food pipe) and stomach is relaxed and the stomach contents leak back into the oesophagus. The contents may then flow back into the stomach or be vomited. The amount the baby spills varies. Often the spills are only small and tend to flow out easily and effortlessly, especially as the baby is put down. The regurgitated stomach contents are acidic and may burn and inflame the oesophagus, causing considerable pain.

Mild reflux – spilling or posseting – is so common that it is considered normal and unimportant if the baby is thriving and not unduly miserable. The spilling is messy and may cause parents worry, but it can be lessened by careful handling.

**Any of the following symptoms can be part of a severe gastric reflux:**

- *C* Your baby may spill more than a little of the feed, gag and vomit. There might be specks of blood in the vomit, and this can be either bright red or, if it has been partly digested, chocolate-coloured and looking like coffee grounds. If unrelieved the baby will fail to thrive.
- *C* The baby might cry in real distress.
- *C* The baby might refuse to feed.
- *C* There may be poor weight gains – your baby's weight may remain stationary or there may be a weight loss.
- *C* You baby could sleep poorly.
- *C* You baby might appear to be in pain, stiffen and arch the back and neck in response to the bitter burning of the acid, gastric contents that are causing inflammation.
- *C* Your baby may have a persistent cough.

Such a baby will need to be seen by a doctor and suitable treatment arranged. An experienced, sympathetic and supportive doctor will lessen the stress that reflux vomiting can cause to both the baby and the parents.

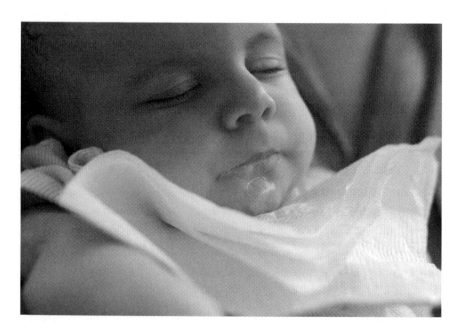

## Managing reflux vomiting

Have plenty of small towels you can use to mop up. Use large absorbent bibs that pull over the head and do not tie. You will need to safety-pin the bib down onto your baby's clothes.

### When feeding your baby, remember the following:

- Keep your baby's head above the level of their tummy.
- Give slower feeds. If you have a fast flow of milk, as it lets down you could express this until the flow slows – your baby may need this milk at the end of the feed.
- Give smaller, more frequent feeds which usually cause less reflux vomiting than large feeds. Appetite-feed your baby to replace the amount vomited.
- If formula-feeding, check that the formula is correctly mixed and give the feed slowly. Do not change the formula without consulting your health adviser.
- If so advised, use a thickened feed, which might lessen the reflux.

## Handling a baby with reflux

- Try to keep your baby quiet and relaxed after a feed. Play quiet games together preferably between feeds or, if your baby is happy, before the feed.
- When fed, place your baby so that you continue to keep the head higher than the tummy.
- When you change the nappy put a pillow beneath the change table mattress to keep the head raised.
- Change your baby before the feed, and do not lift the legs: you can roll your baby gently from side to side. Avoid pressure on the tummy from a tightly pinned or fixed nappy.
- Try carrying your baby upright in a sling or possum pouch for about half an hour after the feed before putting them down.
- Raise the head ends of the cot and change table (if you use one) on stable 10-centimetre blocks (you could use bricks) or you could place a pillow *under* the head of the mattress.
- Handle your baby gently – rub the back rather than pat it to bring up wind.

If you feel that you need even more help it might be possible for your doctor to arrange admission to a postnatal hospital.

You can expect the reflux to lessen as your baby grows and develops, very often between nine and eighteen months. The valve strengthens, your baby starts solid food and learns to sit and stand. These changes help to keep the food down.

## Hives (see 'Urticaria' later in this chapter)

## Infantile acne

Young babies, especially males, may develop a form of acne on their faces which is thought to be caused by hormones. The onset is usually within the first month of life and the spots usually disappear within a few weeks. Do not confuse with milia (see 'Skin' in Chapter 4).

### Managing infantile acne

- Keep your baby clean and dry.
- Avoid squeezing the pimples.
- Discuss this condition with your doctor.

## Infected nails (see 'Paronychia' later in this chapter)

## Jaundice (see 'Jaundice' in Chapter 4)

## Middle ear infection (otitis media)

Many babies and young children develop middle ear infections. The Eustachian tube that connects the middle ear to the back of the throat is straight and relatively wide so it is easy for bacteria from the nose and throat to travel up and reach the middle ear. Likewise, a little of a feed can flow up the Eustachian tube if the baby vomits or if the feed is given with the head level with or lower than the tummy.

The onset of a middle ear infection may be sudden. It often accompanies or follows a cold. The fever can be high and pain extreme. It is not always easy to recognise where a baby is feeling pain. Your baby may or may not pull at the ear when it is aching. If you are doubtful and your baby seems sick or in pain go for a medical check. On examination the doctor will look for an inflamed ear drum and then recommend the appropriate treatment. If the infection progresses, pus can form; the raised pressure will cause acute pain and the ear drum may rupture. Repeated, untreated middle ear infections can lead to hearing loss.

## Preventing middle ear infections

**The following steps can help to prevent middle ear infections:**

- Check your baby's position when feeding. Do not allow your baby to feed lying flat on their back.
- When breastfeeding, particularly if your baby is lying beside you, prop yourself so that your baby feeds with their head a little higher than their tummy.
- Do not allow your baby to feed from a propped-up bottle.
- If your baby has a cold, raise the head of the cot (see earlier, 'Handling a baby with reflux'). This can aid drainage of mucus.

## Managing middle ear infection

Consult your doctor. Do not use 'home remedies' or pain relievers without medical advice.

## *Nappy rash and chafing*

These conditions (to be discussed in order) both involve reddening and tenderness of the skin due to moisture and/or rubbing. Some babies have more sensitive skin than others and so are more prone to developing nappy rash. Nappy rashes can vary between a slightly reddened bottom to a sore, weeping, inflamed area with sores or pustules. The rash may cover a small or large area, even extending onto the inner thighs and the lower abdomen.

## Causes of nappy rash

These include:

- leaving a baby too long in wet or soiled nappies
- using plastic nappy pants, which create warm humid conditions inside
- failing to carefully clean the skin (and creases) when the nappy is changed
- frequent loose bowel motions
- acid stools (possibly due to undigested lactose)
- thrush
- seborrhoeic dermatitis (If the baby has this rash – possibly in the creases around the genitals – it may be evident on other parts of the body too. It is usually greasy, yellowish and there may also be redness. It might have spread from cradle cap, which is the same condition, and might also be present in eyebrows and behind the ears.)
- allergy or sensitivity to some component of a formula or of the mother's diet if breastfed
- sensitivity to detergents, strong soap powders and/or antiseptics used in nappy washing
- ammonia burn: this occurs when bacteria from the stool begin to build up in a wet nappy. They act on the urine and produce ammonia. Ammonia can scald and even blister the skin and has a strong, recognisable smell.

## Managing nappy rash

- Keep your baby as clean and dry as possible by changing nappies frequently.
- Try a dusting of a commercial powder or cornflour.
- Wash the bottom at each nappy change. You can use warm water or if there is soiling use warm olive oil to remove any stool. If the rash is mild you may be able to use a good quality unperfumed soap with warm water.
- Allow your baby times without a nappy in a warm, draught-free place. The air will circulate and reduce humidity and moisture.

- Watch for any signs of thrush; this will need separate treatment with antifungal cream.
- Try a barrier cream such as zinc and castor oil or sorbolene. If the rash is severe you can spread the cream on a piece of cotton material and place it against the sore area. This can be soothing and aid healing. If the rash is extensive and/or there is a raw area, consult your health adviser.
- Avoid using plastic nappy pants while the rash persists. Flannel or woollen nappy pants help to draw urine away from the bottom and keep your baby warm. You can buy flannel 'snap-ons'; they are comfortable but usually expensive. It is easy to make nappy pants from old woollen garments or other woollen material you may have at home.
- Wash cloth nappies using a good quality unperfumed laundry soap instead of detergents or strong soap powders. Careful rinsing is essential. In the final rinse you can add a quarter of a cup of vinegar. This helps to soften the nappies and counteract any alkalinity. If possible, dry the nappies in the sunlight and wind.

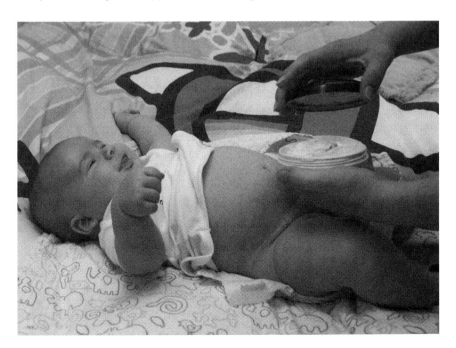

## Chafing

Chafing occurs where two skin surfaces or skin and clothing rub together. The friction results in a reddened area, even in a loss of skin. Under the chin, which often becomes damp from dribbling, is a common site. Other likely sites are in skin folds and creases, around the neck, under the arms, in the groins, thighs and behind the knees and in the elbow creases. Chafing can be troublesome, especially in hot weather.

### Managing chafing

- Bathe and dry carefully.
- Apply a dusting of silky, smooth baby powder or cornflour to the creases – do not use so much that the powder cakes in the creases.
- Ensure your baby does not get overheated and sweaty.
- Increase ventilation and air circulation to the affected areas. If the inside thighs are chafed, time without a nappy will help.

## Paronychia (infected nails)

This is inflammation of the nail bed and can be caused if the nail cuts the surrounding skin and infection gains access to the cuticle. It can occur in both fingers and toes. The infection may be present in just one nail or more. The side of the nail will be swollen, red and angry and pus may gather there as a small yellow blister.

### Managing infected nails

- Bathe in warm, salty water (one teaspoon of salt in a cup of warm, boiled water).
- You can ask your health adviser or pharmacist about a suitable antiseptic lotion.
- If the infection does not respond after 48 hours or you feel that it is becoming worse, get medical advice.

## Posseting (simple spilling of small quantities of milk)

Harmless spills of milk often follow a feed. Sometimes babies overload their tummies and/or gulp their feed. The milk may then come up when you are burping your baby. Certainly spilling is a nuisance you could do without but your main concern will probably be to protect your clothes! Obtain medical advice for larger spills that affect your baby's growth (see 'Gastro-oesophageal reflux' earlier in this chapter).

## Prickly heat

Prickly heat is sometimes referred to as sweat rash. It can be troublesome during summer heat and if a baby is too warmly clothed and covered. It is a fine red rash of tiny papules and the baby can find it very irritating. It will be most marked where there is sweating, particularly in the creases but also on the back of the head and the neck. Shoulders, back, chest and inner thighs can also be affected.

Less common are small white blisters about half the size of a match head. They are not surrounded by inflammation. They most often appear on the scalp, forehead and upper chest.

### Managing prickly heat

- Keep your baby cool. Give tepid baths or sponge baths.
- Dust your baby with a little baby powder or cornflour. If the itching continues try dabbing the rash with calamine lotion.
- Avoid using sticky creams and oils.
- Use a cloth nappy and avoid plastic nappy pants as lack of circulating air and humidity can make the rash worse.
- Dress your baby in a fine cotton shirt or short dress and a cloth nappy.

## Pustules

Very young babies can develop pustules below the umbilical area. They may spread down into the groin. The spots are red and slightly raised with a spot of pus on top. They may be the result of an infection spreading down from the separating umbilical cord or from some remaining bacteria at the site when the cord separates. Sometimes these pustules appear on other parts of the body.

## Managing pustules

- *C* Keep your baby as dry as possible.
- *C* Wash the affected area with an antiseptic soap, rinse well, dab dry and apply a suitable antiseptic (check with your pharmacist).
- *C* If they do not respond to this treatment within 24 to 48 hours, are spreading, or if you feel anxious, obtain medical advice.

## Rashes

A rash can last a day or two, or they can persist. A rash can be mild with no other symptoms, or severe. It may be due to a bacterial or viral infection, allergies (see 'Food allergy and intolerance sensitivity' in Chapter 21), overheating or a local irritation such as a sensitivity to laundry washing powder, to wool or synthetic fabric in clothing. (See also in this chapter 'Eczema', 'Urticaria', 'Infantile acne', 'Nappy rash and chafing', 'Prickly heat' and in Chapter 23 'Bites and stings'.)

A baby dribbling continuously may have a chin rash. You can help protect the skin by using a protective cream such as zinc and castor oil. If the rash is severe, your baby has a raised temperature, there are other signs of illness or you are worried, obtain medical advice. Tell your doctor that you are concerned about your baby's rash and check when it would be best to visit the surgery. Meningococcal C disease can have a rash of red-purple spots or bruises – seek urgent medical advice (see 'Immunisation' Chapter 22). Note that should the rash be rubella there is a risk to any mother in early pregnancy who might come into contact with the rash.

**Reflux** (see 'Gastro-oesophageal reflux' earlier in this chapter)

## Rubella (German measles)

Rubella is an infectious disease with an incubation period of fourteen to 21 days. It is usually a mild disease. Your baby may have a fever and a runny nose. A fine pink rash starts on the face and spreads over the body and arms.

To confirm the diagnosis you need to consult your doctor and probably arrange a home visit rather than go to the surgery. You will want to avoid any contact with anyone who is or might be pregnant because of the risk to the unborn baby. (See also Chapter 22, 'Immunisation'. )

## Snuffles

Snuffles may begin within a few days of birth and continue for a number of weeks. They are not harmful and are not due to a cold. Should they cause difficulty with your baby's feeding or sleeping obtain medical advice. Snuffles rarely last beyond three months of age.

## Squint (strabismus)

Your new baby may take about three months to learn to coordinate the movement of both eyes. You need not be concerned about squinting in these early weeks. Should the squinting continue after six months of age, obtain medical advice as treatment is likely to be needed.

## Thrush (monilia)

Thrush is an infection of the skin or membranes caused by the fungus *Candida albicans* (formerly *Monilia*). It normally occurs harmlessly on the body, but at times when the balance is upset infection flares up. A course of antibiotics or an illness could provide the opportunity.

Moist areas of the body are most likely to be affected by surface growth, but the fungus can invade the breasts. Mothers and babies can infect each other. The source from mothers is often the vagina, where there may be a sticky white dischage with or without irritation. Nipples can also become infected (see 'Nipple problems' in Chapter 21). Cracked skin or wounds that are red and moist and failing to heal may be infected.

The baby can have thrush in the mouth (oral thrush) and it can also appear in the nappy area.

### Signs of oral thrush

In some cases the baby may not seem to be bothered by it but if left untreated oral thrush can spread rapidly. The first signs usually occur on the inside of the cheeks and then over the tongue. White plaques have the appearance of tiny milk curds, but they do not come away easily. If they are scraped off the mucosa, they leave a sore reddened patch underneath. The baby may feel miserable with a sore mouth and even refuse to suck.

The thrush can spread from the mouth through the digestive system. In this way thrush can appear around the anus and even spread out over the nappy area. Obtain medical advice.

## Signs of thrush in the nappy area

The first signs are usually in the form of small red spots on the skin concentrated in one area, particularly around the anus. The reddened area with the surrounding red spots can extend to the buttocks and even the thighs.

## Managing thrush for the baby

- Discuss appropriate treatment with your health adviser. For thrush in the mouth an antifungal medication that the baby can swallow is likely to be prescribed and if there is any sign of thrush around the anus or on the nappy area, a cream to apply will be included.
- Change nappies frequently. Cloth nappies are better than disposables, which are likely to provide the warm moist environment so suited to the growth and spread of thrush. Similarly, avoid the use of plastic nappy pants.
- Allow your baby to lie for short periods without a nappy so that air can circulate freely around the bottom, though avoid chilling the baby.
- Carefully wash and sterilise any teats and dummies that you use. They are best boiled until the infection has completely cleared.

## Managing thrush for the mother

- Obtain medical advice. Thrush usually responds rapidly to treatment. It is likely that an antifungal cream and possibly an oral medication will be advised depending on the site of the infection.
- If you are breastfeeding and using an antifungal cream, wipe it off your nipples with clear water before feeding your baby.
- Re-apply the cream at the end of the feed.

✐ Avoid damp breast pads and allow the air to circulate whenever possible. One method is to use plastic tea strainers with the handles cut off and filed smooth. Place these over your nipples within your bra.

Remember that mothers and babies can infect each other. If one is infected then watch for signs of thrush in the other.

## Urticaria (hives)

These can appear in varying shapes and sizes. They are usually raised, have red margins and white centres and look like insect bites or a sting from a nettle. Sometimes there is a small clear blister on top. The smaller hives appear to be less irritating than the large ones. Sometimes there is a reddening of the nappy area too. Any part of the body can be affected but they often erupt on the face, forearms and legs and appear across the small of the back.

Hives can appear if a baby's formula is unsuitable but they are more common in older children and in infants who are starting on solid foods. Some mothers have noticed that hives come and go when their babies are teething. Food sensitivity or allergic reaction to insect bites or other substances may produce hives.

## Managing hives

You can try:

✐ adding a tablespoon of bicarbonate of soda to the bath water; this can be soothing

✐ dabbing the hives with calamine lotion

✐ dressing your baby with cotton next to the skin

✐ keeping your baby warm but not hot.

If the hives persist, contact your doctor.

## Vomiting

Vomiting, especially if unexpected and more than simple spilling, can indicate the onset of illness. However, both breastfed and formula-fed babies can have vomits that are of no real concern although these simple spills (often called possets) can alarm parents. If your baby appears well, is thriving, gaining weight and growing satisfactorily and is reasonably contented, it is unlikely that you have a problem.

### Assessing vomiting

🖉 Has the onset of the vomiting been sudden? If your baby also has diarrhoea it is likely that the baby has gastroenteritis. This is an emergency because of the risk of dehydration due to fluid loss (see 'Dehydration' earlier in this chapter). Get immediate medical advice even out of surgery hours or go to a hospital.

🖉 Does your baby appear sick? Is there any fever, any sign of pain, loss of appetite? Is your baby unusually miserable, abnormally sleepy and lethargic and/or difficult to settle?

- *Persistent vomiting* calls for medical advice even if your baby does not appear sick.
- If formula feeding, could the formula be the cause? Have you altered the formula?
- Is there a pattern to the vomiting? How often is your baby vomiting and when: between, before, during or immediately following feeds? Is the vomiting much more than any usual spilling and is it effortless or forceful?
- Does the vomitus appear unchanged or is it curd-like?
- Does it contain mucus, bile or blood?
- Does your baby appear easier after vomiting?

## Managing vomiting

- During a vomit turn your baby onto the side or hold the baby up, leaning forward so that the fluid can drain more easily from your baby's mouth.
- While waiting for medical advice, give extra fluid. If breastfeeding offer small feeds frequently. Your breastfed baby may need extra fluid; check with your doctor.
- If formula feeding, stop the formula. You can add a heaped teaspoon of sugar to a cup of cooled, boiled water and offer 30 to 40 millilitres every fifteen to twenty minutes until you obtain medical advice. Your baby may be able to keep small quantities down whereas a larger quantity will be vomited at once.
- Do not give fruit juice. You may be advised to use a mixture of water with sugars and particular salts known as electrolytes. These are available from pharmacies.

## Reflux vomiting

This is discussed in this chapter under 'Gastro-oesophageal reflux'. It can be very mild or become a severe problem needing medical care.

## Projectile vomiting usually due to pyloric stenosis

In this rare condition the baby's vomits emerge with such force that they gush through the nose and mouth and may be thrown as far as 1 metre; these are referred to as projectile vomits. There is a narrowing of the pyloric sphincter, the muscle that controls the flow of stomach contents into the bowel. When it occurs babies are usually between two and six weeks of age. The vomits tend to occur towards the end of, or soon after, a feed. The vomit may contain mucus and even small amounts of dark blood. The baby will be continually hungry and look anxious, have small stools and pass little urine, lose condition and rapidly become dehydrated. This condition calls for medical treatment and is usually relieved by simple and effective surgery.

## Allergic vomiting

Your breastfed baby may be reacting to something you have had to eat or drink. A formula-fed baby may be reacting to a component of the formula, for example the protein in a cow's milk or in a soybean formula (see 'Food allergy and intolerance sensitivity' in Chapter 21).

Allergic vomiting will persist until the cause is removed. The baby will be uncomfortable after feeding and relieved after vomiting. There may be other signs of allergy present such as clear nasal discharge, sneezing or rashes. Often there is a family history of allergy. Get medical advice to help overcome the problem.

# 21

# Feeding problems

If you have a concern with any aspect of the feeding of your baby, whether breastfeeding – this includes your breasts and nipples as well as your baby's actual feeding – or formula feeding, here are suggestions and options you can consider while looking for a solution.

# Recognising a problem

Do you and your baby have a real feeding problem? Look at your baby.

**Is she or he:**

- bright-eyed and responsive and having periods of peaceful sleep
- showing firm, well-rounded limbs
- having five or six good wet nappies in each 24 hours, with pale urine rather than dark
- gaining weight satisfactorily?

If you answered 'yes' to these questions there would appear not to be a major problem with your baby. However, if you answered 'no' to any of these questions, there are several significant medical problems that should be investigated. It is important to have your baby assessed by a healthcare professional to provide you with support and guidance, along with the following suggestions for you to consider (also refer to Chapter 20 'Health and illness').

# Babies who are difficult to feed

A baby's behaviour may affect feeding. There are mothers who have difficulties with an excitable, easily distracted baby or with a tired, sleepy baby. These babies will need to be handled differently. The way you care for your baby can affect the way he or she feeds.

## Caring for the excitable, easily distracted baby

You can keep the environment as peaceful as possible by minimising stimulation such as loud music and other noises. Don't entertain your baby with television – all babies are better off without the visual bombardment of the television screen. Play gentle games – these babies often love noisy, boisterous fun but it can become very difficult to settle your baby so keep play gentle. It is wise to allow your baby some time alone to enjoy an environment of interest. Hang some colourful items within your baby's focus range. If you have a tree outside a window where the baby can watch sunlight on the moving leaves put the pram there (watch that the sun does not shine in on the baby). Meanwhile enjoy your baby's obvious interest in and desire to interact with the world.

## Managing the feed – breast or bottle

Because these babies are curious and excitable they will stop feeding to see what is going on. If you have this problem you will find that your baby's ability to handle distractions can vary from feed to feed. You will soon know what the baby can comfortably accept; then you can plan the feed surroundings accordingly.

**You can:**

- avoid sudden movements: handle the baby smoothly and quietly; talk in a soft voice and aim to feed your baby before he or she becomes distressed
- not stimulate the baby before a feed
- if necessary give the feed without company.

## *A tired, sleepy baby*

If you feel your baby is abnormally sleepy, think of possible causes. Is this sleepiness due to a low birth weight, a difficult birth or jaundice? Sometimes there is no obvious cause – perhaps the baby is simply finding life beyond the uterus difficult or is just tired. It is important to keep a check on the baby's weight (if possible weekly) until it is clear that the feeds are adequate and that the baby is thriving. Your daily care can affect the way your sleepy baby feeds.

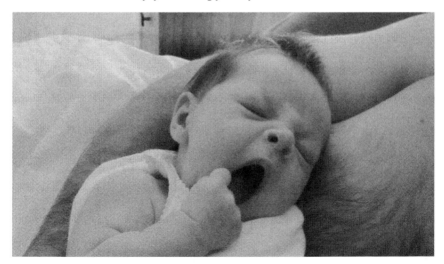

## Caring for your sleepy baby

You can encourage interaction as you gently stimulate, play with, talk to and smile at your baby. You can play games together – clapping hands or you might blow noisily on the tummy when undressing the baby for the bath. Be sensitive to what is fun and what the baby can handle. As the days pass and security and trust grow you can expect your baby to become more alert and show an increasing interest in everything.

## Feeding the sleepy baby

Some sleepy babies respond to extra skin-to-skin contact. Feed time is a good time to provide this. You will be further stimulating the baby's senses of touch and smell as well as taste. With a light cover over both of you, your own body will provide the extra warmth needed. Have a cool, damp face washer on hand to wipe your baby's face if dozing becomes a problem.

**You can help a sleepy baby to feed most easily if you follow these guidelines:**

- Feed as soon as your baby wakens or shows early feeding cues such as putting his or her hand into their mouth, licking their lips or making sucking noises, as crying uses energy.
- During the day, after a sleep of four hours gently wake your baby for a feed.
- If your baby appears uncomfortable after taking just a little of the feed, try to bring up a bubble of wind; or if dozing off to sleep again do your best to rouse your baby. You could wipe the baby's face with a cool damp cloth or get up and walk around for a minute or two.
- Start your milk flowing by rolling your nipples to stimulate let-down and then attach the baby as the milk flows.
- Don't spend extra time encouraging a sleepy baby to 'empty' the first side – move to the second breast when the baby is no longer interested in the first side. You can ensure the first breast is well drained by expressing any remaining milk when the feed ends.

🖋 Have some expressed breastmilk ready to give if your baby stops feeding before taking a reasonable feed. To avoid the baby becoming accustomed to bottle-feeding you can give your expressed milk from a small cup, medicine measure or spoon. You will need to rouse your baby enough to be able to swallow the milk. Have your baby sitting up against you but with the head tilted back a little. Rest the edge of the container on the bottom lip and give the milk slowly between breaths (see 'Complementary feeding' later in this chapter).

🖋 Express what breastmilk is left in your breasts and store it in the refrigerator or deep freezer, if you are likely to need it (see Chapter 15, 'Expressing, using and storing breastmilk').

🖋 If formula-feeding check that the teat is fast enough for easy sucking and slow enough to allow a comfortable swallowing and breathing pattern (associated with the suck-breathe-swallow reflex).

**To ensure your baby is taking enough food:**

🖋 look for five or six good wet nappies in each 24 hours

🖋 check that the urine is pale rather than dark

🖋 check that your baby is gaining weight.

# Nipple problems

As mentioned at the start of this chapter, problems with the nipples or breasts may also cause breastfeeding problems.

## *Flat or inverted nipples*

Many mothers are anxious if they have flat or inverted nipples but often find that they improve during pregnancy (see 'Antenatal care of breasts and nipples' in Chapter 2).

## *Tender or sore nipples*

As you start breastfeeding, your nipples can be quite sensitive during the first few days or even the first week or two while they are adapting to your baby's sucking. This is normal and provided the baby is correctly attached (see Chapter 13, 'How to breastfeed') you can expect the initial soreness to decrease as time passes. You may feel some tenderness as each feed begins.

The most common cause of sore nipples is incorrect positioning and attachment. When the nipple is not drawn well back into the mouth, where it is protected, the baby nipple-sucks rather than breastfeeds. The nipples can become chafed, bruised or squashed. If the nipple is squashed against the hard palate it may be flattened and there may be a 'white stripe' along it after the feed.

Sore nipples can be caused by the use or overuse of some creams. They can also become soggy by the continued wearing of wet or plastic-backed breast pads. Soreness can also be caused by infection, thrush or dermatitis. Sometimes the skin of the nipple is damaged and can appear reddened and covered with tiny raised lumps (papillae), and crusting may occur. Whatever the cause, sore nipples need help before the condition gets worse.

## Managing sore nipples

Do not stoically allow your baby to continue to feed when your nipple is hurting. Interrupt the feed by slipping your little finger into the side of the baby's mouth, press down on the bottom gum to break the suction, and ease your baby's mouth off your breast. Now reposition and reattach your baby. Unless you do this the soreness will rapidly get worse. If severe pain persists take your baby off the breast and express

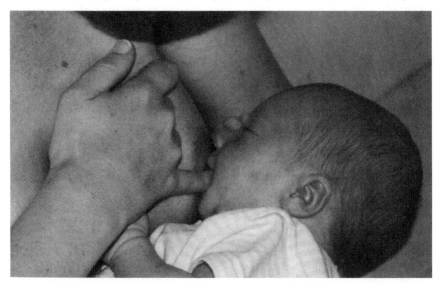

your milk by hand. You can give your expressed breastmilk to your baby. If you express to drain your breasts regularly, your milk will be replaced. Usually resting very sore nipples for 24 hours improves them greatly.

**Here are some suggestions you can try. Find the ones that suit you:**

- If you need help, look for an experienced adviser who can observe your baby at the breast and assess your nipples and advise appropriate management.
- As mentioned above, breastfeed unless the pain is too severe – if it is, you will need to express your milk by hand and rest your nipple/ nipples, giving your baby your expressed milk.
- If pain is still a problem because of nipple tenderness you can take an analgesic about ten minutes before feeding (as advised by your health professional).
- Consider expressing a small amount of breastmilk to lubricate your nipple before attaching your baby; this is helpful in decreasing pain before latching.
- To soften your areola (the darker part of the nipple) express some milk or massage your areola before the feed, as often a deep latch is stopped if your areola is too firm or full of breastmilk.
- Offer shorter, more frequent feeds so that your baby is not ravenously hungry when coming to the breast.
- Limit comfort sucking.
- If only one nipple is sore, feed on the 'good' side first since the baby is likely to suck more gently on the second side.
- If both nipples are sore you can try stimulating the let-down. If possible, gently roll behind your nipples between finger and thumb; otherwise stroke your breast towards the nipple and press behind the areola (see Chapter 15, 'Expressing, using and storing breastmilk') before putting the baby on the breast.
- You can try altering the baby's position on the breast when feeding. You can feed using the cradle position, the 'twin' (or 'football') hold or with your baby straddling your thigh while sitting facing the breast (see 'Different positions for breastfeeding' in Chapter 13). You may

choose to vary the positions during a single feed. Pillows may be useful as you move the baby round the breast to find the least painful position for you.

*✿* Keep your baby very close to you throughout the entire feed. If you can see your baby's bottom lip then your baby is too far away from you. Use your tummy to keep baby close to you: this is a perfect 'pillow' for baby to rest on.

*✿* At the end of the feed express a little milk and allow it to dry on the nipple to aid healing. Some mothers find a purified lanolin helpful, used sparingly just on the nipple. Always avoid applying creams to the areola as this can interfere with nature's own healing. To check that you are not sensitive to it before applying it to your nipple, you can rub a little onto the inside of your wrist.

*✿* Change breast pads often; you can try leaving off your bra for a time and wearing a loose cotton T-shirt to allow air to circulate.

*✿* If clothing against the nipple is painful you can use tea strainers (take a plastic tea strainer, cut off the handle and file the edge smooth) placed inside your bra over the nipple. It holds clothing away from the nipple and allows the air to circulate. This reduces a build-up of moisture and helps healing. Wash the strainer well at each feed.

If none of these suggestions help it is important to get experienced breastfeeding help as soon as possible.

## Fissured (cracked) nipples

Fissures are deep splits into the nipple – either across the surface or at the base. They may develop if sore nipples are not effectively treated and if positioning and attachment are incorrect. They are very painful. It is important to find experienced help.

You do not have to keep breastfeeding if the cracked nipple is causing you pain. You can feed the baby by expressing your milk. Remember to drain the breasts well until you feel you can start breastfeeding again. Usually these cracked nipples heal in 24 to 48 hours although they may take longer.

## Managing fissured nipples

Take any of the steps above in 'Managing sore nipples' that you find helpful. In addition:

- Prevent engorgement either by continuing to breastfeed or by expressing the milk from the problem side.
- Remember the importance of correct positioning and attaching.
- Generally it is better to hand express rather than use a breast pump when breastfeeding is very painful. Breast pumps can drag on the fissure and open it more. However, women whose let-down triggers easily and whose milk flows freely may prefer to use an electric pump operated on a comfortable pressure.
- At the end of the feed or expressing, express a drop or two of your milk and allow it to dry on the affected nipple or nipples.
- If your breasts are extremely painful to touch you can try bathing them in a bowl of warm water and Epsom salts; this is likely to start the flow of milk (see 'Milk engorgement').
- If your sore or fissured nipple persists some mothers find that application of anhydrous purified lanolin or wool fat is very soothing and helps healing. Ask the pharmacist for a brand that meets all the standards of medical-grade purity and check you are not sensitive to it (see above in 'Managing sore nipples').
- If only one nipple is affected start the feed on the other breast. If both are fissured it may help to give the baby some expressed milk before breastfeeding. If a little less hungry, your baby might then feed more gently. If the baby has been off the breast for a day or so and you are trying to breastfeed again you can try stimulating the let-down before putting the baby on the breast. The flowing milk lessens the strain on the healing fissure.
- Watch the fissure and, as it heals, increase the baby's time on the breast. A fissure may heal from within and fail to close fully. Absence of pain and a healthy appearance of the nipple mean that healing has occurred.

Here is one woman's experience.

**Tess:** *'With my first baby, it was only a matter of days after returning home from the hospital that I developed cracked nipples. I had so much milk and I am sure that my baby could not attach properly because of this. I was utterly determined to continue breastfeeding and therefore knew I could not give in to this excruciating pain. However, it got to a point where I only had to think about the next feed and I couldn't stop the tears. It even hurt to have breast pads touching the nipples between feeds.*

*I used something called 'nipple ease' at this time which helped. These are two plastic dome-shaped things that fit over the nipples under the bra and breast pads to prevent the nipples from remaining damp from constant contact with the wet breast pads. They also made sure the purified lanolin I used to help heal the cracks/fissures was not rubbed off onto the breast pads. Anyway, I tried nipple shields with great hope, but they were a total disaster for both me and Matt. I tried to use a manual and an electric pump but these also resulted in the same sort of pain. I could not go on any more and decided that I would need to switch to formula.*

*However, at that time I happened to speak to a brilliant midwife who totally changed the situation around. I learnt that, if left to heal a cracked nipple could do so in 24 to 36 hours. From her directions I started to hand express my milk from both breasts at every feed for the next 24 to 36 hours. There was no pain in my nipples at all, and I fed my milk to my baby in a bottle at each feed. Thankfully he switched between bottle and breast without any difficulty at all! I cried with joy! It was tiring to hand express. Luckily I had observed a friend do this for her baby when I was pregnant and I knew I could do it too. I expressed a bit of extra milk from both breasts between feeds to build up a supply to stay one bottle feed ahead of my baby's needs. It became easier and faster for me to do, with the right instructions and with practice.*

*Believe it or not, I developed more cracked nipples in those first twelve to sixteen weeks, usually on one side only. So I simply fed my baby from the other breast, and expressed the milk by hand from the breast with the cracked nipple, until it healed once again. There came a time when I no longer had pain and breastfeeding my baby was easy and a total pleasure.'*

With help, Tess was able to manage her severely cracked nipples so that she was able to successfully breastfeed her baby. Because she expressed regularly she kept up her supply of breastmilk for her baby while her nipples were healing. There are now ventilated breast shells (which should not be confused with nipple shields as they are quite different) that you can buy from the pharmacy. These breast shells are an alternative option to the cut-off plastic tea strainers mentioned earlier.

## Leaking nipples

Episodes of milk leaking from the nipples are annoying but normal. Nipples stay damp and marks appear on clothing. Leaking often happens in the early days before lactation has settled down when there is an excess of milk. You may have an unexpected let-down. This can occur between feeds through just hearing or thinking about your baby. Persevere with breastfeeding because the leaking usually settles down, although some mothers continue to find it troublesome. This is no reason to wean your baby.

## Managing leaking nipples

𝒞 Wear a comfortable supporting bra; be sure there is no clothing pressure on the breasts.

𝒞 Wear breast pads to catch leaking milk.

𝒞 Avoid plastic-backed breast pads except for short periods on special occasions. If leaking occurs with a let-down between feeds, try to stop it by using gentle pressure on the nipple or nipples with the palms of your hands or by pressure from your forearm which may be enough to stop the leaking.

𝒞 If a significant amount of milk leaks from the other breast during baby's feed and simple pressure does not stop it, you can catch the milk in a sterilised container. If your baby is still hungry at the end of the feed you can use this milk. If you do not want to save it just let it drip onto a small towel or nappy.

𝒞 Bathing nipples with alternate hot and cold water will induce the small muscles around the ducts to relax and contract. This can help to strengthen them and reduce leaking between feeds.

𝒞 Milk shows on plain clothing. Patterned tops, particularly if they are dark, help to conceal damp patches.

## *Nipple blisters*

Occasionally nipple blisters appear, usually due to friction. Poor positioning and attaching and 'nipple sucking' can cause these blisters.

## Managing nipple blisters

𝒞 See that the baby is correctly positioned and attached (see 'Positioning and attaching your baby' in Chapter 13) to the breast as you feed. If you need help and a breastfeeding adviser is available, ask for it.

𝒞 Express a small amount of milk to make sure your areola is soft and elastic so your baby can stretch the areola out, and also make sure your nipple is deep in your baby's mouth.

𝒞 If your nipple feels sore you can stimulate the let-down before putting your baby on the breast.

- If the baby feeds vigorously, try more frequent feeds so he or she feeds more gently.
- At the end of the feed you can allow some hind milk to dry on the nipple.
- If you wish you could try the merest smear of anhydrous purified lanolin – you can discuss this with your health adviser or the pharmacist. You can buy a very small tube. You do not need to wash this off before the next feed.
- Change breast pads frequently.

## *Nipple dermatitis*

Dermatitis refers to an inflammation of the skin covering the nipple. It looks red and is painful throughout the feed. The dermatitis can range from a mild irritation to extreme sensitivity when anything touching the nipple causes acute pain.

Dermatitis can be caused by a variety of substances including solutions, ointments or lotions that have been applied to the nipples. Some soaps and shampoos can be responsible and laundry detergents used when washing bras or other clothing that come into contact with the nipples may affect them. Fabrics used in clothing such as synthetics and wool may also be a cause. (Mothers who are sensitive to wool may react to lanolin.) Dermatitis may also develop in response to medication your baby is having or to a particular item of food as your baby starts on solids.

### Managing nipple dermatitis

- Try to find the cause, then eliminate it.
- Stop using any creams or ointments. Try washing clothes in pure soap and rinse thoroughly. Use a pure soap in the shower and do not put any soap on the nipples themselves. If you are using a bra made of synthetic material and there are signs of dermatitis you can try placing large cotton handkerchiefs within the bra to protect nipples and breasts from contact with the bra.
- Continue to breastfeed if possible. (For pain use any of the methods suggested earlier in 'Managing sore nipples'.)

- Use nipple shells (or tea strainers) to allow circulation of air and to keep clothing off the nipple.
- If the dermatitis persists get medical advice.

## Nipple thrush

Thrush is due to a fungal infection of the skin by the pathogen *Candida albicans* and results in inflammation.

## Signs of nipple thrush

Nipple thrush may be indicated by nipples that are:

- tender, sore and itchy
- bright red, or have very small white spots on the tips
- scaly with traces of white plaque, especially if there are any fissures (cracks) in the underlying nipple.

Unless treated, nipple thrush can spread. The irritation can cause the skin to flake and the nipples to become so sensitive that even clothing causes pain. Thrush on the nipple and in the breast causes pain that has been described as 'burning knives shooting down the breasts'. The infection may spread from the mother to her baby if she has vaginal thrush or from the baby to the mother if it is present in the baby's mouth. Such transfer is made more likely if either has had a course of antibiotics (see below). When thrush is present in either mother or baby the infection can be passed repeatedly between them. If it is found in either one it should be looked for in the other.

## Managing nipple thrush

Nipple thrush is not especially difficult to manage. To treat it you can try the following:

- Take special care with hand washing and hygiene before and after handling the baby or your nipples.
- Wash clothing separately, use hot water and dry in the sun.
- If the baby has thrush and has had an antifungal cream prescribed check with your health adviser, as you might be advised to use this

cream on your nipples and the surrounding area as a preventative measure.

- Keep nipples dry and where possible expose them to the air. You might go without your top and bra for a while or you can use tea strainers in the bra. In this way you reduce the moist, warm conditions that allow thrush to thrive.
- A course of antibiotics can predispose you to thrush until the body re-establishes its normal balance of bacteria in the digestive tract. Try eating cultured yoghurt (with live lactobacilli) or take acidophilus tablets to help re-establish friendly bacteria in the alimentary tract.
- If the thrush is severe and/or resistant obtain medical advice. Depending on the site of infection, oral medication and/or vaginal antifungal ointment will be necessary.

## Blocked nipple openings

Blockages in the nipple openings are uncommon, usually external and fairly easily cleared. They may be due to:

- external dried secretion
- firm white cheesy plugs or thick stringy material within the nipple duct or opening
- a blister forming on the end of the nipple – if the areola is squeezed the blister bulges with milk
- nipple creams or ointments.

## Managing blocked nipple openings

To treat blocked nipple openings you can try the following:

- Gently bathe the dried secretions with warm water.
- Bathe white plugs (which tend to be more difficult to move) with warm water using a face washer, stroking the breast down towards the nipple and exert gentle pressure behind the areola but take care to avoid damage. Try to express some milk. If this does not work you might need to soak the nipple in warm water for up to ten minutes, taking care not to burn it, before expressing again. The plugs can suddenly pop out.

- Stringy threads of colostrum or thickened milk can be removed in the same way as above.
- Creams and ointments can be removed by bathing in warm water using a soft cloth.
- If you do use creams or ointments try to keep them away from the nipple openings.

## Nipple vasospasm

Other names for this condition are Raynaud's phenomenon, disease or syndrome. This is a rare but painful condition involving the circulation in the nipple. During the feed there is a deep stinging pain. The nipple turns white, generally after the feed. At the end of the feed, as the circulation returns, the nipple becomes red and there is a burning pain. When the redness subsides the pain passes. One mother described the pain as similar to a burning chilblain although it soon passed when her baby finished feeding. It can also occur if the nipple is squashed. For some the stinging pain occurs a minute or two after the feed finishes. Warm packs, breast warmers (available at chemists) and manual stimulation of the nipple to encourage circulation can help but the answer is to see that the baby is correctly attached so that the nipple is protected and squashing does not occur.

Some women need medications to manage symptoms of nipple vasospasm due to Raynaud's disease rather than incorrect attachment; discuss this with your doctor.

## Nipple shields

It is wise to regard a nipple shield as a last resort. Try other options first. Use the shield for as short a time as possible. When using a shield be prepared to express, preferably by hand, any milk remaining at the end of a feed.

Nipple shields are devices used to reduce direct contact between sore nipples and the baby during breastfeeding, or to control an excessive flow of milk which would otherwise distress the baby, although they are more likely used for babies having difficulty attaching in the early days or weeks. They are now made of soft latex or silicone and they are certainly better than the older shields made of more rigid rubber.

Although some mothers have successfully used shields, others have not succeeded and as a result have had to wean their babies. Many experienced breastfeeding advisers therefore do not support their use and prefer alternative ways of coping with problems.

**Nipple shields can:**

- chafe the nipples if poorly fitted
- make firm attachment to the breasts difficult
- reduce stimulation of the nipples and areolas, which could result in poor let-down and inadequate supply of milk
- cause the baby to refuse to feed unless a shield is in place
- make the baby tired before obtaining an adequate feed
- prevent effective draining of the breast which can decrease supply or even result in failure of the lactation or lead to engorgement (tight, full breasts), blocked ducts or mastitis
- lead to the baby's failure to thrive because of insufficient milk
- cause infection if not properly cleaned.

## How to use a nipple shield for either purpose

Wash the new shield before using. After use, wash it in hot soapy water, rinse and store in a clean lidded jar. Only if there is thrush on your nipple or in your baby's mouth will there be a need to sterilise the nipple shield.

If necessary, trigger the let-down before applying the shield (see 'Difficulties with let-down' later in this chapter). As the milk begins to flow lean over, turn back the rim of the shield, catch the milk in it and place it gently but fully over the nipple, then flip the rim back onto the breast. If the baby is unwilling to finish the feed without the shield express the remaining milk; offer it if the baby is still hungry. Make sure your breast is well drained (at least one breast at each feed).

## Controlling an excessive milk flow

*   If your baby is not coping with a strong milk ejection reflex and so cannot coordinate the suck-swallow-breathe reflex, she or he will come off the breast. If this happens, wait until the flow settles and reattach your baby. Excess milk can be caught in a cup and kept in the freezer for emergencies.
*   A nipple shield to control excessive flow should only be used when you have tried everything else and only with the guidance of a lactation consultant or your community health nurse.

Some mothers' experiences with nipple shields:

**Crystal:** *'I was having trouble with a fast flow. I couldn't control it. The silicone shield worked really well for me. I put Jay on the breast to trigger the let-down, which took a good minute or so in spite of my breasts being very tense and full of milk. When it did start there was a deluge. As he began to gulp I took him off, grabbed the nipple shield, leant over to catch my jetting milk in it and fixed it over my nipple and onto the breast. A bit leaked out of the shield which was good because he could taste the milk and he was quite willing to go onto it.*

*The first time we tried he was not on far enough and I could feel the shield rubbing against my nipple. I took him off and then waited until he opened his mouth really wide and then got him well on. This time it was comfortable and, instead of drowning in my milk, he could feed without choking. After a couple of minutes when the tingling from my let-down had stopped and my tense breast felt a little easier I took the shield off to see if the free flow had stopped. It hadn't. On went the shield again, another couple of minutes and my breast felt comfortable (such a relief). I took the shield off and put Jay back onto the breast. It still seemed to be flowing fairly fast but he was able to keep up with it so we just went on. He stayed on that breast for about twenty minutes and then just stopped. I did offer him the other side but he wasn't interested. He was full to the gills. I expressed a little from the second breast, felt for any lumps or blocked ducts but there were none. I didn't need the shield in the afternoon or the evening although I had to use it for the 2 a.m. and 6 a.m. feeds for about five or six weeks. Sometimes I did need it for other feeds. When he was around two months he managed without it by clamping onto the breast when the flow was too fast. As long as he was well on the breast it didn't hurt. The shield worked well for me.'*

Crystal successfully managed a nipple shield with the help of her child health nurse who supported her to resolve her fast flow issues with the use of the nipple shield. Crystal did have a cooperative baby and she was wise to take Jay off and reposition him when she felt the shield chafing.

**Jessie:** *'I too had a fast flow but my experience with a nipple shield was a disaster. You'd think I had offered Ruby poison. Mind you, she had never had a dummy or anything from a bottle or teat and I suppose that the feel of the nipple shield (although it was one of those soft ones) was strange and very different from the breast. She went on all right, took a few sucks and then pulled off and yelled.*

*It was funny, really, she looked so outraged. When she quietened I tried again. This time she stiffened and screamed. That was the end of my using the nipple shield. I persevered with my finger and thumb pressure on the areola and eventually got it right.'*

Jessie's experience is not unusual. Many breastfed babies object strongly if offered a teat or nipple shield. Jessie was able to control the fast flow with finger and thumb pressure on her areola – maybe she had experienced help from a breastfeeding adviser or she may have managed alone. She might have also succeeded if she had tried the suggestions listed later in this section, 'Too much milk'.

**Sarah:** *'It took no time for James to learn to use the nipple shield. From the very first feed he was perfectly happy with it, so much so that he totally refused to go onto the breast without it. I had been warned that this could happen so I had tried from the beginning to put him back onto the breast every couple of minutes. He would have none of it. I guess it was because he was so upset by the week we spent struggling with my gallons of milk and then the relief of the comfortable feeding he enjoyed when using the shield that he refused point blank to feed without it. He is now three months old – a happy contented baby, and there is no sign of my lactation decreasing. I still could feed quads I have so much milk. It's funny that it hasn't cut back because I'm not expressing. I'll probably still be breastfeeding him when he is two or three years old and still through a nipple shield.'*

**Tammy:** *'I lost my milk because I used a nipple shield. I still can't believe it. I had this huge supply. I always wanted to breastfeed and felt so confident when my breasts filled up. I didn't even fuss when they became engorged as my milk 'came in'. At first I just expressed enough to allow Alex to go on and I did try to control the flow by* *compressing the areola. The trouble was that this just did not work for me. I then tried expressing a half a cup of milk before putting him to the breast. Whatever I tried I could not stop my milk from fountaining out and he simply could not manage the fast flow.*

*It frightened him and then he would refuse to feed. I bought a soft nipple shield from the chemist and it seemed the perfect answer. Alex took it happily. I did try to get him to finish his feed directly on the breast but he would fight and refuse. He fed comfortably on the shield and would suck for about twenty minutes on each side, which was a rather long time, and he would fall asleep at the breast. When he was four weeks old we went off for a month to the beach so I didn't have him weighed until we came back. He did look a bit thin but I thought he was probably growing in length and, as he didn't complain often, we didn't even think that he might be hungry. While we were away he cut out his 2 a.m. feed which was great for me. I certainly appreciated the extra sleep. All the time we kept on with the shield because the milk still flowed fast out of my nipples. I leaked a lot between feeds too.*

*I went to the clinic when we came home. He had a very poor weight gain. His urine smelt a bit strong and he wasn't always really wet when I changed him but I had not thought that he might be passing too little. The nurse thought that his colour was good but that his limbs were thin and not rounded out. She thought he was probably underfed but suggested I went along to our family doctor for a check and meanwhile try to increase the number of feeds including waking him again during the night. She really wanted me to persevere in trying to get him back onto the breast without the nipple shield. I knew it would be hopeless because I had tried before. He screamed and then wouldn't feed at all for a couple of hours – so much for getting in extra feeds! I tried all the nurse's ideas for breast refusal. Nothing worked. He simply would not go directly onto the breast.*

*My family doctor said there was nothing wrong with Alex that a few good meals wouldn't fix. He wanted to see him again in a week and said that if he had not had a good gain he would have to have some formula because he was undernourished. I was miserable and worried. The nurse visited me over the next three days. She came to see if she could help get him onto the breast. Alex would scream and I would end up in tears. Being upset myself seemed to affect my supply even further. That week he actually lost 90 grams. That was that. He took the complementary bottle as though he'd never had a feed. The doctor said I was to let him have as much formula as he wanted providing that he didn't vomit. He still took what breastmilk he could get through the shield but it dwindled and in just a week he was fully on the bottle. I only wish that I had tried posture feeding and never touched a nipple shield.'*

Tammy needed help but it was difficult for her to attend an early childhood clinic as she lived out of town and could only attend infrequently. Before resorting to the nipple shield Tammy could have phoned for breastfeeding advice; tried posture feeding (see 'Posture feeding' later in this chapter) or expressed just enough milk to allow Alex to fix on the breast. Tammy confused fast flow with a copious supply. If she had expressed at least one breast (alternately) at the end of each feed it is likely that this draining would have kept up her supply.

As it happened, Alex took the nipple shield happily but was underfed. As he did not complain constantly and his weight was not checked, Tammy did not recognise this. She did arrange to stay with a friend for a few days so that the early childhood nurse could visit her to try to get Alex back directly onto the breast but sadly this did not work and Alex had to have more food. In this case Tammy's baby ended up on the bottle.

# Breast problems

The most common breast problems are engorgement, blocked ducts, mastitis and unreliable or difficult let-down. Following birth, aim to prevent breast problems by frequent feeding, correct positioning and attaching, caring for your breasts and avoiding fatigue. Assume that your body is quite able to feed the baby it has just produced.

## *Breast pain*

This can be due to engorgement, blockages in ducts, mastitis, thrush or injury. Another possible cause of persistent severe pain is very strong sucking. You may need to express your milk. This should be painless.

## *Engorgement*

After birth it is usual for the breasts to increase in size. This fullness is normal. At first it is due to increased blood flow and then to the 'coming in' of the milk. If your baby feeds well and frequently and the breasts are well drained, both day and night, breast engorgement problems can usually be avoided and even if over-fullness occurs very soon after birth it is likely to settle down quickly. Sometimes new babies do not feed well because they are born early, or because of medication you had in labour, or because they are jaundiced (yellow).

Engorgement is due to a build-up of pressure in the breasts. They become hard, swollen and lumpy, feel hot and painful and the skin is stretched and shiny. The areola can be involved and the nipple may be unable to stand out. Mothers can be ill and in pain. The breasts need to be handled very gently – they can bruise easily.

There are two types of engorgement: vascular engorgement and milk engorgement.

### Vascular engorgement

Vascular engorgement is said to be present when breasts become painful and swollen in the first 24 to 48 hours following birth. This is usually before the milk 'comes in'. It is due to increased blood flow and congestion. It may affect the breast, or the areola or both. Because it occurs so soon after birth it is likely a midwife will be there to advise you.

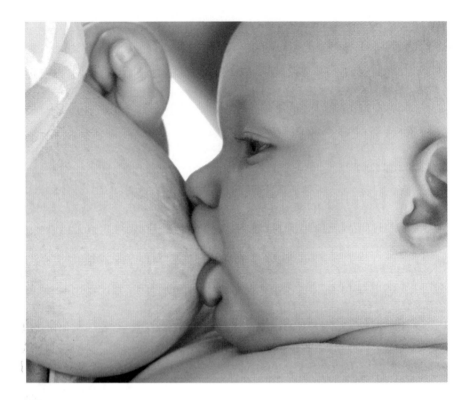

## Managing vascular engorgement

Vascular engorgement is usually a short-lived issue. To manage it, you can try the following:

- Support the breasts with a well-fitting bra with wide shoulder straps, and wear it day and night. Avoid using crop tops during this time, as they can cause mastitis.

- Breastfeed your baby on demand day and night. This is important. In taking colostrum the baby is receiving nourishment and easing pressure within your breasts. This helps the re-absorption of fluid in the engorged tissues. At the same time the baby is stimulating the production of the breastmilk.

- If your baby finds it difficult to attach well, try to soften the areola by very gently expressing a little colostrum by hand. If it will not flow you can try expressing under a shower. The warm water flowing over the breast may help.

**When handling your breasts, care is needed:**

- It is better to express your milk by hand but some women find this difficult or painful in the early days and so they prefer to use a breast pump set on 'their' comfortable setting. Some women use both methods. The disadvantage of the pump is that breastmilk can 'escape' when the pump shield is pulled off.
- Don't restrict fluid. It is very important that you drink enough to satisfy your thirst.
- At the end of the feed you may find that applying cold packs to the breasts brings relief. You can buy a cold pack from the pharmacy which can be chilled in the freezer or even use a packet of frozen peas. A disposable nappy soaked in water and then frozen also works well. Place a cloth on the breast before applying the cold pack. Don't leave it on for more than ten minutes. If it brings relief you can apply the cold pack again after an hour.
- Mothers have had relief from washed and dried cold cabbage leaves from the refrigerator cupped around the breast (seriously!). Again, don't leave on for more than ten minutes.
- The application of heat to ease breasts is not advised in the first ten days as it may continue the vascular engorgement. For pain relief discuss appropriate analgesics with your midwife or doctor. You may be advised to take the medication about ten minutes before feeding your baby. The analgesic is unlikely to reach the breastmilk for around half an hour, thus minimising the amount the baby obtains in the feed. Alternatively it may be suggested that you feed first and then take the analgesic.

## Milk engorgement

This form of engorgement is caused by an over-accumulation of milk in the breasts. It can be made worse or even be caused by poor feeding practices, for example if the baby is not attached well or there is a long interval between feeds. Although it can also happen at other times, a mother is most likely to suffer from engorgement as the milk 'comes in'. This is usually between the second and fourth day after birth.

**The best form of treatment is prevention:**

- Allow your baby unrestricted access to the breasts and feed as often as the baby is willing to feed. Give a minimum of six feeds in 24 hours. Remember to allow the baby to drain the first breast well before offering the second. If the baby takes no milk or very little from the second breast, express enough for comfort.
- Prevent long periods between feeds. A lengthy separation or a long sleep may allow too much milk to collect in the breasts.
- Check that your baby is well attached and feeding efficiently and is given no other fluid, as this can interfere with the appetite for breastmilk.

## Managing milk engorgement

If milk engorgement occurs, the following should relieve your symptoms:

- Feed frequently.
- Remove excess milk. Usually this is done most gently by your baby. If the breasts are too full to allow comfortable attaching, stimulate your let-down by rolling the nipples between fingers and thumb before the baby goes to the breast. As the milk starts to flow stroke the breasts gently towards the nipples. It may jet out and/or you may need to express a little. Allow the forceful flow to ease and then, when the breast is soft enough for the baby to attachs begin the feed. If nipple rolling alone does not produce a let-down you can bathe the breasts in warm water or take a warm shower. The water falling gently on the breasts plus the stimulation of nipple rolling is most likely to prove successful.
- Each breast needs to be drained at least at every other feed. Do not be tempted to feed the baby for a short time on each to ease both; keep the baby on the first side until either the baby is satisfied or has well drained it before offering the second breast. Express to ensure both breasts are well drained.
- If the second breast is still too full at the end of the feed, express enough for comfort. It will be well drained at the next feed when it is offered first.
- At the end of the feed or after an expressing session gently feel the

breasts for lumps or tender areas that can indicate a blocked duct or ducts.

- Unnecessary regular expression will maintain the surplus milk production. However, when milk engorgement persists, as well as trying the suggestions above you might find it helpful to soften both your breasts once in 24 hours to make them comfortable. Expression by an electric pump can make this easy but be careful because you can overstimulate the breasts. Sometimes mothers find that a second complete 'draining' in 24 hours is required if their breasts rapidly become over-full and distended again. This may be most helpful before settling to sleep at night. Discontinue this as you find the engorgement easing.

Remember that the amount of milk present in the breasts is likely to vary from feed to feed. At one feed, particularly if you have been asleep, the breasts may be distended and uncomfortable, while at another there may be no discomfort. At one feed your baby may need only a little or nothing from the second breast and at another may drain both.

If a mother has such painfully engorged breasts that she dreads having them handled at all, there is a simple procedure she can try to start the milk flowing. This procedure is described by P. Hatherly in *Back to the Bath*. In her article she describes the instant and dramatic relief experienced by a woman with a 'caked' breast who filled a deep dish of warm water to which she added a liberal amount of Epsom salts (magnesium sulphate). In this solution she soaked her breast – and the milk flowed. I have seen the same relief experienced by a mother who had grossly engorged breasts (in this case the ducts were not blocked) but her breasts were exceedingly painful to touch. She could not express nor would her milk flow when allowing the warm to hot water in a shower to flow over them. She then placed her breasts in a solution of one tablespoon of Epsom salts added to 4 litres of warm to hot water. Instantly her milk jetted from all the nipple openings. Had this not been effective we would have tried adding a second tablespoon of the salts to the solution, hoping that the milk would be drawn into it. This works because Epsom salts has a tendency to attract water to itself and as 85 per cent of breastmilk is water it is easily drawn into the solution of magnesium sulphate. Should you try this *take extreme care not to burn the breasts*. When enough milk has been drawn out to make you comfortable, bathe the breasts with clear warm water.

Physiotherapists use ultrasound to assist milk movement and this can be helpful in milk engorgement.

## Blockages in ducts

Commonly, blocked ducts are caused by engorgement of the breast that is more than just over-full. It may be tender, tense and lumpy in some parts, pressing on the ducts and blocking the flow of milk. If unrelieved this condition becomes increasingly painful and predisposes the breast to mastitis. Because of pain the let-down may not work readily. There may be inadequate or irregular emptying of a particular duct. It can also result from external pressure on the breast, perhaps from sleeping on it, from a tight bra or restrictive clothing. Some elastic fabrics, when rolled, can stop or slow milk flow leading to block ducts. Occasionally blockage can occur because of a plug of colostrum or thickened breastmilk. Unless cleared, pressure can build up and fluid can leak into the breast tissue and you will feel ill with a raised body temperature.

### Signs of blocked ducts

Blocked ducts may be indicated by a number of things:

- *ℓ* A tender or lumpy area might be felt in the breast, caused by a build-up of milk behind the blockage. This may be near the surface or deep in the breast. It can be very painful as let-down occurs and milk can leak into the breast tissue and even into the bloodstream. Your temperature may then rise and you may feel as if you are getting the flu.
- *ℓ* A distended duct close to the surface may be visible and/or felt as a cord-like hardening in the breast tissue. One mother described it as resembling a small, tightly inflated bicycle tube.
- *ℓ* Your baby might start to feed and then pull away from the breast in frustration if the blockage interferes too much with the flow of milk.

## Managing a blocked duct

Blocked ducts can be difficult to unblock. The following may help you.

- Encourage frequent feeds and offer the affected breast first, when the baby will feed most vigorously. The strong sucking will often clear a blocked duct.

- Position the baby with the lower jaw on the same line as the blockage. Some women find that changing their feeding position from the usual cradle to the 'football' hold or having the baby straddle their thigh facing the breast is helpful. Other women struggle with changing their feeding position and even find it disruptive and difficult.

- Use a little oil on your fingers and massage gently from above the blockage down towards the nipple as the baby feeds. If baby becomes distressed and refuses the breast, change to the other side. You can offer the affected breast when the baby is calm again. Try this technique while expressing with the electric breast pump or hand expressing.

- At the end of the feed, bathe the breast over a bowl of very warm water or apply a small towel which has been dipped in hot water and well wrung out. You may choose to try expressing under a hot shower. Take care not to burn your breast.

- Do some wide-arm exercises (such as the action of swimming breast stroke) followed by a cold compress to the breast when the feed has finished and/or after expressing any milk that will flow.

- If you have not cleared the duct, soak the breast in the solution of Epsom salts described earlier in 'Milk engorgement'; visit a physiotherapist and discuss the use of ultrasound, which may resolve the issue (before the blocked duct causes mastitis).

- If the blockage persists and your partner is willing, ask him to try to clear the duct for you. I have known this to be successful when all else has failed. He can suck as gently or firmly as you direct him. One mother amused me greatly when she was recounting her experience: *'Jack was marvellous. He was a bit doubtful at first but agreed to try. He had to go gently because my whole breast was so painful. Gradually he sucked more strongly and suddenly it cleared and the milk was able to flow again – oh the relief! But I was indignant –*

*he spat out my good breastmilk. Still, I have never forgotten how grateful I was.'*

✐ Watch for signs of mastitis (see under 'Mastitis' below in this chapter).

✐ If a lump persists for more than 24 hours, consult your doctor.

## Breast lumps

Learn how to examine your breasts for lumps and keep checking them throughout your life. While breastfeeding, painless lumps may be felt occasionally and in different areas of the breasts, particularly between feeds when the glands are filling with milk. Efficient feeding or expressing the milk usually removes them.

Lumps can be due to blocked ducts as described above. You will need medical advice for any breast lump which persists or becomes reddened and painful. Today, persistent breast lumps can be investigated using ultrasound or needle biopsy and need not interfere with feeding. Surgery is rarely necessary.

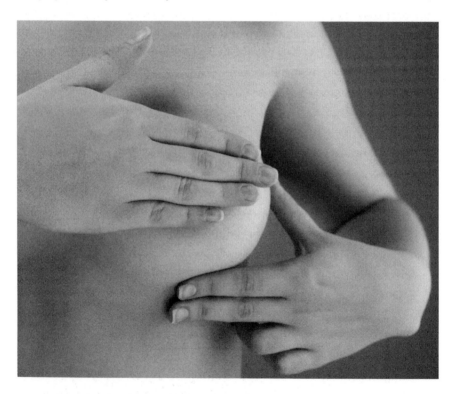

## *Difficulties with let-down*

Even if you suspect let-down problems remember that your body is programmed to produce the milk your baby needs and to deliver it when he or she needs it – believe it! To doubt that you have this ability can inhibit your let-down. If there is difficulty it is just a matter of finding the best solution. A number of external influences can undermine a mother's confidence in her ability to successfully breastfeed. Conflicting, incorrect or unwanted advice, lack of support, partner's opposition, and negative attitudes of other people can all play a part in affecting let-down.

When problems do occur they are more likely in the early stages of lactation but they can occur later. A mother might suspect that she has a let-down problem if her baby becomes frustrated within a minute or two of starting a feed. Her let-down may be normal although slower than her baby likes. The feed may start happily while there is milk available then the baby begins to fuss as this dwindles if the let-down has not occurred. The baby may become restless and miserable, repeatedly attaching and pulling off the breast or even refusing to continue at all. The mother may sense that her let-down has not occurred. She just needs to be patient even if her baby is not being so. Usually the milk will begin to flow within a few minutes.

## Some causes of poor let-down

- Engorgement. In an engorged breast, pressure of milk on the muscle cells around the alveoli can make it difficult for them to contract to squeeze the milk into the ducts.
- Insufficient nipple stimulation. Attachment may be difficult or the baby may be reluctant to work at the breast to trigger the let-down. If you are expressing you may not have stimulated the nerve pathways which trigger the let-down.
- Pain from any source can be a cause, including breast or nipple problems, a sore episiotomy wound or after-pains.
- Fatigue and exhaustion can affect let-down.
- Emotions such as fear, grief, worry, anger, resentment or embarrassment can be inhibiting.

*C* Trying to hurry a feed. This is likely in the evening when others in the family have needs to be met and everyone is tired and hungry.

*C* Being cold.

*C* Drinking alcohol.

## Managing a delayed or unreliable let-down

Start by checking your lifestyle. Try to reduce stress and fatigue, simplify meals and housekeeping and plan some relaxation time for yourself. If anxiety is resulting from opposition to your breastfeeding by anyone close to you, try to persuade them to go with you to a supportive health adviser experienced in breastfeeding to talk about your difficulties. If others are offering unwanted advice, change the subject.

**A routine can help condition the let-down reflex. Here are some suggestions:**

*C* If you are troubled by after-pains then ten or fifteen minutes before you start the next feed, take a suitable analgesic. If nipples are tender you can try the suggestions earlier in this chapter under 'Managing sore nipples'.

*C* Try to arrange that there are no interruptions. You could take the phone off the hook. If you have a toddler you could provide some interesting activity near you. Having a box with special toys, which is only brought out when you are feeding, can help.

*C* Have all you will need for the feed close by you.

*C* Feed in the same familiar, comfortable place.

*C* Take a couple of deep breaths and relax, particularly neck and shoulders. You could put on some favourite music.

*C* Drink a glass of water.

*C* Visualise your milk flowing to the baby.

*C* Be patient while the baby sucks to stimulate the let-down.

*C* Roll your nipples between finger and thumb to stimulate the let-down and remember that this can take a minute or two or even longer. Do this before the baby goes to the breast, particularly if he or she becomes frustrated because it is slow. If the let-down is still slow you can bathe the breasts with warm water, stroking down towards the nipple as you continue to roll it.

Once well established the let-down can be expected to function easily and can survive many problems that mothers encounter.

## A fast or forceful let-down

If the baby is distressed by a fast or very forceful let-down that may last a moment or two or continue during the feed, you can put pressure on the areola with a finger and thumb and this will probably slow the flow so that the baby can feed more easily. If this is not enough, while the forceful flow lasts you could try some of the other methods suggested below in 'Too much milk' in this chapter. Remember that a forceful let-down does not necessarily mean that you have an over-supply.

## *Mastitis*

**Myth:** If you have mastitis you must stop breastfeeding.
**Truth:** It is very important to continue breastfeeding. Breasts must be well drained and the best way is to allow your baby to do this for you.

Mastitis means inflammation of the breast and is most commonly caused by poor drainage of the breast, particularly by a blocked duct. The first signs of mastitis are likely to be tenderness and a faint pink blush on the breast. It is commonly found on the upper, outer part of the breast. The condition can worsen rapidly, the breast becoming swollen and painful. This may be preceded or accompanied by a general body reaction with flu-like symptoms of varying degrees of severity and a raised body temperature. There is a saying that 'flu in a lactating woman is mastitis until proven otherwise'.

There are two types of mastitis: non-infective and infective. The first, if not treated, will lead to the second. In both, care of the breasts is similar: the aim is to reduce pain and congestion by keeping the breasts well drained (preferably by feeding your baby frequently) and by keeping the nipples dry. In addition, infective mastitis is treated with antibiotics.

**Mastitis may be caused by:**

- unrelieved engorgement
- a persistently blocked duct
- poor positioning and attaching, leading to inadequate drainage
- faulty or poor let-down
- long periods between feeds or restricting the baby's feeds
- pressure from clothing (tight straps or bras) or sleeping on the breasts
- trauma, such as a knock to the breast
- bacterial invasion of breast tissue.

## Non-infective mastitis

Non-infective mastitis involves an inflammatory reaction within the breast that occurs when breast fluids leak out of the glands and ducts into the surrounding breast tissue and beyond. It usually begins as a small localised area that is pink or reddened, lumpy and tender to touch. If the inflammation spreads, making more of the breast swollen and painful, the mother will feel generally unwell, with symptoms ranging from lethargy and malaise through to a raised body temperature and flu-like symptoms. This will predispose to infection and needs medical consultation.

## Infective mastitis

In infective mastitis bacteria are present, multiplying and invading the breast tissue. Engorgement, blocked ducts and pre-existing non-infective mastitis can lead to infective mastitis. Lowered immunity may be involved, which can be due to poor nutrition, continued fatigue and stress, smoking and/or any other existing illness.

Bacteria may reach the tissues through a damaged nipple and multiply rapidly. Occasionally, mastitis can occur in association with a wound on the skin which will need to be treated like any other infected wound – cleaned with antiseptic solution and kept dry. Medical attention is necessary because if it is left untreated, bacteria can rapidly multiply and spread throughout the breast.

Signs and symptoms of infective mastitis include redness, swelling, heat and pain in the breasts with additional general symptoms ranging from fatigue, headache and feeling mildly ill to feeling acutely sick with a high body temperature, rigors and muscular aches. It can be difficult to differentiate between non-infective and infective mastitis; however, infective mastitis is likely to be more severe and persistent and will need medication.

## Managing mastitis

Obtain medical advice first. If the condition is mild it is likely to be non-infective and will respond to careful management. Some doctors will want to see if the mastitis can be resolved with rest and careful draining of the breasts. You may be given a script for antibiotics to have on hand so you can start them at once should the mastitis worsen. A specific antibiotic will be necessary and usually two prescriptions are needed. Your doctor will advise you. Most antibiotics do not affect either the baby or the breastmilk as minimal amounts pass into the milk. The breastmilk is not infected or altered in taste to any great degree. It may be a little 'salty' but this does not usually worry the baby.

### You can help by following these steps:

- Continue to breastfeed.
- Maintain personal hygiene, change breast pads to keep breast and nipple dry.
- Drain breasts frequently. Your baby's feeding is usually the gentlest and most efficient way to drain the breasts. If you cannot breastfeed, express by hand or breast pump. The breasts must be drained to help with healing and to prevent a breast abscess.
- Use hot packs on the breast before you feed or express and then apply cold packs when finished.
- Ensure there are no blocked ducts; if you detect these take steps to relieve them.
- Check that there is no pressure on the breast from a tight bra or as you sleep.
- Rest in bed if general symptoms are present.

- Drink extra fluid if the body temperature is raised.
- Try to get and/or accept household help while you are ill.
- If the breasts are painful use an analgesic about ten minutes before feeding. Non-steroidal anti-inflammatory drugs like Nurofen or Voltaren are helpful as well.
- Feed from the affected breast first. You may find it helpful to trigger the let-down before starting the feed.

If the baby still cannot feed from the affected breast because of pain or engorgement, you must express the milk. If it is difficult to get the milk to flow you could try the Epsom salts method explained earlier in this chapter under 'Milk engorgement'. It is most important to drain this breast well by hand or pump. You can give this expressed milk if the baby is still hungry after taking the other breast.

## Preventing a recurrence of mastitis

Maintain good health and boost your immune system by:

- avoiding smoking
- eating well
- planning adequate rest, exercise and relaxation
- keeping fatigue and stress to a minimum. While this may seem impossible with a baby and other children, look after yourself as much as you can. Accept offers of help. Don't stand when you can sit, or sit when you can lie down. Reduce household chores and aim to 'have home just clean enough to be healthy and just tidy enough to be happy'.

**Prevention of a recurrence of mastitis is assisted by preventing breast or nipple damage. This can be achieved by the following:**

- Check that the baby is well positioned on the breast and feeding effectively.
- Check your breasts routinely and act promptly if there are any signs of a problem such as lumps, blocked ducts or any reddened, tender areas.

- Prevent engorgement by frequently and effectively draining the breasts.
- Keep your nipples as dry as possible by changing breast pads when they become moist.
- Avoid tight or restrictive bras and pressure from sleeping on the breasts, and take care to avoid knocks and bumps.
- Handle the breasts gently.
- Avoid rigid feeding schedules and long intervals between feeds.
- Allow the baby to drain the first breast before offering the second. Keep the second breast comfortable by expressing if your baby does not feed from this side.
- Alternate the breast offered first at each feed.

## Breast abscesses

These are very rare because treatment of mastitis is usually effective. They form when bacteria and cells gather to form pus. Medical treatment is needed.

Signs that an abscess has formed include the presence of a lump that may be exquisitely tender. There will be local and general signs and symptoms of infection. A breast abscess is not a reason to stop breastfeeding unless the abscess discharges into the ducts and mixes with the milk, but this is rare. If there is difficulty with the feed, perhaps due to pain, expression will be necessary to prevent engorgement. Gentle manual expression rather than breast pump expression (even on low pressure) is usually a better way to remove the milk from the breast but this can depend on the site of the abscess. Use the less painful method.

### Managing a breast abscess

To manage breast abscesses, try the following:
- Obtain medical advice and follow the treatment prescribed.
- Maintain careful hygiene.
- Continue to breastfeed if possible and feed frequently. Usually healing occurs quickly if breastfeeding is not disrupted. Gently express by hand to drain any residual milk.

- If the abscess has been opened and is draining into a dressing, finish handling this breast completely then wash your hands thoroughly before changing the baby to the second breast.
- With hot soapy water thoroughly wash pump fittings, containers or clothing in contact with your milk or the wound.
- It is normal for breast smells to leak out of an abscess wound. As it heals the smell will go.

## Too much milk

You can expect an over-abundance, which is often present as lactation commences, to reduce to match the baby's appetite. Allow free access to the breasts right from birth. If the over-supply continues and/or the milk flow is too fast or the let-down too forceful, there will be a need for a little careful management.

A fast flow or forceful let-down does not necessarily mean that you have too much milk. Your supply can be adapted to the baby's needs and you may just need to control the rate or reduce the force of the flow.

### What you should *not* do if you have 'too much' milk

The following practices might seem reasonable but they lead to too little milk.

- Do not give the baby a few moments on the first breast and then move to the second simply to relieve discomfort in both breasts. You should allow the baby to feed on the first side until no longer willing to continue. The first breast needs to be drained. (Remember that there are always at least a few drops left in an 'empty breast'.) You can relieve the other breast if necessary by allowing it to drip as the baby feeds on the first, or you can express a little milk.
- You should not restrict the feed to one breast only. You need to offer the second side so that the baby can take more if hungry, but do not pressure baby to continue if satisfied.

When you have a problem with too much milk and the baby wakens crying after only a short time since a feed, do not assume that hunger is the cause. It may be, but look for other possible reasons for the crying (see Chapter 6, 'Communicating') before offering more food. If you need help consult an experienced breastfeeding adviser.

## Consequences of over-supply

In the mother:

- leakage of milk, which is annoying
- mastitis, which can result from unrelieved, over-full breasts.

In the baby:

- increased weight gains, often very large (even 400–500 grams in a week), many wet nappies and frequent large bowel motions
- gasping, spluttering, pulling off the breast or even refusing to continue feeding (but some babies manage to control a flood of milk with their gums)
- an uncomfortably overloaded tummy, possibly leading to a simple vomit of excess
- excessive flatus may be passed, and baby may have colicky pain which is due to a 'false' lactose intolerance because of an increased lactose volume from so much milk; the baby may also search for extra sucking – the feeds may be too short to satisfy the sucking needs, so baby will want to continue even if her or his tummy is already over-full; perhaps the warm breastmilk is briefly soothing, although it soon causes even more discomfort
- unnecessary weaning because undigested lactose in the stools is mistakenly put down to lactose intolerance; the large feeds may simply contain too much lactose for the available lactase to digest (See, in Chapter 20, 'Diarrhoea due to lactose overload'.)

## Managing an excessive flow

You want your baby to feed comfortably, to take an adequate amount without overtaxing the digestion and to drain at least one breast at each feed. Be flexible, for the quantity of milk flowing can vary at different feeds. Flow may be excessive in the morning and less so, or even comfortable, later in the day.

**You can try the following:**

- Attach the baby correctly. Babies can often control the flow by gripping the areola with tongue and gums. A new baby may not be able to do this – proper attachment helps the baby to learn.
- Use finger and thumb to compress the areola (or the breast tissue immediately behind it if your baby has taken areola, and even some breast, into the mouth) to stem the flow. If your baby is well attached and feeding easily and your nipple is comfortable, continue this compression until the fast flow eases, then relax the pressure as the feed continues.
- Have the baby straddle your thigh with the mouth in line with the nipple. In this way the baby may manage the flow by feeding horizontally.

As the flow slows the baby will probably manage to feed easily. You may then be able to move him or her into a more comfortable position. Should the milk flood again, control it using whichever method suits you both. Be sure to allow the baby to feed for as long as willing on the first breast before offering the second. If these steps are still insufficient look for experienced help for an individual assessment of the baby's feeding.

Remember: *a fast and/or forceful flow need not mean an excessive amount of breastmilk* and the baby may need all your milk (that which is taken directly from the breasts plus any you catch in a sterile container as it drips or that you express).

## Posture feeding

This term refers to positions sometimes used when managing a fast flow. However, many breastfeeding advisers are concerned about problems that can occur with posture feeding and are reluctant to advise posture feeding; but there are others who recommend it enthusiastically and many mothers who choose to posture feed do so very successfully. They have found it comfortable both for themselves and their babies. Some continue to posture feed until the baby is weaned.

Posture feeding is a special technique which needs to be carefully followed to be effective. Experienced help is an advantage as you learn.

Posture feeding can be helpful at the beginning of a feed when the breasts are very full. This may be early in the morning or following a long sleep but may or may not be necessary at other times. As the flow eases, mothers need to sit up for the rest of the feed. The baby may then be able to feed comfortably and the breast can be drained more easily. Mothers need to alternate the breast they offer first at successive feeds so that each breast is drained well in turn. They can then express if necessary.

## Full-posture: feeding 'uphill'

This position gives maximum control to a baby taking a very fast or forceful flow. With your head and shoulders supported on pillows you lie flat on your back. The baby lies, more or less diagonally, across your body while you support the head with the palm of your hand.

Feeding 'uphill' may be needed only for the first few minutes of a feed, although some mothers continue because of their persistently copious flow. Because the baby has to suck against gravity it is possible that he or she may become tired after two or three minutes and need a rest before continuing. As the feed progresses you might use the semi-posture position (see below) before sitting up to finish.

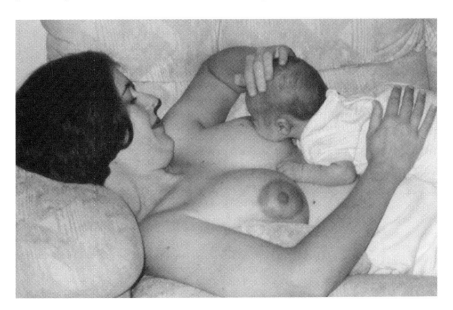

**To full-posture feed:**

- Place pillows for your shoulders and your head on a flat surface (bed or floor) – use two or three pillows, whichever is more comfortable.
- Sitting upright, attach the baby to the breast with the arms one on each side of the breast, so that, when you lie back, the baby is lying across your body supporting him or herself on the forearms (like a little sphinx) with no twist in the neck.
- Start the feed while you are sitting.
- As the baby starts to gulp lie back flat on the bed, head on one pillow, shoulders on the second pillow which is beneath and a little forward of the top one).
- As you feed from the right breast have your right elbow on the bed or a pillow beside you and use the palm of your right hand to support the baby's forehead.
- Allow the baby to rest at any time.
- As the initial fast flow eases you can try rolling onto your side (with the baby still attached) and tucking the baby against your body in the kneeling (semi-posture) position; as soon as possible sit up, or you may be able to go straight to the sitting position.
- Let the baby finish the feed in the cradle position and then repeat the process for the second side.

Be relaxed about the procedure; you will very quickly find what suits you both and do it quite automatically.

Remember when posture feeding to sit up as the baby attaches to the breast, lie down as the milk flows and again sit up when the flow of milk is manageable. See that you are sitting up as the breasts empty. If you find that the baby is satisfied and uninterested in taking more milk while a breast is still uncomfortably full or lumpy, express just enough to reduce lumpiness or discomfort.

## Semi-posture: feeding horizontally

For both of you, this position may be more comfortable than full-posture; it will be less tiring for your baby. The procedure is:

- Place pillows on a flat surface (bed or floor) so that the position is right for your head and shoulders when you lie down on your side with the feeding breast up.
- Attach the baby to the breast while you are sitting.
- Slide down the bed turning onto your side, holding and supporting the baby. Hold the baby's body closely against yours so that the baby is kneeling while feeding.
- Use this position while the flow is fast.
- As the flow eases sit up and nurse your baby in the cradling position until the feed finishes on that breast.
- Turn to the other side and offer the second breast in the same way.

A slightly different semi-posture position has your baby straddling your thigh and facing your breast. As well as helping with a fast flow this position may ease a sore nipple.

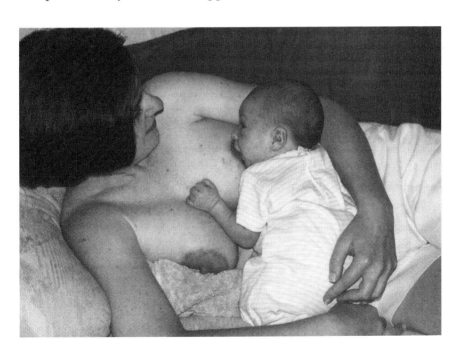

**Concerns with posture feeding are:**

✐ Poor attachment to the breast may possibly lead to 'nipple sucking', the nipple slipping from the mouth, and/or the nipple being chafed.

✐ If posture feeding is continued after the fast flow has ceased it will take more effort to obtain the same amount of milk and the baby may become tired and stop before taking enough to ensure they thrive, and before draining even the first breast, which is needed to maintain supply. At least the first breast offered at a feed should be emptied (preferably by your baby as you sit up to finish the feed, if necessary by expressing). The second breast will have its turn at the next feed, and so on.

If you posture feed be aware of these concerns. If you feel you need help or reassurance and have access to an experienced breastfeeding adviser who will sit with you and observe your baby feeding, you can ask for this help.

## Low milk supply

Frequently, against their better judgement, mothers with unsettled babies are influenced by others to give up breastfeeding. Often they are persuaded that they haven't enough breastmilk and should bottle-feed. Even if more breastmilk is needed, with accurate information and support the great majority of mothers can increase their supply and the benefits of breastfeeding can be retained. Believe in your body's natural ability to feed your baby.

Know that lactation is the natural sequel to birth, so expect your body, which has competently conceived and produced your baby, to produce all the milk needed. An ample supply is normal and it is almost certainly within your reach. If the supply has fallen behind there are ways of increasing it provided that you are relaxed and confident.

Remember that most mothers of twins, or even triplets, are able to produce enough breastmilk to feed them, so feeding only one is unlikely to be a problem.

## Mistaken beliefs about too little milk

The following signs are often misinterpreted as indicating an inadequate supply of milk:

- an unsettled baby
- a sudden demand for more feeds because the baby is growing and needs to stimulate an increase in supply (see 'How do I manage when baby suddenly asks to feed more often?' in Chapter 14)
- small weight gains in a thriving baby (see below)
- the natural reduction in breast size as lactation establishes and adapts to the baby's appetite.

Mothers with sufficient milk often worry needlessly if their very full breasts, which they had in the first few days when lactation was commencing, suddenly become softer and smaller, particularly when it coincides with their return home. They believe their lactation is failing. This change in the breasts is not due to a failing supply of milk. It simply indicates that their lactation is settling down to match the baby's appetite. The size and softness of the breasts will vary from feed to feed, depending on the feed taken and the time of day. In the evening, there is likely to be less milk with breasts being softer than they are in the morning but the milk has increased concentrations of nutrition and immunity factors. Less volume and increased concentrations in the afternoon allow for frequent feeding to stimulate supply.

## When there really is insufficient breastmilk

If the baby is really underfed you will need to provide more milk (see in this chapter, 'Complementary feeding').

A well newborn baby who has lost more than 10 per cent of birth weight and has not regained it, preferably within fourteen days but certainly within 21 days, is usually described as underfed. A mother and her baby who have feeding problems while in hospital or are being visited at home by their midwife, can expect to receive skilled advice. Once on her own and in the days ahead, the mother will be the one observing her baby's behaviour and condition. If available she can visit an early childhood nurse at a clinic. She can look for help from an experienced breastfeeding adviser such as her midwife, a lactation consultant or counsellor from the Australian Breastfeeding Association, or possibly her family doctor. Remember that there is phone help available too.

## Recognising underfeeding

Mothers with insufficient milk are sometimes misled into believing they have plenty because they can express a little from well drained breasts at the end of a feed. You can always expect to express a little from an 'empty' breast after feeding. Generally a well but underfed baby will show signs of hunger and be hard to settle and this will probably alert the mother to look for other signs of underfeeding.

It is not always easy to recognise mildly underfed babies. They can become accustomed to small feeds, remaining alert and responsive and not unduly miserable. As the underfed baby's energy reduces, the baby may feed lethargically at the breast and fall asleep before taking a good feed. This can be mistaken for contentment. The baby is seen as a 'good baby'. In both cases unsatisfactory weight gains, thinness and poor body tone would indicate that the baby is not thriving. It is important to rule out illness and establish that the condition really is due to underfeeding so consult your health adviser.

## Underfeeding consequences

If underfeeding continues, you can expect the following:

- The baby will stop gaining weight and later lose weight. Their irposition on the percentile chart will drop and the baby will look thin with less rounded limbs that are not firm to touch.
- The output of urine will decrease and there will be fewer than six to eight wet nappies in 24 hours. Some of these will be only damp. This is easier to judge when using cloth nappies rather than disposable nappies. The urine may become concentrated and strong-smelling. Bowel motions will be small and usually infrequent.
- The baby is likely to be less bright-eyed and responsive than before.

## Behaviour of the underfed baby

- An underfed baby may cry continually and angrily and be difficult to settle to sleep, and sleeps are likely to be for a short time only before the baby wakens, hungry again.
- The baby might take the breast eagerly only to become frustrated (constantly stopping and starting, possibly pulling away after a short time, even refusing to return to the breast at all) indicating that there is not enough milk. If the baby is offered extra milk it is likely to be taken hungrily.
- He or she might feed unhappily for longer than usual and be unwilling to leave the breast, obviously still hungry when taken off. These babies often suck miserably on hands, fingers or even the bed clothes.
- An underfed baby might grizzle rather than cry vigorously (if energy is low) and the baby may sleep for long periods or lie awake looking tense and strained. The baby is often less responsive and interested in the environment.

## When the baby's low energy is the cause of underfeeding

Should you feel that your baby is lacking energy and therefore feeding poorly, see a doctor to check that there is no medical cause responsible.

### If reassured you can then take the following steps:

- Visit a health adviser experienced in breastfeeding if one is available.
- During the day, allow the baby to sleep for no more than four hours between feeds. Try feeding after three hours if the baby is willing to go to the breast. Feed at least four hourly through the night.
- Be prepared to offer a feed whenever the baby wakens and is willing to go to the breast, even if only for a short time.
- Feed promptly when the baby wakens or shows early signs of interest in feeding (hands going to mouth, sucking fingers or lips), because crying wastes energy.

- Unless the let-down is rapid, initiate it before starting the feed.
- Towards the end of the breastfeed give what complement is needed, preferably with a supply line (see 'Supply line or cup for giving the complement' later in this chapter) cup or spoon.

Both the quantity of milk in your breasts and the baby's energy will vary from feed to feed. A very small, young or lethargic baby may not have the energy or strength to obtain milk directly from the breast, particularly at some feeds. In this case you can give the expressed milk or, if there is none available, some formula. It is wise to obtain advice before offering a formula. Continue to express any milk there is in the breast.

## Maternal causes of low supply

- Sometimes a piece of placenta is retained in the uterus – this inhibits milk production. In the early days following birth, if you are anxious about your supply of breastmilk ask your midwife or doctor if this might be a possible cause.
- Poor positioning and attachment of the baby to the breast can cause low supply, as well as not well draining each breast, at least at alternate feeds. Restricted feeding can interfere with the removal of the milk and the stimulation of the breasts on which supply depends. Periods of engorgement in the early days can also lead to a low supply.
- Use of a soother/dummy instead of offering comfort/short feeds as well as regular feeds can inhibit supply.
- Use of a nipple shield without adequate advice from a lactation consultant or child health nurse can have an adverse affect.
- Unresolved difficulties with nipples may be the cause.
- Illness (for example, hypothyroidism), smoking, or poor nutrition.
- Hormonal changes – a period (or threatened period) or a new pregnancy may cause a temporary upset.
- Oral contraception – the combined progestogen and oestrogen contraceptive pill will reduce lactation but it is believed that the progestogen-only oral contraceptive (the mini-pill) should not affect

lactation. However, some mothers feel that the mini-pill causes a change in their baby's willingness to breastfeed contentedly. This can affect their supply (see 'The progestogen-only oral contraceptive pill' in Chapter 8; for other methods of contraception see the same chapter).

- Drugs – some prescribed medications and social drugs can also reduce supply.
- Not enjoying or wanting to breastfeed can be a factor.
- Anxiety, can create tension. Mothers can doubt their milk away if they worry too much.
- Difficulties with let-down.
- Unrelieved tiredness and fatigue after the return home, particularly when there are other children, can affect supply. There may be unrealistic expectations. Partners can expect too much and offer too little in return. Some mothers are on their own. Women may try to do far more than is reasonable. In the first six weeks at least women need *rest, help and support willingly given. This is so important.*
- Insufficient milk-producing tissue in the breasts is very unusual but can occur.
- The actions of well-meaning support people, who do not recognise early feeding cues and so want to limit the mother's access to her baby or the baby's access to the breast when the baby is demanding a feed, can create supply problems. Some babies will go back to sleep, others become very upset. Both reactions mean baby has missed a feed.
- Surgical augmentation or reduction mammoplasty. Augmentation is sometimes done because of underdeveloped breasts, not just to enhance normal small breasts. Surgery does not necessarily interfere with breastfeeding. Sometimes reduction surgery does make full milk production impossible but most women who have undergone breast surgery will produce some milk and this can often be maximised by using a supply line. Any breastmilk is better than none. However, if the ducts behind the nipple have been cut a mother will not be able to breastfeed. After a surgical removal of one breast a mother can still fully breastfeed from the remaining one.

## How the baby can affect supply

The baby can have an effect on milk supply by:

- feeding inefficiently, resulting in inadequate draining of the breasts
- being sick or sleepy – the baby might be jaundiced in the early days following birth
- having sucking difficulties
- taking less from the breasts because unnecessary extra fluid was given, so reducing the appetite and the needed stimulation of the breasts
- using teats or dummies when learning to breastfeed. This may cause sucking problems. Dummies or pacifiers can limit comfort sucking at the breast and shorten feeds, which reduces stimulation and decreases the amount of milk.

## How to increase your supply

- Look for the cause of the low supply.
- Feel relaxed and confident in your ability to breastfeed; after all, we have survived as a species so most women most of the time must have been able to do it.
- Eat wisely – you may find that eating frequent, nutritious snacks rather than three larger meals suits you better. Drink whenever you feel thirsty.
- Minimise the stresses and anxieties of daily living where you can and increase opportunities for rest and relaxation to avoid fatigue. If stressed and you can arrange it take the Rest Cure – see the following section. You may find it surprisingly helpful.
- Ask for support from your family and your friends.
- Look for support and experienced advice. If it is not readily available you can phone an early childhood clinic, a post-natal hospital, the Lactation Consultants of Australia and New Zealand (LCANZ) or one of the Australian Breastfeeding Association (ABA) groups.
- Look for early feeding cues and feed your baby for comfort or to quench his or her thirst.
- Aim to feed the baby more frequently – through the day at least every three hours and even at other times if the baby is willing. Feed four

hourly during the night or at least twice. Extra night feeding may be necessary for only a few nights while the breasts are responding to the increased demand. It may help to have the baby sleeping in your room beside your bed. You can bring the baby into bed with you to feed if you are both comfortable but check 'Where to sleep' in Chapter 18.

*Check that the baby is well positioned and attached to the breast. At the end of each feed allow a short rest then offer each breast again in the order in which they were given. If willing to try, the baby might obtain a little extra milk and further stimulate the breasts. Then during the day you can try to hand express any remaining milk although it is likely that the baby has taken all there is. It is worth trying for a couple of minutes. The extra stimulation can help.

*At the end of the feed if the baby still seems hungry and you have it, you can offer some expressed breastmilk – perhaps 30 millilitres. Because the breasts need frequent stimulation you do not want to give more than necessary, even of your own expressed milk. You may not need to give the extra in the morning but really need to in the afternoon and evening and as you settle the baby for the night.

*If possible you can check the baby's weight weekly. For an accurate assessment of the baby's progress try to have him or her weighed by your child health nurse at approximately the same time at each visit whether it be just after, midway between feeds or just before a feed. The baby will be more relaxed if it is after the feed. Remember that it is difficult to weigh your baby accurately on home scales. It is best to avoid using scales in a chemist or pharmacy as this may lead to inappropriate advice about weaning or the introduction of formula feeds.

*If still more milk is needed there is something additional that you can do. You can express between the baby's feeds. It will mean planning because this will be even more time-consuming and you may be doing this for two or three days. About an hour after the feed, stimulate the let-down by rolling the nipples and express what you can from each breast. *Even if you express only a teaspoon or two it is worth doing because you are stimulating the breasts to make more milk.* While expressing you can try for two or three let-downs by nipple rolling. Be relaxed about it all and encouraged even if you express only 10 or 15 millilitres. Save this milk and be ready to give it after the next feed – the baby is likely to need it. Don't worry that there may be less milk for the next feed – just encourage the baby to take what you have and then give the expressed milk. With this expressing you can expect a further increase in the supply. Ideally combine the extra expressing with the Rest Cure (see below).

- If you have been advised by your doctor, child health nurse or lactation consultant to give some formula because, for now, your baby is underfed, top-up as necessary.
- You could discuss with your doctor the advisability of using a medication that could increase the prolactin level. Success with this treatment is considered to be most likely in the first three months of lactation.
- Discuss with your doctor other medical reasons for a low milk supply: for example, you may need thyroid function tests and treatment if your thyroid levels are found to be low.

## The Rest Cure

The Rest Cure is simply 48 hours in bed and is a special way to try to increase milk production rapidly. Many mothers have found this plan well worth the effort to arrange. It is particularly valuable when the probable cause of the low supply is fatigue and/or continued stress. It can greatly help to increase milk production, but to maintain the increased supply it is essential to find ways of obtaining more rest in the days ahead. Stress may be more difficult to reduce, but practical and sympathetic support can help. Remember that many people are very willing to help when you let them know you need it.

You will need a supportive partner or another helpful adult to assist you in 'taking the cure' – someone who can and will, willingly take over the household chores and meals and help you with the baby. Be as relaxed and comfortable as possible. There must be no feeling of guilt or that you are being lazy when you try the Rest Cure.

**You can:**

- look on this time as a way to increase your milk supply for the baby
- let yourself and the baby benefit from your rest
- read or, if you enjoy it, listen to relaxing music; it is likely that you will spend much time sleeping if you have someone to care for the baby while you nap
- if you wish, have the baby beside your bed for most of the time; whenever it suits you both, have the baby in bed with you provided that it is safe for the baby (see 'Where to sleep' in Chapter 18)
- share plenty of skin-to-skin contact, which is easiest when feeding; the baby can be in a nappy only and you without bra and top
- feed as frequently as the baby is interested
- during the day waken the baby after three hours and offer a feed
- at the end of the feed express any remaining milk
- if there are restless periods someone may be able to take the baby off for a walk or provide a cuddle to give you the chance to have the extra rest, which is so important
- while resting, review your daily routine and think about ways you can make life easier.

It is most likely that the supply of breastmilkwill increase. As this occurs the baby's condition will improve and protests will be fewer and less frequent. Time between feeds will lengthen and when awake, the baby will be content for longer periods. Once more you can return to simply feeding the baby according to appetite following the principles of good breastfeeding.

Occasionally these efforts do not increase the supply. These mothers need the help of experienced health and breastfeeding advisers to examine carefully other possible causes of their low supply. Meanwhile they may choose to give their babies what breastmilk they have and enough complementary formula for proper nourishment.

## Complementary feeding

Complementary feeding is the giving of extra milk to a breastfed baby. The extra milk is referred to as the complement or supplement. Very few healthy breastfed babies need this. However, if a baby is not thriving because of insufficient breastmilk the food intake must be increased.

If the baby is in immediate need of extra nourishment you will be advised to start it without delay. Ideally this complement will be your expressed breastmilk. If you have some stored, use it. If not, the baby will need some formula while you take steps to increase your supply. The formula you use must be suitable. The options should be discussed with a breastfeeding adviser, midwife, child health nurse or doctor.

### Give a complement carefully

Breastfeed before giving the complement. If you start with the complement it will reduce your baby's interest in the breast and probably reduce the amount taken from it. If you give it before the baby finishes on both breasts they may not be fully drained. The exception occurs when the baby is so underfed that the baby has insufficient energy to obtain the milk from the breast and you must give it using another method. You could try using a supply line or a cup; see below.

### How much complement to give

The complement you give must provide the extra calories/kilojoules needed without reducing the baby's appetite for the breasts. The baby needs to waken readily for the next feed. Because the baby takes different quantities from the breasts at different times, the amount of complement needed will also vary from feed to feed. If your breasts are reasonably full in the morning, and the baby is only a little underfed, it may be enough to give the complement only during the afternoon and evening. If the baby has needed more for some time or you do not have enough breastmilk at any of the feeds then you may need to give a complement after each breastfeed. It may be reasonable to start with 30 to 60 millilitres. If the baby is still hungry offer more but stop as soon as there is any loss of interest. If the baby is taking large complements

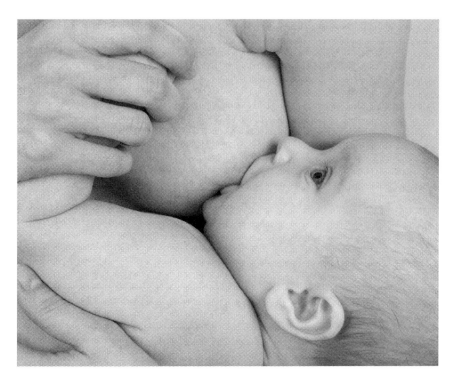

and then sleeping for more than four hours you can assume that you are giving more than necessary. Try giving a little less.

Be guided by the baby's condition and behaviour. As you give the extra needed you can expect the baby to become more contented, stronger, to have more energy and to thrive again. The baby will be able to breastfeed more vigorously and is likely to provide the additional stimulation the breasts need. As the supply increases you can reduce the complements until they are no longer necessary.

## Supply line or cup for giving the complement

Before introducing the different technique of drinking from a bottle and teat, which may make the baby reluctant to go back to the breast, it is worth trying a 'supply line'. If the baby will accept the supply line, and many will, there are advantages in using it because the baby is fixed to the breast while taking the complement from the supply line. The baby continues to associate the breasts with feeding and, at the same time, is stimulating them.

A supply line unit consists of a fine, soft tube and a small container, bottle or plastic bag to hold the complement (expressed milk or formula). The container hangs around the mother's neck and rests between her breasts. One end of the tube lies in the container beneath the level of the complement. The other end leads across the breast and lies beside the nipple. It is taped to the areola to keep it in position.

The baby goes onto the breast and the tube and draws the milk from the container while feeding. It can be helpful to have an experienced midwife, child health nurse or breastfeeding counsellor to assist you at first. A supply line can be obtained from the Australian Breastfeeding Association or from some pharmacies. Another way is to use a small cup or glass, even a spoon. The baby needs to be held comfortably, almost sitting and with the head tilted back just a little. Rest the rim of the container on the lip and gum. Babies should be able to lap the milk with their tongue rather than have it poured into their mouth. It is surprising how easily even new babies manage to learn to swallow from a small cup or medicine measure (see illustration on page 396).

## How long to give complements

Complements may be necessary for only a few days, although some mothers find that they need to continue for longer. Sometimes complementary feeding continues indefinitely while the mother gives whatever breastmilk she can and her baby willingly takes both.

Occasionally, in spite of experienced help and her own determined effort to succeed, a mother finds that she is unable to breastfeed regardless of her wish to do so and has to fully bottle-feed. She may feel deeply distressed and need support and understanding. On the other hand some women feel relieved when they make this decision, often after weeks of struggle when they know that it is just not working out. Regardless of the cause, whether arising in herself or in her baby, there is no place for guilt or blame of either. She can build a loving relationship with her baby and expect the baby to thrive on the formula feeding.

## *Breast refusal*

A baby who has been breastfeeding normally may suddenly refuse the breast for any number of reasons. Be reassured that a solution can usually be found. (If breast refusal occurs in the newborn you will have a midwife on hand to help you.)

The first thing you need to do is: look at the baby – could your baby be sick? You are very likely to know if this is so (see 'Recognising the sick baby' in Chapter 20). Loss of appetite is common in a sick baby and can lead to breast refusal.

A well baby can suddenly refuse the breast for no apparent reason. This may happen at any age and may occur at an occasional feed or the refusal may persist. A mother whose baby refuses the breast is likely to become very distressed, particularly if there is no obvious cause. She may lose confidence and self-esteem and then may feel angry. She needs to feel that she can do something to help the situation – to feel capable rather than helpless.

The baby is too young to be 'naughty' and needs your help. Breast refusal is usually temporary so try to remain calm. If the baby is well this is not an emergency situation. Provide patient, relaxed handling and loving care as you help the baby back to the breast. Ask for help if you need it. If the breast refusal continues, look for a breastfeeding adviser or talk to one on the phone. Also look for extra help from a partner, family member or friend. You might even be able to employ some household help for a day or two.

Babies refusing the breast may start to feed and then pull off, or they may refuse to go to the breast at all. They may become frustrated and fight, obviously distressed; they may scream, stiffen, kick and push away with their hands. They might actually forgo the feed altogether. If this happens at an occasional feed and you feel that the baby is well, and taking other feeds normally, it is unlikely that there is any reason for you to be concerned. This can happen at a feed if your supply is really low – often around 6 p.m. – and the baby is feeling frustrated. Check that, over 24 hours there are still five or six good wet nappies with pale-coloured urine.

Don't label the following behaviour breast refusal: the baby begins the feed but then pulls off for a minute or two only to return and continue. The baby is not upset but may butt the breast, wriggle and look around and then resume feeding – it is likely that the baby is not really hungry and may be feeling playful or perhaps is waiting for the let-down, which may be a little slower than usual. If this is so, when you do let-down and the milk flows the baby will probably latch on and feed contentedly.

## Causes of breast refusal

A well baby refusing to feed may be:

- not yet hungry
- having difficulty attaching to over-full breasts
- distressed by a fast flow of breastmilk
- uncomfortable because about to have a bowel motion, especially if it is a few days since the last one
- reacting to some food or drink the mother has taken
- uninterested in the breast because of having some other fluid that has interfered with the appetite
- suffering from sucking confusion if very young and has been fed with a bottle and teat; if this happens some babies apparently decide that it is easier to take a feed from the bottle
- accustomed to a nipple shield and prefers it to the breast
- frustrated because let-down is slow or inadequate
- restricted by a rigid feeding schedule
- miserable with a sore mouth
- uncomfortable with wind or a colicky pain
- disturbed by some confusing change in routine or overstimulation
- upset, frightened or overtired
- finding breathing difficult because of nasal mucus or a soft breast obstructing the nose
- frustrated because of increased appetite and wanting more milk (see 'How do I manage when baby suddenly asks to feed more often?' in Chapter 14)

- reacting to immunisation that has been given within the last day or so and, although not really sick, feeling miserable and/or has a sore arm or leg
- beginning baby-led weaning (in an older baby).

**Possible causes in the mother include:**
- food or drink that is actually upsetting the baby or has altered the taste of the milk – it may be something new in her diet or a 'binge' on a particular item such as peanuts
- use of nipple creams, a different perfume, deodorant or soap
- hormonal changes
- smoking or the taking of drugs or medications.

## Restless feeding associated with hormonal changes

Some babies appear to react to hormonal changes in the mother. Perhaps there is an alteration in the taste or the flow of the milk. There are women who have reported reactions when they have menstruated, when they took oral contraceptives or became pregnant while breastfeeding. The babies may react by fussy feeding or may refuse to take the breast.

### MENSTRUAL PERIODS

Most women do not recommence menstrual periods while breastfeeding, particularly while their baby has only the breast. However, some women say that at times they feel like they are about to begin a period and a few actually do. If this happens to you, you may find that your baby reacts with fussy feeding. Patience will be needed. Just offer the breast. Check the number of wet nappies and that the urine remains pale. If your baby has taken only a very small feed or has refused altogether you can offer some expressed milk if you have a store of it. If not, you can give a little cooled, boiled water. Try to avoid using any formula. Be prepared to express your breastmilk if the baby refuses to feed.

## PREGNANCY

A new pregnancy and the associated hormonal changes can affect the baby's feeding, although many breastfeed happily from their pregnant mothers. Some pregnant mothers find that their breasts and nipples become painful if they continue to breastfeed but often only in early pregnancy. Increased tiredness can be another problem. Your own wishes and health will determine what you decide to do about continuing to breastfeed. You can discuss this with your health adviser.

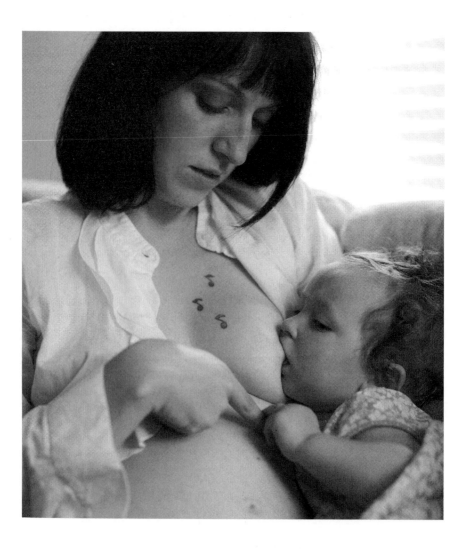

## ORAL CONTRACEPTION

Breastfeeding mothers who use oral contraception are advised to use the mini-pill – the progestogen-only pill. There are those who breastfeed easily when taking this pill but others complain that their babies become upset and some mothers describe the following sequence of events: they commence the mini-pill, then five or six days later their previously contented babies become restless and irritable while feeding at the breast. They repeatedly pull off and then attach again. This is similar behaviour to that seen in some babies whose mothers are having a period. Sometimes they refuse the breast altogether and weight gains may be less than usual. If you wish to avoid the mini-pill you can consider other methods of contraception (see 'Contraception' in Chapter 8).

If the baby is refusing the breast you may feel tense, anxious and worried, perhaps rejected and even angry. This is understandable. Don't feel guilty. Look at priorities and how you can rest and relax so that your tension does not increase the baby's distress as you help him or her back to comfortable breastfeeding.

If you are feeling tense be prepared to put the baby down safely and walk away for a short time. Start by taking several deep breaths, relax your neck and shoulders and shake your arms and hands. You might have a bath or go out and water the garden. Use any method that helps you to relax. When the baby is sleeping, try to rest too. You could have a nutritious snack or a meal with a drink and, if possible, a sleep.

See that your breasts are regularly drained so that they continue to produce milk, and don't allow them to become over-full. Express if necessary. The expressed milk will be available if you need to feed your baby some other way. Any excess can be stored if you have the facilities. Extra support from a partner, an early childhood nurse and/or helpful others will be of great help to you – arrange this if you can.

## Getting the baby back to the breast

Avoid a battle but be ready to offer the breast frequently. Knowledge of your baby will tell you when to stop trying to get the baby on the breast. Allow your baby time to relax and when it is reasonable try again. If the baby is well there will be no harm if a feed is delayed for an hour or so. You can hold, comfort, smile at and talk quietly and lovingly to the baby as you walk around. Try to divert and find something to interest the baby.

It may help to increase skin-to-skin contact between you. Remove the baby's clothes and hold the baby gently against your bare body. Use a light blanket to keep both of you warm. You may like to get into a warm bath together. Without clothes and feeling warm and comfortable with your naked breast dangling in front of the baby's nose, he or she may be tempted to feed. Initiate the let-down and express a little milk onto the nipple so that the baby can lick and taste it – a feed might follow.

Rub some breastmilk into your baby's hands and fingers and some around your areola because the smell of the milk will help your baby to coordinate their feeding reflexes. This is especially helpful for young babies.

If you use a dummy you can try letting the baby suck on it for a while. Carry the baby around and, when quiet and while you are still walking, ease the dummy out of the baby's mouth and immediately offer the breast with a little expressed milk on the nipple. If it is refused again replace the dummy. Continue to walk around. Walking rather than sitting can sometimes prevent the baby from becoming tense and resistant and you can offer the breast while doing so.

If the baby gets upset and continues to refuse whatever you try, do not continue the struggle. Both of you will need a rest. If you have a rocking chair, fast rocking can be very comforting. You can also try pushing the baby in the pram. If wheeling inside the house try pushing the pram back and forth over a bump on the floor (for example a coathanger or the edge of a rug), giving a slightly bumpy ride. Wheeling the pram outside may be even better. If the baby is well and is still having plenty of wet nappies, stop worrying.

Other things to try include giving the baby a deep, warm, relaxing bath (see 'Helping the baby to fall asleep' in Chapter 18). If the baby has been very upset then an exhausted sleep may follow. Allow the baby to sleep; starvation will not set in – the baby might even sleep for three or four hours before waking. Express your milk and have it ready should you need to give it. At the very first sign of the baby stirring, before waking fully, prepare to breastfeed. Express a little milk onto the nipple and then, without changing the nappy, offer the breast. If the baby is still refusing to take the breast you will now need to give a feed, preferably of expressed milk. If you have some, warm and give it with no more delay. If not, just express your breasts and then give that breastmilk.

How you give the expressed milk will depend on the reason for refusal. If the baby is frustrated because let-down is slow or supply really low but is still willing to start at the breast, a supply line might be successful because the milk will flow at once through the tube as the baby begins sucking. If you continue the let-down will probably be stimulated and more milk will flow.

If the baby still refuses to breastfeed you will have to use another method, e.g. a small container such as a cup or medicine measure or a bottle and teat. But if you do use a bottle there is the risk that the baby could decide it is easier than the breast and then refuse to go back to the breast at all.

After this feed carry on with the baby's usual routine. When due for the next feed try the above procedures again. Refreshed from a sleep and hungry, the baby might now go back on the breast. If the refusal continues do not try to force feed. Once more you can give the expressed milk. If you have not discussed your problem with a breastfeeding adviser this could be the time to do so.

As a last resort you might try a nipple shield. If your baby is already using a silicone dummy use a silicone shield. Remember the possible problems that might arise in using a nipple shield (see 'Nipple shields' earlier in this chapter). If the baby accepts the nipple shield and is feeding well you can try to remove it and feed directly on the breast. If unsuccessful you can replace the shield again. At the end of the feed express any milk that is left.

While breast refusal continues, express your milk so that you maintain supply. Once the problem is solved babies usually come back happily to the breast. I have known mothers whose efforts to get their baby back onto the breast were not successful but they expressed enough milk to feed them exclusively on breastmilk for months. When they started giving solid food some changed to a manufactured formula but others continued to express their milk until they felt ready to stop.

### Refusing one side

Sometimes babies who have been feeding well from both breasts suddenly fuss and refuse to feed from one breast. This may just happen at an occasional feed or the baby may continue to refuse to feed on the rejected breast. Feel the breast for any lump that may be blocking the flow of milk (see 'Blockages in ducts' earlier in this chapter). If you find one try to clear it. If not successful get help from your health adviser. If there is no obvious cause, at each feed offer the rejected breast first. Try to trigger the let-down by rolling the nipple between finger and thumb and, as the milk starts to flow, offer the breast. If the baby refuses, give the favoured side holding the baby in the usual cradling position and then, without turning the baby, just slide the baby across to the rejected breast and see if the baby will feed in the 'twin' position. Babies will sometimes accept the breast if you try this method, particularly if you have expressed a little milk onto the nipple beforehand.

Be relaxed as you gently persevere. Don't struggle with your baby. You can express and give this milk if necessary. The baby is very likely to return to both breasts.

Occasionally babies totally refuse to go back to the rejected breast. Mothers can continue to feed from the favoured breast. The supply will increase if you feed the baby frequently. If you think about it, mothers feed twins and one breast for each baby will usually provide ample milk for them. You can continue to express from the other breast if the baby needs this extra milk. Otherwise, if necessary, just express enough to keep the breast comfortable and healthy.

## Difficulties with formula (bottle) feeding

Common problems with bottle-feeding are due to trouble with teats and the technique in giving the bottle, or the formula itself. The formula you use must suit your baby. Don't be rigid in deciding that you will use a particular formula or a set quantity according to the baby's weight and age just because they suit the average baby. If the baby does not seem happy with the feeding or quantity you are giving you can discuss this with your health adviser.

## The baby who is still learning to bottle-feed

Some babies take time to learn to drink from a bottle and teat. When the bottle is first offered the baby may refuse to suck at all, particularly if you have been breastfeeding. The baby may be missing the breast, aware of the different feel of a teat and/or the taste of the formula. Often babies push the teat out of the mouth with the tongue or just let it lie there loosely. Some actually fight the bottle and become very upset. If this happens you will need gentle patience and understanding as you encourage the baby to accept it. (You could read again 'Giving the bottle' in Chapter 16.)

If the baby is refusing to feed be patient. You will not be able to persuade an unwilling, distressed baby to feed, even when hungry. The baby is unlikely to accept the feed until comforted and quietened. You may need to wrap the baby firmly in a bunny rug and even try putting them down for a while. If you use a dummy, try it. If the baby falls asleep following this bout of screaming don't worry, just be ready to try again when you see signs of waking.

If the baby is sucking poorly or is tired, place your index finger lightly under the chin (on the jaw bone, not the soft under-part) while resting the bottle on the palm of your hand. As the baby sucks, your finger can press gently up against the chin. Pull on the bottle slightly. You may then feel that the baby has a better grasp of the teat and is able to suck more effectively. If this is not enough, still with the index finger under the chin try adding a little pressure on each cheek using your thumb against the 'outer' cheek and your middle finger against the cheek next to your body. Again as the baby starts to suck exert a slight pull on the bottle (see illustration over the page). Be aware if the baby is becoming really tired and, if necessary, loosen the screw top a little more or use a teat with a larger hole. If the baby has simply had enough, stop offering the bottle. Be flexible.

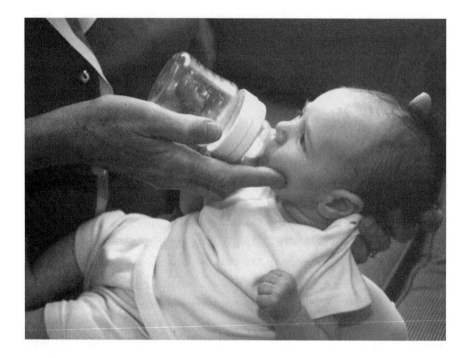

## *Digestive upsets*

Most babies do not have problems with formula. However, some are upset as they begin with a formula. First check that the formula you are using is within its use-by date and correctly prepared.

Sometimes a formula is not suitable. The baby may be finding it difficult to digest or may be sensitive or allergic to some part of the formula.

A baby reacting to the formula may vomit, become pale or flushed, come out in hives or a rash, or suffer abdominal pain. The upset may be in spasms or constant, and even quite distressing. There may be a clear, runny, nasal discharge, noisy wheezing and/or a cough. If the baby looks ill and/or appears to have a severe reaction, contact your doctor at once. The most frequent allergic reaction is due to the protein in the formula. The most common is cow's milk protein, but babies can also react to the protein in a soy formula. The obvious cure is to change the formula, but choosing another one at random may not help. An experienced health adviser will consider many factors, including your family history as well as the baby's history since birth, before suggesting another formula.

The baby might have colic. Is the change in the stools more than the normal change in colour and consistency (see 'Constipation' and 'Diarrhoea' in Chapter 20)? The stools may be frequent, green, possibly explosive and/or curd-like with mucus or the baby might be constipated. There may be behavioural changes in the baby such as a lack of interest in feeds, poor sleeping and an increase in crying.

## *Refusing to feed*

If changing from the breast to the bottle, the baby may start by refusing to feed. Someone other than you, perhaps your partner or a friend, may succeed because the baby is accustomed to receiving breastmilk from you. Babies can often smell their mother's milk. If this occurs the baby will need your loving understanding and patience.

Try for a few minutes then wait until the baby is calm before trying again. *Don't force feed.* Persevere gently but do not let the baby become distressed. If possible give breastmilk in the bottle while the baby is learning to use the teat. When the bottle is accepted you can start adding some formula to the breastmilk until the feed is fully formula.

You could start the feed with a small quantity in the bottle so that a minimum of milk is wasted. When your baby has taken that you can offer more. *Do not save the milk or the formula in the bottle as it might become contaminated.* Use fresh breastmilk or formula when next you try.

If the baby has been taking the bottle well and then refuses to feed, check that the top is not too tightly screwed – try loosening it a little. Are you using a new teat that is firmer than the one you have been using? You can soften it by boiling it gently for half an hour or so but do not let the water in the saucepan boil dry – the smell of burning rubber is more than unpleasant!

Does your baby appear well? At the onset of an illness babies often lose their appetites and are not interested in feeding (see 'Recognising the sick baby' in Chapter 20). If the baby appears well, when did you give the last feed and how willingly was it taken? Perhaps the baby is not yet hungry. Did you give a sweetened drink since the last milk feed? Sweetened drinks can interfere with appetite and are not recommended. You can offer a little cooled, boiled water between feeds if you think your baby may be thirsty.

If restless or crying the cause may be discomfort. The baby may be about to pass a bowel motion particularly if there has been none in the last 24 to 48 hours. Be prepared to wait even an hour or two. The baby may fall asleep as you provide comfort. When the baby wakens the feed might then be taken willingly. Check the mouth for thrush. Could the baby be overtired, overstimulated or upset by a change in routine? If refusal continues offer some cooled, boiled water using a small cup or spoon. If you are still anxious you can phone a help line for advice or, if necessary, consult your doctor.

## Poor weight gains

If the baby is not taking enough formula or the formula is not suitable the baby will not thrive. A visit to the early childhood clinic or your doctor will confirm this. Your health adviser will assess the baby and

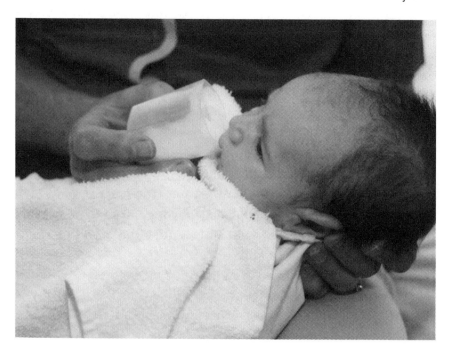

suggest ways to help. A change of formula might be needed. Your doctor will look for other medical problems that could be responsible. An ongoing check can be kept on the baby's progress.

## Food sensitivity (allergy and intolerance)

There are substances that can cause adverse reactions in the body. These are present in the environment and among them are chemicals, detergents, sprays, tobacco smoke, fumes and pollens. We need to be aware and protect our babies and ourselves from these wherever possible. Items that mothers take into their bodies in their food and drink or as drugs, alcohol and cigarette smoke can also affect their babies when breastfed, and bottle-fed babies may react to something in the formula.

Food sensitivity refers to reactions to food or drink. There are two types of reactions. Firstly, there is food allergy which involves the immune system. An example is the formula-fed baby who reacts to a foreign protein in the feed such as cow's milk protein. The second is food intolerance. This is a broader term used to cover reactions not involving the immune system, e.g. lactose intolerance – this occurs when there is an adverse response to undigested lactose (see 'Diarrhoea due to lactose intolerance' in Chapter 20).

Both exclusively breastfed and formula-fed babies can suffer from food sensitivity due to some item that has passed into the breastmilk from the mother or is an ingredient in the formula. Their reactions can be immediate or later, within 24 or even 48 hours after the feed. The incidence of such reactions is greater in formula-fed babies.

An upset in a breastfeeding baby may be an early warning of tendency to allergy. The baby may take the breast hungrily, only to pull off after a moment or two and possibly scream a few minutes later, or may refuse the breast after the first mouthful. Don't reach for a formula because the foreign proteins in the bottle-feed can also lead to the development of allergies. In fact, this is the principal objection to substituting the occasional breastfeed with a formula feed or giving an unnecessary complementary feed of formula to a breastfed baby.

If you are breastfeeding be aware that items you are eating or drinking can cause reactions in the baby. When the offending food or drink is removed from the diet the symptoms will subside. If such a breastfeeding upset occurs, discuss this with your health adviser.

In the breastfed baby the triggers may be things that you eat only occasionally, leading to episodes of upset. Examples of items that cause problems for some babies include eggs, chocolate, peanuts, and cow's milk protein in dairy products. There are others. Be a detective: think about your food and drink over the last 48 hours.

You can try excluding just one possible item at a time. Keep written records of any changes in your diet and of your observation of the baby. Look for an unaccustomed item in your own food, or for a 'binge' on a particular item. Have you had unusual contact with a detergent, spray, or paint or been in a smoke-laden room. These are possible causes of an allergic reaction too. If you find the cause of the upset you can avoid it.

If you cannot find the cause and the upset continues, ask for medical advice. Remember that it is no solution to abandon breastfeeding in favour of bottle-feeding in the hope that the baby will improve. If necessary look for a doctor who has a special interest in allergy problems. The continued exclusion of a whole group (such as dairy products) from your diet may call for the addition of other items to compensate – you could need another source of calcium – so discuss this with your health adviser. Your diet can be assessed.

## If formula-feeding

The formula-fed baby may also start to feed only to stop and refuse to continue, usually becoming very upset. Other reactions in both breastfed and formula-fed babies can include any one or more of the following.

**The baby may:**
- be unusually restless, irritable and difficult to settle
- vomit, or there may be an increase in posseting (spilling small quantities of the food)
- develop a rash, scaly skin patches or come out in hives

- have trouble with breathing and wheeze
- develop a middle ear infection
- have frequent green motions or pale stools, become unexpectedly windy and pass excessive flatus or suffer colic
- have a watery nasal discharge.

Where there is a family history of food sensitivities and/or hay fever, eczema or asthma, exclusive breastfeeding for at least six months may be the best preventative measure you can take for the baby. Not all breastfed babies will avoid such problems but breastfeeding may delay the onset of sensitivity or lessen the severity of reactions.

If your baby is formula-fed and showing signs of an upset it is important to discuss the symptoms with your health adviser. If necessary you will be advised about a change of formula and how this should be done.

# 22

# Immunisation

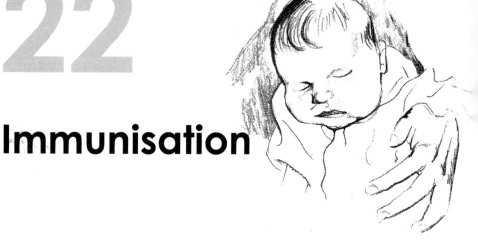

**N**ote: I wish to acknowledge the Australian Government Department of Health and Ageing publications *Understanding Childhood Immunisations* (November 2005) and *Understanding Immunisations booklet* (2004, copyright Commonwealth of Australia). The immunisation schedule is reproduced by permission of the Australian Government.

There are simple measures you can take to protect your child from some dangerous childhood diseases that can lead to paralysis, mental retardation and even death. Ask your health adviser for information and/or you can contact the Commonwealth Department of Health and Ageing, on 1800 671 811. The booklet *Understanding Childhood Immunisation* contains very detailed information. This is available on the Immunise Australia Program website (http://immunise.health.gov. au) or by calling the Immunisation Infoline on 1800 671 811.

Since mass immunisation began, epidemics of infectious diseases have been greatly reduced but babies and children can still succumb to these infections. The more babies and children in the community who have not been immunised the greater is the risk of epidemics.

When immunised, the body produces antibodies to the vaccine that is given. This can take a few weeks to become effective and more than one dose may be needed for maximum effect. If later there is contact with these preventable diseases the immunised body will be ready to fight them; the immunised baby or child will either not develop the disease at all, or the disease can be expected to occur in a very much weaker form.

Parents often wonder if the risks associated with immunisation are enough for them to decide against it. Medical research has shown that the risks of complications from the diseases are far greater than the risks of side effects from immunisation. However, before your child is immunised ask as many questions as you need to make an informed decision for your baby. One question often asked is: 'If my baby is fully breastfed is immunisation still necessary?' The advice is that it is. The breastfed baby should be immunised according to the recommended schedule because breastmilk does not provide specific protection against various diseases. Immunisations won't interfere with breastfeeding.

In some areas you cannot enrol your child in a daycare centre, preschool or school unless you can present an immunisation certificate. Others exclude your child from care during an outbreak. This could be for several weeks. Some government benefits are available for children who meet the immunisation requirements. You can obtain detailed information from a Family Assistance Office. The contact number is 13 61 50 in all states and territories.

Before immunising your baby the health adviser will ask if your baby is unwell in any way, if your baby has any known allergy problems or if there are allergy problems in the family, whether your baby has ever had a fit, has had any other immunisation in the last three weeks

**Australian Government**

**Department of Health and Ageing**

# National Immunisation Program Schedule

## (VALID FROM 1 JULY 2007)

| Age | Vaccine |
|---|---|
| Birth | • Hepatitis B (hepB) [a] |
| 2 months | • Hepatitis B (hepB) [b]<br>• Diphtheria, tetanus and acellular pertussis (DTPa)<br>• *Haemophilus influenzae type b (Hib)* [c,d]<br>• Inactivated poliomyelitis (IPV)<br>• Pneumococcal conjugate (7vPCV)<br>• Rotavirus |
| 4 months | • Hepatitis B (hepB) [b]<br>• Diphtheria, tetanus and acellular pertussis (DTPa)<br>• *Haemophilus influenzae type b (Hib)* [c,d]<br>• Inactivated poliomyelitis (IPV)<br>• Pneumococcal conjugate (7vPCV)<br>• Rotavirus |
| 6 months | • Hepatitis B (hepB) [b]<br>• Diphtheria, tetanus and acellular pertussis (DTPa)<br>• *Haemophilus influenzae type b (Hib)* [c]<br>• Inactivated poliomyelitis (IPV)<br>• Pneumococcal conjugate (7vPCV) [e]<br>• Rotavirus [i] |
| 12 months | • Hepatitis B (hepB) [b]<br>• *Haemophilus influenzae type b (Hib)* [d]<br>• Measles, mumps and rubella (MMR)<br>• Meningococcal C (MenCCV) |
| 12-24 months | • Hepatitis A (Aboriginal and Torres Strait Islander children in high risk areas) [f] |
| 18 months | • Varicella (VZV) |
| 18-24 months | • Pneumococcal polysaccharide (23vPPV) (Aboriginal and Torres Strait Islander children in high risk areas) [g]<br>• Hepatitis A (Aboriginal and Torres Strait Islander children in high risk areas) |
| 4 years | • Diphtheria, tetanus and acellular pertussis (DTPa)<br>• Measles, mumps and rubella (MMR)<br>• Inactivated poliomyelitis (IPV) |
| 10-13 years [h] | • Hepatitis B (hepB)<br>• Varicella (VZV) |
| 12-13 years [i] | • Human Papillomavirus (HPV) |
| 15-17 years [i] | • Diphtheria, tetanus and acellular pertussis (dTpa) |
| 15-49 years | • Influenza (Aboriginal and Torres Strait Islander people medically at-risk)<br>• Pneumococcal polysaccharide (23vPPV) (Aboriginal and Torres Strait Islander people medically at-risk) |
| 50 years and over | • Influenza (Aboriginal and Torres Strait Islander people)<br>• Pneumococcal polysaccharide (23vPPV) (Aboriginal and Torres Strait Islander people) |
| 65 years and over | • Influenza<br>• Pneumococcal polysaccharide (23vPPV) |

\* Please refer to reverse for footnotes

iMMUNiSATiON

or a blood transfusion or an injection of gamma globulin in the last three months. There will be other questions too. When your baby or child is immunised you will be told of possible side effects and what to do about them.

When your baby's immunisation program is commenced you will be given a schedule with space for recording the date and each injection (or dose) your child receives. You will be told when the next immunisation is due. Keep this record safely.

**The following vaccines are currently provided free for all children in Australia through the Immunise Australia Program:**

- hepatitis B
- diphtheria, tetanus and whooping cough (pertussis)
- *haemophilus influenzae type b (Hib)*
- polio (poliomyelitis)
- measles, mumps and rubella (German measles)
- meningococcal C
- pneumococcal
- chickenpox
- rotavirus.

# Description of diseases

Because of vaccination we are no longer familiar with the symptoms and course of many childhood illnesses. The following descriptions highlight the severity of several vaccine-preventable diseases.

## Diphtheria

Diphtheria is caused by bacteria that are found in the mouth, throat and nose of an infected person. Diphtheria can cause a membrane to grow around the inside of the throat which can lead to difficulty in swallowing, breathlessness and suffocation. A powerful poison (toxin) is produced by the bacteria and may spread throughout the body. The toxin may cause serious complications such as paralysis and heart failure. About 7 per cent of people who contract diphtheria die from it.

## *Tetanus*

Tetanus is an often fatal disease caused by a toxin made by bacteria present in soil and manure. You don't catch tetanus from other people. Rather, the bacteria enter the body through a wound that may be as small and insignificant as a pin prick. Tetanus attacks the nervous system, causing severe muscular spasms, first felt in the neck and jaw muscles ('lockjaw'). The effects spread, causing breathing difficulties, painful convulsions and abnormal heart rhythms.

Because of immunisation, tetanus is now rare in children in Australia but it still occurs in adults who have never been immunised against it or who have not had their booster.

## *Whooping cough*

Whooping cough, which is also known as pertussis, is a highly contagious disease caused by bacteria and spread by coughing or sneezing.

Whooping cough affects the air passages and can cause difficulty in breathing. Severe coughing spasms occur and between these spasms, the child gasps for breath causing the characteristic 'whoop' sound. Not all children get the 'whoop' and vomiting often follows a coughing spasm. The cough may last for months. Whooping cough is most serious in babies under twelve months of age, often requiring admission to hospital.

Complications of whooping cough include convulsions, pneumonia, coma, inflammation of the brain, permanent brain damage and long-term lung damage. Around one in every two hundred children under six months of age who catch whooping cough will die. These days, whooping cough is more common in older children and adults in whom the protective effect of the childhood vaccine has worn off.

The Commonwealth Government is addressing this issue by introducing a booster dose of diphtheria-tetanus-pertussis vaccine for adolescents.

## *Poliomyelitis (polio)*

Following the introduction of polio vaccines there has been a dramatic decrease in polio infection. Since 1978 no cases of polio have been reported in Australia. However, it is still important to have your child immunised against polio. There is an ongoing risk of polio being imported from other countries and re-established here if our children and adults are not immunised.

Polio may cause mild symptoms or very severe illness. It is a gastrointestinal virus which causes fever, vomiting and muscle stiffness, and can affect the nerves and cause permanent crippling. Polio can paralyse the breathing and swallowing muscles, leading to death. About 5 per cent of people hospitalised with polio die from it and about half of those who survive suffer permanent paralysis.

## *Measles, mumps and rubella*

These are all serious viral diseases. A combined measles-mumps-rubella (MMR) vaccine is used to protect children against these diseases.

**Measles** is a serious, highly contagious viral illness which causes fever, rash, runny nose, cough and conjunctivitis. Complications following measles, such as pneumonia and inflammation of the brain (encephalitis), can be very dangerous.

**Mumps** is a viral disease which causes fever, headache and inflammation of the salivary glands. It can cause inflammation of the brain or permanent deafness. Adolescent or adult males can develop painful inflammation and swelling of the testes. On rare occasions it can lead to infertility.

**Rubella** (also known as German measles) is highly contagious and is usually a mild disease in childhood. It can affect teenagers and adults. The usual symptoms are a slight fever, swollen glands, joint pain and a rash which appears on the face and neck and lasts for two or three days. If a pregnant woman is infected during the first twenty weeks of pregnancy her baby is at serious risk: deafness, blindness, heart defects and mental retardation can occur.

### Haemophilus influenzae type b (Hib)

Hib can cause infection of the membranes covering the brain (meningitis) and swelling in the throat which can block breathing (epiglottitis) in children under five years of age. It may also cause pneumonia, joint infection or cellulitis. Both meningitis and epiglottitis can develop quickly and cause death.

### Hepatitis B

This is a serious disease that can be contracted throughout life. It is caused by a virus that affects the liver. Babies that get this disease may have only mild symptoms or have no symptoms at all but can become lifetime carriers of the virus and pass it on to other people. Hepatitis B carriers may develop liver cancer or liver failure later in life.

### Meningococcal C disease

This is an uncommon life-threatening disease caused by bacteria that live at the back of the throat or in the nose. Although most people who carry these bacteria remain well, they can spread the meningococcal bacteria to others.

The onset of meningococcal disease is very quick and can rapidly cause meningitis or blood poisoning or a combination of both. The highest rate of meningococcal disease is in children under five years of age. Among the symptoms of this disease are: the sudden onset of fever, severe headache, drowsiness, confusion or coma, neck stiffness, joint pains, rash of red-purple spots or bruises, dislike of bright lights and vomiting. Additional signs to look for in babies: fretfulness, high-pitched moaning cry, difficulty in waking baby, refusal to eat and pale, blotchy skin.

### Pneumococcal disease

This is caused by bacteria that are commonly carried in the back of the throat and nose in healthy children and adults. The disease can lead to meningitis, blood infection, pneumonia and middle ear infections. Pneumococcal disease is most common in children under two years of age.

## Chickenpox

Chickenpox is a highly contagious viral disease. Chickenpox starts with a runny nose, mild fever, cough and fatigue followed by a rash. The rash usually starts on the trunk and face and spreads over the whole body. The rash starts as small red spots which rapidly turn into blisters. It is spread through coughs and sneezes and through direct contact with the fluid in the blisters. In healthy children chickenpox is usually a mild disease which lasts five to ten days. The rash can become very itchy and scratching can lead to bacterial infections of the spots.

## Rotavirus

Rotavirus is the most common cause of severe gastroenteritis in infants and young children, causing around half of all hospitalised cases of gastroenteritis in children less than five years of age. The illness can range from mild, watery diarrhoea to severe dehydrating diarrhoea with vomiting and fever, which can result in death. Children can be infected with rotavirus several times during their lives. Confirmation of rotavirus infection can only be made by laboratory testing of faecal specimens. The most common time for rotavirus disease to cause severe diarrhoea and dehydration is in babies between six and 24 months of age.

# 23

# Safety and first aid

**B**efore starting first aid in any situation, assess continuing danger to your own and others' safety from the hazard that has caused the injury, such as electricity, gas, fumes, smoke, road traffic or deep water.

If your baby clearly is breathing but with marked difficulty, remove any obvious cause. If there is no obvious cause, suspect choking by an obstruction in the airway and follow the steps under 'Choking' (page 417). If the breathing worsens, call the ambulance and begin resuscitation (page 427).

The suggestions in this chapter are particularly for a young baby but very often fit older infants and children too.

# Your awareness – your baby's safety

Most accidents involving babies and young children happen in the home. Great care must be taken to ensure your baby's and child's safety.

- Secure fencing around backyard swimming pools with child-proof locks on gates is vital. Parents need a designated adult to watch little ones at all times in the pool area.
- Cover any water: basins, fish ponds or ornamental ponds.
- Nappy buckets are also a potential source of harm and should be covered and stored out of reach.
- Take particular care in your driveway, especially when you are backing out. It is very easy to miss seeing a small child in your rear-vision mirror.
- Protect your baby from polluted air, especially tobacco smoke, which can lead to respiratory ailments. SIDS (cot death) is less likely in smoke-free environments. A baby need not directly inhale; harmful substances in cigarette smoke can appear in the breastmilk and so reach the baby.
- Harmful chemicals, for example dishwashing powder, laundry detergents and household poisons must be stored up high or in a locked cupboard.

Anticipating dangers beforehand is the first step to prevention. Much is common sense but is worth revisiting in your new role of parent. Consider where your baby is at every moment – and keep yourself always within hearing at least. Aim for prevention of accident and injury at all times.

The new baby has an ongoing, in-built and ever-expanding drive to develop new skills – a relentless curiosity to see, feel, taste, smell and hear anything and everything around them. At first the body movements are random and limited, but abilities develop and the capacity to explore the environment, dangers and all, increases.

Be prepared for new stages, for quick and sudden movements and for increasingly coordinated actions: the arm flung out at random that upsets your hot drink can become deliberate, with leaning forward and grasping added in. Babies cannot know what is harmful and what is safe; they copy what others are doing, while constantly expanding their own range of activity.

Understand how the baby will develop so you can anticipate the next stage such as rolling over, crawling, standing (first with support and then freely), walking (likewise), climbing and so on. Look around the house at the baby's level for the ever widening set of hazards, and identify and remove potential dangers.

The Early Childhood Injury Prevention Program (ECIPP) is available through Kidsafe. If you are faced with an emergency, then having attended a first aid course will increase your confidence and competence in giving first aid. This is particularly true of resuscitation procedures. First aid manuals such as *Australian First Aid* by S. John Ambulance, are a help. A first aid kit both in the home and car is useful. One can be bought from St John Ambulance or Red Cross, or you can put your own together (a pharmacist will help). You can include:

| | |
|---|---|
| antiseptic solution | calamine lotion |
| saline solution | gauze swabs |
| magnifying glass | tweezers |
| sterile gauze dressings | sterile bandages |
| crepe bandages | safety pins |
| band-aids | sling (cotton material 90 cm square) |
| | thermometer |

Pack these things into a waterproof carrying case and keep out of reach of children.

## Some common injuries and hazards

The following alphabetical listing contains common injuries, mishaps and preventions requiring first aid. Most serious are breathing difficulties, which may be life threatening and call for resuscitation.

| Hazard/aid | Page | Hazard/aid | Page |
|---|---|---|---|
| Bites and stings | 412 | Injuries | 425 |
| Bleeding | 413 | Pets | 426 |
| Breathing difficulties | 413 | Poisons | 427 |
| Burns:  superficial<br>deep<br>electrical<br>sunburn | 414<br>414<br>414<br>415 | Resuscitation | 427 |
| Cars and children | 416 | Splinters | 430 |
| Choking | 417 | Strangling | 431 |
| CPR | 427 | Suffocating | 431 |
| Cuts | 421 | Toddlers and young children | 432 |
| Drowning | 421 | | |
| Electric shock | 422 | | |
| Eyes | 423 | | |
| Falls | 423 | | |
| Fire | 424 | | |

## *Bites and stings*

Below are some of the more common instances of bites and stings.

### Bee stings

These are painful. You may be able to scrape out the sting (which remains in the tissue) with your fingernail. Take care not to squeeze the sting since this injects more poison into the site. Ice wrapped in a cloth can help relieve pain. Obtain medical advice if the sting is on the baby's throat or face: it may produce swelling, which could interfere with breathing, and a number of bites could make the baby very ill. Watch for signs of allergy such as difficulty with breathing, vomiting or severe swelling at the site. If the baby shows these signs get help straightaway.

### Ants

Ants can also inflict pain. Some (e.g. bull ants) are worse than others. You can apply ice wrapped in a cloth to ease the pain. If you are worried see your doctor. There are no remnant stings from ants (or wasps).

### Mosquitoes

Protect your baby from them, for they carry such diseases as Ross River fever, dengue fever and encephalitis. Use mosquito nets and suitable screens on doors and windows. Mosquitoes breed in any still water outside – in birdbaths, containers and fish ponds (unless you have fish or tadpoles to eat the larvae).

A cream from the chemist can lessen the itch (and may be needed for sand fly/midge bites that readily become infected). If the baby becomes sick, seek medical advice.

### Spiders

Aim to keep your house free of spiders and use a mosquito net over the pram outside. If the baby is bitten check with the doctor; if possible, take the spider for identification.

## Cats and dogs

Wash the wound. Apply antiseptic; if it is severe or shows signs of inflammation, see the doctor. Check that tetanus immunisation is up to date.

## *Bleeding*

Cover the wound with a clean cloth and press down hard on it. Lessen the flow of blood by raising an arm or leg. If there is a foreign body protruding from the wound place a padded ring around it; then bandage the wound. Do not give the child food or drink and get immediate medical help.

## *Breathing difficulties*

If your baby is not breathing (no chest movement visible, and no sound or feeling on your cheek of airflow from mouth/nose) call the ambulance and begin CPR at once.

Because the body needs a continuous supply of fresh air, interruption to breathing may be dangerous, even life threatening. The body can cope with small reductions in supply due to colds, hay fever or mild choking, but large reductions are beyond it and will soon be fatal unless bystanders help.

**Causes of serious interruptions demanding urgent intervention include:**

- interference with intake of air and its flow down the airway (the tube to the lungs from the mouth/nose); see 'Suffocating', 'Choking', 'Strangling' later in this chapter
- lack of oxygenated air in the surroundings; see 'Suffocating', 'Fire' later in this chapter.
- submergence of the face in water; see 'Drowning' later in this chapter
- breathing may prove to be involved in SIDS; see 'SIDS' in Chapter 18.

*Check for breathing directly as above,* holding your own face near the baby's face.

While some air is still passing, there is likely to be distressed coughing and spluttering. If the condition worsens there will be only occasional gasping, and the skin colour will turn blue and then grey.

The first aid you can give is set out under the headings mentioned above, particularly choking; choking is the most likely cause of interruption to breathing.

## Burns

Treatment for a burn will depend on the type of burn, as outlined below.

### Superficial burns

For small blisters or minor reddening, wash with cold water for 30 minutes, then apply a sterile non-stick dressing and bandage.

### Deep burns

Cut away clothing over the burn, leaving any stuck-on material. Gently pour cold water over the burn (do not chill the baby). Do not use ointments or lotions. Firmly cover the burn with a sterile dressing and bandage. Use a clean sheet for a large area. Get medical aid as soon as possible. Keep the baby warm, and give small drinks of water to a thirsty infant.

### Electrical burns

Check for danger; see 'Electric shock'. Treat an obvious burn as above. There can be deep tissue damage which you cannot see, so have your baby or child immediately checked.

### Prevention of burns and scalds

House fire could expose your baby to flame, so be careful with heaters (and especially electric blankets) in the bedroom; contact with hot objects in everyday situations is more likely, causing localised burning. Kitchen and bathroom are the likely places: stove, toaster, kettle and bath respectively. Set your hot water at 50°C at most. Put cold water first into the bath.

If your heaters are hot spots, put fireguards around them. Be careful with your hot drinks and hot water bottle. Never leave a hot water bottle in bed with your baby. Clothing that flaps or trails is a fire hazard, whether it is on you or the baby or near a flame, and remember that synthetic fabrics, when burning, can melt into the skin.

## Sunburn

Over-exposure to the sun burns the skin and the time, but may result in skin cancer later. The most dangerous rays are the ultraviolet (UV), also affecting eyes. They are present every day, whatever the season or the weather, but are strongest around midday.

**Follow these sun protection guidelines:**
- Avoid direct sun for the two hours each side of noon.
- Cover arms and legs against prolonged sun exposure, and use a hat with a brim to shade face and eyes.
- If outside, move the pram to follow the shade.
- Shade your car windows with stick-on screens.
- Check that the baby's face is shaded by the stroller roof.

Apply a broad spectrum sunscreen (30+) or zinc based sunscreen to all areas of exposed skin (back of hands, neck, ears, etc).

## Cars and children

There are strict national laws about travelling with children in cars, intended to reduce injuries sustained in accidents. Your road safety council or Kidsafe websites, or your local police, have details. Briefly:

- Babies less than six months old must be secured in a rearward-facing restraint.
- Children aged six months to less than four years old must be secured in either a rearward- or forward-facing restraint.
- Children aged four years to less than seven years old must be secured in a forward-facing child restraint or booster seat.
- Children younger than four years old cannot travel in the front seat of a vehicle with two or more rows.
- Children aged four years to less than seven years old cannot travel in the front seat of a vehicle with two or more rows, unless all other back seats are occupied by children younger than seven years in a child restraint or booster seat.

The law provides for Australian Standards to apply to capsule/seat construction, restraints and installation. An anti-slip liner is required; do not wrap your baby before you place and buckle them into the capsule; add covers after you have done so.

Capsules can be hired or bought pre-used. Check the history, especially whether the capsule has been involved in any accident. Kidsafe can help with this.

## Cars in sun

Your baby needs shade as you drive. The temperature rises quickly inside a car on a sunny day with closed windows and can rapidly lead to heat stress and dehydration. Death can occur. Never leave your baby or child unattended in a car.

## Children and driveways

Car drivers simply cannot see short things behind their vehicles, or on the left side. Babies in bassinets, toddlers and small children are at great risk of being run over whenever a car shares common ground with them, particularly if reversing. This applies to household garages and driveways, footpaths and car parks. Do not rely on the driver's vigilance when you have mobile children in your care in such settings. Physically separate the driveway from play areas.

# *Choking*

Choking occurs when some foreign substance enters and lodges in the airway (the tube to the lungs down the throat). It interferes with the flow of air and the body reacts with coughing and spluttering. A complete blockage is rapidly fatal, for the brain must be kept supplied with oxygen by the blood circulation through the lungs.

- Although it is common in children of all ages, most choking is mild and coughing shifts their obstruction.
- Babies and children who do not lose consciousness during a choking event and who have an effective cough just need to be supported and watched closely while coughing. If the obstruction is not relieved call an ambulance.
- For babies or children who remain conscious but who have an ineffective cough call an ambulance and use the back blows and chest thrusts (see below).
- For babies and children who can't be woken (unconsciousness), call an ambulance and perform cardiopulmonary resuscitation (CPR) (see 'Resuscitation'.

**First aid can help. Here is what you can do:**

- First, look into the baby's or child's mouth for the obstruction. If visible, hook it out with your little finger but be sure not to push it down any further.

- Promptly slap the back sharply up to five times between the shoulder blades with the aim of relieving the obstruction. An infant may be placed in a head down position (across your lap) before giving the blows.

- If unsuccessful but coughing (not merely gasping) continues, you have time for another option: that is, giving chest thrusts (some air must be getting through to support the coughing). If coughing ceases and breathing clearly is in great trouble, call the ambulance and begin resuscitation (CPR). You can check breathing by watching for chest movement and feeling for airflow on your cheek.

## Giving back blows and chest thrusts

✎ Place your baby head down across your thigh and in this position give five blows (on the back between the shoulder blades) with the heel of your hand; after each blow check for the obstruction in the mouth (or on the floor).

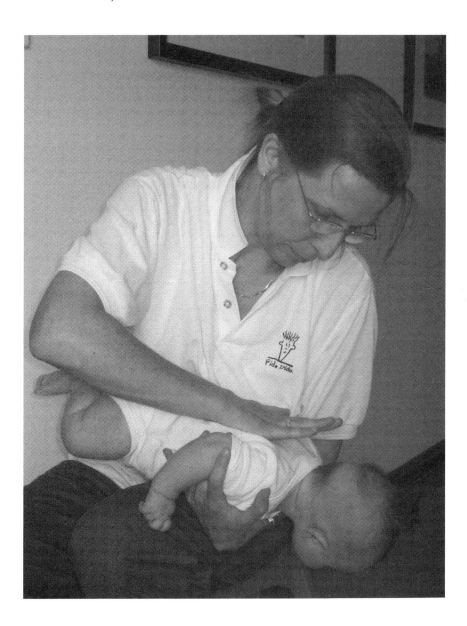

*C* Lie the baby face up on a firm flat surface, tilt the head back (only a little and gently) and pull the chin forward without roughly handling the soft tissues. This should move the tongue clear of the airway. Remove any material from the mouth.

*C* With the baby still face up, if necessary give five chest thrusts (each followed by checking in the mouth) by pushing down sharply with the index and middle finger on the breastbone between the nipples. The downward travel – the amount by which you depress the chest with each thrust – from resting position should be about 1 to 1.5 centimetres depending on the size of your baby; this is about one-third the depth of the chest. Check in the mouth after each thrust.

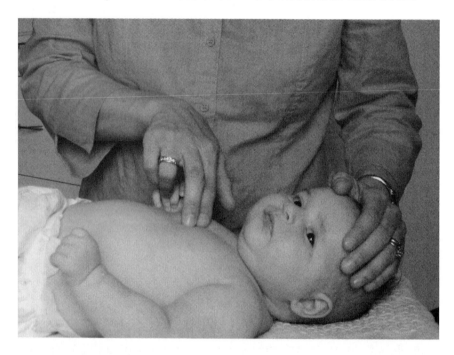

*C* If the obstruction remains, but the baby still has some coughing and breathing, continue alternating the back blows and chest thrusts until help arrives.

*C* Remember to check for breathing at intervals. If breathing lessens and coughing stops, begin CPR at once.

## Prevention of choking

Avoid buttons and ribbons on clothing. If bottle feeding do not prop up bottles. When your baby begins to put things into the mouth, there is an increased risk of choking so try to anticipate the hazards. Do not leave him/her alone while eating solid food – any hard piece of food or fruit is a danger. Nuts are best avoided until your child is aged five years or so. Toys and playthings can shed small parts and pieces, so inspect them carefully before buying. Buy toys that have been approved for sale in Australia as they meet our safety standards.

**CPR** (see under 'Resuscitation' later in this chapter).

## Cuts

First aid: see 'Bleeding' earlier in this chapter. Severe cuts are likely to need gluing or stitching by a doctor or registered nurse.

### Prevention

It may take sustained concentration and effort for new parents to alter their habits in dealing with household objects. Knives, scissors, and tools of various kinds don't mix with small fingers.

## Drowning

Every moment counts in managing drowning, so begin CPR at once as prompt action can save the life of an apparently drowned child; St John Ambulance says that more than half such cases can be saved.

### What to do

Pick up the infant and carry with the head lower than the chest to drain any fluid. Wrap in a dry, warm covering and give CPR. The puffs to inflate the lungs may need to be firmer and slower than called for in cases not involving water in airway and lungs.

First aid classes will instruct you in the details of what to do and why. It is imperative to obtain medical attention even if good recovery apparently has occurred.

## Prevention

Avoid risks. Never leave your infant or small child alone in or near water: 4 or 5 centimetres of water can drown a mobile baby or toddler.

Inside the house are basins, baths, unlidded buckets and toilets. Toddlers can climb around hand basins; safety straps will hold down the toilet lid.

Outside the house are paddling pools, ponds, swimming pools. Although fences are compulsory around swimming pools by law, parents should also check regularly that child-proof gates are working and are never propped open and that there are no chairs or boxes near the fence or gate, so no small children can enter the pool area without supervision. Be vigilant always to prevent what can be a terrible tragedy.

# Electric shock

This occurs if your child contacts an electric current. A minor shock is distressing; a major shock leads to unconsciousness or death. Full flow of house voltage will be fatal.

## What to do

Do not attempt first aid until it is safe to touch the child. Switch off the current or push the child out of danger with dry insulating material, such as rubber gloves, a wooden broom handle or a chair, rolled woollen material, newspaper or plastic. If the child is unconscious, call 000 for the ambulance (111 in New Zealand) and begin CPR at once.

The electricity authority must first disconnect high voltage power lines.

## Prevention

Install a circuit breaker of the earth leakage type. Keep flexes in good order, and keep water away from power. Have no portable electric appliances (e.g. hair dryer) in the bathroom, where they might fall into the bath. Insert flat outlet plugs into empty power outlets, to keep out metal objects that a child could poke in.

## Eyes

Try to protect the eyes from very strong light, which may contain UV radiation. Shade your baby's face if you are out in the sun, especially around the middle of the day, and allow for the shade to move if you have the pram outside. Avoid strong bulb sources of light near the eyes.

A foreign body in the eye will irritate it. The baby will cry; the eye will be watery and later reddened. If you can see the foreign body you can try to remove it with extremely gentle contact. Grandma's method was to lick it out, i.e. pick it up on your own tongue:

- Hold baby's head between your hands and separate the lids with your fingers.
- Try to lick the foreign body out.
- Alternatively you can use dampened gauze twisted to a point.
- If you cannot see the object, try to wash it out with tepid normal saline (which you can buy in 30 millitre ampoules from the chemist for the first aid kit; or you can make normal saline by adding half a teaspoon of salt into 300 millitres of cooled, boiled water), poured across the eye.
- If none of these actions succeed, seek medical help.

### For liquids in eye

Soapy bath water is upsetting but easily washed out. Stronger chemicals should be promptly washed out – the tap is the nearest and quickest method. Continue with gently poured tepid water for 10 minutes and get medical help.

## Falls

If the fall is severe, get medical aid at once. Apply CPR if breathing appears to have stopped. Check limbs for breaks by comparing shape and alignment. Move the child with great care.

## Precautions

Never leave a baby or small child alone on a bed, bench top or table. Even very young babies can move and fall; if in a bouncinette or carry-chair they can bounce or rock off a table or bench.

Put safety gates at top and bottom of stairs, but you will find that an infant who can crawl can be taught stair technique: forwards up, backwards down, always with supervision and frequent practice.

Non-slip soles on shoes and slippers or bare feet are safer than socks for all ages on hard polished floors.

Use safety harnesses (see 'Injuries' later in this chapter) for your baby when in the chair, highchair, pram or stroller. Be careful to keep the pram or stroller upright and do not make it top-heavy by overloading it with shopping or a sibling: it could overturn.

Don't allow infants (or small children) to play or run with things such as pencils, pens, cutlery, scissors or sticks. These could be driven through the roof of the mouth, or into an eye in a fall. Thick colouring pens are safer.

### Fire

The great dangers for persons from actively burning fire are of exposure to flames and to smoke. The flames burn bare skin directly, and by igniting the clothing then affect covered skin; smoke interferes with breathing and sight, and may burn airway and lungs. Smoke can suffocate and carry poisonous fumes, which are formed when many materials in modern houses burn.

## What to do

If clothing is alight roll the child in a woollen blanket to extinguish the flames as you make for fresh air away from the fire. You can use your own body over a small child or baby, provided your own clothes are not likely to flare up. Damp cotton towels are usable in an emergency, and you can keep a regular fire blanket in the kitchen, where so many house fires begin.

(For immediate treatment of burn damage, see 'Burns' earlier in this chapter.) Get medical aid, both for burns and smoke inhalation, especially if toxic.

## Prevention

Install smoke alarms. Have fireguards for open fires and radiators. Keep electrical wiring in good order, and do not overload power points and leads. Do not use electric blankets for children, and be cautious with your own. Use flame-resistant garments that fit closely, both for your infant and yourself; no trailing shawls near the stove. Take care of radiant heaters that come on with a preset timer-control. Keep matches and lighters out of reach of children.

# Injuries: causes and preventions

Your baby could be put at risk by dangerous features of things in everyday use, or by the way you use them.

## *Hazards in equipment or environment*

- Can you isolate the kitchen work-area by installing a gate? If a gate is not feasible, look for a safety rail to fit around the stovetop. Long handles on pots and pans are a bad feature of their design and short double ones are safer; when using them turn the long ones sideways or towards the back of the stove. Child-proof latches on cupboards and drawers will limit access to their contents, such as knives, scissors and the rest.

- Swinging doors invite crushed fingers as they close. Glass doors are often hard to see, but cross rails or stick-on patches at a suitable height are a remedy. Folding furniture such as ironing boards or chairs can collapse onto an infant or trap fingers. Irons are heavy, often hot and trail their cords if power points are low.

- Blind or curtain cords can reach cots, or determined toddlers, and be sucked in or twisted around limbs or neck.

- Are the cot slats 5 to 8.5 centimetres apart? Are there suitable safety straps on bouncinette, pram, highchair etc? (see below and 'Equipping the household' in Chapter 1).

- Many items now meet Australian Standards and are marked accordingly, e.g. cots, prams, strollers and some toys. However, check all items, especially toys, before you buy because small parts or pieces may break off and lead to choking. Dummies should not be so small that they could go completely into the mouth, or have strings or ribbons that can be sucked or swallowed. Bibs should pull over the head and be held in place by a safety pin, not tapes. Knits should not be so open that fingers or toes could push through and risk cutting off circulation.

*𝒞* Sheet plastic in contact with babies and infants is extremely dangerous, especially if it is fine and lodges over the face. Plastic bags (including shopping bags) will speedily suffocate a child if pulled over the head; split them or knot them to make them safer. Cot mattresses come in thick plastic wrapping which looks ideal for keeping them dry, but it is unsafe; moisture-repellent woollen sheets are safer. Fine plastic freezer bags are a hazard in the kitchen; keep them out of children's reach.

## Hazards in use

*𝒞* Harness body straps can slip around the neck if the crotch strap is not secured to resist wriggling down. This danger is especially present with bouncinettes, but also with chairs and strollers.

*𝒞* Pillows and bumpers in the cot could suffocate your baby should they contact the face (either under or over), so don't use them.

*𝒞* A cradle needs stops to keep its movement under control. Otherwise it might roll your baby around inside, or even tip (see 'For sleeping' and 'Equipping the household' in Chapter 1).

*𝒞* A child alone with a bottle or food is at some risk of choking.

*𝒞* Use table mats instead of dangling tablecloths, and move electric leads and kitchen tools to the back of the bench.

*𝒞* Hot items – containers and contents – are an ever-present danger to stretching hands and fingers: your hot drink could seriously burn the baby you nurse while you juggle both.

## Pets

Many cats love to curl up next to, or on, warm sleeping babies. Even if you have no cat of your own, an unscreened window can let in a visitor; so beware of suffocation. Use a strong cat net securely fastened over bassinet or pram.

You may find your dog, used hitherto to your undivided attention, showing signs of jealousy towards the new baby. Protect the baby but involve the dog pleasantly with the baby rather than displace it abruptly (see also 'Toddlers and young children' later in this chapter). If you put your thought and care into the problem, your child will gain a best friend.

Keep pets healthy and clean, free of fleas and worms. Be mindful that some children may become allergic to pets.

Do not trust pets fully with infants or children – or the other way around, perhaps? Even a placid animal will defend itself if teased or hurt. Start early to teach your child the fine art of handling animals gently.

# Poisons

If your child has contacted or swallowed a poisonous substance, ring immediately for guidance. The Australian Poisons Information Centre (a national 24-hour service) can be contacted on 13 11 26; put the number by the phone.

Around the house there are likely to be a number of substances, mostly industrial products, which could poison a child. That is, they could seriously damage body tissue or disrupt vital functions. Among the 'household poisons' are medicines (including contraceptive pills and other tablets), cleaners, alcohol, paints and thinners, kerosene, rat baits, garden sprays, fertilisers, pesticides and mower fuel.

## Precautions

Shut the substances safely away, in containers that have child-proof caps – never in old drink bottles or ex-food containers. There are approved safe cupboards on the market. Be careful in carrying, using or cleaning up afterwards.

# Resuscitation

Resuscitation in first aid is the procedure called cardiopulmonary resuscitation (CPR) by which you use your own breath to inflate the lungs and your hand action on the chest to circulate the blood in someone who has stopped breathing. Provided only a short time has passed since breathing stopped, CPR can sustain life until medical aid arrives; i.e., it postpones death.

The Australian Resuscitation Council (2010), which oversees the matter, has simplified the procedures so that only one schedule (two inflations and 30 chest compressions per set or cycle) applies to casualties of any age. This makes it easier for a novice or occasional first aider, and saves time previously spent in searching for weak pulses and in changing schedules. Like natural breathing, assisted circulation should be continuous; delay in beginning it is to be avoided. It is a great advantage to have attended first aid classes before being called on in an emergency.

## CPR (cardiopulmonary resuscitation)

What to do if your baby is unconscious (in summary):

- Assess the situation for likely ongoing hazard to baby, yourself or others; deal safely with it.
- Call the ambulance – 000 in Australia, 111 in New Zealand. If possible, have somebody else do it; if out of range, go ahead with your own efforts at once rather than attempting dashes by car.
- Quickly check the breathing, and the airway for blockage.
- Urgently begin the (2 + 30) CPR sets and keep them up as long as you can or until the ambulance comes.

The detailed steps follow.

### Checking the breathing

- Note any audible breathing noises. Coughing (but not occasional gasping) indicates that some air is still passing.
- Look at chest and abdomen for movement up and down. If the skin colour is bluish, oxygen/air is lacking.
- Feel for airflow by putting your cheek near your baby's nose and mouth.

### Clearing the airway of possible blockage

- With baby face up on your lap, open baby's mouth without pressing under the chin (which could put the tongue across the airway). Tilt the head only slightly. Look for any obstruction; try to hook out a visible one with your little finger (but do not push it further in).

⌀ If the obstruction is not visible, commence CPR. The chest compressions are similar to chest thrusts so at the end of your 30 compressions check the airway to see if a foreign body is now visible. If not, continue with the CPR. That is, attempt breathing and then go back to doing chest compressions.

## Outcomes

⌀ If breathing resumes, make your baby comfortable but monitor the breathing closely.

⌀ If breathing is not restored, call the ambulance if not already sent for, and begin the (2 + 30) sets as below.

## Inflating and chest compressing (2 + 30)

**1.** Place your baby face up on firm, flat surface (a table top).

**2.** Tilt the head back a little, open the mouth by lifting the chin (which should bring the tongue from the back of the throat); keep your fingers away from the soft tissues under the chin.

**3.** Cover mouth and nose with your own mouth, sealing carefully onto the face with your lips.

**4.** Puff once, gently, with probably no more than a mouthful of air (do not blow with full strength; watch for chest to rise; relax seal; watch for chest to fall back). Re-seal and give a second puff.

**5.** If the chest has not responded to your puffs, check for material in the mouth, re-tilt the head and lift the chin. Always seal carefully onto the face. Depending on the size of the infant, you can cover the mouth only and seal off the nose by pinching it closed with your fingers.

**6.** After the second puff and release, place your index finger and middle finger tips on the baby's breastbone between the nipples. Push downward so that the chest compresses to about two-thirds of its original thickness or depth: movement down 1 to 1.5 centimetres. Allow the same time as the compression took to return to its starting position.

**7.** Repeat the compression and release 29 times, completing the (2 + 30) set. Continue, so that you give about five sets per two minutes. This calls for rapid, shallow compressions, as first aid classes will show you.

Continue until the ambulance or other help arrives, aiming for rhythmic continuity with only brief pauses for breathing checks and handovers to a helper. If natural breathing returns, make your baby comfortable but monitor the breathing carefully until the ambulance arrives.

## Splinters

Children become very upset over the removal of splinters, so you may need another adult to comfort and reassure the child while you are removing the splinter.

If you can grip the end of the splinter with tweezers, gently remove it. If it is just below the skin you may be able to push it towards the point of entry, allowing you to grip the end as it comes within reach. If not, sterilise a needle in a match flame and use it to uncover the end by teasing away the flesh. Grip with the tweezers and pull it out along the line of its entry. If the splinter is too deep to reach, or has sharp edges (being of metal or glass), leave it for your doctor to remove.

# Strangling

Strangling occurs if the airway is compressed by external pressure on or around the neck. For a child, ribbons, power leads or cords might have this effect if twisted tightly around the neck.

## What to do

Deal safely with the cause, call for help and check for breathing. If there is none, begin CPR.

## Prevention

The straps on bouncinettes or strollers are dangerous unless the crotch strap is secured so that the child cannot slide or wriggle down, resulting in the body strap around the neck.

Blind cords are a risk for the older infant if they are hanging loosely within reach. Keep cots away from windows with blind cords.

Avoid using ribbons on clothing – they could also cause choking if sucked in – and check that cords or ropes on outside play equipment are not dangerous for older infants and children.

# Suffocating

Although you may come across the term 'suffocating' to refer to cutting off air in general, it is commonly restricted to the following causes affecting children:

- a barrier of some sort across the face e.g. fine plastic sheet or film; bedclothes; pillows or bumpers in the bed; fall of earth (in a cave-in) across the face
- lack of air in confined spaces e.g. old refrigerators, trunks, car boots (places to hide that might attract children); complete burial in a cave-in
- smoke and leaking gas (other factors such as temperature and toxicity may also be involved in these).

## What you will see

Skin colour will be blue and grey, indicative of lack of oxygen. The child will probably be unconscious. The actual cause will probably be obvious from the circumstances.

## What to do

Remove the child from the scene, into fresh air, and check for breathing. If none, begin CPR at once and call the ambulance.

## Prevention

Keep plastic sheeting and bags in safe places. Avoid using pillows and bumpers in the cot or bassinet, and arrange bedclothes so they will not cover the head. Install smoke alarms. Keep abreast of playtime activities.

# Toddlers and young children

Be aware that toddlers and young children may be jealous of a new arrival in the family and attempt to poke, push or hit (with a toy or similar) the new baby. Older children can be upset until they realise they are still important to you.

Encourage them to observe your baby care, and to join in. Show them acceptable behaviour rather than issue a series of 'don'ts', which merely leave them at a loss: 'Be gentle when you touch', with demonstration, provides guidance, whereas 'Don't be rough' gives none.

## Prevention

Give dedicated time to the older child or children when someone else is able to mind the baby. This reassures the older ones that you love them too. Initially, vigilance in supervision may be necessary to protect your baby and to detect signs of mounting resentment in older siblings. A high catch on the bedroom door while the baby is sleeping could prevent a potential problem. Reading the toddler or young child a favourite book while you breastfeed the new baby keeps everyone happy!

# Endnotes

Page 5. 'Although strictly limited amounts were formerly considered acceptable, it is now widely advised (by the National Health and Medical Research Council, for example) that for women who are pregnant ...' National Health and Medical Research Council, *Australian Guidelines to Reduce Health Risks from Drinking Alcohol*, National Health and Medical Research Council, www.nhmrc.gov.au/_files_mhmrc/publications/attachments/ds10-alcohol.pdf.

Page 8. 'In a safe cot the spaces between the slats will be between 5 and 9.5 centimetres. The sides should be at least 60 centimetres above the level of the mattress and there should be no footholds which a toddler can use to climb out.' Australian Competition and Consumer Commission, *Keeping Baby Safe: A guide to infant and nursery products*, Product Safety Australia, www.productsafety.gov.au/content/index.phtmI/itemId/972363/frmtemId/973424.

Page 9. 'They need to have a locking pin bolted into place and the maximum tilt should be no more than 10 degrees.' Australian Competition and Consumer Commission, Keeping Baby Safe: A guide to infant and nursery products, Product Safety Australia, www.productsafety.gov.au/content/index.phtmI/itemId/972363/frmtemId/973424.

Page 46. 'During your pregnancy you may have heard of, read about or seen a video called *Kangaroo Mother Care (KMC)* by Dr Nils Bergman. Kangaroo mother care is defined by Dr Bergman as a ...' For more information go to www.kangaroomothercare.com and www.skin.kangaroomothercare.com/index.htm.

Page 54. 'For example, the average weight at birth of babies in Australia is around 3400 grams; the 10th and 90th percentiles are about 2600 grams and 3800 grams respectively; and nearly all babies at birth, it is expected, will weigh between these weights.' Australian Bureau of Statistics, *Australian Social Trends 2007: Australia's babies*, Australian Bureau of Statistics, www.abs.gov.au/ausstats/abs@nsf/mf/4102.0.

Page 54. 'The average length at birth is about 50 centimetres, and the head circumference about 35 centimetres. The chest is usually a little less than 35 centimetres...' Birth weight conversion guide, www.birth.com.au.

Page 58. 'Newborn Screening is a publicly funded system which tests for more than thirty rare but treatable diseases...' *The Guthrie test: midwifery basics - Practising Midwife*, Baston, H, vol 5, no 3, March 2002, pp 32-35,

Page 74. 'One well worth reading is You and your Grandchild by Joan Gomez, published by Bloomsbury.' Gomez, J 1996, *You and Your Grandchildren*, Bloomsbury, London, UK.

Page 124. 'The condom has a safety range of around 96 to 99.6 per cent if used correctly and consistently.' Family Planning Queensland, Contraception: Condoms – male and female, Family Planning Queensland, www.fpq.com.au/ Fs_Condoms.pdf and Association of Reproductive Health Professionals, *Health Matters Fact Sheet*, Association of Reproductive Health Professionals, www. arhp.org. www.fpnsw.org.au

Page 124. 'The only reported side effect is latex allergy ... containing a hole or one that is perished or an incorrect fit.' Sexual Health and Family Planning ACT, *Sexual Health Info Sheet: Diaphragms,* Sexual Health and Family Planning ACT, www.shfpact.org.au.

Page 125. 'The female condom can be placed in the vagina up to eight hours prior to intercourse and up to 95 per cent effective.' Family Planning Queensland, *Contraception: Condoms – male and female*, Family Planning Queensland, www.fpq.com.au/Fs_Condoms.pdf, and Association of Reproductive Health Professionals, *Health Matters Fact Sheet*, Association of Reproductive Health Professionals, www.arhp.org.

Page 126. 'The IUD is more than 98 per cent effective but carries with it potential side effects such as cramps, although these usually resolve after a few months.' Family Planning Queensland, *Contraception: Intrauterine contraceptive devices (IUDs)*, Family Planning Queensland, www.fpq.com.au/ Fs_IUDs.pdf.

Page 126. 'Like the non-hormonal IUD ... the contraceptive effect of the hormonal IUD is immediate once inserted into the uterus.' Family Planning Queensland, *Contraception: Intrauterine contraceptive devices (IUDs)*, Family Planning Queensland, www.fpq.com.au/Fs_IUDs.pdf.

Page 126. 'This is a small, flexible plastic rod approximately the size of a matchstick ... is considered safe to use if breastfeeding' Better Health

Channel, *Contraception – implants and injections*, Better Health Channel, www. betterhealth.vic.gov.au.

Page 127. 'This is a soft plastic ring which is self-inserted into ... because oestrogen suppresses prolactin and therefore milk production is reduced.' Better Health Channel, *Contraception – vaginal ring*, Better Health Channel, www.betterhealth.vic.gov.au.

Page 127. 'If you are not breastfeeding it is advisable to wait several weeks prior to commencing the combined oral contraceptive pill.' Family Planning Queensland, *Contraception: Combined oral contraceptive pill*, Family Planning Queensland, www.fpq.com.au/Fs_COCP.pdf.

Page 128. 'Unlike the combined oral contraceptive pill, the mini pill contains only one hormone ...' Family Planning Queensland, *Contraception: Progestogen only contraceptive pill (POP)*, Family Planning Queensland, www.fpq. com.au/Fs-Progestogen_Only.pdf.

Page 130. 'In the presence of these three factors the LAM method is considered to be approximately 98 per cent effective.' Family Planning Queensland, Sexual and Reproductive Health for All, Natural methods of birth control, Family Planning Queensland http://www.fpq.com.au/publications/ fsBrochures/Fs_Natural_Methods.php

Page 131. 'It is about 85 per cent effective if taken within three days of unprotected intercourse and may be effective up to five days after unprotected sex.' Family Planning Queensland, *Contraception: Emergency contraception*, Family Planning Queensland, www.fpq.com.au/Fs_Emergency. pdf.

Page 131. 'A copper IUD (as discussed earlier) can also be used as emergency contraception if inserted within five days of unprotected intercourse.' Family Planning Queensland, *Contraception: Emergency contraception*, Family Planning Queensland, www.fpq.com.au/Fs_Emergency.pdf.

Page 132. 'Micro-inserts are 99.9 per cent effective but there is a three-month delay in the effectiveness of this method of permanent contraception while the tissue grows into the inserts to block the tubes.' Family Planning Queensland, *Contraception: Sterilisation*, Family Planning Queensland, www. fpq.com.au/Fs_Sterilisation.pdf.

Page 132. 'A tubal ligation is has a failure rate of less than 1 per cent and is effective immediately.' Family Planning Queensland, *Contraception: Sterilisation*, Family Planning Queensland, www.fpq.com.au/Fs_Sterilisation. pdf.

Page 132. 'A vasectomy has a failure rate of less than 1 per cent but, unlike female surgical sterilisation ... which will still be in the semen for several ejaculations after the procedure.' Family Planning Queensland, *Contraception: Sterilisation*, Family Planning Queensland, http://www.fpq.com. au/publications/fsBrochures/Fs_Sterilisation.php

Page 134. 'The new baby blues are relatively common and the proportion of mothers affected is thought to be in the range of 50 to 80 per cent.' www.beyondblue.org.au.

Page 137. 'More women than men are likely to suffer depression in their lifetime. It is during their reproductive years that women are at greatest risk.' American Psychological Association, *Women and Depression*, www.apa. org. www.beyondblue.com.au

Page 137. 'For example, research undertaken by beyondblue suggests that up to 10 per cent of pregnant women develop antenatal depression and this increases to around 16 per cent after the birth (postnatal depression).' Beyondblue - Antenatal and Postnatal depression http://www.beyondblue.org. au/index.aspx?link_id=6.1246

Page 139. '...a traumatic/abusive childhood.' Raising Children Network http://raisingchildren.net.au/articles/what_is_postnatal_depression_-_panda. html/context/305

Page 140. 'The following postnatal circumstances may contribute to depression ... lack of family and community support...' Raising Children Network http://raisingchildren.net.au/articles/what_is_postnatal_ depression_-_panda.html/context/305

Page 146. 'This affects only one or two mothers in a thousand ... With good medical care and adequate support most women fully recover.' *Postpartum Care (obstetric-based care)*, The Womens, the Royal Women's Hospital, Victoria, Australia, www.thewomens.org.au.

Page 150. 'An ongoing joint study conducted by Brisbane's Mater Hospital and the University of Queensland examined cognitive development of 3880 children and their experience of breastfeeding. It has found that the longer the duration of breastfeeding the greater the child's skill with language at age five years.' Mater University of Queensland Study of Pregnancy (MUSP), as reported in *UQ News Online*, September 2002.

Page 201. 'It has been suggested by Ruth Lawrence in her book Breastfeeding that the effect in emergency weaning of a sudden drop in prolactin levels in the mother (prolactin is thought to contribute to a feeling of wellbeing) may cause hormone withdrawal syndrome and that this may be associated with depression.' Lawrence, RA & Lawrence, RM 2005, *Breastfeeding: A Guide for the Medical Profession*, Sixth Edition, Elsevier, Philadelphia, USA.

Page 267. 'Back in 1979, Doctor Kerry Callaghan of South Australia wrote of the factors experienced by the infant while still in the uterus just before labour commences – factors which, if we can reproduce them as closely as possible, can help to recreate feelings of security....' Callaghan, K, *Creating Optimal Environments for Newborn Infants and Their Families*, Nairne, Australia.

Page 267. 'A SIDS death is said to have occurred when a baby is put to bed apparently well and later is found dead. Autopsy examinations (a legal requirement) are performed to exclude other causes of death. As yet no specific causes of the syndrome have been identified. A great deal of research continues in this area. For more information go to Sids and Kids, www.sidsandkids.org.' www.sidsandkids.org and www.sids.org./definition.htm.

Page 277. 'The average length at birth is about 50 centimetres, some being a little more and others a little less. The length can be expected to increase by 25 to 30 centimetres during the first year. Head circumference is about 34 to 35 centimetres at birth and will usually reach 47 to 48 centimetres by twelve months.' *Baby's growth – weight, length, head circumference*, www.birth.com.au.

Page 278. 'Research by van de Rijt and Plooij found that all babies appear to take seven major leaps in development during their first year...' Van der Riet, H & Plooij, F 1992, *The Wonder Weeks*, Kiddy World Promotions, Arnhem, The Netherlands; Plooij, F & van der Riet, J 1996, *Why the Cry: Understanding Child Development in the First Year*, Thorsons, England.

Page 279. 'The American Academy of Paediatrics recommends that children are not exposed to the television before the age of two years.' Committee on Public Education Policy 2001, *'Statement American Academy of Pediatrics: Children, Adolescents and Television'*, *Pediatrics*, vol 107, no2, pp 423-426.

Page 355. **This procedure is described by P Hatherly in *Back to the Bath*. In her article she describes ... she soaked her breast – and the milk flowed.** Hatherly, P, 1990, *'Back to the Bath'*, *ALCA News*, vol 2, no 2, p 15.

Page 410. **'First aid manuals, such as Australian First Aid by St. John Ambulance, are a help.'** *Australian First Aid, fourth edition* 2009, St John Ambulance, Barton, Australia.

Page 416. **'Babies less than six months old must be secured in a rearward-facing restraint ... are occupied by children younger than seven years in a child restraint or booster seat.'** NSW Transport Roads and Traffic authority:http://www.rta.nsw.gov.au/roadsafety/children/childrestrains/childrestraintlaws_faqs.html.

# Support Indigenous Midwives

The Rhodanthe Lipsett Trust Fund is a scholarship fund established by the Australian College of Midwives for Aboriginal and Torres Strait Islander women who wish to study to become midwives.

Aboriginal and Torres Strait Islander midwifery students are eligible for some government scholarships, but many students find it challenging to meet the additional incidental expenses often associated with studying such as child care, travel to university and text books. The scholarships from this fund will help students to pay for these incidental expenses and many other expenses that often appear when undertaking studies.

Help make a difference. Your support will help to enhance the birth experience for Aboriginal and Torres Strait Islander woman by supporting more Aboriginal and Torres Strait Islander women to become midwives. Make a donation today at www.amaw.midwives.org.au

# Index